DEAD MEN DO TELL TALES: BOOK 1

BLOODY CHICAGO
BY TROY TAYLOR

- A Whitechapel Productions Press Publication -

To Johnnie --- who was always misunderstood.
I would have always driven the getaway car.

This Book is Published by:
Whitechapel Productions Press
15 Forest Knolls Est. - Decatur, Illinois - 62521
(217) 422-1002 / 1-888-GHOSTLY
Visit us on the Internet at http://www.prairieghosts.com

First Edition - October 2006
ISBN: 1-892523-48-5

Printed in the United States of America

PRAISE FOR HAUNTED ILLINOIS BOOKS BY TROY TAYLOR

Troy Taylor's HAUNTED ILLINOIS manages to capture the spookiest aspects of life on the prairie in a way that no other book has done. For those who believe that Illinois is merely corn fields and forests, he only needs to read this book to realize that strange things are lurking on the midwestern plains.
DAVE GOODWIN, author of **MILITARY GHOSTS** & Others

Troy Taylor has done it yet again. In HAUNTED ILLINOIS, the author has hit that rare (and delightful) middle ground between fascinating paranormal research and compelling storytelling. His stories will put you on the edge of your seat and his insights into the supernatural will keep you there. A rare and delightful find and a must-read from one of the best ghost authors writing today.
MARK MARIMEN, author of the **HAUNTED INDIANA** Series

Troy Taylor works hard to unearth new hauntings and to keep the old lore alive. In spite of this, many of the stories which shaded our cemeteries and lingered over our abandoned buildings are lost. So while some of us wonder about the light burning in the old warehouse, or quicken our step in the dusky graveyard, or pause to make sure those are our own footsteps echoing off the attic wall, most of us won't. Yesterday's stories, like yesterday's spirits, draw their power from being remembered. In the absence of memory, legends die, and like forgotten ghosts are left to fade away.
JOE RICHARDSON --- **ILLINOIS COUNTRY LIVING** Magazine

No other author has managed to capture the mystery, history and hauntings of Illinois and Chicago in the way that Troy Taylor has been able to do. His HAUNTED ILLINOIS books are a surefire hit for tourists, ghost researchers and anyone looking for history that is outside the realm of what we are taught in school.
VINCE WILSON, author of **GHOST TECH** & **MYSTERIOUS MARYLAND**

If you are looking for the real history, hauntings and weird stuff of Illinois, then look no further than Troy Taylor's HAUNTED ILLINOIS titles!
You won't find anything else like them on the market!
KEITH AGE, President of the **LGHS** & Host of Sci-Fi Channel's **SPOOKED**

GHOST BOOKS BY TROY TAYLOR

HAUNTED ILLINOIS BOOKS
HAUNTED ILLINOIS (1999 / 2001 / 2004)
HAUNTED DECATUR (1995)
MORE HAUNTED DECATUR (1996)
GHOSTS OF MILLIKIN (1996 / 2001)
WHERE THE DEAD WALK (1997 / 2002)
DARK HARVEST (1997)
HAUNTED DECATUR REVISITED (2000)
FLICKERING IMAGES (2001)
HAUNTED DECATUR: 13TH ANNIVERSARY EDITION (2006)
HAUNTED ALTON (2000 / 2003)
HAUNTED CHICAGO (2003)
THE HAUNTED PRESIDENT (2005)
MYSTERIOUS ILLINOIS (2005)
DEAD MEN DO TELL TALES: BLOODY CHICAGO (2006)

HAUNTED FIELD GUIDE BOOKS
THE GHOST HUNTER'S GUIDEBOOK (1997/ 1999 / 2001/ 2004)
CONFESSIONS OF A GHOST HUNTER (2002)
FIELD GUIDE TO HAUNTED GRAVEYARDS (2003)
GHOSTS ON FILM (2005)
SO, THERE I WAS (With Len Adams) (2006)

HISTORY & HAUNTINGS SERIES
THE HAUNTING OF AMERICA (2001)
INTO THE SHADOWS (2002)
DOWN IN THE DARKNESS (2003)
OUT PAST THE CAMPFIRE LIGHT (2004)

OTHER GHOSTLY TITLES
SPIRITS OF THE CIVIL WAR (1999)
SEASON OF THE WITCH (1999/ 2002)
HAUNTED NEW ORLEANS (2000)
BEYOND THE GRAVE (2001)
NO REST FOR THE WICKED (2001)
HAUNTED ST. LOUIS (2002)
THE DEVIL CAME TO ST. LOUIS (2006)

BARNES & NOBLE PRESS TITLES
WEIRD U.S. (Co-Author with Mark Moran & Mark Scuerman) (2004)
WEIRD ILLINOIS (Barnes & Noble Press) (2005)
HAUNTING OF AMERICA (2006)

WELCOME TO BLOODY CHICAGO!

Chicago is, and always has been, a lusty, brawling, violent city; a polyglot city, a rich city, a city powerful and unafraid. In a curious, oblique manner, Chicago is proud of her reputation.
Sewell Peaslee Wright

When I sell liquor, they call it bootlegging. When my patrons serve it on silver trays on Lake Shore Drive, they call it hospitality.

You can get much further with a smile, a kind word and a gun than you can get with just a smile and a kind word.
Al Capone

Ah, to hell with them Sicilians...
Dion O'Banion

Nobody shot me.
Frank Gusenberg... mortally wounded in the St. Valentines Day Massacre

Never trust a woman or an automatic pistol.
John Dillinger

I have always been opposed to violence, to shootings. I have fought, yes, I have fought for peace. And I believe that I can take credit for the peace that now exists in the racket game in Chicago. I believe that people can thank me for the fact that gang killings here are probably a thing of the past.
Al Capone ---- in January 1929

FOREWORD

I was 12 years old when I first became interested in Chicago crime. There was a battered copy of John Kobler's excellent biography of Al Capone on my father's bookshelf and I picked it up one day and soon read it from cover to cover. Not once --- but two times.

My interest could not have come along at a better time either. It was the late 1970s and a revived interest in the Prohibition era, and the gangsters of Chicago, was in full swing. I'm sure that it was prompted by the release of the *Godfather* films, and whatever the reason, good reading material was easy to find. It was the heyday of Jay Robert Nash, and many lesser writers, and his writings sparked my interest in the crimes of yesterday. I quickly began to pile up a more than adequate library on Chicago's crime and criminals.

But Chicago crime was not my only interest to come along around that time. I also developed a rabid fascination with American ghosts and hauntings and I soon found out that the two interests combined rather nicely. You see, it has often been said that the events of yesterday create the hauntings of today. Such a statement is especially true when it comes to hauntings that are born of deaths caused by murder and crime. Most ghost enthusiasts would agree that one of the main reasons for a place to become haunted is because a murder, or a violent death, has occurred at the location. As you will soon discover, this is likely the reason that so many have referred to Chicago as "America's Most Haunted" city.

This is not the first book that I have written about Chicago's history and haunted places, and it's unlikely that it will be my last. However, this book will be a little different. The purpose of it is to collect Chicago tales that are connected to the history and hauntings of crime, murder, disappearances, unsolved mysteries and other dark deeds. Even though such a combination has never been attempted before, I can assure you that it's unlikely I have collected them all. Some stories will forever elude me but regardless, I can tell you that I have gathered the most unusual --- and often the bloodiest --- of these stories and will, of course, attempt to chill your blood with the telling of them. However, keep in mind as you turn these pages that not every story in this book will be related to ghosts. Some of them were simply so strange, so mysterious and so horrifying that they had to be included anyway. They may not be about ghosts but you won't find them any less terrifying. As some have said, it's not always the dead that we need to be afraid of --- sometimes it's the living.

In any case, I think you will find the stories ahead of you to be both familiar and strange. Some of them, you will never have heard before and some of them may be old favorites. But every single one of them has left its bloodstained mark on the haunted streets of Chicago. Many of them will frighten you, some will disturb you and others will surely have you looking over your shoulder as you read. These are not tales for the faint of heart but they are all a part of the fabric that has made Chicago great.

It's a strange road to come so sit back, relax and prepare yourself for a side of the city that few ever live long enough to see! Welcome to "Bloody Chicago".

Troy Taylor
Halloween 2006

INTRODUCTION: Born in Blood

Chicago was literally born in blood.

She saw her first settlers slaughtered during a wartime massacre, and watched as the man considered by many to be Chicago's founding father murdered another man during a land dispute. It was a gruesome start for a city that was already founded in chaos.

Chicago was not planned in the way that other great American cities were started. Her birthplace was not carefully chosen and her streets were not laid out with care. Chicago began as nothing more than empty wilderness and open prairie, a desolate and isolated region on the shore of a great lake. The land on both sides of the Chicago River was low and wet, a brackish area of swamp and mud. A large portion of the land spent part of the year under the murky waters of Lake Michigan. The mouth of the river itself was choked with sand, allowing passage by nothing larger than a canoe. The streambed was filled with rice and wild onions, an aromatic vegetable that would give Chicago its name. In 1684, the future city appeared as nothing more than a notation on a French map as "Chekagou", a Potawatomi Indian name that meant "wild onion". It would be more than 100 years later before settlers would come to this place.

The earliest real settlement here would be at the junction of the north and south branches of the Chicago River, a place commonly known as Wolf Point. A small village later grew up around the site, thanks to its close proximity to Fort Dearborn, which was constructed in 1803.

The first settler, Jean Baptiste Point du Sable, a French trader and trapper, came here in 1779 and opened a trading post. He married a Cahokian Indian woman named Catherine in 1788 and they had a daughter two years later. In 1796, after a failed bid to become the head of the Potawatomi Indians, du Sable sold out the inventory of his trading post and moved to Missouri. He died in St. Charles in 1814.

A French trader named Le Mai purchased du Sable's inventory and three or four other traders joined him at Wolf Point. They created a small settlement of shacks, tents and lean-to's. One of the men, Jean Lalime, purchased Du Sable's original trading post and he expanded the operation into a successful enterprise.

By 1803, America had expanded its borders to the west and an outpost called Fort Dearborn was established on the south bank of the Chicago River. The fort, which had been named in honor of Secretary of War Henry Dearborn, was commanded by Captain John Whistler and was held by a company of 66 soldiers.

At the time, this corner of Illinois was one of the most remote regions of the frontier. It was a wilderness that was virtually cut off from all communication with the rest of the country. Access to the area was by river or Indian trail and the closest settlement was Fort Wayne. Today this is a short journey, but in those days, it was a dangerous and difficult trek. The soldiers who came to Fort Dearborn had no idea of the desolation they would face.

The fort was a simple stockade of logs. They were placed in the ground and then sharpened along the upper end. The outer stockade was a solid wall with an entrance in the southern section that was blocked with heavy gates. Another exit, this one underground, was located on the north side. Inside of the fort, there was room for a parade ground, officer's quarters, troop barracks, a guardhouse and a magazine for weapons and ammunition. Two blockhouses were also added at opposite corners of the fort, along with a raised walkway that allowed defenders inside to fire over the top of the wall. It was the largest structure in the entire region at the time and offered substantial protection for the soldiers who were garrisoned here and also for the settlers who needed it for shelter.

In 1804, a man named John Kinzie arrived in the region. He bought out the property of Jean Lalime and over the course of several years, became the self-appointed civilian leader of the settlement. He was known for his sharp dealings with the local Indians over trade goods and furs. He also established close ties with the Potawatomi Indians and even sold them liquor, which created tension among the other settlers. Kinzie managed to become very successful and this seemed to anger Jean Lalime, the man who had sold Kinzie his business. The two became bitter rivals.

A depiction of Fort Dearborn as it looked in 1803. From "History of Chicago from the Earliest Period to the Present Time" (1884) by A.T. Andreas

John Kinzie was regarded for many years as the "Father of Chicago", largely thanks to a book that was written about him by his devoted daughter-in-law, Juliette Magill Kinzie. She painted him in the best light possible but there is little doubt that Kinzie was a much bigger rogue than was originally thought. Perhaps the fact that he was such a scoundrel makes him even more worthy to be the founder of a city like Chicago, which revels in its colorful characters and questionable morals.

John Kinzie was born around 1763 and worked as a silversmith before setting out to trade among the Indians. Shawnee Indians had kidnapped his first wife, Margaret, at age 10 and after spending a decade in captivity, she escaped to Detroit, where she met and married Kinzie. The two of them had three children together but after a chance meeting with her birth father, Margaret abandoned her husband and returned to Virginia with the children. Kinzie never saw or heard from any of them again.

Kinzie later married Eleanor Little, the widow of Daniel McKillip, who supported the British during the American Revolution and who was killed at the Battle of Fallen Timbers. Eleanor's father was also a British loyalist and narrowly escaped being hanged in Pittsburgh in 1783. Kinzie had four children with Eleanor, and in 1804, they arrived in Chicago, where Kinzie purchased the trading post from Lalime.

His business quickly prospered but it was not without problems. A partnership formed with Captain Whistler's son, John Whistler Jr., deteriorated so badly that it caused a major conflict within the community. The disagreement became so heated that word of it reached officials in Detroit and, because of this, Whistler and all of the other officers at the fort were recalled and assigned to various posts across the frontier.

In 1810, Captain Nathan Heald replaced Whistler at Fort Dearborn. He brought with him Lieutenant Linus T. Helm, an man with much experience on the frontier. Not long after arriving, Helm met and married the stepdaughter of John Kinzie. In addition to she and Captain Heald's wife, there were a number of other women at the fort as well, all wives of the men stationed there. More families arrived and within two years, there were 12 women and 20 children at Fort Dearborn.

Throughout the changes at the fort, Kinzie and Lalime remained enemies and in constant conflict with one another. Finally, in April 1812, their animosity boiled over into violence. One day as Lieutenant Helm and Kinzie were leaving the fort, Lieutenant Helm warned him that Lalime was armed ---- and that he was looking for trouble. Kinzie went in search of the other man and soon the two were embroiled in another heated argument. The harsh words quickly turned to violence and a brief struggle ensued. Lalime managed to fire his pis-

tol at point blank range and Kinzie was shot in the shoulder. In spite of his wound, he managed to stab Lalime to death, spilling the first blood in Chicago history.

And once blood was spilled, it seemed that Chicago acquired a taste for it.

In August 1812, tension erupted into violence on the Illinois frontier. War had broken out once more between America and Great Britain and the conflict had created unrest among the local Indian tribes, namely the Potawatomi and their allies. The war brought many of the tribes into alliance with the British because they saw the Americans as invaders on their lands. After the British captured the American garrison at Mackinac, Fort Dearborn was in great danger. Orders came stating that Captain Heald should abandon the fort and take the civilians to Fort Wayne.

Captain Heald delayed in carrying out the orders though, refusing to flee like a coward. He waited six days before making the arrangements to evacuate but, by this time, the Americans were trapped. A large contingent of Indians had come to the fort and they gathered outside, becoming more and more hostile as the soldiers and settlers packed their belongings and prepared to leave.

Heald realized that he was going to have to bargain with the Indians if those in Fort Dearborn were going to safely reach Fort Wayne. On August 12, Heald began several days of bargaining with the assembled tribes. His junior officers refused to attend the meetings. The talks eventually led to an agreement for the Indians to provide safe conduct for the soldiers and settlers to Indiana --- but the cost of this agreement was higher than Heald's men were willing to pay. The commander had agreed to leave behind in the fort all of the supplies, whiskey and ammunition that could not be carried. His officers were understandably alarmed. They questioned the wisdom of handing out guns and ammunition that could easily be turned against them. Heald reluctantly agreed with them and the extra weapons were broken apart and dumped into an abandoned well. The ammunition and the stores of whiskey were dumped into the river. None of this escaped the attention of the Indians outside and they also began making plans that differed from those that had been agreed upon.

On August 14, Captain William Wells arrived at the fort. Wells, along with 30 Miami warriors, had managed to slip past the throng outside and rode through the front gates of the fort. Wells was a frontier legend among early soldiers and settlers in the Illinois territory. He was also the uncle of Captain Heald's wife, Rebekah, and after hearing of the evacuation of Fort Dearborn, and knowing the hostile fervor of the local tribes, he headed straight to the fort to assist them in their escape. Unfortunately, he had arrived too late.

Throughout that night, wagons were loaded for travel and reserve ammunition was distributed, amounting to about 25 rounds per man. Early the next morning, the procession of soldiers, civilians, women and children left the fort. The infantry soldiers led the way, followed by a caravan of wagons and mounted men. Several of Wells' Miami warriors guarded the rear of the column.

Nearly 500 Potawatomi Indians escorted the column of soldiers and settlers. As they marched southward and into a low range of sand hills that separated the beaches of Lake Michigan from the prairie, the Potawatomi moved silently to the right, placing an elevation of sand between them and the Americans. The act was carried out with such subtlety that no one noticed it as the column trudged along the shoreline. The sand ridge was not high and it ended a little further along the beach. At that point, the two groups would come back into one line again --- or so it was believed.

The column traveled along the beach (a line marked by present-day Michigan Avenue) to the area where the intersection of 16th Street and Indiana Avenue is now located. There was a sudden milling about of the scouts at the front of the line and, suddenly, a shout came back from Captain Wells that the Indians were attacking. A line of Potawatomi appeared over the edge of the ridge and fired down at the column. Although completely surprised, the officers still managed to rally the men into a battle line, but it was of little use. So many of them fell from immediate wounds that the line collapsed. The Indians overwhelmed them with sheer numbers, flanking the line and snatching the wagons and horses.

What followed next was butchery. Officers were slain with tomahawks and the fort's surgeon was cut down by gunfire and then literally chopped into pieces. Rebekah Heald was wounded by gunfire but was spared when a sympathetic chief captured her. The wife of one soldier fought so bravely and savagely that she was hacked into pieces before she fell. In the end, cut down to less than half their original number, the garrison surrendered

The monument to the Fort Dearborn Massacre victims was once located in Potter Palmer's backyard, where he insisted the massacre had taken place. After the Prairie Avenue District went into decline, the monument was removed to the Chicago Historical Society where it remains today.

Another monument was once attached to a Kodak warehouse around the site of the massacre but the building has long since been destroyed. Today, relief sculptures on the Michigan Avenue Bridge also serve as monuments to those who died in 1812.

under the promise of safe conduct. In all, 148 members of the column were killed. There had been 86 adults and 12 children slaughtered in the initial attack and the others had fallen in the fighting that followed. One of the dead was Captain Wells, who was captured and had his heart cut out and eaten by his slayers. A Chicago street now bears the name of this brave frontiersman.

In the battle, Captain Heald was wounded twice and his wife was wounded seven times. They were later released and a St. Joseph Indian named Chaudonaire took them to Mackinac, where they were turned over to the British commander there. He sent them to Detroit and they were exchanged with the American authorities.

The surrender that was arranged did not apply to the wounded and it is said that the Indians tortured them throughout the night and then left their bodies on the sand next to those who had already fallen. Many of the other survivors later suffered terribly. One man was tomahawked when he could not keep pace with the rest of the group being marched away from the massacre site. One baby that cried too much during the march was tied to a tree and left to starve. Mrs. Isabella Cooper was pulled from a wagon containing women and children and was actually scalped before being rescued by an Indian woman. She had a small bald spot on her head for the rest of her life. Another man froze to death that winter, while Mrs. John Simmons and her daughter were forced to run a gauntlet, which they both survived. In fact, the girl turned out to be the last survivor of the massacre, dying in 1900.

John Kinzie and his family were spared in the slaughter. Appealing to the Potawatomi chiefs, they were taken away from the massacre site. He would return to Chicago one year later, but found that much had changed. He failed in re-starting his business and soon was working for his largest competitor, the American Fur Company. In time, the fur trade would end and Kinzie worked as a trader and Indian interpreter until his death in 1828.

After the carnage, the victorious Indians burned Fort Dearborn to the ground and the bodies of the massacre victims were left where they had fallen, scattered to decay on the sand dunes of Lake Michigan. When replacement troops arrived at the site of Fort Dearborn a year later, the charred ruins of the old fort ---- and the grinning skeletons of their predecessors ---- greeted them. The bodies were given proper burials and the fort was rebuilt in 1816, only to be abandoned again in 1836 when the city would be able to fend for itself.

Not surprisingly, the horrific massacre spawned its share of ghostly tales. The site where the soldiers and settlers were slain was quiet for many years, long after Chicago had grown into a sizable city. The area later became the fashionable and historic Prairie Avenue district, which was home to Chicago's wealthiest families for several decades. Later, these families abandoned the area when it began to be encroached upon by industry on the near South Side. Warehouses and garages took the place of once opulent mansions, and it would be construction excavation that would unearth a large number of human bones. The bodies were first thought to be victims of a cholera epidemic in the 1840s but when the remains were later dated more closely to the early part of the 1800s, it was realized that the bones belonged to those killed during the massacre.

The bodies were buried elsewhere but, once disturbed, the spirits of the dead refused to rest. Over the course of the next few weeks, people in the area began to report semi-transparent figures dressed in clothing and uniforms from the pioneer era. The apparitions were seen wandering in an empty lot just north of 16th Street and while many seemed to run about haphazardly, others appeared to move in slow motion. Many of them reportedly looked very frightened or were screaming in silence.

The sightings continued for several years throughout the 1980s and were often seen late at night by Chicago Transit Authority drivers who parked their buses in a garage that was once located nearby. They often spotted the ghosts as they drove past the empty lot, their headlights capturing the figures in the darkness. The specters vanished without a trace or, in some cases, disappeared into the walls of nearby buildings.

As time passed though, the sightings became less and less frequent and soon faded away, along with the warehouses and industrial buildings that blighted the area. The once desolate neighborhood has now been filled with luxury lofts and condominiums and the remaining homes of Prairie Avenue have been restored to their former glory.

The victims of the Fort Dearborn Massacre have been all but forgotten --- or have they? There are those living in this neighborhood that claim that on certain nights, shadowy figures still walk these streets, blending into the darkness and vanishing when the lights of automobiles approach. Are these elusive phantoms still lingering from the massacre after all of these years? Perhaps they are and if this is the case, then these victims may not rest in peace.

They may be the first Chicago murder victims to return from beyond the grave --- but they have certainly not been the last.

I. CRIME WAITS FOR NO MAN

The History of Chicago Crime

Chicago may have gotten off to a bloody start, but actual crime in the region came about slowly. This is in spite of the fact that the first white man to build a shelter on the site of the city was a criminal. His name was Pierre Moreau and he was a French bootlegger who sold whiskey and illegal goods to the Indians before vanishing from Chicago history. He is barely remembered today but he was the one who set the stage for the gangsters, killers and thieves who would follow him in the years to come.

The first Chicago settlers were a rough lot but there was no record of criminal activity here until the first real population booms of the early 1830s. Thousands swarmed into the region from the east and among these was Chicago's first thief -- or at least the first one to be caught at it. In addition, the mob of new arrivals also brought with it the first man to be housed in the city jail. This drifter, known only as "Harper", was apparently arrested in the early fall of 1833 for being a vagrant. Thanks to Illinois law at the time, vagrants could be offered for sale into slavery. Public sentiment was opposed to the sale of a white man, and even though a large crowd attended the auction, the only bid came from George White, a black man who was employed as the town crier. Harper was sold to him for a quarter and White led him away at the end of a chain. What became of him after that is unknown, but it's thought that he escaped that night and quickly fled the city.

The name of Chicago's first thief has never been recorded but he reportedly stole $34 from a fellow boarder at the Wolf Tavern. Constable Reed arrested him and the missing funds were discovered when the man was taken to Reed's carpenter shop and ordered to strip. The money was found wadded up in the toe of one of the man's socks. The defendant was held over for trial, which took place at the tavern, and after much argument and speech making, he was found guilty. He was released on a nominal bail, pending a motion for a new trial by his boisterous attorney, Giles Spring, and he promptly disappeared.

By the late 1830s, Chicago newspapers were publishing an increasing number of accounts detailing thefts, hold-ups, drunken disturbances, street brawls and small riots. Other cities began to notice and in the summer of 1839, a newspaper in Jackson, Michigan commented that the "population of Chicago is principally composed of dogs and loafers".

One of these "loafers" was a young Irishman named John Stone who went to the gallows and became the first legal execution in Chicago history. Stone arrived in America at the age of 13 and came to Chicago in 1838, after having served prison time for robbery and murder in Canada. He worked off and on as a woodcutter but spent most of his time in saloons and in the city's first billiard hall. In the spring of 1840, Stone was arrested for the rape and murder of Mrs. Lucretia Thompson, the wife of a Cook County farmer. In May, he was tried and convicted of the crime. On Friday, July 10, Stone handcuffed, chained and taken to a spot on the lakeshore about three miles south of the courthouse. About 200 mounted citizens and 60 armed militiamen, under the command of Colonel Seth Johnson, escorted him to the gallows. He was hanged in front of a large crowd of interested spectators, and after his death, his body was taken by two doctors, Boone and Dyer, and dissected for medical study.

Even from these early days, Chicago thrived on its reputation for being a "wide-open town". As far back as the 1850s, the city gained notoriety for its promotion of vice in every shape and form. It embraced the arrival of prostitutes, gamblers, grifters and an outright criminal element. A commercialized form of vice flourished during the Civil War era and it's believed that an estimated 1,300 prostitutes roamed the dark evening streets of Chicago. Randolph Street was lined with bordellos, wine rooms and cheap dance halls, and the area became known as "Gambler's Row", mostly because a man gambled with his very life when braving the streets of this seedy and dangerous district.

The Great Fire of 1871 swept away the worst of the city's vice areas, destroying both gin rooms and disease-ridden prostitution cribs, but a desire for illicit activities caused it to rebound quickly. By the 1880s, Chicago had gained its place as a mature city and also as a rail center for the nation. Waves of foreigners and immigrants poured into the city and with the arrival of the World's Fair in 1893, thousands of new citizens followed.

During the latter part of the 1800's, random street crimes became the bane of Chicago's citizens. It became a good general rule for residents and visitors to avoid all but the busiest thoroughfares at night. Many places were considered unsafe after dark and the lack of well-lighted streets in many areas added to the danger. It was suggested to travelers that they might always consider walking in the center of the street if possible. That way, they would be out of reach of any hold-up man who might step out of an alley. Weapons among the criminal element could mean anything, from a club to a knife, a canvas bag filled with sand to a pistol. As there were no laws in those days against concealed weapons, any drifter or drunk who got hold of a pistol could become a deadly menace. The thief may have only been looking for a little cash or some jewelry but his "harmless" crime could easily become murder with a gun involved.

But not all of the crime in Chicago was carried out at the wrong end of a gun....

CROOKS, CRIMINALS & CORRUPTION
The Legacy of Chicago Politics

"Vote early and and vote often."
Famous Chicago Political Slogan

There is no city in America that has been as maligned as Chicago when it comes to the city's politics, corruption and questionable voting practices. Even Chicago's most famous nickname of the "Windy City" comes from the hot air that is expelled by the city's politicians, rather than for the speed of the local air currents.

This reputation dates back to the earliest days of the city. Chicago was officially incorporated as a city in August 1833; although no one has any idea just how many inhabitants actually resided here at that time. It is thought that the event of the city's incorporation was the first incident of "voter fraud" in Chicago, and this began a tradition that has besmirched the city's reputation ever since.

A preliminary election and vote on the city's incorporation was held on August 5 but only 13 voters showed up. Only one man voted against incorporating but since he lived outside of the proposed city limits, his vote didn't count anyway. The voters were invited to return to Jolly Mark's tavern on August 10 to vote again and this time, 28 people showed up and 13 of those became candidates for office. The rule of thumb in those days was that each voter represented five other, non-voting persons, meaning that Chicago had about 140 residents at most. Unfortunately, though, 150 inhabitants were needed to incorporate. In spite of this, the vote somehow went through and Chicago became a real city at last. It's no wonder that "vote early and vote often" became a phrase to ridicule Chicago voting habits in years to come.

Since that time, the city has become known for its backroom politics, "smoke-filled" rooms, backhanded favors and outright bribes. Needless to say, Chicago's politicians have long been colorful characters, starting with those who served as mayor.

The mayors of the city were always men of importance. It's true that the early pioneer mayors are barely remembered today but as the later mayors became more entrenched in the city's political system, they became capable of causing riots and firing the entire police force. Some of them were controlled by gamblers, befriended by gangsters or manipulated behind the scenes by merchants and businessmen. Occasionally, good men would be elected to office and each would try valiantly to clean up the town. They would start reform movements to purge the city of corrupt officials, to close down saloons on Sunday and brothels on weeknights, and to raid all of the gambling dens within spitting distance of City Hall. But, in most cases, these good men were not supported by an honest administration and soon, the people of Chicago would be drawn to another man, who spoke louder and made more promises than the rest. For the most part it seems that the best Chicago mayors have been the ones who have more or less let the city run them, rather than to try and run the city. They have been men who have enforced the laws to the point that respectable citizens could walk the streets, but never caused enough trouble to scare off the tourists or irritate the local folks who wanted to drink, gamble or carouse a little.

Some authors have said that Chicago is a religious town, but I wouldn't say it's religious in any traditional way. The town has a moral façade that it maintains to disguise its sinful activities. Chicago loves the money that its reputation for being a bloody city, which is tied to gangsters and ghosts, brings in ---- but the "official" stance on the subject rejects this image. Many of the mayors of the city have epitomized this attitude. They made deals with crooks and gangsters, while issuing self-righteous statements about how awful crime was.

The first mayor of Chicago was a man named William Ogden, who made an amazing impact on the early city. In addition to being the first mayor, he was also the first president of the Union Pacific Railroad, which brought the line to Chicago. He was also responsible for the first drawbridge across the Chicago River, helped to create the Illinois-Michigan Canal, was the first president of Rush Medical College, and was an investor heavily in local real estate. In addition, Ogden bankrolled International Harvester when he gave Cyrus McCormick $25,000 so that he could build his reaper works in Chicago.

He didn't start out with such grand plans, however. Ogden had to be talked into coming to Chicago at all. Some of his relatives had purchased a large amount of property during one of the city's first real estate booms and Ogden had been sent to the region to look it over. He looked out over the muddy wasteland and wrote to his family that they had "been guilty of the grossest folly".

However, he soon changed his mind. Later that summer, Ogden sold a third of the land and gained back the entire initial investment. He began to believe that Chicago had a future; soon his own investments in land and business convinced him of the fact.

He was elected mayor on May 2, 1837, defeating John Kinzie's son for the position. Even then, the local Democratic Party was accused of "large scale election fraud". Ogden weathered problems and scandals during his time, including a period when the state of Illinois went bankrupt. Ogden refused to allow the fledgling city to ignore its debts and arranged for special scrip to be issued that would get Chicago through this rough series of years. Later, Ogden and his friend, Walter L. Newberry, were instrumental in the building of Holy Name Cathedral, the city's most illustrious church. But the two men did not do so for religious reasons. They actually donated the block where the church stands in exchange for the Catholic vote for a new bridge over the Chicago River. The bridge was needed so that land owned by Newberry and Ogden could be developed and sold.

In the early 1850's, a wave of sentiment that claimed to be patriotic swept the country and out of this came the "Know Nothing" political party. Its slogan was: "Put none but Americans on guard", meaning that only native-born Americans could serve on the police force and in politics. Dr. Levi Day Boone, grandnephew of famous Indian fighter Daniel Boone, was the head of the Know Nothing party in Chicago and somehow managed to get himself elected mayor, despite the fact that the city was made up of mostly Irish and German immigrants.

He implemented his new political policy and demanded that all applicants for city employment, especially those on the new police force, be able to prove that they were born on American soil. Many in Chicago were angry with this but not as angry as they were about the enforcement of the old (but seldom enforced) law that closed saloons on Sunday. This might have still been acceptable except for Boone's peculiar manner of enforcing it. Only beer halls, which were mainly located on the north side with its German population, would be closed. Saloons that sold whiskey, on the south side, could remain open. Boone also recommended that licensing fees for beer halls be raised from $50 to $300 each year.

The owners of the German beer halls and gardens refused to close and they refused to pay the higher fee. More than 200 people were arrested over this and put on trial. The hearing was scheduled for April 21, 1855 but on that morning, a mob of over 400 Germans marched on the courthouse. Their representatives entered the courtroom and announced to Judge Henry C. Rucker that if any of the defendants were found guilty, a riot would commence. The mob then left the courthouse and stopped all traffic on Randolph and Clark Streets until a legion of police officers could be summoned. The officers, led by Captain of Police Luther Nichols, charged into the mob with clubs, causing the Germans to break ranks and run. Shots were fired but no one was injured.

Dr. Levi Day Boone, head of the "Know Nothing" Party in Chicago. His skewed legal decisions led to the Lager Beer Riots

Meanwhile, the mob retreated to the north side to make new plans. They returned to the area that afternoon with over 1,000 men and they had armed themselves with shotguns, rifles, pistols, clubs, butcher knives and hammers. Mayor Boone countered this by bringing every police officer in town to the area, plus about 150 deputies. He even ordered that cannons be brought to the courthouse.

The rioters soon marched on the Clark Street Bridge and as they approached it, the mayor ordered that the bridge be opened so that the group would be unable to cross. The mob shouted and yelled until (for some inexplicable reason) the bridge was put back into place. They swarmed across the river and collided with the police officers on the other side. Shots were fired and knives flashed --- and all for the right to drink beer on Sunday! The pitched battle lasted for almost an hour and a number of injuries were later reported, along with a single death. One of the Germans, Peter Martin, fired off a shotgun and Patrolman George Hunt lost his arm from the blast. Martin was then killed where he stood. Rumor persisted for some time that more than one man was killed but this was never confirmed, as the Germans were close-mouthed about their injuries and fatalities. Hunt was later arrested for the murder but then was released and given a $3,000 reward by the city council.

In the end, 60 people were arrested for their part in the Lager Beer Riots but only 14 of them were tried and only two were found guilty of anything. They were later granted new trials but nothing ever came of it.

Eventually, the story faded away into memory -- just as the Know Nothing party did. Boone lost his bid for re-election and two months after the riot, the voters soundly defeated a prohibition law in Chicago.

Long John Wentworth was undoubtedly the most colorful of all of Chicago's mayors. During his tenure in office, he fired the entire city police force, personally caught and arrested gamblers, tore down advertising signs that personally offended him and illegally leveled an entire neighborhood. As author Norman Mark noted, "if he were any more colorful, Chicago might not have been standing after he finished his terms as

15

mayor."

Wentworth was 21 years-old when he arrived barefoot in Chicago. It was October 1836 and the young man had almost nothing to his name. Somehow, though, within four weeks, he was the owner of the local newspaper and, by age 28, was in Congress. He soon was offered his first bribe -- by the people of Wisconsin. They badly wanted to become a state but needed the population of Chicago to do so. They told Wentworth that if he would vote to have the boundaries of Wisconsin redrawn down to the southern tip of Lake Michigan, swallowing up Chicago, they would make him their first senator. Wentworth refused, having no interest in becoming a citizen of Wisconsin.

Eccentric Chicago Mayor "Long John" Wentworth (Chicago Historical Society)

Long John certainly earned his nickname. He stood six feet, six inches tall and weighed over 300 pounds. He would usually order as many as 30 courses for a single dinner and would insist that everything be placed on the table before him when he was ready to eat, from soup to dessert. He always sat alone at a table that had been made for four or five and would spin the table around so that whatever dish he wanted to eat next was always within reach.

He became mayor of Chicago in March 1857, taking office after a violent campaign that saw one man killed and several others wounded near polling places. Early in his administration, he decided that he didn't like low advertising signs. Since he constantly bumped his head on them, he decided that they should be removed. On June 18, 1857, he gathered all of the police officers and express drivers in the city and prepared them for their mission by personally pouring them all shots of bourbon. He then ordered them to remove "every swinging sign, awning post or box found protruding two feet or more beyond the front of buildings". All of the signs were thrown into a large pile on State Street and their owners were allowed to retrieve them if they wished -- and to hang them somewhere else.

This would not be the only time that Wentworth would create his own laws and it was certainly not the last time that he enforced them. One night, Wentworth went along with police officers on a raid of Burrough's Place, a notorious gambling den. When the gamblers inside sounded the alarm, the customers and dealers went running out the front door and into the waiting arms of the city's giant mayor. Wentworth personally supervised the booking of 18 of the prisoners who were captured that night. Later, the gambler's lawyer, a man named Charlie Cameron, appeared at the jail and demanded to speak to his clients. His request was denied so he crept around to the back of the building and whispered a conversation through the barred window. Enraged, Wentworth grabbed the attorney and locked him up too. Police returned to the gambling parlor and stripped the place and Burrough's never re-opened.

That same year, Wentworth went beyond just closing a gambling den; he decided to level an entire neighborhood instead. For years, an area known as the Sands had been a blight on downtown Chicago. This vice district was located along a stretch of lake that was just north of the Chicago River, and had originally been the site of a few lodging houses and some saloons. Gradually it enlarged to between 20 and 30 ramshackle buildings where gambling parlors, saloons and brothels could be found. The *Chicago Tribune* called it "decidedly the vilest and most dangerous place in Chicago." Little could be done about this area because the ownership of the property was tied up in court battles -- or at least that was the case until Long John Wentworth decided to get involved in the matter.

Wentworth led a procession of about 30 policemen, and hundreds of well-meaning citizens, across the Clark Street Bridge one afternoon. They managed to tear nine buildings down and by the time that darkness was starting to fall, they had burned the rest of the district to the ground. Unfortunately, the plan to clean up vice in Chicago backfired. Once the Sands was destroyed, the gamblers, criminals and whores simply spread out all through the city.

This event managed to anger many people in the city and they began to question the authority that Wentworth actually had, especially when it concerned the police force. The mayor was so busy making his own arrests, writing laws and designing uniforms and badges that many had to wonder how he was managing to run the city. Wentworth had overstepped his bounds, many believed, so local citizens convinced the state legislature to create a board of three police commissioners to take control of the Chicago police force out of the mayor's hands.

Undaunted, the mayor then decided to fire the entire police force in protest. On March 26, 1861, the force was assembled in the courthouse and Wentworth discharged them from duty, leaving the streets unprotected and the stations empty and abandoned. Of course, it was all done for show as Wentworth left custodians in all of the police stations and told the men to be ready to be called to action if the town bells were sounded. Symbolically though, Chicago had been turned over to the criminals!

How long the city was actually unprotected is open to debate. Some say that it was for as short a time as 12 hours, while others say that it was for as long as 36 hours before the police board began to rehire the officers. There are those who say that the old police force was so inept, though, that no one ever knew the difference!

One of the most famous statements that Wentworth ever made during his tenure occurred during Chicago's first royal visit. The distinguished guest was the Prince of Wales, who later became King Edward VII. When he came to Chicago in 1860, Wentworth introduced the royal guest from a hotel balcony to a crowd that was gathered on the street. He slapped the prince on the back and said, "Boys, this is the Prince of Wales. He's come to see the city and I'm going to show him around. Prince, these are the boys!"

But Wentworth's ego knew no bounds, even when it came to the Prince of England. When he was asked how he felt sitting next to the future king of England, he corrected the questioner by saying "I was not sitting beside the prince. He sat beside me." An author once submitted a new history of Chicago for his approval and Wentworth scratched out all of the entries in the book that did not pertain to him and handed it back. "There is a correct history of the city," he reportedly said.

Wentworth was even filled with himself when it came to his death. Before he died, he bought a huge burial plot at Rosehill Cemetery that took up nearly two-thirds of an acre. He died on October 16, 1888 and was buried beneath a 70-foot monument of his own design. It remains the largest in the cemetery and, for years, had no inscription on it. When he was asked about this peculiarity, he replied that if nothing was placed on the stone, people would ask whose monument it was and, when told, they would "ransack the libraries to find out who John Wentworth was". Years later though, someone decided that too few people were asking who the stone belonged to so they inscribed his name and a list of accomplishments on the monument. It didn't seem to help though, for few people remember Long John Wentworth today -- and even fewer are ransacking the

A caricature of Mayor Carter Harrison welcoming the public to the 1893 World's Fair --- an event that would come to be regarded as a "criminal's paradise". Harrison was tragically assassinated during the final days of the Exposition.

libraries in search of his history.

Aside from the Daley's, there have been two other mayors in Chicago history that have had the same name. The two men, both named Carter Harrison, were father and son and they held office between them for more than two decades. The elder Harrison was elected first in 1879 and then again in 1893, just in time to preside over the city during the Columbian Exposition. It was believed that Harrison was elected one last time for the fair thanks to the criminal element in the city, which bribed him to allow gambling and prostitution to continue unmolested in Chicago. He may have done so to the city's benefit however. The story persists that he made a deal with Mike McDonald, a longtime leader in the vice community, that agreed that no one's pocket would be picked at the entrance to the fair. The agreement specified that any pickpocket who was arrested at the gates would have to either return the money to their victim and would have to pay a fine of $10. In exchange, any pickpocket arrested in the city's central area during daylight hours would be immediately released from the Central Station House.

The fair was considered to be a great success, by all accounts, and marked the crowning achievement of the elder Carter Harrison's career. Unfortunately though, he met with a tragic and premature end. He was at home one day during the waning days of the fair and because he had no bodyguards of any sort, a man named Patrick Eugene Joseph Prendergast was able to walk right into the house. Before visiting Harrison, Prendergast had visited Adolph Kraus, the Corporation Counsel for the city. Kraus had already received several threatening postcards from Prendergast, who wrote in red ink: "I want your job." "Do not be a fool. Resign" and "Third and final notice. You either resign or I will remove you."

When Prendergast arrived at his home, Kraus immediately humored him by telling him that the job was now his. Unsure of what to do, Prendergast became flustered and insisted that he did not want the job that day. Confused, he wandered out of the house. Obviously unbalanced, Prendergast fancied himself a religious man and a politician but a more apt description would have been "fanatic". He believed that it was his divine duty to force the elevation of streetcar tracks in the city. When he arrived at Harrison's home, he walked in and fired three bullets into the mayor's chest. Hearing the shots, Preston and Sophie Harrison ran to their father's side, while the mayor's valet, William Chalmers, rushed in pursuit of the killer.

Mayor Carter Harrison, Jr.

Prendergast, firing over his shoulder, ran down the street and vanished. He paused long enough to put away his gun and to climb into a streetcar, which he rode until reaching Des Plaines Avenue. Less than 15 minutes after Harrison had been shot, Prendergast strolled into a police station, handed his weapon to the desk sergeant and surrendered. At almost the same moment, Carter Harrison died.

Prendergast was put through two exhausting trials with his sanity being called into question by his attorneys and by Clarence Darrow, who spoke for two hours at the man's sentencing hearing, begging for the killer's life. However, the assassin remained unrepentant and flippant throughout the trials, even while his lawyers were testing the insanity defense for the first time in Illinois criminal history. The jury was unconvinced that he was insane though and Prendergast was sent to the gallows on July 13, 1894. He made the sign of the cross just before the trapdoor sprung open and ended his life.

By most of the accounts, unlike his father, the second Carter Harrison was not as easily swayed by the questionable elements of the city. During his first mayoral campaign in 1897, he was pictured with both of his hands in his pockets, leading citizens to laugh that they might actually get a mayor who could keep his hands in his own pockets for a change.

But Harrison never had a chance when it came to really cleaning up the city and he was not adverse to admitting it. When he took office, he described the city council as being a "'motley crew' of saloon keepers, proprietors of gambling house and undertakers". They had no outstanding characteristics, he said, except for an "unquenchable lust for money". Those interesting characters included "Hot Stove" Jimmy Quinn, who claimed that his cronies would steal anything they could get their hands on; Johnny Powers, who bought the votes of fellow councilmen for about $10 each; "Umbrella Mike" Boyle, who collected bribes in an umbrella; and Mike McInerney, who once said that the smoke from the stockyards was good for babies.

And these were the men running the city! Is it any wonder that Harrison later suggested that good citizens might want to "carry revolvers strapped outside of their clothing" for protection?

Even so, Harrison did manage to clean things up as well as could be expected. By the last year of his final administration, in 1915, Chicago was as empty of vice as it had ever been. His administration had been free from official corruption and none of his friends had gotten rich from bribes or at the expense of the public. But this state of affairs would not continue in city government for long....

Between the second Carter Harrison's first term and what was perhaps the most corrupt administration in Chicago history, there was really only one mayor of note -- Fred A. Busse, a bar brawler, drunk and personal friend of a well-known Chicago gangster. He was a man of few words and never took criticism with style. Once when questioned by a reporter about his close ties to business in the city, he simply smirked and said, "Go to Hell." That summed up his feelings about that!

Busse did achieve some worthwhile accomplishments during his time as mayor, although suspending the closing time of his favorite saloon and raiding the Illinois Athletic Club after he was insulted during a card game there were not among them. He also took some criticism for his relationship with gangster Christian "Barney" Bertsche, who killed a detective and two police officers shortly after Busse took office in 1907. Aside from all of this, Busse did help to create the Chicago Plan Commission, which eventually saved the lakefront for the people, and reluctantly supported the massive 1911 Vice Commission Report. Ironically, that report was considered "pornographic" at that time and was banned by the U.S.

Chicago Mayor Fred "Go to Hell" Busse

Postal Service. Busse also ended the infamous First Ward Ball, a genuine annual orgy that involved many Chicago politicians.

He was considered a "reform mayor" during his time but most recalled him as a crude, overweight ice and coal merchant who had little time for anyone. He never even bothered to make speeches during his campaign; yet he somehow managed to get elected. No real scandals rocked his term in office but it should be noted that when Busse died, his safe-deposit box was opened to reveal a huge block of stock that indicated his ownership in the company that sold all of the manhole covers to the city! Any question as to how they managed to get that particular contract?

William Hale "Big Bill" Thompson served as the mayor of Chicago during what was likely the city's worst and most violent period. When he finally left office after three terms, the *Chicago Tribune* wrote that Thompson's rule had meant "filth, corruption, obscenity, idiocy and bankruptcy" for Chicago. They added that he had "given the city an international reputation for moronic buffoonery, barbaric crime, triumphant hoodlumism,

Chicago Mayor William "Big Bill" Thompson -- the gangster's best friend. At Al Capone's headquarters at the Lexington Hotel, he sat under framed portraits of George Washington, Abraham Lincoln and Big Bill Thompson.

unchecked graft and dejected citizenship. He nearly ruined the property and completely destroyed the pride of the city."

In Thompson's defense though, he did serve as mayor through the most difficult era in Chicago history. In those days, Chicago seemed to be filled with gangsters ---- gangsters that slaughtered one another (214 dead in four years); gangsters killed by the police (160 during the same period); gangsters shooting up buildings, throwing bombs and speeding in big automobiles; gangsters bribing city officials, ward bosses and aldermen; gangsters dining in expensive restaurants and attending plays, operas and baseball games; gangsters with shotguns, rifles, machine guns and convoying beer trucks; pretty much gangsters everywhere -- except in jail!

"That's all newspaper talk," scoffed Mayor Big Bill Thompson. Although, just for the record, according to the Illinois Crime Survey, gangster Al Capone was one of the largest contributors to Thompson's mayoral campaign and at his headquarters in the Lexington Hotel, Capone sat under framed portraits of George Washington, Abraham Lincoln --- and Big Bill Thompson.

But how corrupt was Thompson? Did he purposely allow the criminal element of Chicago to run unchecked during his terms in office? Or was he just so inept that he had no idea of the lawlessness around him? Who can say? But we should note that when he first started his political career, one of his supporters stated that "the worst thing that you can say about him is that he's stupid".

Thompson's early life was spent avoiding education. He went out west as a young man to become a cowboy but returned to Chicago after the death of his father. He later achieved a small amount of fame as captain of the Chicago Athletic Club's water-polo team, which was his only qualification for office when he ran for the first time! He first ran for alderman in 1900 after making a $50 poker bet with friends who said that he was too afraid to run. His speeches were dull, his delivery was listless and he had little idea what he was talking about. In fact, he was so clueless that when it was time for him to smile or laugh, a friend would let a brick fall to the floor as a signal.

Thompson ran for mayor with the naiveté of a cham-

Big Bill Thompson crowns the Queen of the Stockyards in 1921 (Chicago Historical Society)

pion athlete on the side of truth, justice and the American way. He actually vowed in this first campaign that "I am going to clean up Chicago" but by his third campaign, his picture was hanging in Capone's office and the gangster was donating as much as $260,000 for Thompson's re-election. After winning that first time, Chicago once again became a wide-open town as far as vice and crime were concerned.

But Thompson's ability to win elections did not always come from Chicago's criminals. In 1915, he was largely elected due to his pro-German stance. In fact, he was often nicknamed "Kaiser Bill". A short time later, his stance caused a great amount of controversy when he refused to invite Marshall Joffre, hero of the Marne, and Rene Vivani, the French Minster of Justice, to Chicago as part of their national tour to drum up American support for their side in the Great War. Thompson noted that Chicago was the "sixth largest German city in the world" and added that he didn't think many of the residents would be interested in having the Frenchmen here. Joffre and Vivani were finally given the invitation but not before Theodore Roosevelt was heard to say, "We'll hang old Thompson to a sour apple tree."

Even after the visit though, Thompson continued to oppose the United States getting involved in the war. A bishop from Texas was quoted: "I think that Mayor Thompson is guilty of treason and ought to be shot... what this country needs is a few first class hangings, then we could go on with our work without fear of being stabbed in the back."

Scandals continued to plague Thompson through his first two terms as mayor. He employed a henchman of Al Capone as city sealer, the person in charge of honest weights and measures, and a local court once ruled that Thompson and his associates owed the city over $2 million, an amount they had allegedly plundered. He almost had a nervous breakdown over this decision until it was thrown out on appeal.

After his first two terms (he was elected in 1915, 1919 and 1927), there was so many scandals, indictments of friends and signs of obvious corruption that Thompson believed that he would never be able to run again. He decided to leave town and look for headlines instead. He found them by organizing an expedition to the South Seas in search of the legendary "tree climbing fish". Thompson set sail on a ship called the *Big Bill*, with a crew that included a theater owner who wore nothing but a jockstrap on most days. The expedition ended before the Big Bill ever left the Mississippi River.

Thompson decided to run again in 1927 and it was this final campaign and term in office that marked Big Bill as the most irresponsible, dangerous and corrupt mayor that ever presided over Chicago politics -- and that's saying a lot in this city! The 1927 campaign was so out of control that it was only exceeded by Thompson's losing 1931 primary effort.

Thompson was so immersed in the corruption that had plagued his former terms in office by this time that he was oblivious to what was going on around him. He had lost his mentor, Fred Lundin, who ran his campaigns and bossed his patronage throughout most of his career, and also Dr. John Dill Robertson, a long-time supporter. The two men had become supporters of Thompson's rival in the Republican primary, Edward R. Litsinger, and Thompson was not above "slinging mud" in every direction. At one point, he appeared at a theater for a campaign rally and was accompanied by two caged rats that he called "Fred" and "Doc". He also noted that Litsinger "lived back of the gashouse, and when he moved to the North Side, he left his old mother behind". His opponent seemed nonplussed by his comments and simply said that Thompson had "the carcass of a rhinoceros and the brains of a baboon".

During that same campaign, Thompson also spent a lot of time maligning the King of England, who was assuredly not interested in being the mayor of Chicago. He even boasted that he would punch the monarch in the nose if he ever dared set foot in the city. No one seems to know where this bizarre obsession with England came from but even after he was elected, he spent a lot of time trying to get allegedly pro-British history books banned from the Chicago Public Library. A henchman named Urbine J. "Sport" Herrmann even threatened to burn all of the offensive books at the lakefront until a court order stopped him. It wouldn't have been much of a fire anyway since Thompson only found four offending volumes in the library's collection and one of them was dedicated to George Washington.

Thompson's election night victory celebration was as big a farce as his campaign had been. He and his cronies ended the night aboard his Fish Fans Club ship, drinking illegal hooch. The 1,500 followers who came

Big Bill's Fish Fans Club, which was kept docked in the Belmont Harbor. One party here was so wild that the ship actually sank in six feet of water. (Chicago Historical Society)

so overloaded the boat that the ship actually sank in six feet of water. This was perhaps a precursor of things to come, for Thompson nearly sunk the city during his term in office and he assuredly sunk his own career.

All of his terms were marked with criminal activity, especially during election time. The most stunning events occurred during the so-called "Pineapple Primary" in 1928, when "pineapples" (hand grenades) were used to convince voters of which way to cast their ballots. A series of bombings occurred in Chicago when Senator Charles S. Deneen's faction of the Republican Party opposed the faction headed by Thompson and State's Attorney Robert E. Crowe. Thompson's political machine was so powerful by this time that they controlled practically all of the jobs and patronage in the city, county and in association with Governor Len Small, the state of Illinois.

Several bombs were exploded during the early days of the campaign, mostly directed against supporters of Thompson and Crowe. On March 21, 1928, assassins killed Diamond Joe Esposito, a racketeer who was behind the Genna gang of bootleggers. Esposito was also a close friend of Senator Deneen and one of his most influential supporters. On the morning of his funeral, bombs were also set off at the homes of Senator Deneen and Judge John A. Swanson, Deneen's candidate for State's Attorney.

The bombings prompted Crowe to make a huge blunder. He issued a statement saying that he was "satisfied that the bombings were done by the leaders in the Deneen forces... and were done mainly to discredit Mayor Thompson and myself". The mayor made a similar statement a short time later but the reaction against Crowe was tremendous. Newspapers, which had been supporting him, now turned against him, saying that "the callous, cynical note in this led to public exasperation." Meetings were held to denounce his candidacy and the Chicago Crime Commission, which had been friendly to him, now released a letter recommending his defeat. The Deneen faction managed to carry the election and this began to spell the beginning of the end of the rampant days of crime in Chicago.

In 1931, Thompson tried to maintain his hold on the office but failed. He lost to Anton J. Cermak, his Democratic rival. This ended his political career but it did not end the rumors and scandals that would plague him -- even after his death. Thompson passed away on March 19, 1944 and it was thought that his estate amounted to about $150,000, which would have indicated that, despite the stories, his claims of being honest were true and that it had been the newspapers creating scandalous tales about him all along. However, when his safe-deposit boxes were opened, cash literally came tumbling out. One box held $1,466,250 in cash, plus stocks, bonds and gold certificates. Another had $112,000 in stocks and bonds and two other boxes contained nearly $250,000 in stocks and cash made up of $50 and $100 bills. In the end, his estate totaled well over $2 million. No one had any idea how the money had gotten there -- but there were plenty of theories, as the reader can imagine.

To make matters worse, his death also sparked a battle between his mistress of a dozen years, Ethabelle Green, who settled for $250,000 and his wife, Maysie, who got most of the estate. By the time that she paid off all of her attorney bills though, she managed to end up with just $100,000.

The *Daily News* sounded the last note on Thompson in that he "was not a great man, he was highly successful in his field. He was not a statesman, he was a consummate politician. His success was based on deception and distraction. He was the most amazingly unbelievable man in Chicago's history."

Chicago's South Side Levee District took shape during the Columbian Exposition in 1893, when thousands of people from all over the world descended on the city. Many believe that the growth of a vice district on the south side may have been what spurred Potter Palmer to flee the region and to build his castle on North Lake Shore Drive, far from the illicit goings-on. And he was not the only one of the wealthy to flee either. Prairie Avenue soon fell into gradual ruin as the Levee began to grow and prosper in the early 1900's.

Visitors to the district could partake of just about every form of vice imaginable, from drinks to women, and it became a seedbed of crime that would go on to spawn men like Al Capone, Johnny Torrio and the generations that followed them and who became the modern Chicago "outfit". Three vice rings formed the criminal organization that ruled the Levee and also provided the areas various forms of "entertainment".

James Colosimo, an old-world Italian brothel keeper, controlled the street sweeper's union and was linked to the legendary Black Hand. After striking it rich selling the services of young women in two of his bordellos (one of which was named in honor of his wife!), he opened a famous café on South Wabash Avenue that attracted both society patrons and gangsters to its doors. Italian opera stars often dropped in to sample Colosimo's famous pasta, and to rub shoulders with dangerous Levee characters, as well. The café was closed only twice during Prohibition and remained in business long after the proprietor was dead. Colosimo himself was shot to death inside of the vestibule of the restaurant on May 11, 1920 and his garish funeral procession included three judges and nine aldermen as pallbearers. The café was taken over by Mike "The Greek" Potson, a former Indiana saloonkeeper. He kept the restaurant going but after Colosimo was killed, he reportedly gained a new business partner -- Al Capone.

Maurice Van Bever and his wife Julia, who operated an interstate white slavery ring that extended from St. Louis to Chicago, controlled another Levee vice ring. The ring inspired the passage of the Mann Act in 1910. Representative James Robert Mann of Illinois introduced the act and it made it illegal to transport women across state lines for immoral purposes. It was believed that operators in the Levee had imported more than 20,000 young women into the United States to work in their brothels.

Charley Maibum, who ran a "pay by the hour" hotel where the local streetwalkers could take their clients for a quick rendezvous, operated the third vice ring.

In addition to these, there were scores of independent operators in the district. The Levee arcade featured a number of "dollar a girl" joints, where the women provided services on a volume basis. Many of these unfortunate young ladies ended up on the Levee thanks to the smooth charm of oily con men, who lured them away from small-town life with promises of romance and marriage in the big city. Instead of love and excitement, they ended up robbed, beaten and "broken in" at the hellish dives of the Levee. In those days, most could see the need for organized prostitution but saw the methods used to induce women to become prostitutes as far more unwholesome. In Chicago (and in every other major city of the day), vice operators had no problem pay-

Big Jim Colosimo would go on to launch the careers of some of Chicago's greatest criminals.

23

Ada Everleigh, the brains behind the infamous (and elegrant) Everleigh Club in the South Side Levee District, and her sister, Minna Everleigh, who provided the wit and humor of the operation. (Chicago Historical Society)

ing off police officers and politicians for permission to run houses of prostitution. However, the officials were less tolerant of what was called the "procuring" of the girls, although the right amount of money could always get them to look the other way. Chicago's vice trade required so many women that procurers operated here with or without approval and the city became a supply point for other cities in the Midwest.

But not all of the bordellos in this part of town were cheap dives that were filled with "white slavery" victims and broken down old whores. Located at 2131 South Dearborn Street was the famous Everleigh Club, believed to be the most garish and opulent bordello in the city. Ada and Minna Everleigh recruited refined and cultured young women and charged their wealthy patrons as much as $500 a night for their entertainment. The Everleigh opened in 1900 and hired chefs, porters and servants to provide background staffing for the six parlors and 50 bedrooms located on the premises. The rooms were amazingly furnished with tapestries, oriental rugs, impressionist paintings and fine furnishings and there was even a huge library for the education of the young women who worked there. There was a waterfall in one room and orchestras often appeared in the drawing rooms. Upstairs, the Gold Room featured gold-rimmed fish bowls, a miniature gold piano and gold spittoons. The basement was arranged to duplicate the sleeping arrangements of Pullman cars.

The Everleigh circulated brochures all over the Midwest and the bordello attracted a famous, and infamous, trade. The sisters paid an extravagant sum for police protection and this may have been the reason why

Captain Patrick J. Harding ignored a direct order from Mayor Carter Harrison II to shut the place down. It did get padlocked in 1911 however and the sisters, who had amassed a personal fortune in jewelry, stocks and bonds, moved on to the city's west side. The ladies were driven out by their indignant neighbors though and retired to private life in New York. The club was demolished in 1933 to make room for the Hilliard Homes, a public housing project.

The rest of the South Side Levee only lasted a year longer than the Everleigh

The gilded ballroom of the Everleigh Club during the club's height of popularity (UPI)

Club. A massive civil welfare parade that was organized on September 29, 1912 spurred grand jury indictments and complaints to be filed against property owners in the district. This resulted in the end of "segregated vice" in Chicago but the Levee did not completely disappear. Many of the famous resorts from this area were bull-dozed, as they stood in the way of an important east-west railroad corridor, but others remained and became the jazz clubs of the 1920's. A number of deadly occurrences still plagued the district in the years to come but when Colosimo's was finally closed in 1945 (Mike "The Greek" was convicted for income tax evasion) and demolished in 1957, an era in Chicago's sorted history finally came to a close.

The point of this history lesson on the vice of the South Side Levee district is to explain who the real "bosses" behind the Levee were. Michael "Hinky Dink" Kenna and "Bathhouse" John Coughlin, Chicago politicians, ran the notorious, gangster-infested First Ward for almost four decades, between 1897 and 1938. They made a legendary team, collecting graft and doling out favors in the area to those who paid the most. In 1911, when Mayor Harrison gave the word to Captain Patrick J. Harding to order his divisional inspector John Wheeler to close down the Everleigh Club, the inspector did nothing until he received the okay from aldermen Kenna and Coughlin.

Coughlin was known as "Bathhouse" because he had once been a masseur in a Turkish bath and he was a large, poetry-spouting buffoon. He was known for being outgoing and good-hearted and a bizarre dresser, sporting garishly colored waistcoats. His poetry often appeared in Chicago newspapers and in his public statements, many mistook him for being simple-minded. Mayor Harrison once asked his part-ner, Kenna, if Bathhouse was crazy or taken with drugs. Kenna replied that he was neither. "To tell you the god's truth, Mayor, they ain't found a name for it yet."

Kenna was Coughlin's mirror opposite. He was small, glum and quietly dressed and was known for being shrewd and close-mouthed. At Kenna's Workingman's Exchange on Clark Street, patrons were served what was referred to as the "Largest and

"Hinky Dink" Kenna & "Bathhouse" John Coughlin
(Chicago Historical Society)

Coolest Schooner of Beer in the City" and the best free lunch around too. There were no orchestras here, no women, no music and no selling to minors. Here, for more than 20 years, the bums, the homeless and the job-less of the First Ward ate and drank for a nickel. Kenna also found jobs for the down and out and often res-cued them from trouble with the police.

But he also told them how to vote and in more than 40 years, he never lost an election or primary. He and Bathhouse created this astonishing record by marshaling the ward's party workers on Election Day to get votes from railroad hands, tramps, thieves and any other warm bodies that were available. They were taken to a polling place and were given already marked ballots that were deposited in a box. When they returned with the unmarked ballots (taken from the polling place), they could turn them in for a fee of 50 cents or a dollar. Those ballots were then marked and used at another polling place, where the whole scheme was repeated.

The two men made an unlikely pair but were a highly effective and increasingly wealthy duo. In addition to the other services they offered, such as guaranteed voting in the First Ward, they also provided protection for a variety of illicit enterprises. They exacted regular and weekly tributes that ranged from $25 per week from the small houses to as much as $100 from the larger ones. They also received an additional fee if drinks were sold or gambling occurred there. They also offered fees for legal work as well, such as stopping indictments for charges of grand larceny, pandering, theft or kidnapping. These fees could range as high as $500 to $2,000.

They were able to provide such services thanks to the fact that Coughlin and Kenna had men who were beholden to them in every city, county, state and federal office in the city. They controlled the jobs of city workers, including inspectors and the police, and were also, as aldermen, in a position to grant favors to respectable businessmen in Chicago. They could usually count on a routine take of between $15,000 and $30,000 per year, over and above the stipend of $3 per council meeting that they received from the city. Special votes that were purchased bought them in anywhere from $8,000 to $100,000 each, depending on the importance of the matter. The two men went carefully about their business filling the requests that the financiers of Chicago were willing to pay for, such as zoning variances, permits, tax deductions, licenses and other amenities.

However, things didn't always go smoothly and the two men did sometimes manage to get attention brought to them, both personally and professionally. For instance, one of Bathhouse's pet projects in 1902 was the construction of a zoo on land that he owned in Colorado Springs. The zoo featured a refugee elephant from the Lincoln Park Zoo who had managed to lose part of her trunk in a trap door. Princess Alice, as she was called, was purchased by Coughlin and shipped to Colorado, where she caught a severe cold in the winter of 1906. Coughlin suggested that she be given whiskey, which cured his own ailments, so keepers gave the elephant an entire quart, which quickly cured her cold. After that, Princess Alice acquired a serious taste for the hard stuff and began searching the zoo, looking for visitors with flasks. She would beg for drinks from them and when whiskey was given to her, she would sip it daintily, go off somewhere, and pass out.

As mentioned, Bathhouse was also noted for his horrible poetry. Epics that he penned included titles like "She Sleeps by the Drainage Canal", "Ode to a Bathtub", "Why Did They Build the Lovely Lake So Close to the Horrible Shore", "They're Tearing Up Clark Street Again" and others. It was later revealed, though, that John Kelley, a reporter for the *Chicago Tribune*, was the actual author of many of Coughlin's poems, which he read regularly at city council meetings. But only Coughlin would have taken credit for a terrible song that he wrote called "Dear Midnight of Love", which was performed for the first and last time at the Auditorium Theater in October 1899.

Bad poetry aside though, it was not weak prose that brought Coughlin and Kenna to the attention of the public and to every reform organization in Chicago from 1897 onward. It was constantly, and justifiably, assumed that the two of them were corrupt, although nothing was ever proven against them. Their most famous exploit was a party and it was one that was such an outstanding example of public debauchery that it was eventually shut down.

The First Ward Ball, which they organized, was referred to as an "annual underworld orgy". It was required that every prostitute, pimp, pickpocket and thief had to buy at least one ticket, while the owners of brothels and saloons had to purchase large blocks of them. The madams usually had their own boxes, where they could rub shoulders with city officials and politicians. The ball continued a tradition that started around 1880, when there was a charity party to honor Lame Jimmy, a pianist who worked for the renowned madam, Carrie Watson. These parties continued on until 1895, when a drunken detective shot another police officer at the party.

After the end of the charity gatherings, Coughlin and Kenna took responsibility for throwing the annual affair. It grew larger every year until the two aldermen were making as much as $50,000 from the party. They held the ball at the Chicago Coliseum and after one spectacle; the *Tribune* wrote that "if a great disaster had befallen the Coliseum last night, there would not have been a second story worker, a dip or pug ugly, porch climber, dope fiend or scarlet woman remaining in Chicago."

The 1907 First Ward Ball was perhaps the most widely reported and, for this reason, it seemed to raise the most ire among the various reform movements in the city. When the ball opened that year, there were 15,000

The old Chicago Coliseum --- Home of the First Ward Ball for many years (Chicago Historical Society)

people jammed into the Coliseum. One newspaper reported that there were so many drunks inside that when one would pass out; they could not even fall to the floor. Women who fainted from the closeness of the Coliseum were passed over the heads of the crowd toward the exits.

As the event opened, a procession of Levee prostitutes marched into the building, led by Bathhouse John, with a lavender cravat and a red sash across his chest. Authors Lloyd Wendt and Herman Kogan described the parade: "On they came, madams, strumpets, airily clad jockeys, harlequins, Diana's, page boys, female impersonators, tramps, pan handlers, card sharps, mountebanks, pimps, owners of dives and resorts, young bloods and 'older men careless of their reputations'…"

At this point, the party really got started as women draped themselves over railings and ordered men to pour champagne down their throats. "The girls in peekaboo waists, slit skirts, bathing suits and jockey costumes relaxed and tripped to the floor where they danced wildly and drunkenly … drunken men sought to undress young women and met with few objection". This seems to be the first mention of Chicago's "drag queens" of the era too and reformers later described the antics of these men in women's costumes as "unbelievably appalling and nauseating".

Even though there had been 100 policemen detailed to the party, there were only eight arrests and one conviction -- that of Bernard Dooley, who was fined for entering the party without paying! Hinky Dink Kenna later called the party a "lallapalooza" and added that "Chicago ain't no sissy town!"

Reform elements had attempted to stop the ball from taking place every year but had never succeeded. After the 1907 affair though, they were even more determined. In 1908, the rector, warden and vestry of the Grace Episcopal Church asked the Superior Court for an injunction against the event but the court simply stated that the affair was not within its jurisdiction. On December 13, just two days before the ball was to be held, a bomb exploded in the Coliseum, wrecking a two-story building that was used as a warehouse and breaking windows as far as two blocks away. The police who investigated said that it had been the work of "fanatical reformers" and the ball went ahead as scheduled. In fact, Bathhouse John told reporters that it was the "nicest Derby we ever had."

Reverend Melbourne P. Boynton of the Lexington Avenue Baptist Church, who apparently attended, said that it was "unspeakably low, vulgar and immoral". Public opinion sided with the minister and the 1908 First Ward Ball was the last. When Coughlin announced plans for the event in 1909, such a storm of opposition arose that Mayor Fred Busse refused to issue a liquor license. On December 13, Coughlin and Kenna gave a concert in the Coliseum but less than 3,000 people attended and police were on hand to make sure that no liquor was served and that no one got out of hand. It was the dullest affair that the Levee had ever seen and there has been no attempt to hold the First Ward Ball since.

The end came for Chicago's two most colorful aldermen --- not with a bang, but with a sad whisper. Bathhouse John Coughlin died on November 8, 1938, an old and fading politician and a veteran of 46 years on the city council. After all of the money he had had made over the years, he died more than $50,000 in debt, thanks to bad gambling decisions.

Hinky Dink took care of his old friend's funeral arrangements, but there were few people around to do the same thing for Kenna when he passed on in 1946. After more than 50 years as boss of the First Ward, there were only three cars with flowers at the graveside and the mayor didn't even attend. Unlike Coughlin though, Hinky Dink died a millionaire, leaving behind piles of cash (mostly in $1,000 bills), two pints of vintage 1917 bourbon, 11 suits of woolen long underwear and a 1930 Pierce Arrow Limousine. After Coughlin's death though, he rarely ever left his suite at the Blackstone Hotel and toward the end, he never left at all. He died mostly forgotten and if not for the blatant corruption that reigned during his tenure as an alderman, and the debauchery of the First Ward Ball, it's unlikely he would be remembered at all.

COPS & ROBBERS
A History of the Chicago Police Department

Chicago's crime and corruption could not exist without the knowledge of and the approval of its police authorities. There is no such thing as a cop being unaware of any happening on his beat. If he doesn't know, he's asleep on his feet.
Jack Lait & Lee Mortimer, Chicago Confidential (1950)

As crime began to wreak havoc on the city, it came to the realization of many that the police officers that had been hired to offer protection for the citizens were hardly better than the criminals themselves. The Chicago Police Department has been plagued for many years by allegations of corruption and graft --- allegations that were well deserved during the turbulent years of Prohibition -- but in the early years of the city, the complaints about the police force were mostly due to a lack of confidence in their abilities. The job requirements for law enforcement positions were rudimentary at best and it was necessary for the policemen on the beat to be tough. For this reason, other problems were often overlooked in favor of brutality. The behavior of many officers, which ranged from graft taking to covert alliances with criminals, generated public mistrust of policemen at large. Undoubtedly, there were many brave, upstanding and conscientious men in the ranks but the men who were inclined toward violence, or eager for a handout, earned a bad reputation for the force. The good men on the police force often faced an uphill battle from the late 1800s through the early decades of the Twentieth Century.

Chicago had no police officer of any kind until the fall of 1825, when Archibald Clybourne, a native of Virginia and one of the founders of Chicago's meat-packing industry, was appointed the constable of Peoria County, a huge wilderness tract that included all of northeastern Illinois. There is no way that any one person could possibly have patrolled this entire region, even though the white population of the area amounted to less than 100 people at the time. The records say that Clybourne never made an

arrest and his official duties consisted of little more that attending the frontier courts and serving documents that were required by the courts.

There is no mention of a police officer in the roster of town officials at the time of the first municipal election in 1833, and nothing to indicate that there was a police force of any kind for another two years. Constable Reed kept the peace in the settlement and a mysterious figure, referred to in historical records as only "Officer Beach", carried the keys to the jail. Crime was discouraged by signs and placards that were posted at prominent street corners, which notified the residents that violations of the law were punishable by fines and that one-half of the fine would be paid to those who informed on the lawbreakers. Those unable to pay their fines were fitted with a ball and chain and were forced to work on the streets for various lengths of time.

The city's first policeman was O. Morrison, about whom nothing is known, save for the fact that he was elected to the position in 1835 and again in 1836. In 1837, John Shrigley was elected High Constable, an office that had been created when Chicago became a city. Samuel J. Low took over the position (also called Chief of the City Watch) in 1839 and three assistants were appointed, although the city charter allowed for as many as six. This same type of organization was maintained over the next 15 years, when Chicago's police force never numbered more than nine men. Needless to say, the officers were greatly outnumbered by the population of the city, which ranged from 4,500 to nearly 80,000 during that same time period. Is it any wonder that Chicago gained its "wide open town" reputation?

Needless to say, it was impossible for such a small body of men to control the crime of the entire city and yet Chicago had nothing better than the constable and watchmen system until 1855, when the city council adopted ordinances that created an actual police department. Cyrus P. Bradley, a prominent volunteer fireman and later a famous private detective and member of the Secret Service, was appointed as the first Chief of Police. Three precincts were formed, stations were established and about 80 officers were hired. These officers had no insignia to designate their position until 1857, when Mayor John Wentworth issued leather stars and allowed the cops to carry heavy canes in daytime and batons at night. Each man was also equipped with a "creaker", a sort of loud rattle that was later replaced by a whistle. In 1858, Mayor John Haines changed the leather star to brass and introduced the first uniform, which was a blue frock coat and a blue hat with a gold band. He also hired another 20 or so men.

Chicago's new police force received its baptism of fire during the infamous Lager Beer Riot in 1855, the city's first serious disturbance. The protests erupted into violence and a mob of Germans marched on the court house and then stopped traffic on Randolph and Clark Streets. The police officers stood firmly against the mob and managed to repel the rioters and send them back to the north side.

It wasn't long before Chicago's police department became an extension of the local political machine and the men hired for law enforcement jobs depended on the success of their party at election time to retain their jobs. Before the first civil service laws were enacted in Chicago in 1895, an incoming mayor could simply fire everyone on the police force and replace them with men sympathetic to his new administration. The biggest problem was that the Chicago political machine was composed of liquor men, gamblers and tavern owners who saw politicians, and the police force, as a necessary evil. They controlled the politicians; in turn, politics controlled the police.

This made law enforcement in Chicago haphazard at best and a policeman's lot was never a happy one. The hours were long, pay was minimal and the prospects of an early death were many. In addition, he had to be resourceful because his livelihood depended on not only how well he did his job, but how well he pleased his bosses too. In many cases, the policeman's choices were not guided by any moral obligation to the badge but by a desire to survive the complexities of local politics. An officer who was singled out for an appointment by the ward boss, who had a connection with the chief or someone higher up in the department, would be beholden to the party and would pay for it in a variety of ways. He would likely be called on to offer protection to some crony of an alderman, to perform political work or to sell tickets to a fund-raising event that would line the pockets of the politician. The rare honest policeman in those days quickly realized the peril of his convictions when he attempted to arrest gamblers or brothel owners who were protected. One wrong step could mean a transfer to what was called the "woods", which meant working midnight shift in a precinct far from home. The officers who protected these establishments though could expect job longevity and the gratitude of his sponsor's political party -- as long as they continued to be successful on the next Election Day.

As mentioned already, many of the police officers in these days were hired more for their brutality and willingness to work for the party than for their knowledge or skills. Because of this, most officers were the product of poor neighborhoods or drawn from the blue-collar trades. The Irish, because of their familiarity with political strife in their homeland, gravitated toward public sector occupations in America. Such jobs were considered to be low status but for the Irish, were a step up from poverty and they began filling the open political positions in increasing numbers after 1860. By 1865, one-third of the Chicago Police Department was Irish and, for many of these immigrant families, police work was multigenerational and work of good social standing in parish neighborhoods. Even today, fourth and fifth generation Chicago police officers, with little or no connection to green hills of Ireland, faithfully gather to partake in Irish-American traditions that are sponsored by the Emerald Society.

By the late 1800's and early 1900's, Chicago's veteran street officers had become cynical and hardened after years of patrolling the crime-ridden streets and vice districts of the city. They soon gained a reputation for being the toughest police officers in the nation, especially during labor problems and periods of civil unrest. Their aggressive approach to the Haymarket bombings and their dealings with strikers sent a clear message that Chicago cops were not men to be trifled with. Reputations of individual men were built on the streets and Chicago newspaper columnists and crime reporters glorified the exploits of the city's most intimidating officers. By the middle 1900's, Sylvester "Two-Gun-Pete" Washington and Captain Frank Pape were said to have gunned down more felons in the line of duty than "Wyatt Earp, Wild Bill Hickok and Bat Masterson combined."

Captain Pape served the Chicago police force for 39 years and, during his career, was credited with killing nine armed criminals and solving the notorious murder case of Susan Degnan in 1946. The young girl had been snatched right out of her bedroom window and killed. The public applied intense pressure to the police force and the case was finally broken and pinned on a University of Chicago student who always maintained that he was forced to confess by ruthless police tactics. Regardless, Pape and his major crime squad served as the inspiration for the 1950's television series *M-Squad*, starring Lee Marvin as the tough as nails captain.

Perhaps the hardest things for police officers of the era to deal with, outside of the internal politics of the department, were the moral ambiguities of the age. In the fashionable residential and commercial districts, the police were expected to close down the gambling parlors and make sure that the prostitutes stayed off the streets. However, in what was called the "tenderloin" district, vice was allowed to flourish and existed in such a way that police graft was tolerated, if not expected. Everyone seemed to be "on the take" and various services required various forms of payment. Desk sergeants in the various districts maintained index files that contained pertinent information about the prostitutes who worked in their area. A young woman who joined the life was required to come in and register, and pay the required fee, before she could start making her living in one of the local dives. Police inspectors and captains became rich and powerful in their respective neighborhoods, thanks to the nature of the city politics that allowed vice to exist. Corrupt arrangements between the police and the criminal element were inevitable given the contradictions and the lack of definite rules against them.

Over a period of nearly 100 years after the formation of the police department, any improvements in the training, equipment or deployment of the men came following the detection of some scandal in the department. The resulting changes were almost always in reply to a cry for reform from the public, the press or the clergy. Many wondered why the improvements had to be forced in such a way but there seemed to be no other way to accomplish anything, as the department and the local political machine refused to regulate themselves. Even the employment of a civilian review board was judged a failure and disbanded. In 1890, five commissioners were appointed to keep an eye on several district captains who were involved in dealings with gamblers and underworld figures. The scandal was exposed in the newspapers a year later, but it did little to change anything. In 1911, these same commissioners were exposed for accepting their own bribes and the Civil Service Commission recommended that the board of five commissioners be replaced with three deputy inspectors, including one civilian, who would be responsible for upholding public morals. More scandal followed when the civilian deputy became involved in the accidental shooting death of a uniformed officer in 1914. The department was again thrown into an uproar, the city council buckled to pressure from the mayor and the commission was disbanded in 1919.

The city continued looking for answers but major reorganizations in 1920 and 1931 failed to halt the city-wide corruption that took place during Prohibition, a period in which over half the city police department was estimated to have received payoffs. In the long run, the unwelcome intrusion of civilian boards into the department could not succeed and neither could the attempts to recruit "spies" from within the ranks to report on illegal activities. For more than 100 years, graft, bribery and political back dealings continued at the highest levels of the police department. Promotions and appointments were given to those who did favors or who possessed the ability to pay. Captains continued to become wealthy and ordinary patrolmen, not to miss out on the possibility of graft, began shaking down ordi-

nary motorists during routine traffic stops.

A 1961 *Chicago Tribune* article has been extensively quoted from over the years concerning this problem and it included an interview with a Chicago driver who recalled his own encounter with some less than honest cops. "I remember some years ago, driving to work before dawn and being stopped by a police officer who told me I'd been speeding. I hadn't, but they said they would have to take me in. I told them to go ahead but instead they asked me how much money I had. I told them that I had exactly one buck for lunch. They said 'Okay, we'll settle for that, we have to eat too!' And by golly, they took it."

Modern corruption in the department reached its highest point (or rather, its lowest!) in 1960, when a gang of eight officers in the Summerdale Police District organized a burglary gang that looted north side businesses that they were supposed to be protecting. The resulting scandal not only embarrassed Mayor Richard J. Daley but exposed the Chicago Police Department to ridicule that it is still enduring today. Summerdale became a black eye for the department but it did set into motion another reform movement, although this one would finally separate the force from the image of the past.

Orlando Winfield Wilson was chosen as the man to restore order and competence to the department. Wilson was a member of the faculty of the California School of Criminology and had attained international prominence in police administration. He turned his much-needed attentions to the Chicago Police Department and began implementing many changes. Younger, college-educated men were recruited and promoted and officers were encouraged to complete their degree work and pursue graduate studies without fear of ridicule from the old-timers, many of whom were forced into retirement as the Summerdale scandal continued to unfold. The cops who ran their districts under the old methods of political favors and graft were finally being forced out. He also consolidated 38 police districts into 21, diminishing the power of the local aldermen when it came to influence hiring. He also closed down six dilapidated station houses from the 1800's and changed Chicago policing forever by placing the beat cop in a squad car, instead of walking the streets.

Perhaps the main thrust of Wilson's reforms was the creation of the Internal Investigations Division (IID), which was meant to "police the police" and to root out corruption in the force. The unit (later re-named Internal Affairs Division -- IAD) was a daring move for Chicago, a police force that had always imposed stiff sanctions on "rats" and lived by a rather dubious "code of honor" that allowed no one to inform on brother officers, no matter how heinous the grievance. The success of the IAD unit is plainly visible in the decline of major scandals since the time of its inception -- but it by no means stopped corruption completely.

In 1973, at the East Chicago Avenue District, Captain Clarence E. Braasch and 18 men in his command were indicted for collecting payoffs gained from shaking down tavern owners along Rush and Wells Street. No one had seen this coming either. Braasch was a family man and father and had been a shining light in the Wilson administration with a number of commendations and honors.

That same year, in the Austin District, Captain Mark Thanasouras and 18 men who served under him were indicted on charges of extorting thousands of dollars from tavern owners who wanted to operate in the neighborhood. Thanasouras was another respected officer under Wilson but had been exposed, by newspaper columnist Bob Weidrich, for collecting graft in 1968. It took the department five years to make the charges stick and, in 1973, he was relieved of his command. Thanasouras pled guilty and received a three and a half year prison sentence. He was sent to the Terminal Island Prison and into a living hell. Prison turned out to be a nightmare for the former cop and he offered to provide information about police and mob corruption in return for a shorter sentence. After 18 months, he was back out on the street, working as a bartender at the L & L Club in north suburban Lake Bluff and providing testimony that resulted in the indictments of four Austin District watch commanders. He was planning to tell more but was shot to death at his girlfriend's home in the early morning hours of July 21, 1977.

Another scandal hit the department in 1982, when 10 officers from the west side Marquette District were caught allowing a multi-million dollar drug ring to operate in their area. In 1996, the Austin District once again made the news when it was revealed that seven police officers in the district had been robbing and extorting independent drug dealers who threatened the large-scale narcotics operation protected by the cops. These scandals revealed the changes that had come to corruption in the Chicago police department. It was no longer about segregated vice districts, gambling, bootlegging and prostitution; it was about the immense power of the drug trade. Police corruption now comes from the willingness of dirty cops to provide protection to the drug dealers in return for staggering amounts of bribe money -- sums that most officers would never see in a lifetime. This makes the work of the Internal Affairs Division and the honest police officers more difficult, but certainly not impossible.

It's true that the Chicago Police Department still has a long way to go before it can remove the tarnished image that it gained in years gone by, but great strides have been made over the last few decades. Today, the department is better managed and a far superior force than at any point in its history. Unfortunately, so many people only think of the corruption and the graft of the past when they think of the Chicago Police Department and they forget about the brave and honorable men and women who have been the majority of the force, even from the beginning. Perhaps in the future, we'll see that image begin to change.

"BLOODY MAXWELL"
Chicago's Most Infamous Police District

The neighborhood of the old Maxwell Street police district has never been short on either dark history or hauntings. This notorious district earned the nickname of "Bloody Maxwell" in the early 1900's, thanks to the escalating murder rate. All matter of vice could be found here and one of the most famous spots in the district was "Deadman's Corner" -- a moniker whose meaning should be obvious to the reader. The community was a thriving one though, consisting of row after row of tenement houses that were filled with Greeks, Jews and Italians. All of these are gone now, having been consumed by the University of Illinois at Chicago, but their memories remain -- as do the legends.

By the time that the Maxwell Street police station became known to people all over America, it had already garnered a nearly century old reputation in Chicago. In the early 1980's, television watchers saw the station house appear as the fictional *Hill Street Blues* precinct house on NBC; however, people in Chicago had long been privy to the rumors, stories and lore of the old building.

It had been constructed in 1889 to replace the old Second Precinct station, which had been located in the heart of the "Terror District" and abandoned that same year. This new building cost more than $50,000 to build from red and gray stone and it was meant to be a refuge in the

Chicago's Old Maxwell Street

"wickedest police district to be found within the confines of civilization."

Captain William Ward, who commanded the column of police officers who were blown up by the Haymarket Square bomb in 1886, was placed in command of Maxwell Street that first year. It had been because of the unrest at Haymarket Square, a bloody and violent protest by laborers over workplace conditions, that the

33

police force had greatly expanded its numbers and had built two new stations, including the one at Maxwell Street. The station was meant to serve as a threat to worker unrest and also as a buffer between the central business district and the heavily populated immigrant areas that encroached from the south and west.

At that time, thousands of Jews, Italians, Greeks, Poles, Irish, Germans and other refugees from Europe came to the frenzied neighborhoods along Roosevelt Road, Taylor Street and Halsted. This was during the great wave of immigration that occurred between 1880 and 1920 and with the new arrivals came poverty, violence and crime. The *Chicago Tribune* said that all around the neighborhood "are corners, saloons and houses that have seen the rise, the operations, and even the deaths of some of the worst criminals the land has ever known."

At the southern end of the area was the Walsh School, a public institution and the scene of one of the bloodiest feuds in American history -- a war between rival gangs of schoolboys that started in 1881 and continued for almost 30 years. During this time, several were killed and numerous others were shot, stabbed and beaten. The gangs called themselves the "Irishers" and the "Bohemians". The allegiance was not determined, as one might think, by nationality but rather by place of residence. The Irishers lived east of Johnson Street and those who lived west of Johnson were the Bohemians. For years, the boys carried knives and revolvers to school and occasionally slashed one another, or shot it out, in the classrooms, the streets and the playground. The last of the gun battles was fought in December 1905, when some 25 Irishers, led by Mike and George McGinnis, marched against an almost equal number of Bohemians, commanded by Joe Fischer. Between 40 and 50 shots were fired before the police arrived, but no one was hit. The ages of the gangsters ranged between 10 and 15 years-old and many of them were so small that they had to use both hands to raise their revolvers to fire them. For many years after this last climatic battle, every boy who attended Walsh School had to be searched before he was allowed to enter.

A gathering of Gennas. From Far Left is Sam, "Bloody" Angelo, Pete, Tony and the hand at the far right, holding the wine glass, belongs to Jim. The Gennas were feared on the west side and escalated gang wars in the city that woudl last for many years. (UPI)

Just north of the Maxwell Street Station was the liquor warehouse of the six "Terrible" Genna brothers: Angelo, Pete, Tony, Jim, Sam and Mike. On the eve of Prohibition, they had been granted a special dispensation from the government to sell industrial alcohol from a location on Taylor Street. Their brother-in-law, Harry Spignola, had invented the formula for the alcohol and the Gennas paid neighborhood residents $15 a week to cook up a home brew, which contained rotgut whiskey with caramel or coal tar added for color. The result was so vile that it actually killed the warehouse rats that were curious enough to sample it. From the filthy warehouse, the Gennas paid off the cops to leave them alone after it became apparent that the alcohol was not for "industrial" purposes. The Gennas sold the mixture for $3 a barrel, which was half the going rate that was being charged by Irish bootlegger, Dion O'Banion, who hated the Gennas. However, the brothers managed to maintain a neutrality with not only O'Banion but with Al Capone as well. That ended when they began selling their brew to north side barkeeps however. The Gennas had stumbled too far into O'Banion's territory and war erupted. The Gennas were all but wiped out in a few short years and the warehouse was closed down in 1926.

Around 1905, the term "Bloody Maxwell" was actually coined. Thanks to the horrific murder rate and the threats of the Black Hand, a crime organization that terrorized the Italian immigrants in the neighborhood, the west side was starting to gain an even more fearsome reputation. Things were especially frightening for the immigrants here, who feared not only the criminals but the police, as well. Thanks to the rumors that were circulating about the station, the immigrants were terrified of being arrested on some pretense and tossed into the rat-infested dungeon of the Maxwell Street station.

Prisoners who lacked the resources to buy their way out of this "hole" were often savagely beaten and this brutal treatment spawned many other shocking stories. For years, the prisoners in the dungeon urinated and bled into troughs that had been dug into the floors and which flowed beneath the cells of the other convicts. There were also stories of prisoners who "accidentally" fell down the two flights of stairs to the front desk, were beaten with telephone books (so as not to leave marks) and suddenly turned up dead in their cells, even though nothing had been wrong with them when arrested. In 1921, Health Commissioner Herman Bundsen declared the Maxwell Street dungeon as unfit for human habitation and a few years later, the basement was closed down. However, rumors that the dungeon continued to be used as a punishment for the worst offenders went on into the 1970's. The city of Chicago and station officials denied the charges.

The Maxwell Street Station closed down in December 1997, marking the end of an era on the west side. By this time, there was no longer a neighborhood to protect. The university had long ago reduced it to empty lots, tennis courts and campus housing. The station house was saved though and is now being used by the UICC campus police as their headquarters.

Although the cops and robbers of yesterday are now gone, the legendary stories of the Maxwell Street dungeon still linger -- in more ways than one. Accounts

Maxwell Street Police Station

persist in saying that the prisoners who were beaten and so hideously abused in the station's basement still linger here. As the years have gone by, police officers and passersby claim to have heard the sound of bloodcurdling screams coming from this part of the building. Moaning and crying sounds are commonplace, although when anyone checks to see who might be wandering about this darkened space, the rooms are always found to be abandoned.

Whether or not they are actually empty is another matter entirely!

35

"WHERE GOOD MEN FEARED TO WALK...."
Chicago's Famous Crime & Vice Districts

By the late 1850s, Chicago was able to boast almost 1,500 businesses within its borders, dozens of banks, railroad lines, millions of dollars worth of imports and exports, 40 newspapers and periodicals, a half-dozen theaters, 80 ballrooms "where bands played from morning to night" and a still-growing population of more than 93,000 people. But not all of Chicago's accomplishments were ones to be proud of. Crime of every description had increased dramatically in just two decades and a national bank panic was spreading throughout the country, causing businesses to fail and widespread unemployment in the Windy City. This led to burglaries, shootings and holdups by bands of young men who had once been respectable laborers. They were driven, according to one lurid newspaper account "from sheer want and by the sufferings of their families to try their fortunes as garrotters, highwaymen, burglars and thieves."

The newspapers published accounts of these and other criminals with almost hysterical warnings of worse to come. People became panic-stricken and the *Chicago Tribune* advocated a mass meeting of citizens to hire Alan Pinkerton and his detectives to clean up the city. This was never done but a group of businessmen did hire Pinkerton to stop gangs of vandals who were raiding the old City Cemetery on the north side, desecrating the graves and digging up the corpses to sell to medical students.

But such incidents of thievery and murder were not the real scourge of Chicago crime -- and certainly not where questionable fortunes were being made. The real problems came from the vice and red-light districts. There has been some mention made of these districts already, like the "Sands", but there were many others, including some that have become legendary in Chicago history.

The *Tribune* called the Sands was called the "vilest and most dangerous place in Chicago" and, by 1857, it consisted of a few dozen ramshackle buildings, each housing gambling parlors, saloons and brothels, in which a charge for services ranged between 25 and 50 cents. Originally, the area, which was located on a stretch of lake shore just north of the Chicago River, catered mostly to sailors and canal men but expanded into a resort area and a hiding place for all manner of criminals. The leaders of this unsavory community were Dutch Frank, who operated dog fights; Freddy Webster; Mike O'Brien; a burglar and former fighter; his son Mike, a pickpocket and a pimp for his four sisters; and John Hill and his wife, Mary.

The Hill's were said to be the first operators in Chicago to work the "badger game", an old-time sex swindle in which a woman picks up a man and brings him home. Her husband then "accidentally" comes in and catches them in the act, demanding satisfaction from the man, which comes in the form of the sucker's money. Unfortunately, John Hill had a wide jealous streak and after every con, he always tried to kill his wife for encouraging the victim in the racket to get into bed with her!

Freddy Webster, another operator mentioned, owned a brothel that was incredibly vicious, even for the Sands. One of his girls, Margaret McGinness, was said to have been neither sober nor out of the house for five years, and to have been naked for three of those years! She customarily entertained between 10 and 40 men each night. She died in March 1857 from drunkenness and was the seventh unnatural death in the Sands during the week of her passing.

The Sands came to an end during a period of violence that marked the tenure of Mayor "Long John" Wentworth. Even before Wentworth was elected mayor, there had already been talk of demolishing the haphazard shacks of the Sands but the land on which they stood was tied up in litigation with the courts. As the *Tribune* explained it: "In view of the uncertainty of the law, the litigants were disinclined to take violent measures to eject the occupants". In other words, the landowners were too scared, or were being too well paid, to run the brothel and saloon keepers off the property. Finally, in April 1857, William B. Ogden bought out several of the landowners, notified the denizens of the Sands to vacate the buildings, and also told those who owned their own buildings that he would gladly purchase their shacks as well. A few sold out but most of the squatters vowed that they would never leave. This was reported to the mayor and he promised to take action as soon as he could without risking bloodshed.

The opportunity came during a dogfight between one of Dutch Frank's dogs and an animal owned by Bill Gallagher, a Market Street butcher. The event was to be held at the Brighton racetrack and, on April 20, every able-bodied man in the Sands accompanied Dutch Frank to the scene. Chicago legend has it that Mayor Wentworth may have arranged this fight and caused it to be advertised, but no one really knows for sure. Regardless, he did take advantage of it. Dutch Frank and his cohorts had barely left the Sands before Wentworth led a procession of about 100 well-meaning citizens, a Deputy Sheriff bearing orders of eviction, 30 or so police officers and a team of horses drawing a wagon that was loaded with hooks and chains. They managed to tear nine buildings down by evening and by the time that darkness was starting to fall, they burned the rest of the district to the ground. When the male inhabitants of the Sands returned from the dogfight later that night, all they found of the district was ashes.

As mentioned earlier, Wentworth's plan to clean up the city's vice backfired. Once the Sands was destroyed, the gamblers, criminals and whores who called the place simply crossed the Chicago River and, instead of being mostly confined to one small area, spread out all through the city.

As already explored, it was largely due to the helplessness of the Chicago police force during the 1860s that the city acquired a reputation for being "the wickedest city in the United States". Attracted by the easy money of a boomtown, by thousands of soldiers on the loose with Army payrolls and by the knowledge that there was little to fear from the police, human refuse from cities all over America swarmed into Chicago.

The newcomers took over and enlarged the resorts that had been formed by the refugees from the Sands and, within a year after the start of the Civil War, there was hardly a downtown street that didn't have a row of brothels, saloons, gambling dens and cheap boarding houses. The criminal class almost wholly occupied the south side below Madison Street, from the lake to the river, until the Great Fire finally burned them out.

One journalist of the period stated that the "very core of this corruption" was Roger Plant's resort on the northeast corner of Wells and Monroe Streets. Originally, the dive was situated in a single, two-story house but when one after another of the adjoining establishments was added on, the resort was extended about halfway down the block by the middle 1860s. The police called the place "Roger's Barracks" but Plant referred to it as "Under the Willow", thanks to a lone willow tree that drooped at one corner of the main building, and the name stuck. The appearance of the place was further enhanced by a bright blue shade at each of the windows that bore the words "Why Not?" in gold lettering. This became a catch phrase all over the city.

Under the Willow was described by author Fredrick Francis Cook as "one of the most talked about, if not actually one of the wickedest places on the continent." It was believed that a tunnel ran from the resort under Wells Street to a number of underground dens that were located along Wells and along the south branch of the river. There were at least 60 rooms in the sprawling place and it offered just about every vice imaginable. It included a saloon; two or three brothels where customers were often stripped, robbed and dumped into alleys; rooms for the men to meet the ladies of the night; cubicles that were rented to streetwalkers; and hideaways that were used by various species of crooks.

Roger Plant, the landlord, was a diminutive Englishman who only stood an inch above five feet and never weighed more than 100 pounds. In spite of this, he came to be regarded as a deadly fighter, adept with all kinds of weapons, especially his teeth. Ordinarily, he carried a knife and a gun secreted on his person but when he got drunk, he would put aside his weapons and ceremonially drench the willow tree outside with a mixture of whiskey and water. He managed to keep his customers in line but he was dominated by his wife, a huge woman who tipped the scales at nearly 300 pounds. She was said to frequently tuck her spouse under one arm and spank him with her free hand. Mrs. Plant organized the affairs of the prostitutes in the resort and when she was not busy with this, she was producing children. No one knows the exact number of children the Plant's raised, but it was generally believed to be about 15. Each of them learned to pick pockets not long after learning to walk!

Under the Willow operated for about 10 years with no interference. In 1868, having made more money that he ever expected to, Plant closed the resort, bought a house in the country and began living a respectable life.

The Great Fire in 1871 destroyed the worst of the city's vice areas, burning the dangerous saloons and the disease-ridden brothels but within half a decade after the rebuilding of Chicago had begun, a dozen vice districts that were even more vicious had been established. To the inhabitants and to the police, they were known by colorful nicknames like the Black Hole, Little Cheyenne, the Bad Lands, Satan's Mile, Hell's Half Acre, the Levee and more. Most of these areas were on the west and south sides and became places of renown in the annals of Chicago's criminal history.

The Black Hole

The infamous Black Hole district was a group of saloons, cribs and bordellos that were reserved for black customers only. They were located near Washington and Halsted Streets in the heart of a vice district that was bounded by Sangamon, Halsted, Lake and Monroe Streets. The "pride" of the Black Hole in the 1870s and 1880s was a placed called Noah's Ark, on Washington near Halsted. The place was described as a "queer old three story mansion" that was owned by Chicago alderman Jacob Beidler, a wealthy lumber dealer from a rich and devoutly religious family. The place was said to be a seething hive of corruption with two saloons and a half dozen brothels. A former drawing room of the old mansion had been curtained off into cubicles that were just large enough to hold single cots. These cribs were rented out to streetwalkers, who charged from 25 to 35 cents to a customer for a tumble -- depending on whether he removed his shoes or not. Noah's Ark became quite famous for robberies during its time in operation, thanks to the methods devised by two of the denizens of the place. One of the girls, seizing on a moment when she knew the man was completely distracted, would hold him by the arms while her partner cracked him over the head. Once relieved of the contents of his pockets, he was hurriedly deposited in the alley outside.

The largest whorehouse in the Black Hole was Ham's Place, a second floor dive that was famous for its company of uniformed women who were always clad only in white tights and green blouses. No one knew who really owned the place but it was believed to be an establishment under the control of Diddie Biggs, who ran another brothel on Halsted, in which the most popular girl was a midget named Julie Johnson. A member of the staff at Ham's was a 300-pound piano player named Del Mason. Her husband, a thief known as both Joe Dehlmar and Bill Allen, became a central figure in what some have called one of the most memorable incidents in the history of the Chicago Police Department.

On November 20, 1882, Bill Allen became involved in a fight that resulted in the death of one black man and serious injuries to another. Later that same night, Allen also killed a police officer named Clarence E. Wright when Wright attempted to arrest him in a shack at Washington and Clinton Streets. Allen fled to the basement of Diddie Biggs' whorehouse on Halstead and hid out there until December 3. On that day, Allen gave Julie Johnson a nickel and told her to go out and buy a newspaper for him. Instead, she informed the police of where Allen was hiding and, for $2, sold the nickel to the famous gambler Mike McDonald, who thereafter carried the coin as a lucky piece. The coin turned out to be anything but lucky for Bill Allen.

A patrolman named Patrick Mulvihill followed up on the information provided by Julie Johnson and went straight to the brothel basement. Before he could get inside though, Allen opened fire on him through a window and then fled down an alley. Help was summoned from the closest precinct station and, within a half hour, about 200 policemen had shown up and were ripping apart the Black Hole in search of the fugitive. Meanwhile, word spread that the man who killed a police officer had been flushed out and was loose and a mob began to form. According to reports, as many as 10,000 armed men soon joined the police in the hunt.

Late that same afternoon, Allen was discovered hiding in a feedbox in the back yard of a house on Kinzie Street. Shots were fired and, before he could flee, Signal Sergeant John Wheeler gunned down the fugitive. Allen's body was then dumped into a patrol wagon and taken to the DesPlaines Street station. Conflicting reports started to circulate though, saying that Allen had been captured instead of killed and when the patrol wagon reached the station, it was met by an angry mob. Shouts and cries demanded that the dead man be taken from the wagon and lynched!

As the crowd worked itself into a frenzy, Captain John Bonfield and a half dozen officers frantically tried to fend off the mob with revolvers. At a break in the furor, the wagon darted into the alley next to the station, Allen's body was shunted out of the wagon and was taken inside through a window. The mob outside grew even more heated, threatening to tear down the police station, and soon it looked as though a riot was going to break out. Chief Doyle mounted a wagon and tried to quiet the crowd. He insisted that Allen was dead but soon hoots and yells from the crowd drowned out his pleas for calm. The enraged mob shouted that the police were concealing the killer and encouraged one another to break out the station windows and force their way inside.

Doyle and the other officers retreated inside and it was the Chief who finally figured out the best way to calm the situation. Allen's body was stripped naked and placed on a mattress in front of the barred windows so that it could be seen from the alley. Then, he and his men forced the crowd into a line and spent the afternoon filing them down the alley and past the window so that each of them could get a glimpse of the dead man. An eerie silence fell over this grim procession as one person after another filed past the bloody and bullet-riddled body of the black man. Not surprisingly, the crowd grew larger instead of smaller as the word spread of the display. After dark, a gas jet was used to illuminate the scene and the procession lasted all through the night and into the next morning.

Allen's body remained on display for 48 hours and then, after an inquest was held, it was offered to his wife, Del Mason, for a funeral. She refused it. "I wouldn't give a dollar to help bury the stiff!" she reportedly said.

The Bad Lands & Little Cheyenne

There were few who could tell the difference between where the Bad Lands ended and where Little Cheyenne began. They were both located on Clark Street between Van Buren and Twelfth but the police considered the section south of Taylor Street to be the worst, so they dubbed the area the Bad Lands. Police detectives described the whole stretch of Clark Street as being "about as tough and vicious a place as there was on the face of the earth".

The area was filled with saloons, dance halls and brothels and one of the most famous characters of the Bad Lands was Black Susan Winslow, who ran a brothel in a broken down, two-story shack on Clark Street, under the approach to the Twelfth Street viaduct. The roof of the place was level with the sidewalk, so entrance had to be gained by way of a rickety staircase. Winslow paid $40 a month in rent for the place, except during the 1893 Columbian Exposition, when the price was raised to $125. She had from two to five girls living with her and they employed all manner of methods of attracting the attention of men passing along the sidewalk. For a long time, they would ring a sheep bell and then started setting off an alarm clock at regular intervals. Then, (for some reason) they began tapping on the windows and hissing like snakes. Finally, they rigged up an electric battery and attached it to the figure of a woman with a hinged arm. The figure would strike the window and then swing back again, making a motion to theoretically invite customers inside.

There were so many complaints made about robberies at Black Susan's that scores of arrest warrants were issued for her over the years. But every officer who attempted to actually arrest her returned to the station house with no idea as to how he was actually going to do so. The problem was that Susan weighed over 450 pounds and was wider than any door or entrance of her brothel. Officers often wondered how she could have gotten inside in the first place! Clifton R. Woolridge, the famous police detective of the 1890s who billed himself as the "Sherlock Holmes of Chicago", finally solved the problem. He made it a mission to take Susan into custody so he journeyed to her bordello in a patrol wagon, passing through an alley to the back door. After reading the arrest warrant to Winslow, who laughed at him the entire time, he removed the back door from its hinges, and using a handsaw, cut out the frame along with about two feet of the wall. Then he placed two oak planks, each about 16 feet long and a foot wide, on the door sill and on the rear end of the wagon. One of the horses was unhitched, a heavy rope was attached to the animal's collar, and the other end was looped around Black Susan's waist. At Woolridge's command, the horse lurched forward and pulled the enormous woman from her chair. She was dragged about three feet up the planks before she began to scream. Woolridge had used rough timber and Black Susan was now pierced with splinters. Finally, she agreed to enter the wagon on her own and thundered gloomily up the planks. As they rode to the police station, Susan lay prone on the floor of the police wagon while one of her girls carefully removed the splinters from her large behind.

"After this", Woolridge later wrote, "the police had no more trouble with Susan Winslow."

Little Cheyenne was named in honor of Cheyenne, Wyoming, which was considered to be the toughest of the "railroad end towns" that sprang up during the building of the Union Pacific line. Just north of the Bad Lands was a gin mill owned by Larry Gavin and a place called the Alhambra, which was next door. They were typical of the establishments in this area. The Alhambra was a place that was then called a "goosing slum", meaning that it was a small room with a low ceiling and sawdust on the floor. The liquor was of the cheapest sort and the building was staffed by the lowest of the area's streetwalkers. They would sit at the tables and wait for someone to buy them a drink or to make a proposal for anything else. In the 1870s, three old women ran the Alhambra, one of whom boasted that she was once the "belle" of Mother Herrick's Prairie Queen.

Gavin's place was just as bad and one newspaperman called it "about as tough a place as you would want to visit". He stated that the "rickety old chairs are occupied by females even more dilapidated.... it was one of the vilest of places." The reporter took samples of liquor from Gavin's and from the Alhambra and had them analyzed. He reported that Gavin's whiskey was full of "pepper and acids" and that the Alhambra's brandy actually contained rat poison!

As bad as these places were though, they were no worse than the other joints in the district, like one placed called the Pacific Garden Saloon, Concert Hall & Oyster Parlor at Van Buren Street. This joint was not as classy as it sounded and was nothing more than a typical vice district dive. Later on, the place closed down and became, of all things, a religious mission. It is worth noting that it was in this mission that famous evangelist Billy Sunday was converted, decided to quit professional baseball and become a preacher.

Other establishments included the 50-cent brothels of Nellie St. Clair and Candy Molly Jones, who gave a stick of candy to every customer as a souvenir of her place. One clever newspaper writer commented that it was "probably not the only thing a patron took home from her place but those souvenirs usually lasted a bit longer".

Hell's Half Acre

The fabled Hell's Half Acre was comprised of an entire block that was bounded by Polk, State and Taylor Streets and Plymouth Place. It was said that every building here was occupied by a saloon, bordello or gambling den and that the area was so dangerous that police officers never entered save in pairs ---- and seldom even then. The center of Hell's Half Acre's social activity was the Apollo Theater and Dance Hall, on Plymouth Place, which was noted in the 1870s and 1880s for the masquerade balls that were sponsored by the brothel musicians, or "professors". The balls became so famous because, at midnight, the dancers would remove not only their masks, but all of their clothing, as well. The Apollo was in existence as late as 1910 but by the late 1890s was frequented by mostly low-class prostitutes and their pimps.

In the middle of Hell's Half Acre was Dead Man's Alley, a narrow passage that ran from Polk to Taylor Street between State and Plymouth Place. The dark and forbidding passage was always filled with trash and scattered debris and on one side of it were a number of abandoned carriages that were used by prostitutes. Thieves and cutthroats also frequented the alley and a man who dared to walk through it, having no business there, was almost inevitably robbed. For more than a decade, the leader of the gang that operated in this area was a man named Henry Foster, who was better known as Black Bear. His usual method of robbery was to sneak up on a passerby from behind, wrap his massive arms around him, fling him to the ground and then rifle through his pockets.

This type of strong arm work was done by Foster and male members of the gang but the "brains" behind the operation was a skinny woman named Minnie Shouse, who lured men to the mouth of the alley and then divided the loot of those foolish enough to follow her into the shadows. She was arrested more than 300 times in a half dozen years but usually escaped punishment by returning a portion of the stolen money or by paying a policemen to threaten her victim with arrest for consorting with a prostitute. She managed to elude capture until early 1895, when she was finally sent to prison for robbing a farmer. Black Bear got into serious trouble not long after Minnie was locked up. He was hanged on July 1, 1895 for the murder of a saloon-keeper.

Custom House Place

Adjacent to Hell's Half Acre was Custom House Place. During the Civil War, there had been perhaps eight or nine brothels in the northern part of this district but after the Great Fire, this portion of the area was mostly taken over by businesses and the vice moved south of Harrison Street. The Custom House vice district that became renowned as one of the most famous red-light districts in America, sprang from the ashes of the Great Fire. For nearly 30 years, the area would be regarded as a blight on the downtown area. Like most segregated vice areas, where gambling, liquor and prostitution were indulged, the Custom House thrived on not only its proximity to the railroads but on an alliance with the police as well. The closest station could be found at the nearby Armory station and they turned a blind eye to questionable activity in the district --- for a price, of course.

The Dearborn Street Station was once essential to vice operations in the Custom House Place district (Chicago Historical Society)

The Custom House district existed between Harrison Street to the north and Polk Street and the Dearborn train station to the south. It is an area more popularly known as "Printer's Row" today. The boundaries of the area tended to change and expand with the opening of each new saloon or house of ill repute. It also tended to shrink when any of the owners neglected to make their protection payments. A police raid usually followed such absent-minded behavior.

The Dearborn Station became essential to operations in the area as it made a perfect recruiting spot for prostitutes during the gaslight era. Naive young women who stepped off the train were often greeted by one of the army of "pimps" who waited in the station. From that point, they were introduced to immoral acts and lured into the "scarlet patch" of the Custom House district.

The most infamous bordello here was Carrie Watson's place on South Clark Street. Despite the seediness of the area, the beautiful Miss Watson's "house" enjoyed a wide reputation for being a charming place, with Carrie having 60 women in her employ. Over the years, she has become a character of legend in the annals of Chicago vice and her beginnings in Chicago have long been the subject of fascination.

Caroline Victoria Watson was the daughter of an upper middle-class family in Buffalo, New York, where she was born in 1850. According to the lore, she grew up and saw her older sisters and their friends doing little more than eking out a living working in stores or as servants. Knowing that such a life was not for her, Carrie was said to have taken stock of her capabilities and decided that her greatest opportunity lay in the field of prostitution. So, in 1866, 16 years-old and still a virgin, she came to Chicago and began working at a brothel called the Mansion in order to learn the business and to prepare herself for her future career as a madame. She remained in the house for two years, hoarding away her money and learning the ways of the customers.

When a madame named Annie Stewart left Chicago in 1868 after the killing of a police officer, Carrie Watson took over the lease of her bordello on South Clark Street, between Polk and Taylor. She immediately installed new beds and furnishings, and hired new girls as well. She later bought the building with the help of her security man, Al Smith, who ran a saloon and gambling house up the street. Annie Stewart had run her brothel as a wide-open operation, admitting any customer who came calling, but, from the beginning, Carrie catered exclusively to the carriage trade and was just beginning to build up a wealthy clientele when the Great Fire disrupted businesses of every type and description. According to legend, the fire destroyed the house but in fact, it was almost two blocks south of the burned area and was not damaged. It hurt her business badly though and it took nearly two years for Carrie to recover.

Early in 1873, Carrie made extensive alterations to the property and, when they were completed, she re-opened what must have been the finest resort of its kind in America. The three-story brownstone mansion had five parlors, more than 20 bedrooms, a billiard room and, reportedly, a bowling alley in the basement. The furniture was expensively upholstered, imported rugs covered the floors, the walls were hung with rare artwork and European tapestries, a three-piece orchestra played music, and wine was brought into the parlors in silver buckets and served in gold goblets for $10 per bottle. The girls, which numbered 10 to 20 ordinarily but twice that during the World's Fair, received callers while wearing silk gowns and performed on linen sheets. The business of the house was conducted with great subtlety and there was no red light over the door, no red curtains and no hawkers hustling men in off the street.

Carrie's brothel operated for nearly 25 years and enjoyed worldwide fame, thanks to its high prices, the loveliness of the ladies who worked there and the luxurious surroundings of the building. Carrie Watson herself, who was extremely rich by the time she retired, was renowned for her silks and diamonds, her two white carriages with bright yellow wheels, her charities and the fact that she paid a larger personal property tax than most Chicago millionaires. Shang Andrews' *Sporting Life* stated with enthusiasm that "In all the world, there is not another Carrie Watson!"

There were other resorts in Custom House Place that were not so elegant or refined though. Of all of the brothels in the red-light districts, the ones that gave the police the most trouble were the "panel houses", which were more robbing dens than brothels. Often an unsophisticated visitor would stumble into one of these places, where he might be drugged and tied up while an accomplice slipped through a hidden panel in the wall and liberated him of his valuables. More often, the secret panels hid thieves with long hooks who

A diagram showing the interior of a Panel House from Herbert Asbury's "Gem of the Prairie" could lift a customer's wallet from pants hanging on the bed-post, placed there while he was "in the act". Few of these victims would report the robbery to the police, lest they suffer the humiliation of having their names printed in the newspaper.

This system of robbery was said to have been devised by a notorious New York thief and brothel-keeper known as Moll Hodges, who operated several panel houses in New York and later in Philadelphia. The first such resort in Chicago was opened at Clark and Adams Streets around 1865 by Lizzie Clifford, who worked for Hodges in New York. Clifford's house was destroyed during the Great Fire and Chicago seemed to be free of them until the middle 1880s, when they began to appear again in large numbers. By 1890, there were almost 200 of them in the city, most on Custom House Place and in Hell's Half Acre. As much as $10,000 was being taken from panel houses and reported to the Harrison Street police station in a single night. Police officers there logged from 50 to 100 complaints. One can only wonder how many robberies were never reported at all.

In 1896, the police managed to shut down 52 panel houses and they closed about 45 more in 1898. During that same year, the keepers of 28 of these places were arrested and while there is no record to say that any of them were ever punished, by centering the attack on such establishments, the police soon put an end to the business.

By the time of the Columbian Exposition in 1893, Chicago had become known as the "Paris of America" because its many illicit attractions. Reformist W.T. Stead, in his book *If Christ Came to Chicago*, counted 37 bordellos, 46 saloons, 11 pawnbrokers, an opium den and numerous gambling parlors in the Custom House district while writing his expose on Chicago vice.

British reformer W.t. Stead (shown here with his wife) was so shocked at the vice in the city during the 1893 Columbian Exposition that he wrote a book called "If Christ Came to Chicago", which exposed the rampant crime. Stead later became a devoted Spiritualist and died on board the *Titanic* in 1912.

The official stance on such districts was to leave them alone, as long as the operators, thieves and undesirables stayed in the district and kept to themselves. However, this was rarely the case. Granted a wide berth by city officers, the dealers in vice exploited the situation with prostitutes being arrested in the theater district and posing as sales girls in reputable stores. By 1903, conditions had become intolerable and reformers would no longer stand for it. A wave of criminal indictments, pushed through by church groups and the mayor himself, sent the vice operators reeling. Most of them moved to the South Side Levee District where they were welcomed with open arms. The Custom House Place Levee had vanished completely by 1910.

After that, the deserted area was slowly taken over by commercial printing houses and bookbinderies, creating the name the district bears today, "Printer's Row". Eventually, the printing houses joined the bordellos and they too faded away. The area finally gained its dignity around 1979 when it converted into the condominium and rental community that exists today. The railroad freight yards have also disappeared, although Dearborn station remains. It has been converted into a small shopping mall, serving the residents of this quiet street. The Custom House Levee is now only a memory.

CHICAGO'S "MICKEY FINN"

There are many names connected to Chicago crime that have endured throughout history but how many of them, save perhaps for Big Jim Colosimo, have been as well known for their restaurant or drinking establishment as they have been for their ties to Windy City crime? There is only one other man, the proprietor of the Lone Star Saloon & Palm Garden, whose name has endured over the decades. In fact, his name has been immortalized in the American language and it is a name that has been spoken by literally thousands of people who have no idea that he was an actual person. This terrible little man, who stood only five feet, five inches tall and weighed less than 140 pounds, was named Mickey Finn and his name is now used everywhere as a synonym for a knockout drink.

Little is known about the life of Mickey Finn but he was born in either Ireland or Peoria, depending on his mood, and he first came to Chicago during the 1893 World's Fair as a "lush worker", which meant that he robbed drunks in the Bad Lands and the Little Cheyenne vice districts of South Clark Street. Not long after, he began working in a bar owned by Toronto Jim in the Custom House Levee District but only lasted here for a few months. Finn was too tough for even this notorious hangout and was constantly fighting with customers, who were mostly hoodlums and thieves. He was finally fired after knocking out a man's eyeball with a board when the customer failed to produce the money to pay for a round of drinks that he had ordered.

For the next year or two, Finn operated as a pickpocket and as a fence for small-time thieves and burglars. In 1896, he opened the Lone Star Saloon & Palm Garden at the southern end of Whiskey Row. This infamous area was a stretch that ran along the west side of State Street from Van Buren to Harrison and where for almost 30 years, every building was occupied by a saloon, wine room, gambling house or all three combined. A police inspector named Lavin once called the place "a low dive, a hangout for colored and white people of the lowest type." Finn ran the Lone Star for about eight years and during most of this time, continued working as a fence too, handling stolen goods. He also took in money instructing pickpockets in the "art of the lift" and taught thievery to streetwalkers, whom he encouraged to rob the men they picked up at the Lone Star.

Finn's wife, Kate Roses, also handled "house girls" for the place. They were supposed to induce the customers to drink and to entertain them in any other manner for which they were willing to pay. Two of the in-house prostitutes, Isabelle "Dummy" Fyffe and "Gold Tooth" Mary Thornton, would later be Finn's downfall when they testified against him during a 1903 vice investigation.

But the saloon's claim to fame came from Finn's novel approach to fleecing his customers. From the beginning, the Lone Star Saloon & Palm Garden (the garden was a back room that was decorated with a sickly palm tree in a pot) was a robbing den. For the first year or two, Finn and his associates contented themselves with picking pockets and rolling drunks, but they soon moved on to bigger things. In 1898, Finn met a black "voodoo doctor" named Hall, who sold love potions and charms to girls in bawdy houses and sold cocaine and morphine to dope addicts. From the voodoo man, Finn purchased a bottle that contained "some sort of white stuff". The police never identified it but it was probably chloral hydrate.

With the "white stuff" as the prime ingredient, Mickey Finn invented two knockout drinks that would become his trademark. One of them, the "Mickey Finn Special", was made from raw alcohol, water, snuff and a liberal amount of the voodoo powder. The other drink, which he dubbed "Number Two", was beer that was mixed with the powder and fortified with snuff water. Finn brazenly put up a sign behind the bar that read "Try the Mickey Finn Special" and the house girls and whores who worked for him were instructed to push the concoction on every man with whom they drank. Finn was so proud of the drink that he named in his own honor that even the luckless customers who insisted on drinking beer only were given the "Number Two" in retaliation.

A customer who might be given one of the paralyzing potions usually just slumped over in his chair and slept until he could be given the proper attention by the proprietor. The bartender, or one of the house girls, would then drag the man into one of the rear rooms behind the Palm Garden, which Finn called his "operating room". Finn and Kate Roses would do the actual robbing. Finn would always put on a derby hat and a clean white apron and would go to work on the man, first stripping him to the skin and searching for a money belt or anything in his pockets. If his clothing was of good quality, Finn would take it and substitute rags in its place. After that, the man would be tossed into the alley out back or left on the floor of the "operating room" until the next morning. The victims were not hard to handle when awakened and were usually befuddled for a day or two afterwards as well. Few of them ever remembered when or where they were robbed.

Occasionally though, a few of the men gave Finn problems and he always kept a club at hand in case one started to show signs of stirring. Dummy Fyffe stated that Finn was "terribly brutal" with the men that he doped but Gold Tooth Mary later testified that things sometimes took a darker turn. "I saw Finn take a gold watch and $35 from Billy Miller, a trainman," she told the vice commission. "Finn gave him a dope and he lay in a stupor in the saloon for 12 hours. When he recovered he demanded his money, but Finn had gone… Miller was found afterward along the railroad tracks with his head cut off." Mary also talked of many other men that she had seen drugged and robbed in the Lone Star and explained that she had quit working in the bar in the fall of 1903 because of Finn's increasing violence.

She also reported that Finn told her that he would never be arrested because he paid the police for protection and possessed influence with corrupt aldermen Hinky Dink McKenna and Bathhouse John Coughlin. Strangely, no one was ever asked by to explain or deny these boastings by Finn. Not long after the prostitutes appeared before the commission, the police raided the Lone Star but found nothing save for a few bottles of liniment and some cough medicine. With no real evidence, they said, they were unable to arrest Finn. The only action the commission could take was to revoke Finn's saloon license and on December 16, 1903, the doors of the Lone Star were closed.

Mickey Finn left Chicago for a few months but returned in the summer of 1904. He tended bar in a place on South Dearborn Street and, while he refrained from administering it himself, he sold the formula for his "Special" to a number of ambitious saloonkeepers throughout the city. To the underworld, the potion was known simply as a "mickey finn". To this day, it's a name that's applied to knockout drinks of every type --- earning one of Chicago's own a rather dubious place in history.

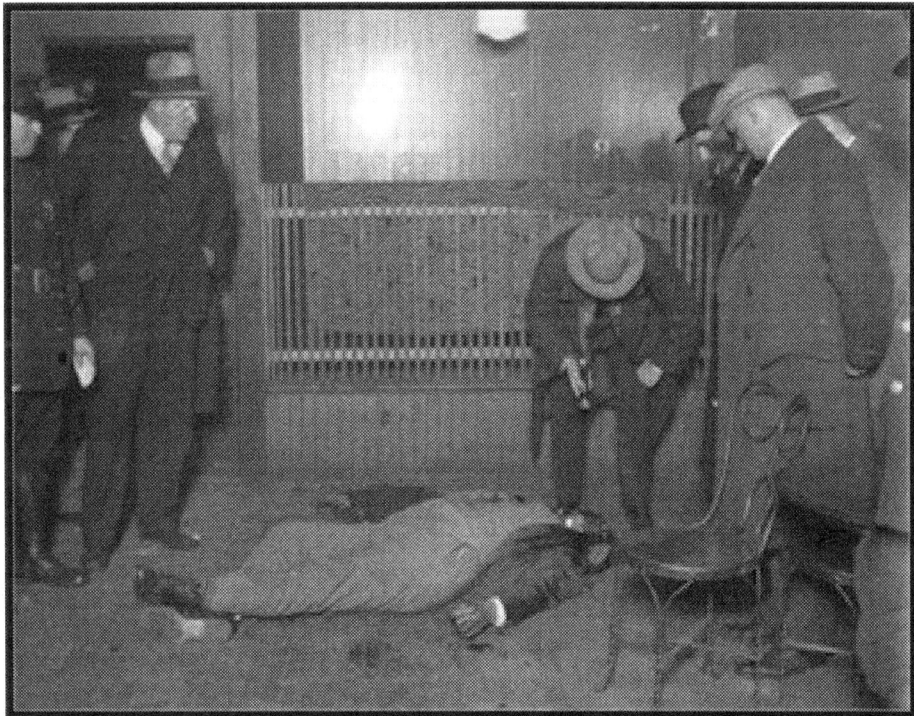

2. BEYOND THE STRANGE

Chicago's Most Famous Bloody Murders & Unsolved Mysteries

Chicago is a man with a conservative and eminently respectable business, a good wife and a wonderful family of kiddies, who looks back with nostalgic tenderness upon his purple past, and pardons the escapades of his youth and peccadilloes of middle age with a shrug and a murmured, "Well, a guy's only human, ain't he?"
Sewell Peaslee Wright

Chicago has never been legit!
Al Capone

From its very beginnings, Chicago has been a city with secrets to hide.

Sadly, it has been a place that has never kept them well. In 1945, author Sewell Peaslee Wright pointed out that Chicago is proud of her soiled reputation. The dwellers of this city never tire of raking up Chicago's political garbage heap so that the stench rises for the entire world to smell. We exhibit our prostitutes against a background of graft, lust and murder, and record in detail the reign of the Prohibition gangsters and how they drenched the streets of the city with blood. Not much has changed since 1945 --- Chicago's crime still fascinates us and we still dwell on her savage, murderous violence and her complicated secret life.

Chicago is a place that has seen nearly every type of crime known to man, including murder. The city has had her share, perhaps more than her share, of not only murders of the common variety but murders that are so strange, bizarre and disturbing that they have often been referred to by students of mystery as "classics". They are murders not only linked to Chicago's bizarre past but are, in some cases, so strange that I could not help but include them in this book.

The chapter that follows chronicles just these types of murders. They are among the strangest to ever occur in the city and are rife with elements of the unknown and in some cases, tinged with the supernatural, as well. In other tales, you will find murders that remain unsolved to this day.

You will likely be both intrigued and disturbed by the stories to come. Remember though, as mentioned in the first pages of the book, not every story to come will be "haunted" by restless specters. Most of those tales will be confined to later chapters but the cases in this chapter were simply so strange, so mysterious and so horrifying that they had to be included anyway.

I have a feeling that you won't be disappointed!

THE "HOUSE OF WEIRD DEATH"

The street where the Wynekoop Mansion was once located is a beaten and forlorn area on Chicago's west side. It was once a place of opulence and prestige but it is now a scene of silent desolation. The weather-beaten old homes here stand with an almost ghost-like presence that hearkens back to days of past elegance. The Wynekoop Mansion was destroyed many years ago, but its memory and reputation still lingers today --- best remembered for its notorious nickname, "The House of Weird Death".

Doctors Frank and Alice Wynekoop built the mansion at 3406 West Monroe Street in 1901. They closely supervised the construction, planning to turn the red brick home into a safe and loving environment for their family. The house seemed to be a warm and welcoming place for a time, but then events conspired to make words like "haunted" and "cursed" better adjectives to describe the place. The house was marked by death, illness and scandal but no single occurrence affected the house like the death of Rheta Wynekoop in 1933.

In the years before this horrific event though, it seemed to be a wonderful place for the family. Another son and a daughter were added to the family and, later on, another daughter was added, this time by adoption. All of the children, who brought Alice many years of happiness, thrived in the environment of learning and respect that was fostered in the family home. Their only sadness came with the death of Dr. Frank Wynekoop, who died while several of the children were still young. He left them in the care of their more than capable mother.

Dr. Alice Lindsay Wynekoop was an early advocate of women's rights and promoter of the suffrage movement. In addition to being a graduate of the Women's Medical School at Northwestern University, she was a pillar of the community and was much loved and admired for her charitable deeds and work on behalf of those in need. She was also a civic leader and a pioneer in the movement for children's health. Dr. Alice maintained her office in a basement suite of her home that had been built for that purpose and which was accessible from West Monroe Street.

Her children continued to bring her joy as adults. Her oldest son, Walker, became a respected businessman in Wilmette, married, and had two children of his own. Catherine, the youngest of the family, also studied medicine and became a surgeon and highly respected member of the staff of the Cook County Hospital. The pride of Dr. Wynekoop's life, though, was her son, Earle. Most considered him a lazy, good-for-nothing leech that continued to be a source of embarrassment to the family. Alice

The brownstone Wynekoop Mansion that would come to be known as "The House of Weird Death" in the sensational newspaper stories of the day.
(True Detective Magazine)

Charming son but errant husband, Earle Wynekoop.

(Below) Earle's young, lovely and ill-fated wife, Rheta Gardner Wynekoop.

never saw this side of him though because, in spite of his many faults, Earle was quite charming and attentive to his mother.

At the age of 27, Earle was still being supported by his mother and residing in her fashionable brownstone. By this time, his younger sister was finishing her medical training and his brother had married and settled in Wilmette. Earle was living a carefree life of travel and, while visiting Indianapolis, met and attractive, well-to-do redheaded heiress named Rheta Gardner. She was an entertainer at a concert he attended and when he returned to Chicago, began corresponding with her. Less than a year later, he had coaxed her into coming to Chicago and had convinced her that they should be married. Since Rheta was only 18, Alice insisted that Earle obtain consent for the marriage from the girl's father, an Indianapolis flour and salt merchant named Burdine H. Gardner. It was given, somewhat grudgingly, and Gardner did attend the wedding.

A celebration was held on the day of the wedding but Rheta refused to spend her wedding night in the Wynekoop mansion. After a night in a hotel, they left on their honeymoon. While they were away on their trip, Alice redecorated and refinished a suite of rooms on the second floor so that it would be ready for the newly-weds when they returned.

Rheta would come home to the mansion and take her place among the rather unusual group of people residing there, including her husband, who made no plans to look for employment now that he was married. But what of the others? There was, of course, Alice Wynekoop, a well-thought of but rather eccentric woman who would soon became a central figure in a strange murder case. There was also her daughter, Catherine, who was studying to become a doctor herself. There was Marie Louise, the adopted daughter, a shadowy and unfortunate young girl who lived a short life. There was a Miss Catherine Porter, a woman of about Alice's age, who was rooming there and being treated by Alice for cancer and heart disease, and who also shared a $2,000 bank account with her doctor and devoted friend. There was also another tenant named Miss Enid Hennessey, a middle-aged schoolteacher, who shared rooms with her elderly father.

After the couple returned to Chicago, Rheta was largely abandoned by Earle, who had quickly fallen out of love (or lust) with the pretty young woman. He was rarely at home and Rheta was forced to make the best of a bad situation, stranded in Alice's dark and gloomy mansion, pining away and playing her violin. She was an accomplished musician and hoped to one day pursue a music career.

In the mean time, the only thing that Earle was pursuing was a string of young women. His "black book" contained the names of more than 50 young women that he had wooed and bedded during the 1933 World's Fair. The handsome rake had proposed marriage to several of these poor and lovesick young girls, who worked at concession stands on the fairgrounds. He escorted them about, buying them food and small trinkets and whispering of the future they would have together. He took special care to avoid areas of the fair where his other "sweethearts" might be working. According to reports, when the details of Earle's many affairs were later revealed, his numerous "fiancées" accused him of making love to them in strange ways that were "shocking and repulsive".

Earle's bizarre behavior just made things worse for Rheta. Since the time of the wedding and subsequent return to Chicago, she had become more and more unhappy. She had been all but forgotten by her handsome husband and had been left with the companionship of her aging mother-in-law and a middle-aged schoolteacher. The only bright spots in her life were her music and the friendship of her "sisters", Marie Louise and Catherine. Tragically, though, Marie Louise died and the deaths of Alice's friend, Miss Porter, and the father of Miss Hennessey followed the death of her sister-in-law. Soon after, Catherine escaped from the household to become a resident physician at Cook County Hospital.

Rheta plunged into depression, a state that she lived in mortal fear of. When she was only seven years-old, her mother had been confined to an insane asylum and she had died there, some 10 years later, from tuberculosis. Because of this, Rheta had a great fear of illness and an even greater fear of going insane herself. One cannot help but wonder what was going through her mind as she wandered around the old mansion each day, wondering where her husband was spending his nights and wondering what would become of her in the future. Sadly, though, she would not wonder about her future for long.

Dr. Alice Wynekoop at the time of Rheta's Murder (True Detective Magazine)

On November 21, 1933, around 10:00 p.m., police officers from the Fillmore Street Station were summoned to the mansion on West Monroe Street. The officer in charge of Squad Car 15 later reported: "We went directly there and were met at the front door by a lady who told us to come inside. The lady we met first we later found to be Miss Enid Hennessey, a schoolteacher and roomer there. When we got inside, we met the defendant, Dr. Wynekoop. She was seated in a chair in the library. Mr. Ahearn, an undertaker, was there. We asked the defendant what happened. She said 'something terrible has happened; come on downstairs and I will show you.' We went downstairs."

The officers found Rheta lying facedown on Dr. Alice's emergency operating table in the basement. She was partially nude and she had a bullet wound in her back, just under her left shoulder. Next to the body, they found a chloroform mask and the murder weapon. Three shots had been fired from it and it had been left just above the girl's head.

The crowd of police attracted onlookers outside and it made things very tense inside of the house. Detectives, who soon arrived on the scene, began questioning everyone, including Alice. As she began speaking, she continually changed her story, confusing the police, the coroner and even members of the household. Many wondered if the beloved doctor might be incoherent over the girl's death. She advanced the theory that Rheta may have killed herself in a fit of depression, and then suggested that a burglar was responsible for the crime, declaring that both money and drugs were missing from the house. But to Captain John Stege, the manner of Rheta's murder didn't agree with the theory of a burglar. He had also ruled out suicide because of the

Veteran Chicago Police Captain
John Stege

angle of the shot and because of chloroform burns that were present on the girl's face.

There was a lot that Captain Stege needed to know and, as word leaked out about the murder, a lot that the public and press wanted to know, as well. For instance, where was Earle Wynekoop on the night of the murder?

According to Earle's version of events, he was traveling west to photograph the Grand Canyon for the Santa Fe Railroad, accompanied by a friend name Stanley, at the time of his wife's death. He claimed that he had started west for Arizona several days before the murder but rumor had it that he had been seen in Chicago not more than a day before the crime. He was taken into custody when he arrived from Kansas City by train and with him was not a friend named "Stanley" but an attractive young girl he had met at the fair. She had known him as Michael Wynekoop and he had told her that he was not married. She was soon released but Earle was taken in for questioning.

Reports stated that he was cooperative with the police interviews and gave an opinion that "a moron" had murdered Rheta. He added other, even more interesting, details about his married life. The marriage, Earle said, was a failure. Rheta, at one time, had attempted to poison the family by putting iron fillings and drugs in the food. She had tuberculosis, he added, and was mentally deranged.

While Earle was making wild, and far from, helpful statements in the press and to the police, Rheta's father, Burdine H. Gardner, was rushing to Chicago. He met with Alice and then dramatically took his daughter's body home for burial. Alice had advised him to tell others that Rheta's death had been caused by complications from tuberculosis! He would later state that he found the living arrangements at the Wynekoop house to be rather odd, and Dr. Alice even more so. "She struck me as a most peculiar person," he told a newspaper reporter.

The police continued the investigation, grilling Alice and the other members of the household. Confused by the large and eccentric collection of characters that lived in the house, they simply began questioning all of them. They turned out to be a bizarre group, each one fiercely loyal to Dr. Alice. When detectives hinted to Miss Hennessey that Alice might have been responsible for Rheta's death, she became hysterical and began screaming, "It's a lie! It's a lie!". She stood faithfully by the doctor through the trial that followed and even invented an alibi to protect her friend.

Alice continued to invent her own stories to explain her daughter-in-law's death. Her "burglars" became "drug fiends" and were responsible for the murder. In recent months, she claimed, her basement office had been broken into and drugs had been stolen. She suggested that Rheta might have caught them in the act. Detectives grilled Alice for hours but she refused to say or do anything to incriminate herself or Earle. Eventually, detectives told her that they had just learned that Earle had taken out a $5,000 life insurance policy on Rheta, so he must have been the killer.

At that point, she confessed.

Her concern for Earle finally caused Alice to break. She confessed that it had been she, not Earle, who had pulled the trigger, but only after Rheta had already expired from deadly anesthetic. Wynekoop explained that she had been about to perform a painful surgical procedure on the young woman (possibly an abortion, although it was never said). She said that she had asked Rheta herself to pour some chloroform into the mask to ease the pain of the surgery but the dosage had proven to be too much. Minutes later, the girl had lapsed into a coma. Fearing public humiliation and a ruined reputation, Wynekoop had panicked and had fired the fatal shot into the girl. She would blame the crime on imaginary "drug fiends".

The sensational confession raised doubts among the detectives. They still believed that "charming" Earle had masterminded the crime and his mother had taken the blame to save her "little boy". Love letters between the mother and son revealed a relationship that went well beyond the norm. One such letter became public and it had been written after a secret meeting between Alice and Earle that had taken place between on the Sunday evening before the murder. Assistant State's Attorney Charles S. Doughtery believed that Alice had made up her mind to murder Rheta after this meeting. No one actually knows what was said that night --- and never will --- but after her return home, Alice wrote Earle a frantic note that read:

Sunday night ---

Precious ----
I'm choked --- you are gone --- you have called me up ----
and after 10 minutes or so, I called and called ---- no answer ----
maybe you are sleeping ---- you need to be ---- but I want to hear
your voice again tonight ---- I would give anything I had ---
to spend an hour ---- in real talk with you ---- tonight ---
and I cannot ----
Good night.

But why would Alice have killed Rheta? Jealousy about her interference with Alice's relationship with her own son? State's Attorney Doughtery believed that there was "another girl", one that Earle truly loved and that she was not Rheta or his mother. Earle had given this girl a diamond engagement ring, said to be the one he had previously given to Rheta. For religious reasons, neither his family nor hers believed in divorce.

Doughtery cited this as a motive for the murder with a demented Alice trying to insure the happiness of her son by getting rid of his unwanted wife. He also added that Alice was deeply in debt and, by killing Rheta, she could collect on an insurance policy that she had taken out on the girl.

After hearing of his mother's confession, Earle made five obviously false confessions of his own, culminating in a wild story about how he had slipped into the Wynekoop home on Tuesday afternoon, hid in the basement, waited for his wife, seized her, threw her onto the operating table, killed her and then fled by airplane to Kansas City. He tried to re-enact how he had done all of this but so badly bungled the "crime" that detectives actually laughed at him. Needless to say, his entire story was dismissed and his confession debunked when it was also proven that his alibi was intact. He really was out of state at the time of the murder. Prosecutors still believed that Alice was responsible for the murder, killing Rheta because she needed money and hated her daughter-in-law for making her son so miserable.

The Wynekoop case stayed in the newspaper headlines. On November 28, Alice became seriously ill with a bronchial cough and high blood pressure. From her sickbed in the prison hospital, she reversed her confession and claimed that the police had coerced her into making it after 60 hours of questioning. During that time, she said, she had been given no food or drink, save for a single cup of coffee. Two days later, she changed her story again and, this time, stated that she had only made the confession because she did not think she would live to stand trial.

The trial was scheduled for January but, in the meantime, the Wynekoops stayed in the public eye. On December 2, Earle announced that the family had hired a private detective to solve the mystery and prove his mother's innocence. Apparently, though, nothing ever came of the investigation for it was never spoken of again.

A few days later, newspapers carried reports that Rheta's body had been exhumed in Indianapolis and the coroner announced that there was no trace of chloroform in her body, thus repudiating one portion of Alice's story.

In the middle of December, two events occurred that, while having nothing to do with Rheta's murder,

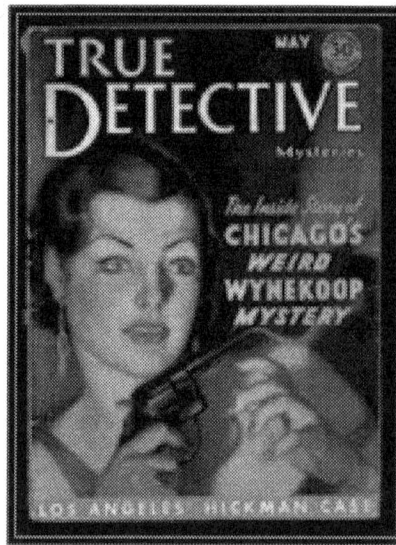
Two of the wildly sensational magazines of the day that covered the
Wynekoop Murder Case.

managed to keep the Wynekoops in the headlines. On December 14, Earle ran over a nine year-old boy with his automobile and his sister, Dr. Catherine Wynekoop, was in the car with him at the time. Shortly after, Alice's brother-in-law, Dr. Gilbert Wynekoop, was found to be insane by a jury that was trying him for attacking a nurse. He was sent to St. Luke's Hospital for the insane.

These happenings helped to put Chicago into a state of great excitement by the time the trial opened in January. The case dragged on for weeks, attracting great public attention. Nearly six months after the weird murder, a jury returned a verdict of guilty against the doctor on March 6, 1934. The press and the public were strongly divided over whether or not justice had been served with the verdict. Alice was sentenced to 25 years in prison but was granted parole from the Women's Reformatory in Dwight in 1949. She was 79 years-old at the time and she died two years later, her life and reputation destroyed.

Somehow, the rest of the family was not destroyed along with her. Walter Wynekoop went on to a successful business career and Catherine became an esteemed physician, long associated with the Children's Clinic of the Cook County Hospital.

Only Earle vanished from the public eye completely. In 1945, he was working as an auto mechanic but that was the last time that anyone heard from him. Most likely, he died many years ago.

The "House of Weird Death", as the newspapers called it, was torn down many decades ago. For years, rumors about the house circulated. It was considered by many to be haunted and stories went around that the ghostly strains of Rheta's violin could sometimes be heard coming from the ruins of the building.

How much of this story was true and how much was legend is now a mystery. The neighborhood itself, the Fillmore district, is now a crime-ridden area and where the graceful mansions once stood, only empty lots remain. Rheta Wynekoop, along with the rest of this strange clan, is now long forgotten.

And if her ghost still walks here, it walks alone.

THE WIZARD OF CHICAGO

One of the most mysterious killers in Chicago history is one of the least remembered today. He may not have claimed dozens of victims or carried out gruesome, bloody crimes but he certainly aroused public interest at the time of the murders that were connected to him.

Herman Billik was a stout, handsome Bohemian with piercing black eyes and a devilish way with women. He was also a fortuneteller who read the future for a small sum and carried on a lively trade in charms and potions. In addition, he was undoubtedly an accomplished hypnotist and claimed to possess strange occult powers that he said were inherited from his mother, who was allegedly a witch. However, when Billik carried out the murders of six people -- a father, mother and their four daughters -- he did so without any sort of supernatural forces and relied on poison instead.

Herman Billik, whose real name was Vajicek, came to Chicago from Cleveland in 1904, where his mother had worked as a fortuneteller (not as a witch, as he often claimed) for many years. He established himself and his family (which consisted of his wife, two sons and a daughter) in a small house on West 19th Street. He immediately hung out a sign that announced that he was the "Great Billik, Card-Reader and Seer". Soon, he began to receive callers from the neighborhood, and from the surrounding area, who wanted to avail themselves of his services. As his reputation spread, he began calling himself the "Wizard of Chicago" and people began to talk about the uncanny accuracy of his predictions and the worthiness of the love charms and spells that he peddled. There were also whispers of his skills as a lover for a number of women went away satisfied by more than just a card reading. It's likely not a coincidence that Billik was an expert hypnotist as well as a "seer".

Located three doors away from the Billik residence was the modest home of Martin Vzral, who lived there with his wife, Rose, and their seven children. Vzral was a milk dealer and one of the more prosperous inhabitants of the neighborhood in that he owned his own home, operated a successful business and had over $2,000 in the bank, a tidy sum in those

Herman Billik -- the so-called
"Wizard of Chicago"

days. Later, it was established that Billik had chosen the Vzrals for his victims before he moved into the neighborhood but he made no attempt to approach them for nearly a week after moving onto the street. Not surprisingly, the Vzrals knew who he was when he finally did make contact with them, as he surrounded his movements with an air of mystery and had become the topic of gossip for blocks around. One day, he walked into the milk depot and ordered a can of milk. As Vzral filled the container, Billik started at him intensely, muttered a few words of gibberish and then said with great gravity: "You have an enemy. I see him. He is trying to destroy you."

Billik would tell him nothing else. He left the milk stand and let Vzral worry about his words for a few days. Then he called on him at his home and told him that Vzral's enemy was another milkman who lived across the street from him. Not to worry, though -- Billik offered to use his supernatural powers in his new friend's defense. Later, at the stroke of midnight, with the entire Vzral family looking on, Billik concocted a horrible smelling potion on the kitchen stove and then tossed the mixture onto the other milkman's front stoop. "Now you will prosper," he told them. "He cannot harm you."

And Vzral did prosper. Not because of any magic spells, but because he was a hard-working and industrious man. He didn't see through the illusion though and credited Billik with his increase in business. He spread the word about the "wizard", even though Billik refused to accept payment for the "great service" that he had done for the milkman. The Vzrals were a strict Catholic family but were also very superstitious and saw no reason that Billik could not be everything that he claimed to be. They listened, night after night, to the litany of supernatural wonders he had allegedly performed and within a few weeks, his domination of the family was complete.

According to reports, he seduced Mrs. Vzral and her daughters and had sex with them in the same room where Martin Vzral stood watching! It was said that Mrs. Vzral's obsession with Billik was so intense that she refused to leave the house for days, fearing that he might come by while she was away. Billik also "borrowed" money from Vzral with every visit and, by January 1905, had stripped him of his bank account, and was siphoning off the profits from the milk business, too. To provide more money to give to Billik, three of the Vzral girls went to work as domestic servants, turning over all of the money they earned to him.

Meanwhile, Billik bought new clothing, purchased a fashionable carriage, and made frequent trips to New York and California, all of which the Vzrals paid for. At his suggestion, Mrs. Vzral insured the lives of her husband and four of her daughters and made Billik the beneficiary. The only members of the family who were not insured were the oldest daughter, Emma, the son, Jerry, and their infant daughter. It's no coincidence that they were the only ones to survive Billik's evil plans.

Early in March 1905, Martin Vzral began to show signs of realizing what was happening to himself and his family. He began to worry about money and the deplorable state of his business and even asked Billik for a loan -- money that he had given to the charlatan in the first place! Billik wondered if perhaps he had pressed the milkman too hard and, to cure the man's "unsettled feelings", he gave Mrs. Vzral a white powder (which he told her was a charm) and told her to put it into her husband's food. A few days later, Vzral began to complain of sharp pains in his abdomen and Billik diagnosed his ailment as mere "stomach trouble". He treated him with his own concoction -- the same white powder, which was later revealed to be arsenic -- and Vzral slipped into a coma and died on March 27, 1905. Mrs. Vzral collected $2,000 in life insurance, which she immediately turned over to her depraved lover. Billik allowed her to keep $100 of it for burial expenses.

A few weeks passed and Emma and Mary Vzral, two of the late milkman's daughters, went to see Billik at Riverside, where he was telling fortunes in a tent. He showed Emma a strangely marked card and explained to her that it was a "death omen" and that "Mary will die soon". He was correct -- Mary died of "stomach trouble" on July 22, 1905. Her life had been insured for $800 and, again, Billik took all but the money that was needed to pay for the poor girl's funeral.

By this time, Jerry Vzral had decided to speak up. He demanded that Billik be banned from their house and his anger provoked his mother to agree that she wouldn't see him anymore. Two days later, Jerry became very ill but his sister Emma insisted on calling a doctor and he soon recovered. The police later came to believe that Billik had not intended to kill the boy but had only administered a small dose of poison to frighten him.

In December of that same year, Billik struck again. Tillie Vzral was the next to die, succumbing to "stomach trouble" and raising $620 in life insurance for Billik. For some reason, he stayed quiet until the following August, when 14 year-old Rose died of the same ailment. She was insured for $300. Three months later, Ella died. Her tender age of only 12 managed to garner Billik a mere $105. As with all of the previous deaths, Mrs. Vzral turned over all of the money to the "wizard", save for the expenses for the funerals.

Now, with no more insurance money in sight, and with the milk business taken over by creditors, Billik persuaded Mrs. Vzral to put her home up for sale. She received $2,900 in cash and gave every bit of it to Billik. He took a leisurely trip to Niagara Falls with the windfall and told Mrs. Vzral that he planned to stop in Cleveland on his way back to "fix" his mother. That way, he could inherit what he claimed was a sizable fortune.

When Billik did return to Chicago, he found the befuddled remains of the Vzral family with no

Chicago Police Inspector George M. Shippy

money, no food and waiting to be thrown out of a house that was no longer theirs to live in. On the night that Billik returned, he called on Mrs. Vzral during the early morning hours. By daybreak, she was dead.

During the two-year period that Billik preyed on the Vzrals, no one in the neighborhood realized that anything out of the ordinary was going on. It seemed that the family was experiencing more than their share of misfortune but no one suspected foul play until a girl employed as a maid in a north side home was overheard by her employer remarking to another servant that "someone ought to look into all of the deaths in that family". The chance remark led the woman to question the maid and she learned that the girl had known Mary Vzral, who, although afraid of Billik, had been unable to resist him.

The girl's mistress repeated the conversation to her

Herman Billik (center) during his trial

husband and he was so troubled by it that he contacted a policeman that he knew who patrolled the neighborhood. The policeman included it in his daily report and eventually this report reached Inspector George M. Shippy of the Hyde Park station. He, in turn, assigned detectives to start an inquiry.

After a few days of investigation, the detectives were curious enough to obtain an order to have Mary Vzral's body exhumed. Chemists who examined the contents of her stomach discovered a number of grains of arsenic and Billik was immediately arrested. He was placed on trial in the early summer of 1907 and was found guilty of murder in the first degree. In July, he was sentenced to death but was reprieved by the governor. More appeals followed, even to the United States Supreme Court, and the case dragged out for another two years. During this time, Billik was held in the Cook County Jail, where he curiously became one of the most popular men, with prisoners and guards alike, to ever be incarcerated there.

While Billik's case was strange from the beginning, it became even more bizarre in the months to come. What was so unusual was the extraordinary fight that was waged to save the "wizard's" life. A Catholic priest, Father P.J. O'Callaghan of the Paulist Fathers, and a nun, Sister Rose of the Order of the Sacred Heart, led the battle. They arranged mass meetings and prayer vigils and, through private solicitation, raised considerable sums of money for Billik's legal expenses.

In June 1908, just before the appeal to the Supreme Court, a prayer service was held by Father O' Callaghan at the County jail. It was reported that 400 of the prisoners attended, praying for God to save Billik from the gallows. Another service was held at the jail on June 9, at which Father O'Callaghan, Billik, Billik's wife and daughter and, unbelievably, Jerry Vzral offered prayers on his behalf. Many of the prisoners wept and moaned and Billik's cellmate, an infamous burglar, wrapped his arms around Billik, kissed him repeatedly and wept openly throughout the service. After the prayer session was over, the prisoners presented flowers to Father O'Callaghan, Sister Rose and even the jailer.

Jerry Vzral, one of the only surviving members of the Vzral family, at the time of Billik's trial. Strangely, Jerry would later become an outspoken supporter of Billik as groups tried to save him from the death penalty.

Father P.J. O'Callaghan, who organized rallies to try and keep Billik off death row.

On June 10, a petition that was signed by 20,000 people was presented to the State Board of Pardons and five rallies were held on Billik's behalf on the west side. Hundreds of women wept and screamed that he should not be hanged. They carried on to the point that many of them had to be treated for hysteria. Father O'Callaghan spoke at all of the meetings and was joined by Jerry Vzral, who tearfully claimed that he had committed perjury at Billik's trial.

Inspector Shippy was nonplussed by the rallies and weird performances. "Billik is a cold-blooded murderer of the worst type," he stated. "He is simply deceiving the people who are working in his behalf."

Guilty or not, the mass meetings, which revolted the police officers in charge of the case, had the desired result. Governor Charles S. Deneen commuted Billik's death sentence to life imprisonment in January 1909. He claimed to do so on the recommendation of the Board of Pardons but it's likely that the hysterical atmosphere of the rallies frightened the politicians into thinking that they would be losing votes if they failed to spare the influential "seer".

Billik was sent to the state prison at Joliet but eight years later, in 1917, the murderer of almost an entire family was pardoned by Governor Edward F. Dunne and set free. The Church, which had never let up on its crusade for him, headed a huge voting bloc in Chicago and the governor was never one to ignore any large group that threatened to vote against him or the party.

There is no record as to what became of Herman Billik after his release from prison. He vanished completely into the historical record -- leaving six victims in his wake. One has to wonder about this killer's appeal and how he managed to not only seduce and kill the greater part of one family but also how he ensnared the general public in the way that he did. How did he create a faithful following to do his bidding, beyond all reason and logic? Did he really possess some sort of strange, supernatural power or more likely, was he but one of the madmen who managed to create a "cult of personality" in modern history?

And, most chilling of all, what could Billik have accomplished if he had been of a later generation? Would he have been the leader of some terrifying cult? Another Charles Manson, Jim Jones or David Koresh? Or, perhaps, something even worse...

Billik is shown here shaking hands with Warden Michael Zimmer after his relase from Joilet Prison. After only eight years in prison, he was pardoned by Illinois governor Edward F. Dunne. Even eight years must have been hard on the "Wizard" as the man leaving prison looks much older and more worn that the robust man who poisoned, seduced and dstroyed the Vzral family.

DR. THOMAS NEILL CREAM
Was Jack the Ripper a "Gentleman from Chicago"?

In the year 1888, a killer who called himself "Jack the Ripper" terrorized the city of London, England. The mysterious madman prowled the streets of the Whitechapel District in East London and slaughtered a number of prostitutes, carving his way into the historical record as the first "modern serial killer". As the years have passed, the Ripper has held the morbid curiosity of professional and amateur sleuths, armchair detectives and crime buffs alike. Having eluded capture in the 1880s, his identity has been debated ever since. Not surprisingly, many suspects have been named as the Ripper over the years with the vast majority of them being British. Many readers, who may have only a "bare bones" knowledge of the case, may be surprised to learn that there are those who believe that Jack the Ripper may actually have been an American!

Perhaps the most insane and devious of the American Jack the Ripper suspects was a man named Dr. Thomas Neill Cream. He thought of himself as a master criminal and his ego knew no bounds. He seemed to love to do evil and he was said to have revolutionized the concept of murder in the late 1800s. His motives would later give much in the way of study to crime psychologists and just what he may have done (and when) continues to baffle crime historians to this day. He specialized in the murder of women and, perhaps for this reason and the fact that he was so adept at covering his trail, Cream emerged in John Cashman's 1973 book *The Gentleman from Chicago* as a Ripper suspect. And while many have disputed these charges, Cream is worthy of mention as an American (and Chicago) connection to the most heinous murders of the Victorian era.

Cream was born in Scotland in 1850 and immigrated with his parents to Canada four years later. Though little is known about his early life, his parents were hardworking and decent folks and Cream lacked for nothing when it came to education and comfort. Somewhere along the way though, some twist in his makeup caused him to develop an overwhelming hatred of women. Perhaps it developed in childhood or perhaps later, when he attended McGill University in Montreal to study to be a doctor. He qualified as a physician but, years later, the college would remove his name from the graduate rolls to avoid being connected to his crimes.

During his senior year of college, Cream met and seduced a young woman named Flora Eliza Brooks. When she became pregnant as a result of the affair, Cream performed a crude abortion on her. This botched operation left her permanently scarred and physically weak for the rest of her life. Her parents,

The Whitechapel District of London, where Jack the Ripper plied his bloody trade.

when they discovered what had occurred, forced Cream to marry the girl but he vanished soon after the nuptials and sailed for England in 1876.

In London, Cream enrolled in a post-graduate course at St. Thomas' Hospital, which was located in the Waterloo-Lambeth section of the city, an area teeming with diseased prostitutes. It is believed that it is here

Mad Doctor --- Dr. Thomas Neill Cream

where Cream first came into contact with the whores of London and where he also contracted syphilis. The effects of the disease on his brain have been blamed for his constant thoughts of murder and his psychopathic rages. However, it's more likely that he was simply mad from the beginning.

Cream returned to Canada a few years later and set up practice in Ontario. He learned that his wife had passed away and while she is listed as having died of consumption, the horrific abortion at Cream's hands undoubtedly contributed to her early demise. His medical practice was anything but savory and he soon earned a reputation for insurance fraud and performing illegal operations on women, especially abortions. He began a prosperous practice among local prostitutes and young women in trouble until the body of a young hotel chambermaid was discovered in his apartment one night with a bottle of chloroform beside her body. Cream had performed a savage abortion on her and it had failed, claiming her life. He was arrested and despite the evidence against him, the girl's death was ruled a suicide and Cream was freed.

This would be the first of a series of miraculous escapes for Cream but it would not be the last. He now took his operation to the teeming red-light districts of Chicago. His career as an abortionist found him plenty of new patients among the dirty and sickly prostitutes of Chicago's Levee districts. He seemed to enjoy inflicting pain on these women but his deviant desires were truly inflamed by the opportunity that sometimes arose to work on proper young ladies who had been compromised. One such woman was Julia Faulkner, who died on Cream's operating table in August 1880. He was charged with murder but the Chicago authorities lacked proof and Cream was released once again. Detectives suspected that Cream had given Miss Faulkner a poison called strychnine in the guise of a painkiller.

In 1881, Cream struck again. After another abortion on a Miss Stack, she also perished after taking medicine that Cream prescribed and which was also laced with strychnine. Cream attempted to blackmail the chemist that he got the medicine from (some medicines contained a small amount of the poison in those days), stating that if he were paid off, he would keep silent about the bad mixture. The chemist, knowing that he was not at fault, turned the blackmail letter over to the police and Cream was arrested. Again, he was questioned and again he was turned loose for lack of evidence.

Cream then began marketing a special elixir that he had created, which he claimed would cure epilepsy. Amazingly, he acquired a considerable following of patients who swore by the medicine. Then, into his office one day walked Julia Stott, an attractive young woman who was looking for Cream's epilepsy cure. Her husband, Daniel Stott, was a station agent on the Northeastern Railway and suffered from epilepsy. Cream began making advances toward Julia and found the woman receptive. She said that her husband's illness, and his advanced age, had ruined her sex life.

It's hard to imagine what could have attracted the beautiful woman to Cream. The doctor was a slight and scrawny man with thinning hair and gold-rimmed glasses through which he constantly squinted. His saving grace was that he often gave off an appearance of being from the upper crust with upscale dress, expensive suits and a bushy mustache that he kept waxed and turned up at the ends. Likely, though, Julia's attraction to him went beyond just looks as she spoke of the doctor as being "insatiable" and stated later that he "ravished" her several times during their first meeting.

Daniel Stott began to grow suspicious of his wife's frequent trips to Cream's office and suspected that he was giving Julia more than just medicine on these visits. Not surprisingly, Cream repaid the man's suspicions by adding strychnine to his medicine and Stott died on June 14, 1881.

Originally, Stott's death was attributed to epilepsy but, for some bizarre reason, Cream wrote to the coroner and stated that a pharmacist was responsible, having given Stott some bad medicine. He suggested that Stott's body be exhumed. The coroner dismissed the letter, not knowing that Cream was trying to collect on Stott's life insurance. Cream had also sent a letter to the district attorney with the same advice. The prosecutor decided to check into the letter and had the body exhumed. An exam discovered that there was poison in Stott's stomach, something that would never have been found if not for the letter!

Cream may have realized his blunder once the letters were sent and he soon fled the city with the widow Stott. The police quickly apprehended them. Cream insisted at his trial that Stott's death had been the pharmacist's fault but Julia turned state's evidence against him and testified that she had seen Cream "put some white powder" into her husband's medicine bottle. This time, Cream's luck didn't hold and he was sentenced to life imprisonment at Joliet Prison. He was admitted in 1881 and was regarded as a model prisoner who spoke little to the other inmates and always did as the officers told him. Over the years, the only complaints ever filed about him came from other prisoners who claimed to be awakened in the middle of the night to the sound of low, hissing laughter coming from his cell. At such times, he could be found sitting on his bunk, speaking to phantom women that appeared in his cell and promising them slow and agonizing deaths. He created detailed plans of revenge and of what sexual savagery he would wreak should he ever be released.

And then fate reared its ugly head in Thomas Neill Cream's life again. In 1887, his father died and left his son a sizable sum of money. His accountant and bookkeeper, Thomas Davidson, wrote to Illinois authorities and requested the complete records of Cream's trial. After studying the case, he became convinced that Cream was innocent of the charges that had sent him to Joliet. He began petitioning for Cream's release and a number of family friends in Canada took up the cause, perhaps never realizing what sort of man their friend's son had become. The petitions and letters arrived in Illinois by the bagful and finally, Governor Joseph W. Fifer relented and he commuted Cream's sentence. He was released from Joliet on July 31, 1891.

Cream immediately went to Quebec and collected his inheritance. It's likely that the accountant finally realized his mistake. He later wrote: "In my first interview with him, I concluded that he was unmistakably insane."

Of course, by that time, it was too late for the victims that still lay ahead.

Wealthy and free to do what he wished, Cream returned to England. He arrived in October 1891 and took rooms in a boarding house on Lambeth Palace Road, back in the slums that he had once reveled in. He told his landlady that he was at work on his postgraduate studies at St. Thomas' Hospital but when he failed to see any patients, or keep any sort of office hours, he had to tell her that he had been ill and was recovering from a strange disease. His eyes bothered him constantly, he explained, forcing him to take large doses of morphine and cocaine. His landlady replied that she hoped his health would improve.

A short time after his arrival, Cream went to work. He began visiting the local prostitutes and began killing them, too. He met one such woman, Matilda Clover, just two days after he arrived and she later died from *nux vomica* poisoning. The substance was a liquid that caused vomiting, which was often prescribed by doctors as a tonic. Matilda had received an overdose fo it. The same fate also befell a woman named Ellen Donworth but as in the past, Cream was not charged with anything.

After a short break from murder, and an even shorter attempt at a love affair with a woman named Laura Sabbatini, Cream poisoned two other women, Alice Marsh and Emma Shrivell. He would have escaped detection in these crimes also but, as he did in Chicago, he inexplicably tried to place blame for the crimes on someone else. This time, he accused his neighbor of the murders and tried to blackmail him. He told Walter J. Harper, a medical student who lived in the same boarding house, that he had incriminating evidence against him but for a large sum of money, he would not notify the police. He wrote a letter to Harper's father also and told him that his son was a murderer. The elder Harper did not respond, but he held onto the letter. Cream then wrote to the coroner and told him that Harper had committed the murders and that he had proof. He also wrote to John Haynes, a photographer who lived in his building, and told him the same thing. He constantly talked of the two dead women, often shocking his landlady with his vile descriptions of Harper's alleged crimes.

It was finally John Haynes (after Cream took him on a guided tour of the murder sites) who went to detectives at Scotland Yard and told them of his suspicions about Cream being the killer. At that point, his attempts to blackmail Harper were also revealed and Cream was finally arrested. He went to trial in October 1892, proclaiming his innocence and capturing newspaper headlines across the nation. A number of people testified against him and only a sobbing Laura Sabbatini testified on his behalf. Cream's tin box that contained vials of poison was placed on display in the courtroom and was later added to Scotland Yard's infamous "Black Museum".

There was a strange incident that jarred the proceedings of the trial. A letter was received and was read aloud in court by coroner Braxton Hicks. It read:

Dear Sir.... The man that you have in your power, Dr. Neill, is as innocent as you are. Knowing him by sight, I disguised myself like him, and made the acquaintance of the girls that have been poisoned. I gave them pills to cure them of all their earthly miseries, and they died.... If I were you, I would release Dr. T. Neill, or you might get into trouble. His innocence will be declared sooner or later, and when he is free, he might sue you for damages. Beware all. I warn but once.
Yours Respectfully,
Juan Pollen,
alias Jack the Ripper

The mere utterance of the name attached to the letter caused the entire assemblage to gasp, except for Cream, who smiled widely. The letter later turned out to be the work of a crank, as Cream could not have sent it himself from his cell, but it stayed in Cream's mind until the end of his life.

It only took the jury 10 minutes to find Cream guilty and Judge Sir Henry Hawkins lived up to his reputation as the "hanging judge" by ordering Cream to be executed on the gallows on November 15, 1892.

While awaiting execution, Cream talked incessantly to his jailers, insisting to them that he was a great man and that the world had refused to recognize it. He also claimed to have killed many more than he was found guilty of and that he had done them in to end their misery and to aid society, hinting at even darker things than those he was to be executed for.

On the night before his execution, Cream could be heard moaning in his cell, no longer bragging of his crimes but now protesting his innocence. At dawn on the 15th though, he went calmly to the gallows. He was bound hand and foot and placed on the trap as the black hood was slipped over his head. Cream saved his most dramatic and strange proclamation for the end. The lever was pushed to release the trap, and moments before he plunged to his doom, Cream shouted out: "I am Jack the....."

The rope cut him off before he could finish and, in that split second, Cream created an enigma that has inspired many to believe that he was confessing to having been the killer Jack the Ripper. And in death, Cream became as mysterious as he was in life.

Cream's last words have plagued both crime historians and "Ripperologists" for years. There have been a number of theorists who have concocted some convincing (and some not so convincing) theories to show that Cream may have been the Whitechapel killer. Sir Edward Marshall Hall, who had once defended Cream on a charge of bigamy, later wrote that he believed Cream sometimes employed a "double" who used his name and that both men "used each other's terms of imprisonment as alibis for each other". Cream had earlier told Hall that he refused to plead guilty to charges against him because he was in prison at the time of the offenses. A check with officials did reveal that a man matching Cream's description had been in prison at the same time and Cream was released.

Ripper expert Donald Rumbelow stated that this has led to the suggestion that even though Cream was serving time in Joliet Prison as the Whitechapel murders were taking place, he may have actually been in England. His double could have been imprisoned, or vice versa. As the double had given Cream an alibi for the bigamy charges, Cream then tried to repay the debt by shouting those last words from the scaffold. Others have suggested that the letter that was read at Cream's trial could have been from Cream's double, the real Jack the Ripper, attempting to save the doctor's life.

Unfortunately for those who feel they have solved the Whitechapel murders by pinning them on Cream, the idea of the "doppelganger" is not very convincing and neither is the other theory as to how the good doctor could have committed the crimes from behind the walls of Joliet prison.

In some accounts, Cream was able to bribe his way out of what was a corrupt prison in the middle 1880s, journey to London, commit the murders, and then return to his cell in order to be released in 1891. Author and crime historian Jay Robert Nash personally checked the records at Joliet prison in the late 1970s and found that the ledger from the era was still intact, although Cream's personal files had long ago been destroyed in a fire. The ledger states that Thomas Neill Cream, prisoner no. 4374, was imprisoned at Joliet on November 1, 1881 and not released until July 31, 1891. There are also records attached about the commuting of Cream's sentence by the governor but nothing to indicate that he was ever released. The idea that he bribed his way out of the prison is merely a theory and no real evidence exists to support it.

And perhaps the biggest problem with the idea of Cream being the Ripper is his method of murder. Although he was a brutish and bloody abortionist, his method of dispatching young women was by poison, not the knife. It seems unlikely that he would poison his victims prior to 1888 and then suddenly go on a wild mutilating spree, only to go back to poisoning them again a few years later.

So, it seems that we have to look beyond Dr. Cream when seeking the identity of Jack the Ripper. Admittedly, the two killers did have some similarities in that both enjoyed killing prostitutes and then writing letters about their deeds to the authorities, but beyond that, the comparisons end --- continuing a mystery that will not be solved anytime soon!

THE MYSTERIOUS DEATH OF MARSHALL FIELD, JR.

If there could be only one name to epitomize the rise of business in Chicago, it would be that of Marshall Field. Dubbed the "Merchant Prince", he began creating an empire in the city before the Civil War and went on to found the world's first department store in downtown Chicago, a structure that still bore his name until 2006. Both glorified and feared, Marshall Field was considered a Chicago icon and one of the richest men in the world in his day, having an estate of more than $140 million. He made a fortune from the city of Chicago but gave much of it back, including the lakefront museum that was established and named in his honor. He also largely founded the Art Institute and laid the groundwork for the University of Chicago.

But despite all of his achievements, a single event occurred in 1905 that would both shorten his life and overshadow many of his accomplishments. The death of his son, Marshall Field, Jr. --- under what can

Marshall Field -- his department store in Chicago made him America's 'Merchant Prince" (UPI)

be called mysterious circumstances, at best --- not only sent Field to an early grave but it also created one of the great unsolved mysteries of Chicago history.

Marshall Field Home at 1905 South Prairie Avenue

Marshall Field came to Chicago in 1856 and went to work as a clerk in a dry goods store with a salary of $400 per year, half of which he saved. A pioneer of new merchandising methods, he went on to coin the ultimate customer service slogan of "Give the Lady What She Wants". He and a partner, Levi Z. Leiter, purchased Potter Palmer's store in 1865 and it became Marshall Field and Company. Even before becoming the premiere dry goods merchant in the country though, he looked for other ways to make money and discovered real estate investment. He was known for being an affable, serious, mild-looking man and was well-liked, even though he never praised his employees and paid them low wages -- never a cent more than he had agreed to pay them, no matter how well they performed. Thanks to this, he did not keep partners for long. At each year's end, he held a dinner in his house for partners and members of the upper management. Over after-dinner brandy, he would make simple announcements to the assembled group as to which of them would not be celebrating the holidays with the company the following year. If an employee had not measured up, he would no longer be required by Marshall Field and Company.

In 1876, Field constructed a luxurious mansion with a prestigious address at 1905 South Prairie Avenue. The house cost over $2 million to build and was the first home in Chicago to have electric lights. Field lived here with his wife, the former Nannie Scott of Ironton, Ohio, and she became known as the social queen of the city. Here, the Fields reared their son, Marshall Field, Jr. and their daughter, Ethel. The family entertained both famous and infamous American and European personages and held many notable parties and balls. Perhaps the most noted event was staged in January 1886 and the party was held in honor of the two Field children. More than 500 guests were present and as Gilbert and Sullivan's operetta Mikado was then all the rage in the fashionable world, the Field event was designated as a "Mikado Ball". Wealthy children and their parents attended the party in colorful, Oriental costumes and their carriages passed beneath special calcium lights that had been erected for the evening. The ball was said to have cost $75,000 and it was talked about for years afterward.

But not everything connected to the Marshall Field family was bright and filled with joy -- and the Mikado Ball was certainly not the only thing spoken of in the city for years after it took place.

In 1890, Marshall Field, Jr. married a young woman named Albertine Huck and, with his father's help, purchased a Prairie Avenue home just a few doors down from the family mansion. The house, located at 1919 South Prairie Avenue,

Albertine Huck Field, wife of Marshall Field, Jr., and their children

62

had been known in the neighborhood as the William H. Murray House, and had been built in 1884. The younger Field purchased the house, with his father's assistance, for $65,000.

The Fields lived happily in the house for a number of years, entertaining and welcoming only the best people on the Chicago social register. However, tragedy came to call at the Field mansion on November 22, 1905. Just before dinner that evening, Marshall Field, Jr. fired a bullet into his left side while he was seated in his dressing room. The shot would eventually prove to be fatal. According to the newspapers the following morning, the gunshot had been a tragic accident. Field had been examining a loaded revolver in anticipation of an upcoming hunting trip to Wisconsin when the gun accidentally discharged. The bullet lodged in his side, piercing his liver. Field was rushed to Mercy Hospital, where he lingered at death's door for several days. His parents, when notified of the shooting, rushed back to Chicago.

The police were summoned to the house and the servants were closely questioned but no one had witnessed the shooting and Mrs. Field had been away for the afternoon. The parents of the critically wounded man were vacationing in New York at the time. Satisfied with the "cleaning the gun" story, the police looked no further into the incident.

Marshall Field, Jr. died on November 27, 1905. Although he at first showed signs of improvement, he weakened with a high fever and then finally succumbed to his wound at a little before 5:00 p.m. According to a newspaper report: "Kneeling beside his death bed in Mercy Hospital, holding his left hand in both of hers, was his wife. His father stood at the foot of the bed, his face wet with tears. Mr. Field passed away quietly, holding to his lips a crucifix." It was said that Albertine collapsed in hysterics after her husband's death and that she threw her arms around her father-in-law, who escorted her to his carriage and drove her home.

A private wake was held in the house at 1919 South Prairie Avenue, where Field had been shot just days before. He was buried in a lavish ceremony at Graceland Cemetery on the city's north side and was soon joined there by his father. On January 16, 1906, the "Merchant Prince", still mourning his son, died from complications of pneumonia and from old age.

His death brought an end to a chapter in Chicago history and created a mystery that few would have talked about while the elder Field was still alive.

Rumors & Legends

While police detectives may have accepted the "accidental discharge" story of how Marshall Field, Jr. died, many reporters and members of the general public were not so quick to do so. While Field was lingering near death at Mercy Hospital, reporters and photographers swarmed the hallways of the place, taking photographs and looking for information from doctors, nurses, cops and even distressed family members. The 87 year-old Marshall Field took to fending them off with his walking stick!

It would be these reporters who first began looking into rumors that were swirling around the city --- rumors that claimed the younger Field was not the family man that his friends, family and colleagues made him out to be. After his death, he was eulogized in the newspapers by his friends and colleagues as a man of "gentle refinements, possessing a quiet and retiring disposition". They spoke of his Harvard education (which Field actually ended after just two years because of health reasons), his enthusiasm for sports and the great outdoors and his abiding love for his wife and children. This was Field on the surface, some said, because rumors around town were telling a much different story about his private life.

Stories circulated that Field had actually been shot, not in his dressing room, but in one of Chicago's most fashionable brothels (the Everleigh Club was usually mentioned). The stories varied, stating that he had either been involved in an altercation in the brothel and was shot by one of the bouncers, or that he was shot by one of the prostitutes when he became violent with her. Regardless, his body was then smuggled home to avoid scandal for the Field family. He was later found in his room "having had an accident while cleaning his gun". This story spread like wildfire but if there was any evidence of this having actually happened, it has long since vanished.

The Marshall Field, Jr. Mansion as it looked during its many years of decline and ruin. (Below) The house as it looks today, restored and preparing for new condiminiums

And this was not the only story that circulated in Chicago about Field's death. The other rumor was even more scandalous and, had it been widely believed, would have been even more damaging to the reputation of the Fields. This rumor claimed that Field had not been killed by accident; that he had shot himself and committed suicide. The possible scandal was then covered up as an "accident" ---- not because Field had killed himself but for the reason that he had taken his own life.

According to the story, he had committed suicide after receiving the horrific news that his wife had been engaged in a long-running affair. This would have been shocking enough, but the story goes on to say that the man she had been having an affair with was none other than her father-in-law, Marshall Field! The clandestine affair had been carried out by way of the tunnel that existed below Prairie Avenue, running from the basement of the mansion at 1905 South Prairie Avenue to that of the younger Field's home at 1919. Enraged and despondent, Marshall Field, Jr. committed suicide rather than face the betrayal by his wife and father.

Of course, absolutely no evidence of this "affair" exists and even if it had, it would have been destroyed long ago. It was a story that widely circulated though, and there are many who maintain the story to be true to this day. We will never know if it was merely a story to scandalize the Fields or if it had any elements of truth. I can vouch for the fact that a tunnel entrance did once exist in the basement of the mansion at 1919 South Prairie Avenue, but if it was used for anything other than mundane purposes, I cannot say.

No matter what the reader might believe though, the circumstances of Field's death can definitely be considered mysterious and the "accidental shooting" leaves a number of questions in its wake. For instance, why was Field checking his gun in his dressing room? If he were preparing for a hunting trip, which would commonly call for a rifle, why would he be worried about his pistol? And there are many more....

Unfortunately, too much time has passed for any of the questions to ever be answered, leaving a Chicago mystery behind that will never be solved.

THE WRIGLEYVILLE TORSO MURDER

Chicago is a city that has long been plagued by strange and unusual crimes, but there is probably no murder as bizarre as the so-called "torso murder" that occurred on the city's north side in 1935. This blood-soaked and grisly murder was made all the more strange by the cast of characters involved, including a desperate woman in love with her daughter's husband; a sickly young woman; her unwitting spouse; a former burlesque dancer and cold-blooded killer; and others.

Chicagoans were shocked and horrified when details of the complicated case reached the newspapers but, as usual, clamored for more. And, as is always the case in Chicago, the press was happy to oblige.

The story of the "torso murder" began in a backyard flat on West Waveland Avenue in the Wrigleyville neighborhood, an area near Wrigley Field, the famous Cubs ballpark. The small apartment belonged to Blanche Dunkel, a semi-attractive, 42 year-old survivor of four failed marriages. She shared it with her daughter, Mallie, and son-in-law, Ervin J. Lang, a grocery store clerk who could not afford a place of his own during the days of the Great Depression. Mallie was a delicate young woman with a "weak constitution" and, because of this, she was unable to work. Blanche largely supported the family by working in the linen supply room of Passavant Hospital.

She was a hard worker but not terribly bright. Blanche had managed to make it most of the way through the eighth grade before she dropped out of school and newspapers later reported that she had an I.Q. of 79. It's likely that she had some additional mental issues as well, as would be evidenced by the events to come.

A newspaper photo of Ervin Lang from the time of the murder.

(Left) A posed photo of Ervin with Blanche Dunkel, shortly after Mallie Lang had passed away. At this point, Ervin was already dating Josephine McKinley and is shown here in the photo with her young son.

Living in close quarters in the cluttered apartment, Blanche soon found herself falling in love with her daughter's charming husband. She described his nature as "gentle and refined" and she mistook his kindnesses toward her as something other than innocent affection for his wife's mother. She was later quoted as saying: "My God, it was selfish of me but no one will ever understand the thrill I got when I looked at that boy." Blanche constantly fantasized about Ervin making love to her. "I had to fight with myself to control my anger when I saw him with her," Blanche said.

Mallie Lang soon began to notice the extra attention that her mother was paying to Ervin and the way that she looked at him whenever she thought her daughter wasn't looking. She and Blanche began to argue and she threatened to move out if her mother persisted with her foolish crush. Blanche angrily dared her to leave, knowing there was no way that the young couple could afford their own flat. Blanche even went as far as to borrow some money from friends to give to Mallie as a deposit for the first month's rent in an apartment of her own. Mallie gave up on her threat to leave. She felt trapped but knew that she and Ervin could not afford to move out. To make matters worse, Mallie's health, never good to start with, was failing. Some days, she was barely able to get out of bed. All that she could do was try and ignore her mother's behavior but it was becoming increasingly harder to do.

One night at a neighborhood party, Blanche saw Ervin sitting quietly, holding Mallie's hand. She later

recalled: "Something came over me, something I don't understand. I jumped up from the table and ran over to him and smothered him with kisses. I was sorry then, she was already ill. And at the same time I wanted her to suffer because she had made me suffer --- making me jealous."

Blanche began working harder and harder to seduce her son-in-law. Eventually it worked and Ervin succumbed to her advances. No one knows how she finally succeeded but it's thought that perhaps she used the fact that Mallie had been too weak to engage in relations with her husband for a very long time. But whatever happened, Ervin found himself ravaging Blanche on every occasion when Mallie was away from the house --- and sometimes when she wasn't.

It all became too much for the delicate young woman to take. Mallie's health continued to decline and she died, some say from a "broken heart", on December 20, 1934.

The simple-minded Blanche was shattered by her daughter's death and began her descent into madness. She began to blame herself for the fact that Mallie had died and turned her frenzied hatred toward Ervin. He had wasted no time in tossing the older woman aside and finding a new lover. He began to date a woman closer to his own age, a 21 year-old named Josephine McKinley, who had a young son. Blanche, likely delusional by this time, imagined that Ervin had killed Mallie in order for him to be close to Josephine. It was a lie, of course. Blanche really just wanted Ervin for herself but he had quickly lost interest in her. She would later claim that her hate for Ervin was not because he had broken things off with her, but because he had failed to remain loyal to the memory of his late wife.

Half-crazed with jealously, Blanche took her suspicions about Ervin murdering Mallie to her sister, Mrs. Jessie Langdon. Her sister then put her in touch with a woman named Evelyn Smith, a laundry worker at the Medinah Club. Smith was a retired striptease dancer and became the strangest figure in this odd collection of characters. Her weird past was later revealed to investigators in the case.

Smith had been born in Berlin, Germany and had been brought to North Dakota at a young age. Soon after, her father died from pneumonia and her sister burned to death in a horrible "bonfire accident". Her mother went mad with grief and died herself a short time later. Evelyn was sent to live with a foster family but did not stay with them for long. At the age of 10, she began riding the rails of America, traveling in boxcars and living the life of a hobo. In the big cities, she wound up wherever there was a Chinatown district, thanks to the fact that the Chinese were always willing to provide shelter and food.

In 1929, Evelyn and another traveling woman ended up in Minneapolis, where they learned the laundry trade. Three years later, Evelyn drifted to Chicago and met a man named Harry Jung. Harry Jung and his brothers had established a successful chain of laundries and Evelyn saw him as the perfect "mark", a man she could con into providing her with a comfortable living. After a short acquaintance, they were married.

But Evelyn could not have been more wrong about Jung. He had plenty of money but he wasn't willing to share it with his new wife. After she suffered a miscarriage, Jung forced her to go out and look for work. She supported herself through a series of odd jobs and, eventually, began dancing in a burlesque house under the stage name of "Trixie". Her striptease career was short-lived, mostly thanks to the fact that Evelyn was a plain-looking woman with a rough face, wire-rimmed glasses and auburn hair that she kept close-cropped like a man's. She was living in an apartment near the intersection of Clark and West Barry when she first met Blanche Dunkel.

Smith later claimed that she fell "under the spell" of Blanche when they met and she was eager to help her out of the situation that she was in with Ervin. The police files in the case allude to the fact that Evelyn was a lesbian and that the "spell" she was under was one of sexual attraction. She had fallen for Blanche and would do anything to win her over. A short time later, she asked Jessie Langdon why Blanche didn't just have Ervin killed. "I could get it done for $500," she told her. By now, Evelyn was very familiar with the inner workings of Chicago's south side Chinatown and offered the services of her husband and his associates for a sum of money that she knew Blanche would be able to obtain.

Blanche was able to get the money and got it from an unbelievable source ---- Ervin himself! She approached Lang's naïve little brother, William, for a key to a safety-deposit box that Ervin kept at the Lake View Trust & Savings Bank. She withdrew $100 of Ervin's own money as a down payment for his own murder. Blanche met Evelyn at the corner of Belmont and Lincoln and handed her a plain brown envelope with the cash inside. She instructed Blanche to bring the young man over to her house that evening.

That evening, Blanche managed to entice Ervin over to Evelyn's apartment with the promise of a night of drinking and card playing. Over the course of a few hours, he was served four whiskey highballs, each of which contained knockout drops. The women waited until nearly 4:30 a.m. before he finally passed out. Irritated and impatient, Evelyn slapped him hard across the face to see if he was really out or if he had just nodded off. Satisfied that he was really unconscious by this time, Evelyn sent Blanche on her way. She promised to take care of Ervin from that point on. "You might as well go home," she reportedly said. " I got him now."

Blanche, filled with as much regret as when she had hurt her daughter, fled the apartment. Meanwhile, Evelyn dosed Ervin with ether, tied him securely, and then dragged him into a closet, where she strangled him to death. The next morning, Harry Jung arrived with a saw and the two of them set to their bloody work. Evelyn cut off Ervin's legs at the hip so that he would fit into a large trunk that Jung had purchased at a Salvation Army store. They loaded the trunk into Jung's car and then set out for the southeast side, eventually crossing into Indiana where they would leave Ervin's legs in a roadside ditch near Munster. The torso was taken to Wolf Lake, which straddles the Illinois-Indiana border, and dumped into one of the many swampy areas nearby. The newspapers referred to the lake as a "gangland cemetery" because of the number of bodies that had been dumped there over the years.

Evelyn and Jung were sure that the body would never be found but the severed corpse was discovered just four days later. The trunk that had been used to transport the body was found in a Chinatown warehouse at 231 West 22nd Street.

Once Ervin's body was identified, the police began to investigate and the first break came in the case within 24 hours. Blanche's sister, Jessie Langdon, told Chief Investigator Thomas Kelly of the state's attorney police about Blanche's hiring of Evelyn Smith to kill Ervin. The unmistakable smell of laundry soap on Ervin's clothing confirmed the story and led the police to the Jung laundry business. Harry Jung vanished but Evelyn was arrested in New York two weeks later.

Blanche was arrested and freely admitted to her part in the crime. She confessed after being taken out to Wolf Lake to view the remains. "I am his common-law wife," she said, imagining that their relationship had gone much further than it had. She continued to talk of how much she loved the young man as the police led her away to jail.

States Attorney Charles S. Doughtery easily convinced a grand jury to return murder indictments against Blanche and Evelyn. "I am ready for the chair," Evelyn sighed wearily in a public statement after the indictments were handed down. "It's better than putting up with all that happened. It wouldn't break my heart,

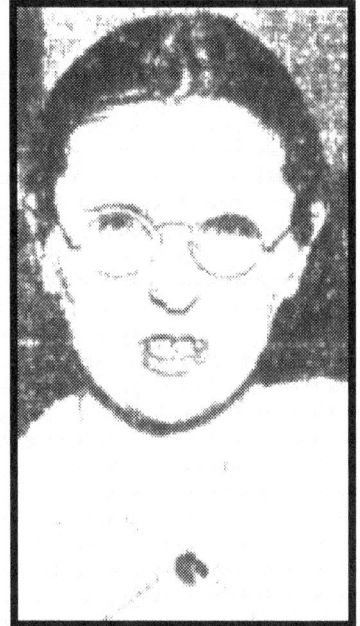

"I Am Ready for the Chair!"
This is the caption that ran below this newspaper photo of former stripper Evelyn Smith at the time of her trial for Ervin Lang's murder. Hard to believe that she gave up stripping, isn't it?

A swampy area around Wolf Lake. It was here, in what the press called "a gangland cemetery" that Ervin's body was found.

though, if Blanche walks up to the chair with me." The news reporter went on to add that "Mrs. Dunkel anticipated the prospect of death with different feelings."

The judge at their trial, Cornelius J. Harrington, did not sentence the women to death, however. He felt that it was too good for them. Instead, he imposed a 180 year sentence to be served at the Dwight Reformatory for women. He added another grim addendum to the sentence. Beginning on July 6, 1936, and for every year after, the women were ordered to spend the anniversary of Ervin's murder in solitary confinement.

In 1955, on the twentieth anniversary of the murder, a reporter for the *Chicago American* visited the two women in Dwight. Blanche, who was now 63, held a bible and praised Jesus a number of times throughout the interview. She had devoted her life to the Lord, she said, and had great remorse for the act that she had committed.

Evelyn Smith, however, was unrepentant. She told the reporter that her conscience was clear and her only interest in life these days was growing flowers. In the past 20 years, the only visitor to Evelyn's cell, expect for the reporter, was a Catholic priest. She had turned him away.

Blanche was paroled from Dwight on March 6, 1961, with a final discharge from Governor Otto Kerner three years later. Evelyn was also paroled, more than a year later, on December 12, 1962. The two "women from hell" as the cops dubbed them, were now senior citizens and both of them vanished from history, leaving a dark stain on the annals of crime in Chicago.

THE CRIME THAT FOREVER CHANGED CHICAGO
The Schuessler-Peterson Murders

One of the most shocking, and terrifying, events in the history of Chicago took place in October 1955, when the bodies of the three boys were discovered in a virtually crime-free community on the northwest side of the city. The Schuessler-Peterson murders stunned the city and the horrific events --- which would remain unsolved for 40 years ---- changed the face of Chicago forever.

The terrifying events began on a cool Sunday afternoon in the fall of 1955 when three boys from the northwest side of the city headed downtown to catch a matinee performance of a Walt Disney nature film called *The African Lion* at the Loop Theater. The boys made the trip with their parent's consent because, in those days, parents thought little of their responsible children going off on excursions by themselves. The boys had always proven dependable in the past and this time would have been no exception, if tragedy had not occurred. Bobby Peterson's mother had chosen the film for he and his two friends, Anton and John Schuessler, and had sent them

Newspaper photos that ran after the discovery of the bodies at Robinson Woods. (Left to Right) Robert Peterson, John Schuessler & his brother, Anton

on their way with $4 in loose change between them. It should have been plenty of money to keep them occupied for an afternoon and safely get them back home again.

What happened when the movie ended, though, is a still shrouded in mystery.

The matinee ended that afternoon but for some reason, at around 6:00 p.m. that evening, the boys were reported in the lobby of the Garland Building at 111 North Wabash. There was no explanation for what they might have been doing there, other than that Bobby's eye doctor had an office in the building. It seems unlikely that he would have been visiting the optometrist on a Sunday afternoon but his signature did appear on the lobby registry for that day, so he was obviously there. The Garland did have a reputation in those days for being a hangout for gays, prostitutes and hustlers but if that had anything to do with the boys being there, no one knows.

Some have surmised that they only stopped long enough to use the restroom since Bobby knew there was one available on the ninth floor, where his optometrist's office was located. They may have hurried up to the ninth floor and then went right back out again because they were only believed to be at the Garland for less than five minutes.

Around 7:45 pm, the three entered the Monte Cristo Bowling Alley at 3226 West Montrose Avenue. The parlor was a neighborhood eating place and the proprietor later recalled that he remembered seeing the boys and that a "fifty-ish" looking man was showing an "abnormal interest" in several younger boys who were bowling. He was unable to say if this man had contact with the trio. They left the bowling alley and walked down Montrose to another bowling alley but, were turned away here because a league had taken over all of the available lanes for the evening.

Out of money, but for some reason not headed toward home, the boys hitched a ride at the intersection of Lawrence and Milwaukee Avenue. It was now 9:05 in the evening and their parents were beginning to get worried. They had reason to be, for the boys were never seen alive again.

Two days later, the boy's naked and bound bodies were discovered in a shallow ditch near a parking lot and about 100 feet east of the Des Plaines River. A salesman, who had stopped to eat his lunch at the Robinson Wood's Indian Burial Grounds nearby, spotted them and called the police. Coroner Walter McCarron stated that the cause of death was "asphyxiation by suffocation". The three boys had been dead for about 36 hours when they were discovered. He also declared that the killing had been a "sex crime" and the work of a "madman" or a "teen gang." It was, he stated, "the most horrible sex crime in years".

Bobby Peterson had been struck repeatedly and had been strangled with a rope or a necktie. Newspaper reports said that he had been slashed across the head 14 times with a knife or an ax. The Schuessler brothers, it appeared, had been strangled by hand and had been hit on their faces with what appeared to be the flat side of a knife. The killer had used adhesive tape to cover the eyes of all three victims. They had then been dragged or thrown from a vehicle. Their clothing was never discovered.

The city of Chicago was thrown into a panic. Police officials reported that they had never seen such a horrible crime. The fears of parents all over the city were summed up by the shaken Anton Schuessler, Sr. who said, "When you get to the point that children cannot go to the movies in the afternoon and get home safely, something is wrong with this country."

Police officers combed the area, conducting door-to-door searches and neighborhood interrogations. Search

The Schuessler-Peterson crime scene at Robinson Woods. Within hours of the bodies being discovered, any possible clues were destroyed by well-meaning police officers and volunteers.

The grieving parents of two of the boys, John and Anton Schuessler. (Charleston Daily Mail Photo)

teams combed Robinson's Woods, looking for clues or items of clothing. The killer (or killers) had gone to great length to get rid of any signs of fingerprints or traces of evidence. More than 100 officers, joined by 50 soldiers from the nearby Army anti-aircraft base, gathered near Robinson Woods at daybreak and walked in lines spaced four or five feet apart, looking for anything out of place. Divers were sent into the depths of the Des Plaines River for clues but they found nothing.

By this time, various city and suburban police departments had descended on the scene, running into each other and further hampering the search for clues. There was little or no cooperation between the separate agencies and if anything had been discovered, it would have likely been lost in the confusion.

Away from the scene, patrolmen and detectives conducted a huge roundup of known "sex deviates", especially those known to work in, or frequent, bowling alleys. They were convinced that this is where the boys had come into contact with the killer or killers. Most of the cops were convinced that a "gang" of some sort had been at work, finding it hard to believe that all three boys could have been killed otherwise. Coroner McCarron extended the possibility that they "fell into the hands of a group of older boys and were manhandled."

While the city remained in stunned shock, the investigation stumbled along under the leadership of Cook County Sheriff Joseph D. Lohman, who searched in desperation for some answers in the case. He even offered $2,500 from his personal bank account for information leading to an arrest. Lohman was over his head with this baffling case and he found himself under unwanted scrutiny by the newspapers (which sensationalized the murders) and the general public (which was collectively terrified).

Lohman was quoted in the press as stating: "Chances are, the attackers were persons close to the boys' own age, who might have known them." He also pointed to indications that the victims had been held captive before they were killed, and may have been slain because something had "gone wrong" and the captors wanted to make sure they were not identified. He said that Bobby, who took the worst beating, might have been killed first.

Not to leave out any possible theories though, Lohman also went the other way and later, also surmised that the slayer was a "burly madman" or that two men had committed the crime. He noted that the "bodies had been thrown like bags of potatoes" and that this "would suggest that at least two persons or one very powerful person did it."

The first suspect picked up in the case was an unemployed schoolteacher, who was brought in for questioning early in the morning. He lived five blocks from the Schuessler home and had been named in an anonymous telephone call to the police. He was questioned vigorously, offered to take a lie detector test, and was soon released. He would not be the last "person of interest" to be questioned in the case but time after time, the men were interrogated and let go.

While investigators were coming up empty, newspaper reporters hounded the grief-stricken parents of the three boys. The press descended on their neighborhood of modest bungalow homes, a place where crime --- of any kind ---- was rare. It was almost impossible for them to even fathom what had occurred. Murder was something that happened in the newspapers, not in their own hometown.

Mrs. Schuessler, described as a "frail 37 year-old woman", rocked back and forth on her living room couch on the day the bodies were found, surrounded by friends and neighbors. Reporters pushed into the room, looking for comments but she only murmured things like "My life, my arms... my legs... now gone." One she shrieked out, "I want my boys! I want my...." before collapsing into hysterics.

Mr. Schuessler rushed into the room and fell to his knees in front of the couch where his wife was sitting. He shuddered with pain and apparent agony. "Mother, mother," he cried. "What kind of land do we live in?" He buried his face in her lap and sobbed.

The investigation continued with no results while the last days of Bobby Peterson and Anton and John Schuessler ended on a grim note. An honor guard of Boy Scouts carried the coffins of the three boys from the St. Tarcissus Roman Catholic Church to a hearse that would take them to St. Joseph Cemetery. The church was filled to capacity with an estimated 1,200 mourners and even more people joined the families at the graveside service, numbering over 3,500. Reverend Raymond G. Carey told the gathering that "God has permitted sin, evil and suffering because He knows that He can bring good from the suffering."

No one present could see much in the way of good from the deaths of three innocent young boys however. This marked the end of innocence in Chicago --- it was now apparent to all that America had changed for the worse.

Years passed. As there is no statute of limitations for murder, the case officially remained open but there seemed to be little chance that it would ever be solved. The Schuessler-Peterson murders became sort of a cautionary tale in Chicagoland, painting a bloody picture of what happens when children talk to strangers.

Then, four decades later, and long after the principals in the case had long since passed away, a bizarre turn of events occurred that would finally offer closure for the cold case. In the middle 1990s, a government informant named William "Red" Wemette accused a man named Kenneth Hansen of the murders during a police investigation into the 1977 disappearance of candy heiress Helen Vorhees Brach.

In 1955, Hansen, then 22 years-old, worked as a stable hand for Silas Jayne, a millionaire from Kane County. Jayne himself was wild and reckless and had been suspected of many violent and devious dealings during his rise to power in the horse-breeding world. He went to prison in 1973 for the murder of his half brother, George, and died of leukemia in 1987, escaping punishment for many of the crimes that were later laid at his doorstep.

Hansen had certainly committed plenty of crimes himself. The homosexual hustler would later admit to molesting as many as 1,000 young boys and investigators were easily able to build a case against him, thanks to the missing pieces filled in by Wemette. The renewed investigation resulted in his arrest in August 1994.

Cook County prosecutors showed jurors how Hansen had lured the Schuessler brothers and Bobby Peterson into his car under false pretenses around the intersection of Lawrence and Milwaukee Avenues. They retraced the path of the killer to Silas Jayne's Idle Hour Stables in the 8600 block of Higgins Road. His story was that he wanted to show the boys some prize horses that were being kept there. According to the testimony of several men that Hansen had bragged to, he had molested and then killed Anton, John and Bobby one by one.

The boys were killed in the tack room when they tried to fight Hansen off and then he tied up the bodies and he and, allegedly, his brother dumped them at Robinson Woods. In the spring of 1956, the Idle Hours Stables burned to the ground. The week before the fire, the Cook County Coroner announced to the press that he planned to exhume the bodies of the three boys in a search for trace evidence. Silas Jayne, after seeing the newspaper report, became convinced that remnants of his stables might remain on the boys. Police detectives had previously visited the stable as they followed up on reports of boy's screams coming from the building at night and Jayne thought they might put it all together and Hansen's crime would bring him down. Out of fear, he torched the

Kenneth Hansen following his arrest for the murder of the Schuessler - Peterson boys. (ATF)

building to obliterate all of the evidence. The detectives never connected the arson to the murders and Hansen escaped from the long arm of the law for nearly 40 years.

As the case came to trial in 1995, four decades of silence were broken and many of Hansen's other victims came forward, recalling promises of jobs made to young men in return for sexual favors. He forced their silence with threats that included warnings that they might end up "like the Peterson boy". Even without evidence and eyewitnesses to corroborate the prosecution's allegations against him, in September 1995 a Cook County jury convicted Kenneth Hansen of the murders. They deliberated for less than two hours and Hansen was sentenced for 200-300 years in prison.

But the case was not yet over. In May 2000, the Illinois Appellate Court overturned Hansen's conviction. Two of the three justices found that the judge in the case erred when he allowed evidence to be submitted that showed that Hansen regularly picked up hitchhikers and sexually abused them. Despite what some saw as a close call, Hansen was almost routinely convicted again and once more, he received the 200-300 year sentence. The Illinois Appellate Court affirmed the conviction in 2004 and, this time, it appears that Hansen will deservedly die behind bars.

Bobby, John and Anton could finally rest in peace.

BORN TO RAISE HELL
The Life & Crimes of Richard Speck

On the hot summer night of July 13, 1966, a brutal and dim-witted drifter butchered his way into the annals of Chicago crime with the murders of eight nursing students on the southeast side of the city. From that point on, the name of "Richard Speck" would strike terror into the hearts of young women living alone and few would ever forget the words inked onto his arm as a burning tattoo.

"Born to Raise Hell", the tattoo read, and it was a fitting description of his life.

Richard Speck was born in Kirkwood, Illinois in December 1941, the seventh of eight children. Over the years, dozens have speculated about the reason behind Speck's brutal crimes and whether he turned evil somewhere along the way, or if he was simply born bad -- as the tattoo scrawled on his arm claimed. Many have also wondered if perhaps things might have turned out different in the lives of eight nursing students if Speck's father, whom he adored, had not died when Speck was only 6 years-old. Regardless, Speck was raised by his mother in a strict Baptist setting that forbade alcohol and worldly influences. She later married Carl Lindberg, a violent man with an arrest record, and they moved to Dallas, Texas, where Lindberg began taking out his drunken rages on his stepson. By this time, Speck was a slow-witted failure with schoolwork and on the fast track to nowhere. He started running with some older boys, drinking, fighting and getting into trouble.

In November 1962, Speck married Shirley Malone and they had a daughter, Bobby Lynn, soon after. Their married bliss was short-lived, however, and Speck began abusing both his wife and his mother-in-law. According to Shirley's later accounts, he often raped her at knifepoint, claiming that he needed sex four to five times each day. Likely to Shirley's relief, Speck ended up in jail for theft and check fraud in 1963. He was paroled in January 1965 but, after only four weeks, he was arrested again for aggravated assault. He was sentenced to serve another 16 months but was released after only six.

During this period, he had had the words "Born to Raise Hell" tattooed on his arm, which his wife Shirley had already experienced firsthand. She filed for divorce in January 1966. When Speck was arrested for burglary and assault, a couple of months later, he fled from Dallas with the help of his sister, Carolyn. He was on his way to his sister Martha's home in Chicago. Once again, we have to wonder how the fates of those young women may have changed if the authorities had gotten to Speck before he could leave.

He only stayed in Chicago with Martha for a few days and then went to Monmouth, Illinois, a small town where he had lived as a boy. He stayed with family friends and worked as a carpenter for a month. He soon quit his job in order to spend his time hanging out in a local tavern, the Palace Tap. Speck only managed to stay out of trouble until April 2, when Mrs. Virgil Harris, 65, was attacked in her home. The man grabbed her from behind, cut her house-coat into strips, tied her up with them and raped her. Mrs. Harris told police that her assailant spoke with a southern drawl, as Speck did after his years in Texas.

On April 13, Mary Kay Pierce, a barmaid at Frank's Place, was found dead in a shed behind the tavern. Her liver had been ruptured from a blow to the abdomen. Speck was brought in for questioning but the interrogation was cut short when he got sick. He promised to return on April 19 for more questions, but he never did. Investigators traced him to the Christy Hotel and, when they entered his room, they found jewelry and a radio that had been stolen from Mrs. Harris' home, as well as items from other burglaries in town. They did not find Speck, however. The hotel manager told police that he had seen Speck leaving with two suit-cases a few hours before they arrived. He told the manager that he was going to the laundromat, but he caught a bus instead -- heading for Chicago.

Speck now returned to the home of his sister, Martha, and his brother-in-law, Gene Thornton. Their second floor apartment on the city's northwest side was crowded but Speck didn't plan to be there much. He announced his intentions to search for work as a merchant seaman but after several days of doing nothing, Thornton got frustrated and drove his unwanted houseguest to the National Maritime Union Hall, located at 2315 East One Hundredth Street. The building is now a church and was then located just a few

Richard Speck, the deviant loser who killed 8 nurses on a Chicago summer night in 1966. Why did he do it? According to Speck, "it just wasn't their night." (UPI)

doors away from three residential townhouses, including number 2319, which had been rented by the South Chicago Community Hospital for 24 of its 155 student nurses.

Thornton brought Speck to the Maritime Union Hall in hopes that there was still an open berth on a ship that was bound for Vietnam. As it turned out though, fate intervened once more. The position went to a man with greater seniority, leaving Speck without a spot. Disappointed, but unwilling to take Speck back in, Thornton handed him $25 and wished him well. He then drove off and left his brother-in-law to fend for himself.

A short time later, Speck managed to get a position aboard an iron ore ship on the Great Lakes, where he was stricken with appendicitis and hospitalized in Hancock, Michigan. When he returned to Chicago in mid-June, he was fired for being drunk and disorderly. He had been warned repeatedly about his drinking and violent behavior but he disregarded the threats. After that, he spent the next three weeks in cheap hotels, sleeping in the park, and financing his liquor and his visits to prostitutes with whatever odd jobs he could come up with.

On July 13, a depressed and angry Speck was drinking heavily in the Shipyard Inn on the southeast side. After a volatile combination of pills and liquor, he suddenly got the urge to "raise some hell". He would later say that he remembered nothing after this point.

Speck left the bar with a hunting knife, a pocketknife and a borrowed .22 caliber pistol and walked over to one of the nearby student dormitories. For the past several weeks, the drifter had seen the women coming and

A current view of the townhouse apartment on the southeast side where the 8 nurses were killed by Richard Speck.

going from the buildings, sunbathing in Luella Park and walking back and forth to their classes. He was familiar enough with their schedules to know that, at nearly 11:00 p.m., they would be home in bed.

A loud rapping came at the door of one of the townhouses and Corazon Amurao, who shared a second floor bedroom with two other young women, went to the door and opened it. She found a tall, lean stranger standing on the doorstep. He smelled of liquor and had a knife in one hand and a gun in the other. He slurred that he was not going to hurt her. "I'm only going to tie you up," he said. "I need money to go to New Orleans."

He shoved his way into the townhouse and ordered the three Filipino students --- Valentina Paison, Merlita Garguilo and Corazon --- into a bedroom at the back of the building, where Pamela Wilkening, Nina Schmale and Pat Matusek were getting ready for bed. Speck took the sheets from the beds and cut them into strips, which he used to bind the women by their wrists and ankles. At 11:30, a seventh nurse, Gloria Davy, returned home from a date and she was also imprisoned. Then, a half-hour later, Suzanne Farris and her friend, Mary Ann Jordan, came to the front door. Speck pulled them inside and led them into the back bedroom at gunpoint.

In the course of the hour, Speck had systematically tied and gagged each of the women. How he managed to do this with almost no resistance remains one of the great unsolved mysteries in Chicago crime. Why did none of the women try to escape? Why did they not try and overpower Speck as he was tying another victim? Why did none of the women in the other townhouses hear anything that was taking place? No one knows and to this day, it remains a mystery.

By 3:30 a.m., Speck's lust was finally spent. One by one, he had taken the eight young women out of the bedroom and had killed them. Only one of them, Gloria Davy, had been raped but all were dead --- save for Cora Amurao, who had managed to roll under a bunk bed and cower there in fear and shock until Speck finally left. Apparently, in his frenzy, he had lost count of the women in the house. Amurao remained hidden, frozen in terror, until nearly 6:00 in the morning. When she finally emerged from her hiding place, she climbed out of the apartment window and, perched on a ledge, began to scream. "My friends are all dead!" she cried. "I'm the only one alive! Oh God, I'm the only one alive!"

Her screams caught the attention of Judy Dykton, a student who lived across the street. She had gotten up early to study and was startled by the cries from outside. Snatching her robe, she ran over to find Cora shaking and crying on the window ledge. Judy entered the open door of the townhouse and stepped into the living room. She first discovered the naked body of Gloria Davy, her hands tied behind her and a strip of cloth wrapped tightly around her throat. Her skin had turned cold and a dusty blue color. She was obviously dead. She turned and fled to the apartment of the housemother, Mrs. Bisone. "There's trouble in 19!" she screamed.

The housemother woke up the other student nurses and ran toward 2319. She brought Leona Bonczak with her, who entered the house. She first checked to see if Gloria showed any signs of life and then mounted the stairs and looked down the hall. In the bathroom, she found the body of Pat Matusek and then crept into the other bedrooms, where she discovered the rest of the students so drenched in blood that she was unable to recognize any of them, save for Nina Schmale. A pillow covered most of the girl's face but she lay on her back,

74

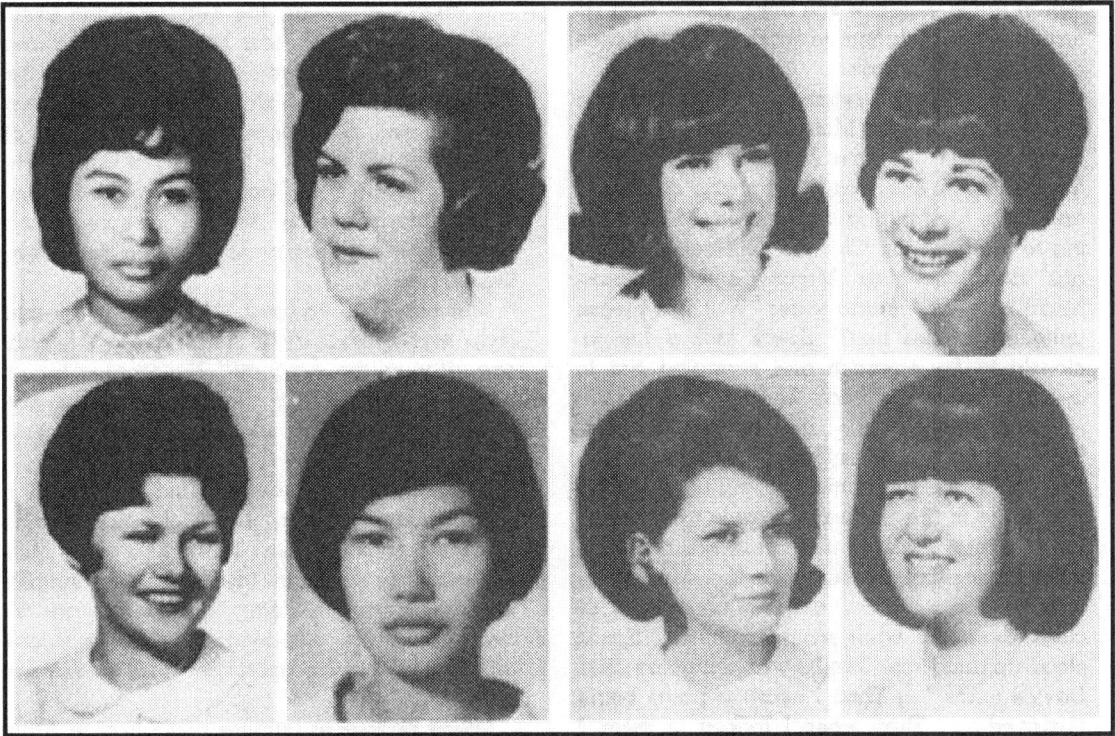

Speck's Eight Victims (Top Row, Left to Right) Valentina Paison, Pamela Wilkening, Patricia Matusek, Suzanne Farris (Bottom Row) Mary Ann Jordan, Merlita Garguilo, Gloria Davy, Nina Schmale (UPI)

hands tied behind her, a cloth around her neck, legs spread apart -- and a fatal knife wound to her heart.

Stunned, she went downstairs and numbly told Mrs. Bisone that everyone was dead. The housemother, shaking and sick, picked up the phone, called South Chicago Community Hospital, and told them that all of her girls had been murdered. When the hospital asked her who had been killed, she was unable to tell them. The only words she uttered were "send help!"

Someone on the street managed to flag down police officer Daniel Kelly, a young patrolman who had only been on the job for 18 months. He radioed in that there was trouble and then entered the house. He was shocked to discover the body of Gloria Davy in the living room. Kelly had dated her sister some time back. Upset, he drew his gun, searched the house and found the other bodies. The townhouse looked like a charnel house and in places, the blood in the carpeting was so thick that it pooled over Kelly's shoes. He ran outside to his car radio and called it in. Soon, Kelly heard the comforting sounds of approaching sirens beginning to fill the air.

The street outside filled with police cars and cops and people ran from door to door, alerting their neighbors of the horror found in 2319. The first detective on the scene was Jack Wallenda, a big powerful man with a soft voice who was shocked by the utter brutality of the killings. He entered the house and viewed the bodies one by one.

He found Gloria first. She was nude, belly down on the couch and tied with double-knotted bed sheets. He noticed what appeared to be semen between her buttocks and found buttons from her blouse strewn down the stairs. The killer had apparently torn them off her as he pulled her to the living room. Also tossed on the floor was a man's white t-shirt, size 38-40.

Wallenda then checked the upstairs bedroom and found the body of Pamela Wilkening. She had been gagged and stabbed through the heart. Suzanne Farris lay nearby in a pool of blood and a white nurse's stocking had been twisted around her neck. The detective counted 18 stab wounds to her chest and neck. He studied Mary Ann Jordan next. She had been stabbed three times in the chest and once in the neck.

In the northwest bedroom, he found Nina Schmale with her nightgown pulled up to her breasts and her legs pulled apart. She had also been tied and stabbed, and it looked as though her neck might be broken. Valentina Paison was found under a blue cover, lying face down. Her throat had been cut. Tossed carelessly on top of her was the body of Merlita Garguilo, who had been stabbed and strangled.

Wallenda walked out the door and to the right and saw the legs of Patricia Matusek protruding from the bathroom. She was lying on her back with her hands bound behind her. She had been strangled with a piece of the bed sheet, double knotted, and her nightgown had been dragged up over her breasts. Her white panties had been pulled down to expose her pubic hair. Blood-soaked towels were strewn all over the bathroom floor.

Wallenda's hands were shaking as he left the townhouse. It was the worst crime scene that he had ever witnessed.

The police immediately went to work and, within hours, were on the trail of Richard Speck. Cora, although heavily sedated, had managed to give an excellent description of the killer and a gas station attendant who worked nearby remembered one of his managers talking about a guy of the same description who had been complaining about missing a ship and losing out on a job just a couple of days before. Police sketch artist Otis Rathel put together an uncanny likeness of Speck. Investigators took the sketch to the Maritime Union Hall and questioned the agent in charge. He remembered an irate seaman who lost out on a double booking -- two guys sent for one job -- and he fished the crumpled assignment sheet from the wastebasket. The sheet gave the name of Richard Speck.

State's Attorney Daniel P. Ward would later call the manhunt for Speck the "finest bit of police work" he had ever seen. The Chicago Police, Sheriff's deputies, the Coroner and a number of amateur investigators managed to neatly compile the case and detectives began tracking his movements.

After the murders, Speck moved from bar to bar, drinking himself into oblivion, not knowing that the police were on his trail. Detectives had convinced the agent at the Maritime Hall to call Speck's last known telephone number, his sister's, to tell him that he was needed to ship out. The agent connected with Gene Thornton, who agreed to try and track Speck down. He managed to find him at the Shipyard Inn and told him that the union hall had a job for him. Speck called the union hall and was told to come down for an assignment on a ship that Speck knew had shipped out several days before. Suspecting a trick, he told the agent that he was up north and it would take him at least an hour to get there. He never showed up.

Immediately, Speck went upstairs, packed his bags, and called a cab. He waited in the tavern, playing pool, and three detectives came in looking for a tall blond man with a southern accent. The bartender was no help and Speck stayed quiet, listening and shooting pool just 10 feet away from them. When the cab arrived, he refused to give the driver an address and told him he wanted to go to his sister's house, which he said was in a poor and slummy section of town. The cabbie drove north and again asked Speck for an address. Clueless, he pointed to a building that turned out to be part of the Cabrini Green housing project. He got out of the cab and watched the cabbie drive away.

Speck started walking and ended up on Dearborn Street at the Raleigh Hotel, a flophouse that had once been a luxury apartment building. He registered under the name of "John Stayton", one of his friends in Texas. A desk clerk later recalled a drunken Speck and his "cracker" accent coming in with a prostitute and giving him the wrong room number. He didn't want to wake his boss, so he let the couple go. Just before the elevator door closed, he heard the girl call him "Richard". A half hour later, the girl came back downstairs and told the clerk that her "date" had a gun. This prompted a call to the police and two officers from the 18th District police station showed up at the hotel at 8:30 a.m. Speck, still drunk, awoke to find two cops standing over him. He had the gun tucked into the waistband of his pants and when asked why he had it, he told the officers that it belonged to the prostitute. When asked what his name was, he told them that it was Richard Speck. They checked his wallet and found his seaman's I.D. and passport but, unfortunately, not all of the police had been notified of the identity of the student nurses' killer yet. He was questioned for 15 minutes and the officers confiscated the gun but never reported it. When they left the hotel, they told the desk clerk that he was "harmless".

Not realizing that Speck had narrowly escaped capture, the police searched the south side. They managed to track him from the Shipyard Inn to the cab company to Cabrini Green. But while they canvassed the housing project, Speck drank himself into another stupor. Later in the afternoon, he ran into some old friends who suggested that he hop a freight train with them and head out of town. Speck went back to the Raleigh, packed his bags and, on his way out, told the manager that he was going to do some laundry. He never returned. Just 15 minutes after he walked out though, two detectives came in and flashed a photo of Speck in front of the manager. Her eyes widened. "It's him," she said. "It's Richard; he just left!"

Oblivious, Speck then headed for the Starr Hotel, a rundown dive on West Madison Street that offered temporary refuge to winos and bums. The "rooms" were nothing more than cubicles that were portioned off by plywood and had "doors" made from chicken wire. For the rate of 90 cents per night, the occupant was provided with a cot, a wall locker, a metal stool and a 15-watt bulb that dangled from the ceiling on a wire. Here, losers could sleep off a drunken stupor amidst the sounds of coughing and moaning and the smells of sweat, booze and vomit. It was the last rung on the ladder for the dregs of humanity and Speck fit right in.

He tossed his bags on a cot and went out to sell some of his belongings to raise money for another night of drinking. He picked up some wine at a local liquor store and several newspapers with his name and photo splashed across them. Speck stumbled back to the Starr Hotel and finished off the entire bottle of wine. He then walked down the hall to the bathroom, smashed the wine bottle and used the broken glass to cut his wrist and inner elbow. Blood splashed the wall and onto the floor and Speck wobbled down the corridor to his cubicle. He collapsed onto the bed, still bleeding badly and then called out to his neighbors for water and for help. They ignored him.

An anonymous call was made to the police but no patrol car was sent. Eventually, Speck was taken to Cook County Hospital. The ambulance drivers ignored Speck's cries for water and missed the police bulletin on their dashboard that had the injured man's photo on it. In the emergency room, Nurse Kathy O'Connor prepped Speck and first year resident Leroy Smith checked his wounds. He noticed something familiar about the man. He checked his arm, looking for a tattoo and saw it there, as he suspected --- "Born to Raise Hell". He compared a newspaper photo with the man and realized that he had the killer on his table.

Speck pleaded with the young man for water but Smith grabbed him by the back of the neck and squeezed it as hard as he could. "Did you give water to those nurses?" he demanded. He dropped Speck's head back onto the gurney and called in a policeman who was guarding another patient down the hall. He told him that Richard Speck, the suspect in the murders, was there on the table. The stunned officer started making telephone calls and then all hell broke loose.

Speck was in police custody a few hours later and William J. Martin, a young and hard-working state's attorney, was faced with putting together and trying the case. He based most of it on the sincere and compelling testimony of Corazon Amurao, who had to be persuaded to remain in the United States long enough to secure the conviction of the monster who had killed her friends. She was understandably unhinged from her ordeal and she wanted nothing more than to return to the Philippines to try and forget the horrific experience. Martin brought her mother and a cousin to Chicago for moral support and kept them in a secret location away from the press. Her quiet testimony galvanized the courtroom and convinced a jury in Peoria (the defense had argued that Speck could not get a fair trial in Chicago) to convict him in just 49 minutes. Speck was given the death sentence for the murders.

Although sentenced to die in the electric chair, the Illinois Supreme Court voided the death penalty in 1971 and Speck was back in court again. This time, he was sentenced to 400 to 1,200 years at the Stateville Penitentiary in Joliet. It was the longest prison sentence ever given to an Illinois inmate and one that he would fall far short of serving.

During his incarceration, Speck never admitted his guilt in the murders. He died on December 5, 1991 from a massive heart attack. His autopsy showed that he had an enlarged heart and occluded arteries, having blown up to 220 pounds by the time of his death. No one claimed his body and he was cremated. His ashes were disposed of in an undisclosed location.

But unfortunately, in 1996, Speck was back.

In May of that year, television journalist Bill Kurtis went behind the walls of Stateville prison and came back with a secret videotape (originally filmed in the middle 1980s) that showed a bizarre Richard Speck with women's breasts -- apparently from hormone treatments -- wearing blue panties and having sex with another inmate. Segments of the video, which also showed sex and drug orgies, were shown on the program *American Justice* and it plunged the Illinois Department of Corrections into a major scandal. Viewers were as repulsed to see what had become of Speck as they were by his bloody crimes.

Even after death, he was still raising hell.

UNSOLVED!
The Washington Park Murders of 1972

A mysterious rash of murders involving young women plagued the Chicagoland area in the summer of 1972. As the last days of summer began to fade, the region could record the deaths of four teenaged girls, two women and one 18-month-old baby girl. The police were baffled, especially by the final murders, which remain unsolved to this day.

The first was discovered in June when the body of Kathleen Morecraft, 18, of Elgin was found in a forest preserve near Streamwood. She had last been seen riding her bike, on her way to visit a friend, when she was attacked and killed. A month later, Julie Hanson, 15, was found stabbed to death in a cornfield south of her Naperville home. She was also last seen riding her bike, this time only a short distance from her house.

Over Labor Day weekend, Judith Bettekey, 24, from Stoke-on-Trent, England, was enjoying her visit to Chicago and decided to take a stroll through Grant Park. She was dragged into the bushes and beaten to death. There seemed to be no clear motive for the murder. On September 11, the bodies of Mrs. Barbara Flanagan, 27, of Mount Prospect, and her 18-month-old daughter, Renee, were found in a church parking lot. Barbara had reportedly gone to meet a man who wanted to hire her as a babysitter. She was attacked and her skull was beaten to a pulp on the pavement. The baby had died from an apparent sexual attack.

Two days later, on September 13, Sally Kandel, 14, of Carol Stream, was found bludgeoned to death in a nearby cornfield. Like Kathleen Morecraft and Julie Hanson, she was last seen riding her bike. Police were puzzled, wondering if perhaps the murders were connected in some way. There was no evidence of any kind to link them but the sheer number of strange murders had put investigators on edge.

Then, on September 23, the most perplexing of the murders occurred, leaving a lingering mystery that has yet to be solved.

Carolyn Van Der Molen, 13, and Deborah Kozlarek, 17, were residents of a rundown neighborhood on the southeast side near Washington Park. The park had been opened just in time for the World's Columbian Exposition in 1893 and had been designed by eminent landscape architect, Frederick Law Olmstead. Its intention was to show off the natural beauty of Chicago but, by 1972, the neighborhood was

Carolyn Van Der Molen, 13 (right) and Deborah Kozlarek, 17 (left) vansihed and were later found dead in the Washington Park neighborhood on Chicago's south side.

anything but beautiful. Much of the area had turned into slums by the 1950s and crime often ran rampant, personified by muggings, robberies and gang violence. The murders of the two girls seemed to blend into the darkness of the area and, perhaps because of this, no one was ever arrested or charged with the crime. In fact, the case was either so baffling ---- or so forgettable ---- that the police were not even sure what led to the girl's initial disappearance.

Carolyn was an eighth-grade student at St. Augustine Grammar School. The semester had only just started but she was remembered by her principal and teachers as a "friendly girl, but a loner." She lived with her parents in a brick three-flat on South Elizabeth Street, near Sherman Park. Carolyn's friend, Deborah, was a high school dropout who lived with her parents and three siblings on South Racine. She worked as a waitress at MotorWorld Lounge, a busy truck stop and motel that was located near Midway Airport. The structure later became the Crossroads Hotel Plaza and the Great Wall Chinese restaurant.

It was reported at the time that the girls were both troublesome, perhaps influenced by one another, and had difficulty getting along with their parents. Deborah had dropped out of school after being stabbed during a racial altercation, a problem that was not uncommon in that part of the city at the time. Tensions between black and white teenagers ran high in 1972. Sherman Park was the domain of the Gaylords, a tough, Irish street gang. Washington Park, and points further east, was the turf of the Black Gangster Disciples and the Black P Stone Nation. Deborah did the best that she could to get along in this volatile neighborhood and was often described as "worldly beyond her years". Co-workers at the truck stop were surprised to learn that she was only 17.

The bodies of the two girls were discovered in Washington Park on Saturday morning. A jogger that was passing by around 7:30 a.m. spotted them and immediately called the police. The bodies were fully clothed, there was no sign of sexual molestation, and ballistic tests revealed that they had been shot to death with .32 caliber bullets. The autopsy revealed that they had eaten a full meal not long before they were killed. The detectives speculated that they had either known their killer, or had trusted a stranger enough to let him buy them dinner. They often hitched rides but none of their friends believed they would have gone willingly into Washington Park so late on a Friday night. How had they gotten there? And why? Investigators began piecing together their last hours, hoping to find a clue.

The girls were not identified at first. In fact, Coroner Andrew J. Toman publicly identified one of the victims as a teenage runaway named Rosemarie Pilewicz. The embarrassed coroner had a lot of explaining to do when the Pilewicz girl turned up alive the following day in the far north side Foster Avenue police district.

Mrs. Van Der Molen, who had asked two police friends to help search for the girls when Carolyn did not come home over the weekend, had made the identification. On Monday afternoon, she went to the police station and reported them missing. After listening to her report, she was taken to the morgue. She then identified her daughter and made a tentative identification of Deborah, which the girl's father later confirmed.

Once correct identification was made, the girls were laid to rest at Resurrection Cemetery and the police stepped up their efforts to find out what happened --- at least for a while. After that, the case rapidly went cold and, unfortunately, outside of the girl's families, no one seemed to care.

On the afternoon of her disappearance, detectives learned, Carolyn asked for her father's permission to spend the night at Deborah's house. When he refused, she stomped out of the house and was later seen at the Down Beat Tap buying pop and candy around 9:00 p.m. Deborah had worked at the truck stop until the end of her shift at 5:00 p.m. and was scheduled to be off the following day. She was last seen by neighbors walking down Elizabeth Street with Carolyn just a little after 11:00 p.m. that night. What happened after that remains a mystery....

This is where the trail went cold and the case dissolved into useless leads and eerie silence. To this day, there has not been a single arrest or formal charge made in the murder case of Carolyn Van Der Molen and Deborah Kozlarek. What scant interest that existed in the case has long since faded with time and it seems unlikely that we will ever know what happened to these young girls.

The city of Chicago holds many secrets and who killed Carolyn and Deborah is one secret that will probably never be told.

3. GANGLAND GHOSTS

History & Hauntings of the Prohibition Era in Chicago

Whatever they may say, my booze has been good and my games have been on the square. Public service has been my motto, I've been spending the best years of my life as a public benefactor. I've given people the light pleasures, shown them a good time. All I get is abuse.
Al Capone

I hope when my time comes, that I die decently in bed. I don't want to be murdered beside the garbage cans in some Chicago alley.
George Moran

There are few periods of American history as fascinating to crime buffs as that of the "gangster era" of the 1920s and 1930s. During this period, organized crime gained a foothold in America, especially in the larger cities, where gangsters became celebrities and "graft" being paid to cops and politicians was an everyday happening. During the years of Prohibition, the mob came into its own, "giving the people what they wanted" and then diversifying into other criminal pursuits once the liquor began to legally flow again.

But organized crime had come to America long before the years of Prohibition. Its American roots were born in the city of New Orleans, but the "Mafia" was created in Sicily around 1282. At that time, it was a secret brotherhood that was dedicated to freeing the country from the French. For years, the Mafia was a champion of the people, waging guerilla warfare against the French and other invaders. The country's chief city, Palermo, became the hub of Mafia activity, and the "dons" of the organization sent recruiters out across the land in search of young and ardent patriots who were skilled in the art of killing.

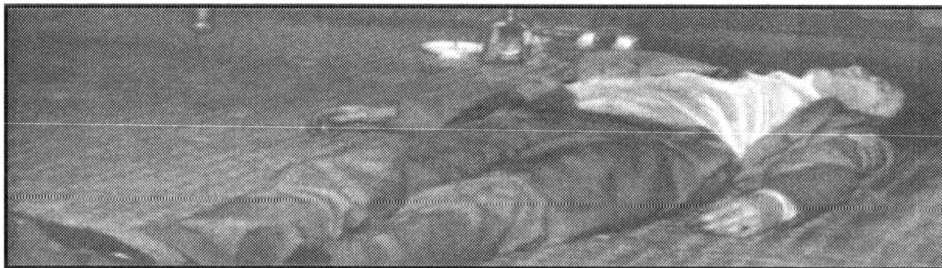

By the early 1800s, the Mafia had evolved from a benevolent society that fed the hungry and sheltered the homeless to an organization that extorted money and power from landowners and peasants alike. Its leaders, known as "capos", directed the group to intimidate and threaten business owners, government officials and even military officers.

By 1889, the Mafia had come to America and it has been said that it came first to New Orleans. At that time, New Orleans was probably the most anti-Italian city in America. The city had recently been flooded with thousands of Italian immigrants and statements from the mayor's office didn't help matters any. In one letter, Mayor Joseph A. Shakespeare called Southern Italians and Sicilians ".... the most idle, vicious and worthless people among us". Of course, not all of the blame could be laid at the city government's door either. In addition to dirty politicians and cops on the take, late 1800s New Orleans was also filled with Italian criminals. There was no denying that the French Quarter ghetto was turning out productive Italian citizens, but it was also turning out lawbreakers too. Undoubtedly, many of these criminals were not "Mafia", but it has long been conceded that New Orleans represented one of the main ports of entry for the Mafia into the United States. Between 1888 and 1890, the New Orleans Mafia, made up of several Sicilian groups, committed an estimated 40 murders without opposition. From New Orleans, organized crime and the Mafia spread across America, gaining footholds in Kansas City, New York, St. Louis and, of course, Chicago.

THE BLACK HAND

The Black Hand first became associated with Chicago crime around 1900. The area where this menace has been most associated was a tenement area that was known as "Smoky Hollow" in the early 1890s. At that time, this was a quiet and hard-working community that was mostly free of serious crime, save for family squabbles and the occasional clash between rival Irish gangs. By the end of the decade, most of the Irish had left the area though and it had largely been taken over by poor, working-class Italians. It would be during this period, when the Italian immigrants began to be terrorized by the Black Hand, that the neighborhood became better known as "Little Hell".

During a period that lasted from roughly 1900 to 1920, there were an alleged 400 murders in Chicago ascribed to a shadowy entity known as the Black Hand. The gangs that made up the Black Hand preyed on the Italian and Sicilian immigrants who lived along Oak and West Taylor Streets and along Grand and Wentworth Avenue. So many murders were committed near the intersection of Milton and Oak Streets that the locality became popularly known as "Death Corner". This was the favorite killing field of a vicious and mysterious killer called the "Shotgun Man" and he was believed to be responsible for at least one-third of the 38 unsolved murders that occurred between January 1910 and March 1911. Four of the victims were killed during the last three days of that final month.

There were probably as many as 60 or 80 Black Hand gangs at work in Chicago during the first two decades of the Twentieth Century but all of them appeared to be independent units so the police were never able to connect one with another. And despite the magnitude of their operations, none of the extensive investigations conducted by the police ever revealed a Black Hand organization that reached national or even citywide proportions. The "Black Hand" was not an actual group, it was realized, but a

The legendary spot known as "Death Corner", at the intersection of Oak & West Taylor Streets. The killing field of the "Shotgun Man".

Police detectives lead a Black Hand suspect to jail. Unfortunately, most arrests were not effective as the shadowy organizations were almost impossible to track down and prosecute.

method of crime. It was used by individuals, by small groups and by large and organized gangs. In Italy and Sicily, it was employed by the Mafia and called the Black Hand because as a general rule, extortion letters, which formed the initial phase of the terrorism, bore the imprint of a hand in black ink. The letters were also sometimes marked with crude drawings of a skull and crossbones or sometimes crosses and daggers.

The way the Black Hand operated was both simple and direct. First, a victim that showed signs of prosperity would be chosen from among the Italian immigrant population. For instance, if a man purchased any property and that fact became public knowledge, he could almost count on the attention of the Black Hand. A letter, bearing a signature of the Black Hand was then sent to the victim demanding money. If the letter was ignored, or the victim refused to pay, his home, office or business would be bombed. If he still refused to pay, then he would be murdered. Most of the letters were blunt instructions about sums of money and where they were to be delivered. Others were more clever and worded with politeness and Italian courtesy. No matter how they were phrased though, each brought the promise of death if the instructions were not carried out to the letter.

Dozens of bombs were exploded in the Italian quarter in retaliation for non-payment of extortion. In 1910, the *Chicago Tribune* reported that there had been 25 unsolved murders connected to the Black Hand, 43 murders in 1911, 33 in 1912, 31 in 1913 and 42 in 1914. During the first six months of 1915, six men were killed and 12 bombs were detonated.

As the police attempted to combat the Black Hand gangs, they were faced with impossible obstacles. Hundreds of arrests were made but suspects were usually released within hours because no evidence connecting them with specific crimes could be secured. Many cases of murder and extortion were brought into the courts but convictions were nearly impossible to obtain and those few who were sent to prison were usually quickly paroled thanks to payoffs to corrupt politicians. The reason that it was so hard to prosecute the Black Hand gang leaders was for the same reason they were so terrifying in the first place. As soon as a Black Hand suspect was arrested, witnesses and members of the victim's family were threatened with death if they gave information to the police. Judges, jurors, members of the prosecutor's staff, and even their families received threats. In one case, a witness was about to give the details of a Black Hand extortion plot when a man entered the courtroom and waved a red handkerchief at him. The witness froze and refused to speak anymore. The state was then forced to abandon the case.

According to the *Tribune*, "the police, hampered at every turn by the silence of the Italian colony, are compelled to resign themselves... at present the police acknowledge the futility of further investigation."

By the latter part of the 1910s, the police officials were forced to try and downplay the Black Hand. They simply had no way of controlling the situation and no way to combat the threats or apprehend the killers when the extortion went one step too far. Most Chicago cops paid them a grudging respect as an elusive and resourceful prey, while others denied their existence altogether, as the Federal Bureau of Investigation would do a few years later when forced to confront the reality of the Mafia. The prejudices of those in the city government who sought to dismiss the Black Hand failed to take into account the helplessness and despair of the Italian immigrants as they tried to cope with the hardships of life in a new and unpredictable country -- only to be faced with being terrorized on top of it.

Because of this, some of the Italian business and professional men decided to try and take matters into their own hands. They formed what was called the White Hand Society, an organization that was sponsored by wealthy businessmen, the Italian Chamber of Commerce, Italian newspapers, and several fraternal orders of Italians and Sicilians. It was formed to work with the police and to try and exterminate the Black Hand. Although virtually every member of the society was threatened with death at one time or another, it was active for several years. Private detectives were employed to help the police investigate Black Hand cases and agents were even sent to Italy and Sicily to look into past histories of the most notorious gangsters. They also arranged for protection for witnesses and their family members. Several murderers and extortionists were sent to prison through the efforts of the White Hand, but they were soon paroled and resumed their activities. For this reason, this society of neighborhood vigilantes was more of a symbolic gesture than anything else. Their intentions were good but they were up against a much too difficult adversary. The White Hand faded out of existence around 1912.

The Black Hand gangs endured for about another eight years and it was finally a federal law that forced them out of existence. Once the federal government began prosecuting extortion as the misuse of the United States mail, dozens of Black Hand gangsters began to be convicted, fined and sent to Federal prisons. The corrupt politicians were unable to help them and most of the convicted men served their full sentences. Thanks to government intervention, the bombings, murders and extortion that still took place were carried out by other methods than the mail and soon the Black Hand began to disappear. By 1920, and the coming of Prohibition, most of the extortionist gangs found that bootlegging and rum-running was a greater field for their talents and the Black Hand became a thing of the past.

THE CURSE OF THE "GREEN CHAIR"

Organized crime in Chicago had been involved in gambling, prostitution and extortion since the early days of the city but it would be an American law that would actually bring the underworld its greatest power.

When the 18th Amendment to the Constitution, which abolished the sale and distribution of alcohol, took effect on January 16, 1920, many believed that it would cure the social ills of America. Little did they know at the time, but it would actually do just the opposite. America's great thirst for the forbidden liquor bred corruption in every corner. Law enforcement officials became open to bribes because the majority of the men just did not believe in the law but, worse yet, Prohibition gave birth to the great days of organized crime. The gangsters of America had previously concerned themselves with acts of violence, racketeering and prostitution but the huge profits that came to be made with the sale of illegal liquor built criminal empires.

Across the country, over 200,000 "speakeasys" opened. These drinking

Chief of Detectives William Shoemaker (Left) in 1928

establishments were so named because many of them were located behind, above or below legitimate businesses and patrons often drank in silence. Huge bootlegging operations sprang into existence to supply the speakeasys and those who chose to ignore the new law. In addition, ordinary people began brewing their own beer and distilling their own liquor. Some of them even sold the stuff from home, and the product called "bathtub gin" came into existence. Disrespect for the law became the fashion as people who would have never dreamed of doing anything illegal in the past were now serving illicit liquor in their homes or drinking in neighborhood speakeasys.

Most considered Prohibition to be largely doomed by 1928, but it hung on for another five years before being repealed in 1933. By then, it had taken its toll, leaving law enforcement in disarray and leaving the mobster organizations so powerful that they were able to move onto other pursuits, like legalized gambling, with wide public approval.

In Chicago, names like Al Capone and Dion O'Banion were no longer spoken in merely the poor neighborhoods, but also among the rich of Lake Shore Drive and the Gold Coast. Newspapers carried accounts of gangland slayings and bootleg wars across the country. Author Herbert Asbury wrote that "the average tourist felt that his trip to Chicago was a failure unless it included a view of Capone out for a spin. The mere whisper: 'Here comes Al', was sufficient to stop traffic and to set thousands of curious citizens craning their necks along the curbing."

Crime ran rampant during this period and even inspired phrases that are still in use today among law enforcement officials. The term "Chicago Amnesia" is still used to describe the reticence of witnesses to testify against organized crime. In Chicago of the 1920s, law enforcement officials found it almost impossible to prosecute gangsters because of the fear that they instilled in witnesses. Even eyewitnesses who eagerly came forward after seeing a crime take place suddenly developed a memory loss when they learned the identities of the culprits. And it seemed that the disease was contagious, often contracted through bribes, but usually through threats and even murder attempts.

The Prohibition era also spawned a number of curious legends among Chicago underworld figures. Perhaps one of the strangest was that of the "Green Chair Curse", also referred to as the "Undertaker's Friend". The curse was named after a green leather chair found in the office of William "Shoes" Shoemaker, who became the Chicago chief of detectives in 1924. Several of the city's top gangsters were hauled into Shoemaker's office for questioning and ordered to sit in the green chair. Several of them died violent deaths a short time later.

This could hardly be that surprising, given the death rate during the gang wars in Chicago, but the newspapers quickly seized on the story and a belief in the "curse" of the chair began to grow. Shoemaker, probably delighted with the attention, stated that he was now keeping track of the criminals who sat in the chair and later died violently. When the inevitable later occurred, he would put an "X" by the gangster's name. These men included the Genna brothers (Angelo, Tony and Mike), "Porky" Lavenuto, "Mop Head" Russo, "Samoots" Amatuna, Antonio "The Scourge" Lombardo, John Scalise, Albert Anselmi, Antonio "The Cavalier" Spano and others. Legend had it that other well-known gangsters, even Al Capone, absolutely refused to sit down in the chair.

When Shoemaker retired in 1934, there were 35 names in his notebook and 34 of them had an "X" after their name. Only one criminal, Red Holden, was still among the living and he was doing time in Alcatraz for train robbery. "My prediction still stands", Shoes told reporters upon his retirement. "He'll die a violent death. Maybe it'll happen in prison. Maybe he'll have to wait until he gets out. But, mark my words, it'll happen."

But Holden managed to outlive Shoes. The detective died four years later and the green chair was passed on to Captain John Warren, who had been Shoemaker's aide. He continued to seat an occasional hoodlum in it, perhaps hoping to "scare them straight" with the eerie legend. By the time that Warren died in September 1953, the chair's death rate stood at 56 out of 57 men.

Red Holden had been released from Alcatraz in 1948 and, afterwards, he was involved in several shootouts, all of which he survived. Then, he was convicted on murder charges and was sent to prison for a 25 year sentence. He died in the infirmary of Illinois' Statesville Prison on December 18, 1953. According to the newspapers, he was smiling when he passed -- because he had beaten the green chair!

Holden's death set off a search for the mysterious green chair. No one knew what had happened to it after Captain Warren had died. Finally, it was discovered that the chair had been destroyed. It was traced to the Chicago Avenue police station, where it had been confined to the cellar after the death of Captain Warren. Later found to be infested with cockroaches, it was broken apart and burned in the station's furnace.

This had happened shortly before Red Holden had died in his hospital bed. Otherwise, some claimed, he would have never escaped the curse!

GUNS, ROSES & VALENTINES
The Rise & Fall of Chicago's Criminal Empires

If the rise of Chicago's mobs came with the start of Prohibition in 1920, then the decline of these criminal organizations began almost a decade later in February 1929. It was on St. Valentine's Day of that year that the general public no longer saw the mob as "public benefactors", offering alcohol to a thirsty city, but as the collection of killers and thugs that it truly was.

Of course, the St. Valentine's Day Massacre (along with the destruction of the North Side mob and the conviction of Al Capone for income tax evasion) was not the death knell for the mob in Chicago. Organized crime will always be with us but it was this bloody event that changed the face of crime in the city forever. In the years that followed, empires crumbled and lives were destroyed, bringing an end to the "glory days" of the mob in Chicago.

The story of the Chicago mob truly begins with one of the most important criminals in pre-Prohibition Chicago, Big Jim Colosimo. In addition to running a popular restaurant in the South Side Levee District, Colosimo was also an influential brothel-keeper and he kept close ties to a number of important city officials. In this way, he insured his political clout and maintained his ability to operate his criminal enterprises without interference. By 1915, he was the acknowledged overlord of prostitution on the south side and thanks to his political powers, he was important in other sections of the city as well.

While operating his string of whorehouses, Colosimo brought a young man named Johnny Torrio from New York to be his bodyguard and right-hand man. It would be Torrio's ambitions that would lead to Colosimo's violent death.

Ironically, Colosimo's downfall came at the same time that he developed a romantic interest

Colosimo's Restaurant in the South Side's Levee District. It was long regarded as one of the finest Italian restaurants in Chicago.

in one of the few respectable women that he had ever known. Her name was Dale Winter, a young musical-comedy actress who had been stranded in Chicago after an unsuccessful theatrical tour. She accepted an invitation to perform in one of Colosimo's establishments and the two fell in love. In 1920, he divorced his wife and married Dale three weeks later. They took a two-week honeymoon in Crown Point, Indiana and returned to Chicago.

Big Jim Colosimo is shot dead in his restaurant, paving the way for Johnny Torrio and Al Capone.

On the afternoon of May 11, 1920, Colosimo left for his restaurant with plans to meet his new wife later that night for dinner. When he arrived, he went to his office and spoke with his secretary, Frank Camilla, who had been meeting with the chef about that evening's dinner. Colosimo spoke with them for a few minutes and then, about 4:30 p.m., he allegedly took a telephone call from Johnny Torrio that explained that a shipment of whiskey was being delivered to the restaurant and Colosimo had to sign for it personally. Colosimo left the office and walked out in the lobby, likely preparing to step outside. A moment later, two shots were fired and Frank Camilla went to investigate the sounds. He found Colosimo's dead body lying on the floor of the lobby with a bullet wound to the back of his head. The second bullet was lodged in the plaster wall. From the angle of the shots, the killer, the police concluded, must have been hiding in the cloak room.

The funeral of Big Jim Colosimo was held on May 15 and was the first of the gaudy burial displays that were the fashion in Chicago's underworld throughout the 1920s. Thousands attended, including both gangsters and politicians, further underscoring the alliances between the two.

The murder of Colosimo remained a mystery, at least as far as legal evidence was concerned. However, most everyone believed that Johnny Torrio had carried out the murder in an effort to take over Colosimo's operation. And who was the trigger man? According to all accounts, it was a young man who had worked for Torrio in New York named Alphonse Capone. He had been working for Colosimo since coming to Chicago and a waiter saw him fleeing the scene after Colosimo's murder but he identified him to the police only as a "stranger".

Alphonse Capone was born in Brooklyn in 1899 and made a name for himself as a slugger and a gunman with the famous Five Points gang in New York, of which several of his cousins were members. Capone was only 23 when he came to Chicago but Torrio soon promoted him to the post of manager in one of his toughest dives, the Four Deuces on South Wabash Avenue. It was a brick building with a saloon on the first floor, Torrio's offices on the second, a gambling den on the third and a brothel on the fourth. During his time at the Four Deuces, Capone became Torrio's first lieutenant and the chief of his gunmen.

As far as the general public was concerned though, he remained an obscure member of Torrio's organization for the first two years he was in Chicago. As late as August 1922, he was still so little known that when he became involved in an automobile accident, the newspaper account referred to him as "Alfred Caponi". In those days, he was rough and brutal but there was little to indicate that he was destined for criminal greatness in the years to come. In the underworld, he was generally known as "Scarface Al Brown", a nickname that was due to the two parallel scars on his left cheek that had been left behind during a knife fight. Soon though, all of Chicago would be familiar with his name.

Torrio and Capone moved up quickly after Colosimo's death. The gangs on the south side, where Torrio had his greatest influence and Capone had the most muscle, quickly fell in line with their plans. Torrio's beer began to flow to the local gangs at $45 a barrel (each costing about $5 to produce) and were distributed by Ragen's Colts and Ralph Sheldon's gang on the south and by the Circus Gang, led by Claude Maddox, Marty Guilfoyle's gang and the Druggan-Lake mob on the west side.

Up until 1922, the Chicago gangland remained at peace. Then, a south side gang, then led by Spike O'Donnell, decided to rise up against Torrio. They were massacred back into their place over a period of about two years, between 1923 and 1925. Not long after, the Genna Brothers, who supplied Torrio with poorly made liquor that was manufactured in neighborhood stills, began to get greedy and demanded a larger piece of the action. Wars began to erupt but most of the trouble seemed to come from the North Side mob, an eccentric legion of mostly Irish gunmen led by Dion O'Banion. The high quality Canadian liquor that was sent to Torrio by the Purple Gang in Detroit was constantly being hijacked by the North Siders. O'Banion also moved his bootlegging operation into Cicero, which Torrio and Capone had already staked out as their exclusive territory.

Dean Charles O'Banion was born in 1892 in the small Central Illinois town of Maroa. His father, Charles, was a barber by trade who hailed from Lincoln and his mother, Emma Brophy, was the Chicago-born daughter of an Irish immigrant father and American mother. She had been just eight months old when the Great Chicago Fire had leveled the city in 1871. Charles and Emma had married in 1886 and moved to Maroa the following year, where Charles' parents lived.

Dean spent the early years of his life in Maroa but soon after the birth of his sister, Ruth, his mother contracted tuberculosis and died in 1901. Dean was only nine years-old at the time and the loss was a devastating one to both he and his remaining family. They packed up and moved to Chicago, where Emma's parents had a place for them. Dean (soon to be known as Dion) saw the end of his innocent years. The hard times ---- and the legend --- were about to begin.

Upon moving to Chicago, O'Banion found himself turning to the streets for a playground. He became involved with a street gang known as the Little Hellions and began picking pockets and rolling drunks. At the same time, he sang in the choir at the Holy Name Cathedral and, on Sunday, he served as an altar boy. Some of the priests at the church believed that perhaps his devotion might lead to the priesthood but O'Banion soon learned to ration his religion to Sundays and to devote his remaining time to robbery and, as he reached young adulthood, to burglary --- "a man's profession."

For a time, O'Banion worked as a singing waiter at the McGovern brother's café and saloon on North Clark Street, crooning and balancing a hefty tray of beer glasses. McGovern's was a rough place and was filled with crooks. It was here that O'Banion met, and befriended, notorious safecrackers and thieves like George

FAVORITE SIDETRIPS INTO CHICAGO'S GANGLAND HISTORY
The Lexington Hotel

In 1986, television reporter and talk show host Geraldo Rivera took a national television audience into what was then one of the last remaining landmarks of the Chicago crime era and the reign of Al Capone ---- the old Lexington Hotel at the corner of Michigan Avenue and 22nd Street. Rivera was in search of lost treasure, a fortune that Capone had allegedly left behind in secret vaults in the hotel. Earlier in the 1980's, a local women's construction company had investigated the possibility of restoring the hotel, which was by then merely a shadow of its former self. As they searched the building, they discovered a shooting gallery that had been used by Capone's cronies for target practice and dozens of secret passages and stairways, including one behind Capone's medicine chest. The passages led to hidden tunnels that connected taverns and whorehouses on the Levee, and also led to the immediate west. The tunnels had been designed to provide elaborate escape routes from police raids and attacks by rivals.

This led to more interest in the hotel and soon researcher Harold Rubin came to the crumbling old building and began his own search of the premises. In addition to recovering many priceless artifacts from the days of the hotel's glory, Rubin also stumbled across one of the great secrets of the place when exploring the escape tunnels. It was said that Capone also had vaults in the lower levels of the Lexington where he had stashed away some of his loot. These vaults were so well hidden that even Capone's closest accomplices were not aware of them. Rubin's discoveries led to a newspaper article in the *Chicago Tribune* but his excellent research would be overshadowed by Geraldo Rivera, who stated that if the secret money vaults could be found, he would discover them --- and would do so on national television.

The Lexington Hotel had opened in 1892 and had been designed by Clinton Warren, the architect of the famed Congress Plaza Hotel. The brick and terra cotta building had been hurriedly opened to serve the masses of visitors who came to Chicago for the 1893 World's Fair. These were boom years on the city's south side and the fine hotel attracted scores of wealthy and famous visitors, including President Benjamin Harrison, who once addressed an audience from the balcony.

Al Capone, who became the Lexington's most famous resident, abandoned the Metropole Hotel (one block to the south) in July 1928 and moved into a luxurious fifth-floor suite of rooms at the Lexington. He registered under the innocuous name of "George Phillips" and ran his operations from the hotel until he was escorted off to prison in October 1931. Capone held court in an office that overlooked Michigan Avenue while in the Lexington's lobby, armed gunman kept a careful eye on the front doors. Additional guards with machine guns patrolled the upper floors and were hidden away in closets.

Capone was ensconced at the Lexington at the time of his downfall, immediately following the infamous St. Valentine's Day Massacre. While this bloody event marked the end of any significant gang opposition to Capone, it was also the act that finally began the decline of Capone's criminal empire. He had just gone too far and the authorities, and even Capone's adoring public, were ready to put an end to the bootleg wars. The massacre started a wave of reform that would send Capone out of power.

Capone's days at the Lexington were numbered by this time because in 1930, the United States government got involved in Chicago's dilemma over how to get rid of Al Capone. Washington dispatched a group of treasury agents to harass Capone and try to find a way to bring down his operation.

In the end though, it would not be murder or illegal liquor that would get Capone, it would be income tax evasion. He was sentenced to spend 11 years in a federal prison and eventually ended up in the infamous "escape-proof" penitentiary of Alcatraz.

The remnants of Capone's gang abandoned the Lexington in 1932 and after that, the ownership of the hotel changed several times as the state of the place declined with the surrounding neighborhood. It was re-named the New Michigan Hotel in the 1950's but soon after it became a bordello, a transient hotel and finally, a crumbling eyesore. By the 1980's -- and the arrival of Geraldo Rivera -- it was scheduled for demolition. But the Lexington had one last act still left in its old bones.

On that night in 1986, Rivera and his camera crew went out live to America from the deserted and empty hotel. The place had already been picked clean by vandals and souvenir hunters, but Rivera was sure that secrets from the past still remained in the place. In a basement chamber, the crew blasted away a 7,000-pound concrete wall that was believed to be hiding a secret compartment that contained thousands, perhaps millions, of dollars. Even the Internal Revenue Service had agents on hand to claim their share of the loot. When the smoke cleared though, only a few empty bottles and an old sign were found. The fortune, if it had ever been there at all, had long since been spirited away.

After Geraldo managed to try and upstage everyone in Chicago who had researched Capone for years, the person who actually discovered the location of the vault, Harold Rubin, got the last laugh. He worked for the production company that produced one of the most watched television specials ever and was interviewed by CBS on the night of Geraldo's blunder. To this day, no one has ever done as much research into the history of the Lexington and Rubin stands as the man who discovered the old place's greatest secrets -- whether the vaults were empty or not.

The Lexington Hotel finally "gave up the ghost" in November 1995. By that time, the ten-story hotel had fallen into ruin after years of neglect and it was torn down. Another chapter in the history of Chicago crime had been closed for good.

"Bugs" Moran, Earl "Hymie" Weiss, Vincent "The Schemer" Drucci and Samuel "Nails" Morton. With these men at his side, O'Banion put together one of the most devastating gangs in Chicago. They centered their activities on the north side, around the Lincoln Park neighborhood and the Gold Coast.

When Prohibition came along, O'Banion purchased several of the best breweries and distilleries on the north side. Where Capone and Torrio on the south side were forced to either import beer and whiskey at high prices or rely on rotgut produced by the Gennas to supply their outlets, O'Banion had the finest beer and booze available.

All over the city, society people and the owners of better restaurants bought from O'Banion. The quality of his product was better and it was thought that he was more trustworthy than Capone, who was also running brothels and floating gambling operations. O'Banion publicly agreed to keep his operations north of the "dividing line", or Madison Street, but still serviced his special customers on the south side as well.

At first, this encroachment on Capone-Torrio territory was tolerated. Capone attempted to negotiate with him, stating that if O'Banion was going to run booze on the south side, then Capone should be allowed to have liquor warehouses in Lincoln Park. O'Banion refused --- not because he couldn't deal with Capone, but because he was morally offended by Capone's dealings in prostitution. During the tenure of the O'Banion operation (and later the Weiss and Moran gangs), not one professional brothel operated in the opulent northeast section of Chicago. However, O'Banion's religious compunctions did not apply to hijacking Capone's trucks, robberies, gambling casinos and the killing of anyone who got in his way.

Torrio constantly tried to negotiate with O'Banion, rather than use the violence that Capone began to urge. Dozens of meetings were held between Torrio, Capone and the North Siders, and each ended with the same results. O'Banion always promised to recognize the territory of the South Siders and then turned right around and began encroaching upon it again. O'Banion insulted the Gennas and they came to Torrio seeking retribution but Torrio insisted that they wait. O'Banion killed several of Capone's gunmen but when Capone urged Torrio to hit O'Banion, his boss again asked him to wait.

Torrio knew that if he killed O'Banion, it would mean all-out war in Chicago.

But his hesitation backfired on him in May 1924 when O'Banion came to him and told him that he planned to retire and wanted to sell Torrio his largest gambling den and his favorite brewery, Sieben's. He had a good excuse for doing so, stating that he planned to retire from bootlegging and work in his flower shop. As everyone knew, despite the fact that he had one of the largest liquor operations in the city, O'Banion hated liquor and beer. He did love flowers though, so he purchased a half interest in the Schofield Flower Shop at 738 North State Street, directly across the street from Holy Name Cathedral. O'Banion easily convinced Torrio that he planned to get out of the liquor business because of this.

Torrio agreed to buy up O'Banion's concerns and reportedly paid him a half-million dollars in cash two days later. The gang leaders agreed to meet at Sieben's on May 19, as Torrio wanted to inspect his new property. But he had not been there for more than 10 minutes before Police Chief Collins, leading 20 officers, raided the place and arrested O'Banion, Earl "Hymie" Weiss and Torrio. This was Torrio's second arrest for violating prohibition. He had been arrested once and fined in June 1923 but a second arrest could mean jail time -- a fact that O'Banion had been very much aware of. Torrio also realized that O'Banion had no intention of retiring. He had conned Torrio into buying a brewery that he knew the police were about to shut down.

O'Banion was very amused by the "joke" he had pulled on Torrio but Hymie Weiss pleaded with his boss to "take it easy with those guys".

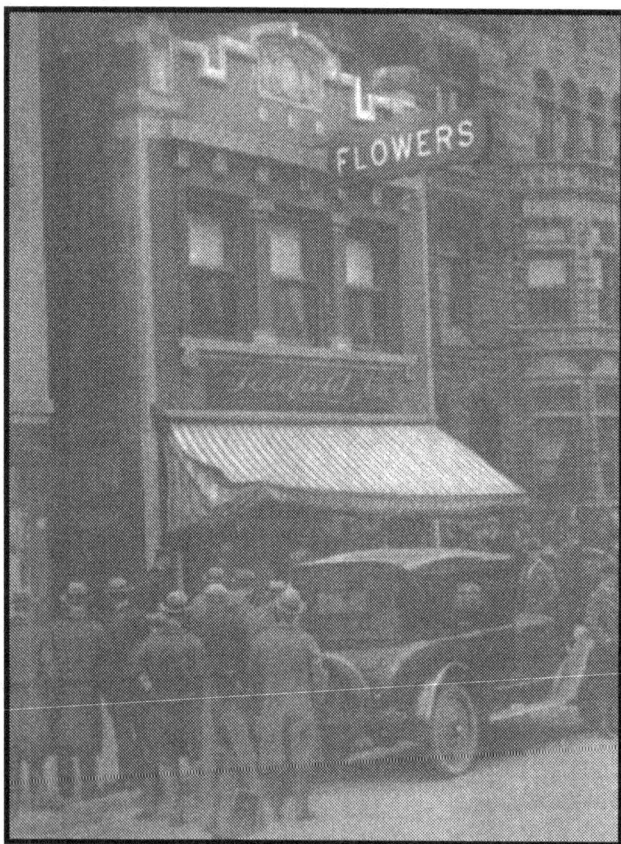

O'Banion laughed. "When are you gonna learn?" he asked his friend. "Those people are gutter rats, dumb bastards all of 'em, Torrio, Capone, them Gennas... To hell with them Sicilians!"

It was time, Torrio finally decided, to get rid of O'Banion. When Mike Merlo, a close friend of O'Banion and the founder and president of the powerful *Unione Sicilian* --- an ethnic group that controlled Sicilian gangster operations which Capone fought for years to dominate --- died in November 1924, Torrio saw a way to kill the north side gang leader.

On November 10, James Genna and Carmen Vacco entered O'Banion's flower shop and ordered a wreath for Merlo's funeral. They gave O'Banion $750 to pay for the arrangement. They told him that they would send some boys back to pick it up a little later. Then they left the shop.

Five minutes later, the telephone rang and an unknown caller wanted to know if O'Banion had the flowers ready. He promised that they would be ready at noon and at five minutes past the hour, a blue Jewett touring car pulled up in front of the shop.

One of the shop's employees, a black man

The scene outside of the Schofield Flower Shop on the day that O'Banion recieved the first "Chicago Handshake" named William Crutchfield, who was sweeping up flower petals in the back room, looked up to see three men get out of the car and walk into the shop. Another man remained at the wheel of the car outside.

O'Banion, dressed in a long white smock and holding a pair of florist's shears in his left hand, came out from behind the counter and extended his hand in greeting. "Hello, boys," O'Banion greeted them. "You from Mike Merlo's?"

The three men walked abreast and approached O'Banion with smiles on their faces. The man in the center was tall, clean-shaven and wearing an expensive overcoat and fedora. It was determined years later that this man was Frankie Yale. The other two, believed to be John Scalise and Albert Anselmi, were shorter and stockier, with dark complexions.

"Yes, for Merlo's flowers," Crutchfield heard Frankie Yale say before he stepped closer to O'Banion. Yale grabbed the other man's hand in greeting and pulled O'Banion toward him. The two men at his sides moved around him and drew pistols. Then, at close range, Yale rammed his own pistol into O'Banion's stomach and, holding his arm in a vice-like grip, opened fire. The other two men also fired their weapons and the bullets ripped into O'Banion. Two slugs struck him in the right breast, two hit him in the throat and one passed through each side of his face. The shots were fired so close that powder burns were found at the opening of each wound. From that point on, this method of murder became known as the "Chicago Handshake."

O'Banion fell, dead on his feet, into a display of geraniums. The three pistols that he had hidden on his body were unfired, not even drawn. The three men fled from the store and climbed into the car outside, which drove slowly away from the scene.

The Genna brothers, Capone and Torrio were all arrested on suspicion of homicide but were all soon released after supplying airtight alibis. Frankie Yale was arrested at the La Salle Station, departing for points unknown, after the shooting but he was also released. The investigation, headed by ace Detective Captain William "Shoes" Shoemaker, went nowhere.

At an elaborate funeral service, O'Banion's friends filed past his body, tough gangsters weeping as they walked into Sbarbaro's Funeral Home. He was placed inside of a $10,000 bronze casket that had been fitted with bronze and silver double walls. A heavy plate glass window had been fitted over O'Banion's patched-up face and his men could peer down and see his head where it reclined on a white, satin pillow.

O'Banion's funeral was the most lavish in Chicago gangland history. The hearse was led to Mount Carmel Cemetery by 26 trucks filled with flowers, worth more than $50,000. The scene at the cemetery was even more bizarre. On one side of the grave, lowering the body to rest, were Hymie Weiss, George Moran, and Vincent Drucci; on the other, Al Capone, Johnny Torrio and Angelo Genna. The North Siders glared at the South Siders but no one made a move toward their guns ----- not yet, anyway.

Torrio was right about one thing --- O'Banion's death ignited an all-out war in Chicago. It would be Torrio who got the first taste of the wrath of the north side gang.

A few days after O'Banion's funeral, in November 1924, Torrio and his wife got out of a chauffer-driven limousine in front of their house at 7011 Clyde Avenue (Torrio lived here under the name Frank Langley) and Anna Torrio began to walk inside. As Torrio reached in to pick up some packages from their shopping trip, a black Cadillac screeched to a stop across the street. Inside, four men with pistols and shotguns watched for a moment and then two of them, George "Bugs" Moran and Hymie Weiss, jumped from the car and ran towards Torrio with their guns blazing.

Torrio fell immediately with a bullet in his chest and one in his neck. The other two men in the Cadillac, Vincent Drucci and Frank Gusenberg, jumped out and opened fire on the limousine with their shotguns. Meanwhile, Moran and Weiss ran to the fallen Torrio and, standing above him, fired bullets into his right arm and another into his groin. Moran leaned over to put the next one into Torrio's head but his gun was empty. As he reached for another clip, Drucci began honking the horn of the Cadillac, signaling frantically that they needed to leave. Moran and Weiss ran to the car and they sped away.

Somehow, Torrio managed to start crawling to the house and his wife, who was screaming, came out and pulled him inside. A neighbor, who witnessed the shooting, called an ambulance and Torrio was raced to the

Newspaper photographers captured Johnny Torrio wearing a scarf to hide the bandages on his throat when he appeared in federal court.

hospital. Unbelievably, he survived with a permanent scar to his neck. Reporters soon surrounded his hospital bed, demanding more information. Torrio stated that he knew all four of the assailants involved but "I'll never tell their names," he said.

In February, Torrio (still bandaged) was sent to federal court for the Sieben's brewery fiasco and he received a nine-month jail sentence to be served in the Waukegan County jail, which had medical services for the still ailing mobster. Earl Weiss, who had taken over the leadership of the North Side gang, was fined for his first offense on violation of Prohibition charges and when the clerk called the name of Dion O'Banion and the prosecutor announced that he was "deceased", Weiss shot Torrio an evil look. Torrio got the hint ---- the North Siders may have botched their first attempt to kill him but they wouldn't miss the second time. He left for Waukegan filled with fear.

However, the treatment that Torrio received in prison was equal to the status of the gangland boss. The windows of his cell were covered with bulletproof glass and extra deputies guarded him day and night. Easy chairs, throw rugs, books and other luxuries were added as well. Torrio also received the special privilege of taking his evening meals in the sheriff's home and was allowed to relax on the sheriff's front porch for awhile each night, visiting with his wife and his associates, such as Al Capone.

As he finished serving his time, Torrio had a lot of time to think. When he got out, he announced that he was tired of the rackets and that he was turning his entire operation over to Capone. All that he needed, he told his younger friend, was to get out of Chicago alive. Capone promised that he would, and he made good on his assurances. Torrio and Anna left the city in an armor-plated limousine and were escorted by two roadsters filled with gunmen. When they reached a train station, just over the Indiana state line, Capone's men patrolled the station with shotguns and machine guns until the train, which held the Torrios, departed for Florida. After that, they went on to Italy, living in Naples for three years.

Torrio got bored in Italy but knowing that he couldn't return to Chicago, he went to New York instead, where he went into the real estate business with the blessing of Meyer Lansky and Charles "Lucky" Luciano. He also helped to establish a liquor cartel along the Atlantic Seaboard and established himself as an elder statesman of the underworld. He lived a sedate and quiet life after Prohibition was repealed but, in 1936, he was arrested for income tax evasion. After a series of trials and appeals, he served two years in Leavenworth and was paroled in 1941. He died in a barber's chair (of natural causes) in 1957.

Torrio's departure from Chicago shoved Al Capone into the violent spotlight of the Chicago underworld and it also made him the top man in the city at only 25 years of age. He now had an annual income that would actually land him a place in the Guinness Book of World Records. And he also had a bloody gang war on his hands. Hymie Weiss offered to stem further violence by having Capone hand John Scalise and Albert Anselmi over to him. It was a poorly kept secret that they had been in the flower shop when O'Banion had been murdered. Capone refused and made plans to knock off Hymie Weiss instead. He was too slow though ---- Weiss and Bugs Moran had already planned their next move.

Capone was sitting with his most trusted bodyguard, Frank Rio, in the restaurant of the Hawthorne Hotel in Cicero on September 20, 1926. The street outside was filled with shoppers and automobiles and, at first, no one noticed as nine cars filled with north side gangsters slowly cruised down Twenty-Second Street. One of the cars accelerated away from the others and as it passed the windows of the restaurant, black barrels of machine guns appeared from the windows and opened fire. Glass shattered and wood splintered as bullets riddled the restaurant! The car sped off and Rio jumped to his feet, gun in hand. But as Capone started to get up from the floor, his bodyguard pushed him back down again because he spotted the other cars in the procession.

The other eight touring cars were filled with men and machine guns. They opened fire on Capone's Cicero stronghold, emptying clip after clip into the hotel, spraying everything in sight. Hymie Weiss boldly climbed from his car with Moran close behind him. Capone had over 100 men inside of the heavily armed fortress and yet none of them faced the withering fire from outside. Weiss ran up to the door of the hotel and opened fire with his machine gun, waving the weapon back and forth across the width of the passageway beyond the doors. When he finished firing, he walked coolly back to the car and with honking and shouts, the

The Hawthorne Hotel, Capone headquarters in Cicero

North Siders drove away. Over 1,000 rounds had been fired into the building and every window in the place was shattered. Amazingly, no one had been killed.

That violent incident was Hymie's one moment of glory and revenge for O'Banion's murder. And while he continued to live a fearless life (to the point of stupidity) and to goad Capone at every opportunity, his days were numbered.

On October 11, Weiss was attending the murder trial of "Polack Joe" Saltis and his driver Frank "Lefty" Koncil, and decided to take a break and return to his office above O'Banion's old flower shop. As Weiss, and gunman Patrick Murray, drove toward the office, they had no idea that four machine gunners were waiting for them. These men, believed to be John Scalise, Albert Anselmi, Frank Diamond and Frank Nitti, were hiding on the third floor of a nearby building. Weiss was a marked man as soon as he left his car on Superior Street, just south of the Holy Name Cathedral. He approached the flower shop with Murray by his side and at the deafening sound of Tommy guns, the pedestrians on the street scattered.

Murray died instantly but Weiss took 10 bullets and survived long enough to be pronounced dead at Henrotin Hospital without regaining consciousness. The bullets that killed Weiss tore away portions of the inscription on the church's cornerstone and left bullet holes as a graphic reminder of the event. The church

(Right) Holy Name Cathedral at the time of the Weiss assassination. Bullet holes still mark a corner of the building. (Left) Police officers take away Patrick Murray's body from the scene. Hymie Weiss was hit 10 times and died on the way to the hospital.

FAVORITE SIDETRIPS INTO CHICAGO'S GANGLAND HISTORY

The Green Mill

If I were forced (perhaps at gunpoint?) to name only one location in Chicago as my favorite spot connected to the days of Al Capone, it would be the legendary jazz club on North Boradway known as the Green Mill. As the city's oldest night-club, it's been offering continuous entertainment since 1907 and remains as an authentic link to not only Al Capone but to the club's former manager ---- and Capone henchman ---- "Machine Gun" Jack McGurn.

The Green Mill opened in 1907 as Pop Morse's Roadhouse and, from the very beginning, was a favorite hangout for show business people in Chicago. In those days, actors from the north side's Essanay Studios made the roadhouse a second home. One of the most popular stars to frequent the place was "Bronco Billy" Anderson, the star of dozens of Western silents from Essanay. Anderson often rode his horse to Pop Morse's and the proprietor even installed a hitching post that Anderson's horse shared with those of other stars like Wallace Beery and William S. Hart. Back then, even screen greats like Charlie Chaplin stopped in sometimes for a drink.

Around 1910, the Chamales Brothers purchased the club from the original owners. They installed a huge, green windmill on the roof and re-named the place the Green Mill Gardens. The choice of the name "Green Mill" was inspired by the infamous Moulin Rouge in Paris (French for "Red Mill") but green was chosen so that it would not be confused with any of the red light districts in Chicago. The new owners added outdoor dancing and live entertainment in the enlarged sunken gardens and also added a rhumba room next door. The Green Mill Gardens was more of a roadhouse that spanned an entire block than a cocktail lounge in those days. Tom Chamales later went on to construct the Riviera Theater, around the corner from the Green Mill. He and his brother leased the Green Mill to Henry Van Horne and it soon began to attract the best --- and worst --- of the late-night denizens of Chicago.

Vintage postcard of the old Green Mill Gardens

By the time that Prohibition arrived, the Green Mill had become known as the most jumping place on the north side. Jazz fans flocked to the club to savor this new and evolving musical art form, which had been born in the south but had been re-created in Chicago after World War I. The jazz crowd ignored the laws against alcohol and hid their bootleg whiskey away in hip flasks, which they eagerly sipped at the Green Mill. The club helped to launch the careers of singers who went on to become legends like Helen Morgan, Anita O'Day, and Billie Holliday. It also offered an endless procession of swinging jazz combos and vaudevillians, who dropped in to jam or just to relax between sets at other, lesser clubs.

94

In the middle 1920s, Van Horne gave up his interest in the place and the Chamales Brothers leased the club to Al Capone's south side mob. Capone himself, although straying into the enemy's territory on the north side, often enjoyed hanging out at the club, listening to the music and drinking with friends.

In the case of the Green Mill though, it's not the remnants of Al Capone that attracts crime buffs to the club; it's the legend of Jack McGurn, who managed the club for Capone in the 1920s.

James Vincenzo De Mora, or Jack McGurn as he later became known, was born in Chicago's Little Italy in 1904. He grew up as a clean-cut kid from the slums who excelled in school and was an excellent boxer. A fight promoter managed to get him promoted into the ranks of professional fighters and at the man's suggestion; James adopted the ring name of "Jack McGurn". He seemed to have a great career ahead, until his father, Angelo De Mora, a grocer with a store on Halsted Street, ran into trouble with the terrible Genna brothers and McGurn stepped over the line into the world of crime.

At the start of Prohibition, the Gennas had transformed all of Little Italy into a vast commercial area of alcohol cookers. Stills were set up in almost every home, franchised by the Gennas, making homemade rotgut whiskey that was popular in neighborhood speakeasies. Angelo De Mora sold sugar to the Gennas for their operations, a relatively safe enterprise until some competitors for the position appeared on January 8, 1923. Angelo was found shot to death in front of his store.

Jack McGurn and his regular squeeze and favorite alibi, Louise Rolfe

McGurn rushed home when he heard about his father's death. He was only 19 but he immediately took the role of head of the household, shielding his mother and five brothers from the police. The police asked him if he was afraid for his life now that he was the man of the house.

"No," McGurn answered ominously. "I'm big enough to take care of this case myself."

McGurn never got back into the ring. He picked up a gun and started working for Al Capone, who regarded him as his most trustworthy gunman and the man to carry out the most dangerous and grisly assignments. Within a few years, "Machine Gun" Jack McGurn was the most feared of Capone's killers.

McGurn relished his work, especially when six of his targets were part of the Genna mob, which he believed were responsible for his father' death. In just over a month's time, he wiped out the Gennas top men and he learned that one of these men had referred to his father as "a nickel and dimmer." So, after each of them had been machine-gunned to death, McGurn pressed a nickel into each of their palms, his sign of contempt and a trademark that would be forever linked to his murders.

McGurn continued to earn his pay --- and his reputation. Joe Aiello's feud with Capone over west side beer territories reached its peak when Aiello offered a $50,000 reward for Capone's murder. He imported four out-of-town killers to do the job when no one in Chicago took him up on his offer. Days after their arrival, the four men met with the wrath of Jack McGurn. All of them were found riddled with machine gun bullets --- and with nickels pressed into their palms.

When not working for Capone, McGurn frequented Chicago's hottest jazz spots and managed to become part owner of several of them through intimidation and violence. By the time he was 23, McGurn owned pieces of at least five nightclubs and managed a number of other lucrative properties. He also managed the Green Mill for Capone and was later given 25 percent of its ownership in exchange for his loyalty. This became his usual hangout and he could often be found sipping liquor in one of the green-plush upholstered booths.

McGurn was fiercely loyal to the Green Mill so, in 1927, he became enraged when the club's star attraction, singer and comedian Joe E. Lewis, refused to renew his contract, stating that he was going to work for a rival club. He opened to a packed house at the New Rendezvous the next night. Days later, McGurn took Lewis aside as he was about to enter his hotel, the New Commonwealth. McGurn had two friends with him and all three of them had their hands shoved into their pockets.

McGurn told Lewis that they missed him at the club and that "the old Mill's a morgue without you".

Lewis assured him that he would find another headliner and when McGurn told him that he had made his point and needed to come back, Lewis refused. He bravely turned his back on the killer and walked away.

On November 27, three of McGurn's men stormed into Lewis' hotel suite, beat him, and then cut his throat almost from ear to ear. The comedian survived the attack, managed to recover his singing voice and continued with his career. Capone, unhappy with McGurn's actions but unable to rebuke one of his best men, was said to have advanced Lewis $10,000 so that the performer could get back on his feet.

A short time later, McGurn's own career was almost cut short. Two machine gunners for George Moran --- Pete and Frank Gusenberg (both killed during the St. Valentine's Day Massacre) --- caught up with McGurn in a phone booth inside of the McCormick Inn. Several bursts from their tommy guns almost finished McGurn for good but major surgery, and a long period of secluded convalescence, saved the killer. Interestingly, this phone booth can now be found in a little inn called the Ruebel Hotel in Grafton, Illinois. How it managed to end up here is anyone's guess.

In early February 1929, McGurn visited Capone at his Palm Island, Florida home for a discussion about the north side gang run by George Moran. Ten days later, the St. Valentine's Day Massacre took place. This hardly seems to be a coincidence!

McGurn has always been connected to the massacre, as has Fred R. "Killer" Burke. George Brichet, a teenager, was walking past the garage when the five men entered on February 14 and overheard one of the men say to another one: "Come on, Mac." He picked out McGurn's photograph from police mug shots. Armed with an arrest warrant, police broke into McGurn's suite at the Stevens Hotel on February 27. As they hauled the gangster away, they were cussed out by McGurn's sweetheart, showgirl Louise Rolfe. The press dubbed her "the blonde alibi" and she swore that McGurn was with her at the time of the murders. He was later indicted but he married Louise soon after and thanks to this, she was not required to testify against him.

McGurn's defense attorneys insisted four times that their client be brought to trial --- so that he could prove his innocence, of course. Each time, the prosecution stated that it was not ready to proceed. Under Illinois law, the prosecution was only allowed four legal delays of this kind. After that, they had to drop the case. McGurn was set free on December 2, 1929.

McGurn's likely role in the St. Valentine's Day Massacre led to Capone putting him "on ice". He was just too hot to use again as an enforcer. He began to be seen less and less with the boss, and was not seen at all during Capone's tax trial, the job of bodyguard given over to Phil D'Andrea.

Once Capone went to prison, McGurn's prestige started to slip. He busied himself with his nightclubs, most of which went under during the Depression, and Louise left him when his money ran out. Alone and flat broke, McGurn met his end on February 13, 1936 ---- the eve of the anniversary of the St. Valentine's Day Massacre.

McGurn was in the middle of his third frame at the Avenue Recreation Parlor, a bowling alley located at 805 North Milwaukee Avenue, when remnants from the old Moran gang finally caught up with him. Five men burst into the place and while three of them pretended to rob the place, the other two machine-gunned McGurn to death on the hardwood lanes.

In his left hand, the killers had placed a comic valentine, which read:

You've lost your job.
You've lost your dough,
Your jewels and handsome houses.
But things could be worse, you know.
You haven't lost your trousers.

In the palm of "Machine Gun" Jack McGurn's right hand, the killers had placed a solitary nickel.

tried to obliterate them years later but the chips and marks have managed to stay. They can still be seen on the corner of the cathedral today.

Meanwhile, the assassins fled their third-floor lair, exited the rear of the building and disappeared into the crowds along Dearborn Street. A discarded machine gun was found in an alley off Dearborn but it couldn't be traced back to the killers.

And one has to wonder how hard the police looked for them. Chief Morgan Collins issued a gruff statement. "I don't want to encourage the business, but if somebody has to be killed," he said, "it's a good thing the gangsters are murdering themselves off. It saves trouble for the police."

The other partners in the North Side gang were, one by one, wiped out or forced to flee from Chicago, leaving only Bugs Moran.

George "Bugs" Moran was born in Minnesota in 1893 but moved to Chicago with his parents around the turn-of-the-century. Here, he joined up with one of the North Side Irish gangs and was befriended by a young tough named Dion O'Banion. The two began working together, robbing warehouses, but after one fouled-up job, Moran was captured. He kept his silence and served two years in Joliet prison without implicating O'Banion in the crime. He was released at age 19 and went back to work with his friend. He was soon captured again and, once more, he kept silent about who he worked with. He stayed in jail this time until 1923.

When Moran, known as "Bugs" because of his quick temper, got out of prison, he joined up with O'Banion's now formidable north side mob. They had become a powerful organization, supplying liquor to Chicago's wealthy Gold Coast. Moran became a valuable asset, hijacking Capone's liquor trucks at will. He became known as O'Banion's right hand man, always impeccably dressed, right down to the two guns that he always wore. When O'Banion was killed in his flower shop in 1924, Moran swore revenge. The war that followed claimed many lives and almost got Moran killed in 1925 when he was wounded in an ambush on Congress Street.

By 1927, Moran stood alone against the Capone mob, most of his allies having succumbed in the fighting. He continued to taunt his powerful enemy, always looking for ways to destroy him. In early 1929, Moran sided with Joe Aiello in another war against Capone. He and Aiello reportedly gunned down Pasquillano Lolordo, one of Capone's men, and Capone vowed that he would have him wiped out on February 14. He was living on his estate outside of Miami at the time and put in a call to Chicago. Capone had a very special "valentine" that we wanted delivered to Moran.

Through a contact in Detroit (reportedly Abe Bernstein, the leader of the Purple Gang) Capone arranged for someone to call Moran and tell him that a special shipment of hijacked whiskey was going to be delivered to one of Moran's garages on the north side. Adam Heyer, a friend of Moran, owned the garage and it was used as a distribution point for north side liquor. A sign out front read "S-M-C Cartage Co. Shipping - Packing - Long Distance Hauling".

Moran received a call at the garage on the morning of February 13, probably from Bernstein, or at least from someone that he knew and trusted. Bernstein, who had always been Capone's supplier, likely would have been sending Moran quality liquor for a month or two to gain his confidence before St. Valentine's Day. Whoever made the call, Moran went along with it and planned the delivery for the next day.

The legendary S-M-C Cartage Company as it looked in the 1930's. The site is an open lot today but the apartment building on the left still stands. The distinctive pillars in front are still easily recognizable on North Clark Street today.

On the morning of February 14, a group of Moran's men gathered at the Clark Street garage. One of the men was Johnny May, an ex-safecracker who had been hired by Moran as an auto mechanic. He was working on a truck that morning with his dog, a German Shepherd named Highball, tied to the bumper. In addition, six other men waited for the truck of hijacked whiskey to arrive. The men were Frank and Pete Gusenberg, who were supposed to meet Moran and pick up two empty trucks to drive to Detroit and pick up smuggled Canadian whiskey; James Clark, Moran's brother-in-law; Adam Heyer; Al Weinshank; and Reinhardt Schwimmer, a young optometrist who had befriended Moran and hung around the liquor warehouse just for the thrill of rubbing shoulders with gangsters.

Bugs Moran was already late for the morning meeting. He was due to arrive at 10:30 but didn't even leave for the rendezvous, in the company of Willie Marks and Ted Newberry, until several minutes after that.

While the seven men waited inside of the warehouse, they had no idea that a police car had pulled up outside, or that Moran had spotted the car as he was driving south on Clark Street and rather than deal with what he believed was a shakedown, he stopped at the next corner for a cup of coffee.

Five men got out of the police car, two of them in uniform and three in civilian clothing. They entered the building and, a few moments later, the clatter of machine gun fire broke the stillness of the snowy morning. Soon after, five figures emerged and they drove away. May's dog, inside of the warehouse, began barking and howling.

The landlady in the next building, Mrs. Jeanette Landesman, was bothered by the sound of the dog and she sent one of her boarders, C.L. McAllister, to the garage to see what was going on. He came outside two minutes later, his face a pale white color. He ran frantically up the stairs to beg Mrs. Landesman to call the police. He cried that the garage was full of dead men!

The police were quickly summoned and, upon entering the garage, they were stunned by the carnage. Moran's men had been lined up against the rear wall of the garage and had been sprayed with machine-guns. Pete Gusenberg had died kneeling, slumped over a chair. James Clark had fallen on his face with half of his head blown away and Heyer, Schwimmer, Weinshank and May were thrown lifeless onto their backs. Only one of

The widely circulated close-up view of the massacre. Chicago newspapers printed it upside down to save the readers the trouble of turning the page to identify the victims.

(Above) A crowd gathers in the alley behind the S-M-C Cartage Co. as the bodies of the massacre victims are removed from the garage.

(Left) Investigators and reporters re-enact the events of the morning of February 14. Men are lined up against the same wall where Moran's men were slaughtered.

The automobile that the massacre killers had been driving was found in a rented garage on Wood Street. The car had been wrecked and then set on fire to hide any trace of its occupants.

the men survived the slaughter but only for a few hours. Frank Gusenberg had crawled from the blood-sprayed wall where he had fallen and ended up out in the middle of the dirty floor. He was rushed to the Alexian Brothers Hospital, barely hanging on. Police sergeant Clarence Sweeney leaned down close to him and asked who had shot him.

"No one --- nobody shot me," he groaned and he died later that night.

Police canvassed Clark Street between Webster and Garfield (now Dickens) Avenues. In 1929, this was a district of mostly rooming houses and there were dozens of landlords and tenants to interview. Transients came and went, the detectives were told, but a couple of women did remember that teams of suspicious men had recently rented rooms, with street views, for $8 per day.

The car that the murderers had been driving, turned into a smoldering wreck, was found in a rented garage on Wood Street. It had been set on fire with acetylene torches and chopped up with a hacksaw. Ownership of the car was traced to Cook County Commissioner Frank J. Wilson, who had sold it to an auto dealership on Irving Park Road a short time before.

The death toll of the massacre stood at seven, but the killers had missed Moran. When the police contacted him later and asked who had sent the men to the garage, he "raved like a madman". To the newspapers, Moran targeted Capone as ordering the hit. The authorities claimed to be baffled though, since Capone was in Florida at the time of the massacre. When he was asked to comment on the news, Capone stated, "The only man who kills like that is Bugs Moran". At the same time, Moran was proclaiming that "Only Capone kills guys like that."

And Moran was undoubtedly right. The murders broke the power of the north side gang and while there have been many claims as to who the actual shooters were that day, most likely they included Scalise, Anselmi and "Machine Gun" Jack McGurn, all of whom were some of Capone's most trusted men. All three men, along with Joseph Guinta, were arrested but McGurn had an alibi and Scalise and Guinta were killed before they could be tried.

The St. Valentine's Day Massacre marked the end of any significant gang opposition to Capone, but it was also the act that finally began the decline of Capone's criminal empire. He had just gone too far and the authorities, and even Capone's adoring public, were ready to put an end to the bootleg wars. The massacre started a wave of reform that would send Capone out of power for good.

Perhaps the strangest bit of history in regards to the massacre involves the fact that Capone had not seen the last of the men who

Capone bodyguard, Frank Rio

were killed on that fateful day. In May 1929, Capone slipped out of town to avoid the heat that was still coming down from the massacre and to avoid being suspected in the deaths of several of the men believed responsible for the killing of the Moran gang. While in Philadelphia, he and Frankie Rio were picked up on charges of carrying concealed weapons and were sentenced to a year in prison. They eventually ended up in the Eastern Penitentiary.

Capone continued to conduct business from prison. He was given a private cell and allowed to make long-distance telephone calls from the warden's office and to meet with his lawyers and with Frank Nitti, Jake Guzik and his brother, Ralph, all of whom made frequent trips to Philadelphia. He was released two months early on good behavior but when he returned to Chicago, he found himself branded Public Enemy Number One.

It was while he was incarcerated in Pennsylvania that Capone first began to be haunted by the ghost of James Clark, one of the massacre victims and the brother-in-law of Bugs

Capone's cell at Eastern State had a radio, private desk, Oriental rugs, an easy chair and all of the comforts of home. It was far removed from the other cells at the Penitentiary in those days. It was here that Capone claimed that he began to be haunted by the ghost of James Clark.

Moran. While in prison, other inmates reported that they could hear Capone screaming in his cell, begging "Jimmy" to go away and leave him alone. After his release, while living at the Lexington Hotel, there were many times when his men would hear him begging for the ghost to leave him in peace. On several occasions, bodyguards broke into his rooms, fearing that someone had gotten to their boss. Capone would then tell them of Clark's ghost. Did Capone imagine the whole thing, or was he already showing signs of the psychosis that would haunt him after his release from Alcatraz prison?

Whether the ghost was real or not, Capone certainly believed that he was. The crime boss even went so far as to contact a psychic named Alice Britt to get rid of Clark's angry spirit. Not long after a séance was conducted to try and rid Capone of the vengeful ghost, Hymie Cornish, Capone's personal valet also believed that he saw the ghost. He entered the lounge of Capone's apartment and spotted a tall man standing near the window. Whoever the man was, he simply vanished.

Years later, Capone would state that Clark followed him to the grave.

On May 8, 1929, just a little more than a week before Capone was arrested on gun charges in Philadelphia, the bodies of Joseph Guinta, John Scalise and Albert Anselmi were found on the floor of an automobile that was parked near Wolf Lake, southeast of the city. Each of the men had been shot several times and had been badly beaten. The crime was never solved but it was thought that either Moran and his men had gotten their revenge for the killings in the Clark Street garage; that Capone had killed the men in order to keep the peace with the remnants of the north side mob; or, most likely, that Capone had killed the men for his own reasons. It is believed that Capone wanted to silence the men because they were becoming too powerful on their own, especially Scalise. It's believed that Capone feared the three men were plotting to move against him and that the three were bludgeoned to death and then shot at a gangland banquet given to celebrate the victory over the Moran gang.

When Capone returned to Chicago in March 1930, he found the climate of the city had changed considerably during the time he had been away. His popularity had waned and the police were adamant about putting his operations out of business. Police Captain John Stege even posted a guard of 25 policemen in front of the

Capone's modest home on South Prairie Avenue

Capone home on Prairie Avenue with orders to arrest him as soon as he arrived from Pennsylvania. Capone slipped quietly into the city though, and took up residence at the Hawthorne Inn in Cicero, where he spent four days answering mail and getting caught up on the state of operations. Then, he and his attorneys blatantly called on Captain Stege, and the United States District Attorney, and found that neither of them had an actual warrant for his arrest. With that settled, he returned to Chicago.

While no charges had actually been filed against Capone, there was nothing to prevent the police from keeping him under surveillance. Two unformed policemen were assigned to follow Capone everywhere he went, day and night. Capone's empire was starting to crumble and even his hangers-on were getting out of control. Eccentric newspaperman Jake Lingle of the *Chicago Tribune* bragged that he was the man who actually fixed the price of beer in town --- and he was on Capone's payroll.

Lingle was found in a subway underpass on Michigan Avenue with his brains blown out. Capone lamented that "Jake was a dear friend of mine" but his sentiments fell on deaf ears as it was widely known that Capone had given Lingle $50,000 to use his influence to clear a dog track operation in the city. Lingle, who referred to himself as the "unofficial chief of police", never delivered. After Lingle's death, it was found that the reporter, who earned $65 a week, actually had an income of more than $65,000 per year. He drove a new car, owned an expensive summer home, bet heavily at the races and maintained suites at one of the city's most expensive hotels. Leo Brothers, a St. Louis gunman, was convicted of Lingle's murder and sentenced to prison for 14 years but served just 10.

Capone began losing some of his men as well. Fred "Killer" Burke was one of the most deadly of Capone's gunmen and was allegedly one of the machine gunners at the St. Valentine's Day Massacre. He was a known murderer and he and his partner, James Ray, had robbed several banks in Ohio dressed as policemen --- the same m.o. used by the St. Valentine's Day killers. In December 1929, St. Joseph, Michigan policeman Charles Skelly spotted Burke fleeing the scene of a traffic

Chicago Tribune reporter Jake Lingle was shot to death in 1930 on his way to the racetrack. The reporter, who made only $65 a week, owned an expensive summer home on Lake Michigan, had a chauffeur-driven limo, wore expensive clothes and was worth more than $65,000 at the time of his death. His connections to Capone likely got him killed. A man named Leo Brothers was later prosecuted for the murder but most feel the real culprits behind it got away.

accident. Skelly curbed Burke's car and jumped on the running board. Burke shot him in the stomach three times and drove away. Skelly died three hours later.

The gunman was badly unnerved by the policeman's murder and he crashed his car into a telephone pole, where it was later found and traced to his address. In the house, they found a machine gun that was later traced to the guns used during the St. Valentine's Day massacre. Burke was captured in April 1930 but was never convicted for the massacre. He was convicted of Officer Skelly's murder instead and was sent to the Michigan State Penitentiary for life.

Michael "Mike da Pike" Heitler was another Capone hench-man, although Heitler turned on Capone after he was ignored and demoted in 1931. Angry, he wrote a letter to State's Attorney John A. Swanson and disclosed all that he knew about Capone's prostitu-tion organization. A few days later, Capone had Heitler brought to his headquarters at the Lexington Hotel and threw the unsigned let-ter in the gunman's face. He told Heitler that he knew that only "Mike da Pike" could have sent the letter but Capone never explained how he had gotten his hands on it. On April 29, 1931, Heitler's corpse was found in a burned-out house in Barrington. Investigators reported that Heitler had been burned alive.

Frank Rio was Capone's most trusted bodyguard, having saved his boss' life during the attack on the Hawthorne Hotel. It was also Rio who learned about the plot being hatched by Guinta, Scalise and Anselmi, and informed Capone about it. According to the story, Rio heard Scalise bragging about being a "big shot" and he managed to convince Capone of a possible plot after a fake argument in which Capone slapped Rio in front of Scalise and Anselmi. Scalise later approached Rio and told him that the Aiello brothers had a $50,000 reward for anyone who would kill Capone. They wanted to know if Rio would join them in collecting the reward. Three days later, the bodies of the would-be assassins were found dumped in a car. Rio's loyalty apparently faded when Capone went on trial for tax evasion

"Mike da Pike" Heitler was burned to death in a house in Barrington for betraying Capone.

in 1931. One report has it that he smarted off to Capone as the mobster was being fitted for some new suits, remarking that he wouldn't need them in prison. Capone was enraged and Rio vanished shortly after.

By 1930, the United States government had gotten involved in Chicago's dilemma over how to get rid of Al Capone. Washington dispatched a group of treasury agents (Eliot Ness and his "Untouchables") to harass Capone and try to find a way to bring down his operation. In the end though, it would not be murder or illegal liquor that would get Capone --- it would be income tax evasion. He was arrested on October 6, 1931 and indict-ed. On October 17, he was convicted on five counts, three of evading taxes from 1925 to 1928 and two of fail-ing to file tax returns in 1928 and 1929. He was sentenced to spend 11 years in a federal prison and was first sent to Leavenworth; then, in 1934 was transferred to the brutal, "escape proof" prison known as Alcatraz.

The prison was a place of total punishment and few privileges. One of the most terrible methods of pun-ishment was the "hole", a dungeon where prisoners were housed naked on stone floors with no blankets or toi-lets and only bread and water for nourishment. The slightest infraction could earn a beating. Capone spent three stretches in the "hole", twice for speaking and once for trying to bribe a guard. He returned from the "hole" just a little worse for wear each time. Eventually, it would break him.

Many of the prisoners at Alcatraz went insane from the harsh conditions and Capone was probably one of them. The beatings, attempts on his life and the prison routine took a terrible toll on Capone's mind. After he was nearly stabbed to death in the yard, he was excused from outdoor exercise and usually stayed inside and played a banjo that was given to him by his wife. He later joined the four-man prison band. After five years though, Capone's mind snapped. He would often refuse to leave his cell and would sometimes crouch down in the corner and talk to himself. Another inmate recalled that, on some days, Capone would simply make and re-make his bunk all day long. He spent the last portion of his stay in the prison hospital ward, being treated for an advanced case of syphilis. He left Alcatraz in 1939.

Jake "Greasy Thumb" Guzik, who helped run the south side mob in Capone's absence, was asked by a reporter if Capone would take control again when he was released. "Al," said Guzik, "is nuttier than a fruit-cake."

The February 1929 massacre may have been the beginning of the end for Al Capone but it began the decline of Bugs Moran as well. With the remnants of his gang, he attempted to take back control of the Gold Coast, but Capone's men were too powerful. His lot did improve somewhat after Capone went to prison in 1931 but it didn't last long. Although Moran did drift into oblivion after Capone was sent to prison, he did have one small piece of revenge for the events on Clark Street. According to reports, Bugs and two others caught up to "Machine Gun" Jack McGurn in a bowling alley on February 13, 1936. McGurn was machine-gunned to death with his sleeves rolled up and a bowling ball in his hand. A small paper valentine was found on his bloody corpse.

The end of World War II reduced the once powerful gangster to petty burglaries. He first moved to down-state Illinois, St. Louis and then Ohio before a failed robbery got him arrested by the F.B.I. He was sentenced to serve 10 years in prison in 1946 and his release found him quickly re-arrested for another robbery. This time, he was sent to Leavenworth, where he died from lung cancer in February 1957.

It was a sad, and almost pathetic, ending for the gangster who was known, after St. Valentine's Day 1929, as "the man who got away."

Chicago, in its own way, memorialized the warehouse on Clark Street where the massacre took place. It became a tourist attraction and the newspapers even printed the photos of the corpses upside-down so that readers would not have to turn their papers around to identify the bodies.

In 1949, the front portion of the S-M-C Garage was turned into an antique furniture storage business by a couple that had no idea of the building's bloody past. They soon found that tourists, curiosity-seekers and crime buffs visited the place much more often than antiques customers and they eventually closed the business.

In 1967, the building was demolished. However, the bricks from the bullet-marked rear wall were purchased and saved by a Canadian businessman named George Patey. In 1972, he opened a nightclub with a Roaring 20's theme called the Banjo Palace and rebuilt the wall, for some strange reason, in the men's restroom. Three nights each week, women were allowed to peek inside at this macabre attraction.

The club continued to operate for a few years and when it closed, the owner placed the 417 bricks into storage. He then offered them for sale with a written account of the massacre but had trouble selling the entire wall in one large piece. Patey, along with a friend named Guy Whitford, who contacted me about the wall in 2002, tried to sell the single piece for some time. The original lot came with a diagram that explained how to restore the wall to its original form. The bricks were even numbered for reassembly. They remained on the market for nearly three decades, but there were no buyers. Eventually, Patey broke up the set and began selling them one brick at a time for $1,000 each. Patey passed away in December 2004 and

George Patey with the bricks from the "death wall" of the Clark Street Warehouse in 1967 (Courtesy George Patey)

had sold most of the bricks by that time. According to legend, he even sold some of the bricks more than once!

The stories say that some of the bricks were returned after he sold them. It seemed that anyone who bought one was suddenly stricken with bad luck in the form of illness, financial ruin, divorce and even death. According to the stories, the bricks themselves had somehow been infested with the powerful negative energy of the massacre! May have called this story a "journalistic embellishment" but there are many who maintain that it's the truth.

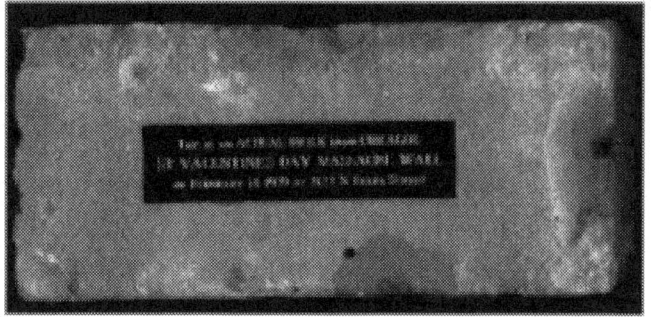

One of the bricks sold by George Patey from the St. Valentine's Day Massacre

These same people maintain that Patey's 417 bricks were not the only surviving bricks from the warehouse!

In recent years, other bricks have emerged that claim to have come from the wall and from the building itself. These were not bricks purchased from Patey; rather they were bricks smuggled out of the lot by construction workers and curiosity-seekers. It was said that from these bricks come the legends of misfortune and bad luck. Are these bricks authentic? The owners say they are, but the reader will have to judge for himself.

Whatever the legend of the bricks, and whether or not they have somehow been "haunted" by what happened, there is little doubt about the site on Clark Street itself. Even today, people walking along the street at night have reported the sounds of screams and machine guns as they pass the site. The building is long gone now, demolished in some misguided attempt by city officials to erase all vestiges of Chicago's gangster past. A portion of the block was taken over by the Chicago Housing Authority and a fenced-in lawn that belongs to a senior citizen's development now marks the area where the garage once stood. Five trees are scattered about the area and the one in the center actually marks the point where the rear wall once stood -- where Moran's men were lined up and gunned down. The apartment building, where Mrs. Landesman lived and heard the sound of Highball barking in the garage, still stands but all remnants of the S-M-C Cartage Co. have vanished.

Or have they?

According to reports, residents of the senior housing complex built on one end of the old lot have had strange encounters in the building, especially those who live on the side of the building that faces the former massacre site. A television reporter from Canada interviewed a woman who once lived in an apartment that overlooked the small park area and she often complained that, at night, she would hear strange voices, sounds and knocking on her door and her window. She complained to the management, who dismissed her claims as imagination but assigned her another apartment. A new tenant moved into the rooms and she also complained of odd happenings, including knocking sounds that would come at her door at night. When she opened the door to see who was there, she never found anyone nearby. One night, the new tenant even stated that she saw a dark figure that was wearing an old style hat. He remained in place for a few moments and then faded away. Most of the strange phenomena experienced by the new tenant also faded away and soon eerie events either stopped completely -- or she got so used to them that they no longer bothered her anymore.

Outside, along Clark Street, passersby and the curious have sometimes reported strange sounds, like weeping and moaning, and the indescribable feeling of fear as they walk past the former site of the garage. Skeptics have tried to laugh this off, saying that the sounds are nothing more than the overactive imaginations of those who know what once occurred on this site but based on the reports of those who had no idea of the history of the place, something strange was apparently occurring.

And those who were accompanied by their dogs also reported their share of weirdness too. The animals seemed to be especially bothered by this piece of lawn, sometimes barking and howling, sometimes whining in fear. Their sense of what happened here many years ago seems to be much greater than our own.

However, many (including myself) believe that what dogs are sensing here is not the human trauma experienced at the massacre site, but rather the trauma that must have been experienced by Johnny May's German Shepherd, Highball. The poor animal must have been terrified by what occurred that morning, from the deafening sounds of the tommy-guns to the bloody slaying of his beloved owner. Tied to the front bumper of the truck, Highball had nowhere to run. It should be noted again that it was not the sound of machine-gun fire that alerted Mrs. Landesman to the horror inside of the garage --- it was the howling and barking of the terrified dog.

Could the animals that now pass by this empty lot be sensing the trauma suffered by Highball so many years ago? As any ghost buff can tell you, it's the events of yesterday that create the hauntings of today and sometimes, those who live in the past can leave a little piece of themselves behind to be experienced in the present over and over again.

Even after all of these years, the violent events of the city's gangster era still reverberate over time. Men like Al Capone, whether city officials want to admit it or not, left an indelible mark on Chicago. It seems that the events of St. Valentine's Day 1929 have left one too!

LAST WALK OF CAPONE'S ENFORCER

On the evening of March 19, 1943, a lone figure left his home in Riverside and began strolling along the streets of his quiet neighborhood. It was a cool, early spring night and the man seemed to have no cares in the world as he walked along, his hands tucked into his pockets and a soft whistle on his lips. His casual manner gave no hint to the turmoil that he felt inside though. Or that he had a loaded handgun weighting down the pocket of his coat.

The man left the street and began walking along the Illinois Central Railroad tracks that ran west of Harlem Avenue and around Cermak Avenue. He carefully picked his way over the railroad ties and walked along until the shadows seemed to envelope him. Darkness was just beginning to fall and this seemed as good a time as any for one last look at the world. The man took the gun from his pocket and he raised it to his head. His hand began to tremble as he squeezed the trigger and then a deafening roar filled his ears and echoed in the stillness of the city around him.

When the first shot was fired, railroad workers who were standing just a little further along the line, doing routine maintenance, looked up to see the walking man. His hands shook as he held the pistol and a thin ribbon of smoke curled from the barrel of it. The gun had been aimed at his head but the first shot had somehow missed. One of the railroad men started to call out to the man as he saw him calmly lift the gun again. Before the words could leave the railroader's lips, though, the man pulled the trigger again and, this time, when the gun went off, the bullet did not miss. It blew apart the top of the man's head and he stumbled over the railroad ties and collapsed against the fence that ran next to the tracks. The man's blood began to seep into the grass and ground, looking black in the fading light.

Frank Nitti, once thought of as one of the most powerful men in

Chicago and an enforcer to Al Capone, lay dead on the ground, slain by his own hand.

Frank Nitti (or Nitto, which was the preferred family spelling) was a man of mystery. Intensely private and quiet, he is only scarcely remembered today as being part of the legendary Capone gang. If not for the television series based on the exploits of Eliot Ness and his "Untouchables", it's possible that he would only be known to the most dedicated gangster buffs and researchers and not to the general public at all. Nitti was a small man but one with incredible will. He maintained discipline in the ranks and acted as Capone's enforcer and troubleshooter. He was also one of the only gangsters in the organization who never used an assumed name, which got him into trouble when investigators discovered a check that he had endorsed. This put him into prison for 18 months in the early 1930's, an experience that had a lasting effect on him.

Nitti was born in 1888 and started out in crime as a barber who also fenced stolen goods. His methods of peddling stolen whiskey put him in touch with Capone and Johnny Torrio at the start of Prohibition and he was a high-ranking member of Capone's organization by the middle 1920's.

After Capone went to prison, the newspapers looked for a new leader for the mob and Nitti was hailed as that man. It's possible that he may have even believed this himself but insiders knew that the remaining men in Capone's gang would not take orders from Nitti. While an efficient organizer under Capone, it had been his job to make sure that Capone's orders had been carried out, not to give them himself. Other mobsters, including Lucky Luciano and Meyer Lansky, when establishing a national crime network in the 1930's, dealt with Paul "The Waiter" Ricca as the leader of the Chicago mob and not with Nitti.

However, Ricca and the others did use Nitti's high profile with the press to keep the heat off the real inner workings of the mob. He became a valuable man to take the heat. Chicago mayor Anton Cermak even dispatched his own police "hit men" to try and take out Nitti so that he could replace him with other gangsters that kept him on the payroll. On December 19, 1932, two police officers invaded Nitti's headquarters, allegedly under orders from new mayor Cermak, who was determined to assist Ted Newberry (who had taken over the O'Banion and Moran mob) redistribute the territories of the Capone gang. Shots were fired and Nitti was badly wounded. He lingered near death for a time but recovered only to end up standing trial for the shooting of one of the cops during the gun battle. However, the jury was convinced that the officer had actually shot himself in the finger in order to look like a hero and the trial ended in a hung jury. Nitti walked away a free man and the officer lost his job.

This was not the end of story though. Rumors lingered for a time that Al Capone himself reached out from the walls of the penitentiary to get revenge on Cermak a few months later.

Anton Cermak was a dynamic, albeit somewhat typical, Chicago mayor of days gone by. He was the city's first foreign-born mayor, emigrating from Prague to work in the Illinois coal mines. He started a real estate company and for years spoke out against banning alcohol. He also organized the "wet vote", which would help to defeat Prohibition and it won him the appreciation of Franklin Delano Roosevelt, whom Cermak was accompanying when the mayor was assassinated.

On February 15, 1933, a fanatic named Guiseppe Zangara shot Cermak at Bayfront Park in Miami, Florida. He was there with President Roosevelt, who had asked Cermak to join him on the reviewing stand. Shots rang out and Cermak was hit while standing next to the president. He was rushed to the hospital but died a short time later. As he was taken from the reviewing stand, Cermak supposedly said to the president "I am glad that

Anton J. Cermak --- rumors still linger that his assassination was arranged by Al Capone.

it was me instead of you" and they became the most famous words that Cermak ever uttered -- or they would have been if he had really said them. A reporter who was there that day, Ed Gilbreth, stated that the phrase was created by the *Chicago Herald-American* to make a good headline and sell some papers. Cermak never actually said anything before he died.

Although some words uttered by another reporter who was standing nearby might have provided more of a clue in the shooting than officials would admit. Just as the shots rang out, a reporter who was nearby allegedly joked to Cermak: "Just like Chicago, eh Mayor?"

And perhaps the event was more like Chicago than anyone knew, for the death of Cermak achieved subtle vengeance for the near murder of Frank Nitti. Ted Newberry had been killed just a few weeks earlier. He had been shot to death along Lake Shore Drive and his body had been dumped in a ditch in Porter County, Indiana. Some said that Al Capone had arranged the shooting of Cermak.

Nitti served prison time for an income tax charge, related to the check that was discovered bearing his name, but stayed out of the newspapers until November 1940, when he was indicted for influencing the Chicago Bartenders and Beverage Dispensers Union of the AFL. Nitti was accused of putting mob members into positions of power in the union and then forcing the sale of beer from mob-owned breweries. The trial rested on the testimony of one man, George McLane, the president of the union. He allegedly was forced to follow Nitti's orders but the pressure got to him and he went to the authorities and explained what the mob was doing. McLane was all set to testify until two mob soldiers showed up at his door and told him that if he talked in court, his wife would be mailed to him in small pieces. When the day came, McLane pleaded for his rights under the Fifth Amendment and the case was dropped.

The heat was on Nitti again in 1943 during what came to be called the "Hollywood Extortion case". Nitti's name was used as a terror tactic during a shakedown of movie moguls in Hollywood. Nitti and several other mobsters managed to get control of the International Alliance of Theatrical Stage Employees and began forcing the movie studios to pay huge sums of money to keep the union at work. A prolonged strike could have ruined any of them, a fact that the studios were well aware of. At that time, the movie studios controlled most of the theaters that exhibited their films and if the union went on strike, there would be no place to show the films that had cost thousands to make. In a short time, Warner Brothers, MGM, RKO, Fox and a number of smaller studios forked over the money and the racket turned out to be a big money maker for the mob. Things began to fall apart when a Chicago reporter, a nationally syndicated writer named Westbrook Pegler, started

asking questions after spotting Willie Bioff and George Browne at a big Hollywood party. He recognized Bioff as a former Chicago pimp and couldn't figure out what he was doing at such a party. He started asking around and discovered that Bioff had moved up the criminal chain and he also began to hear about the extortion racket. He took his information to the federal authorities and the whole enterprise began to unravel.

The investigators were soon able to get evidence against the Chicago gangsters and faced with hard prison

Nitti's body was discovered along the railroad tracks. He had been killed by an apparent self-inflicted gunshot wound.

108

time, Bioff and Browne decided to talk. As a result, indictments were brought against Nitti, Paul Ricca and a number of others. A meeting was called at Nitti's home in Riverside and Ricca decided that now was the perfect time to take advantage of Nitti's perceived top position in the mob. He ordered Nitti to plead guilty in the extortion case and to take the rap for everyone. He would be taken care of when he got out --- as long as he kept his mouth shut while he was inside.

But there was no "inside" for Nitti. He refused to go back to prison. His earlier jail time had so traumatized the gangster that he now had a terrible fear of small, confined spaces. He urged Ricca to come up with another plan or to allow some of the others to share the responsibility with him. Ricca was enraged and demanded that Nitti be a "stand up guy". When Nitti still refused, Ricca told him that "he was asking for it." Nitti took these words to mean his death sentence but he simply couldn't face another stretch in prison. He made a last-ditch effort to try and bribe the prosecutor in the case, M.F. Correa, but his attempt was coldly rebuffed.

So, on March 19, the day after the meeting, Frank Nitti placed a gun in his pocket and went for one last walk through his neighborhood. When he made it as far as the Illinois Central Railroad tracks, his journey came to an end -- or did it?

After his death, Nitti was laid to rest in Mount Carmel Cemetery, not far from where the body of Al Capone also lies. His simple stone is marked with his family name of "Nitto" and bears a direct and ominous inscription: "There is no life except by death". But it has never been believed that Nitti rests here in peace.

For many years, it has been a local legend in the North Riverside and Forest Park areas that the ghost of Frank Nitti still walks along the railroad tracks where he committed suicide in 1943. There are many who claim to have not only sensed the last anguished moments of Nitti but also state that they have seen the eerie figure of a man here as well. The figure often appears along the railroad tracks at Cermak Avenue and begins walking west (eventually towards Mount Carmel Cemetery), plainly visible under the harsh lights of a shopping center that is located nearby. The tracks, which are seldom used these days, can be found next to a toy store, a restaurant and a large shopping mall. The area that marks Nitti's suicide is almost remote and isolated from the activity of the retail area, despite the fact that it's so close by.

I spoke to a man who became curious about this area after reading about it in a Chicago crime book and he decided to go out there one night and have a look for himself. Although a believer in ghosts, this had nothing to do with his survey of the railroad tracks. He was more interested in Nitti himself and never expected to see anything out of the ordinary during his outing. The man parked his car at the nearby toy store and walked over to the tracks. As he stood there and looked down them, he explained to me that he could imagine what Nitti must have felt like during his last journey. Rumor had it that, in addition to facing prison time, Nitti was also suffering from stomach cancer and this may have also led to his decision to end his life.

As the man walked slowly along the tracks, he froze for a moment at what he saw ahead of him. Keeping pace with his own walk, he claimed to see a dark silhouette about 15 yards ahead of him. He saw the figure step high to avoid the rails and it even stumbled once or twice as it moved along. He was unable to describe the figure for me and only said that "it gave the impression of a man who was wearing a thigh-length coat". The witness followed the figure for a short distance and then he described to me that it seemed to "spin" around and fall towards the ground. Moments later, it was gone.

The startled observer blinked once or twice, unable to believe what he had seen. Could he have just witnessed a re-enactment of the last moments of Frank Nitti? "I never went there expecting to see anything," he wrote to me a few months after the encounter took place. "And while I believed that some places and people might be haunted, I never thought that I would ever see anything like that. I am sure that it must have been Frank Nitti's ghost that I saw that night. It's up to you whether you want to believe me or not but I am sure about what I saw. I think he's [Nitti] haunting those railroad tracks."

ROADHOUSE GHOSTS
The Haunting of Rico D's

Located near the southern end of Archer Avenue, a highway that offers more hauntings per capita than any other roadway in the Chicago area, is an imposing yellow brick building that sits nestled against a wooded hillside. It's an inviting place with an air about it that makes you want to stop and have a drink and some great Italian food. At least this is what you see on the surface! There is much more to Rico D's Ristoraunte than first meets the eye.

It is a place with a dark Chicago history that is filled with gangland violence, blood and ghosts!

The old Oh Henry's Roadhouse as it looks today.
(Courtesy Rico D's Ristoraunte)

According to local legend, the building that has come to be known as Rico D's was once a speakeasy and criminal operation that was run by infamous gangster, Al Capone. During the 1920's, Capone's criminal empire stretched all over Chicago and into the suburbs of northern Illinois. It is believed that Capone set up shop in this building along Archer Avenue, and may have even had a hand in some of the unique additions to the structure.

That's the local legend anyway and while it turns out to not be entirely accurate, this is a place with unique connections to Capone's south side Outfit and a location where history has left its presence behind in the form of bullet holes, bloodstains and an ominous secret that is hidden in the restaurant's basement.

The building began its existence in Willow Springs as the Oh Henry Roadhouse some time around 1936, long after Al Capone was sentenced to prison. The original owner of the tavern was John Verderbar, who was also the owner of the Oh Henry Ballroom (which became the Willowbrook Ballroom in 1959), which is still located directly across Archer Avenue.

It was constructed on a piece of land that was known locally as Spatis Grove, which served as a

The Oh Henry Dance Park was started by John Verderbar in 1921. After a fire, the ballroom was constructed and by the 1930's was considered the "swingingest" place on the southwest side.

110

picnic area along Archer Avenue. This grove was an extension of the Civilian Conservation Corp Camp Chicago - Lemont, which was built on the hill above Archer Avenue in 1933. It lasted for three years and, when the land was sold off, John Verderbar purchased the corner where the picnic area was located.

The roadhouse served late night liquor to not only patrons from the Ballroom but, locals and travelers on the roadway, as well. It was also said to provide other forms of entertainment. During the years of Prohibition, the south side mob, which was run by Al Capone, provided liquor to the Ballroom. They also provided gambling and prostitution to many of their customers and, for many years, the Oh Henry Ballroom was well known for its small casino. Gambling was also available at the roadhouse. In addition, there were also prostitutes available on the third floor of the building, which was used as a brothel.

The roadhouse went through several ownership changes, always as a tavern, over the years and then became a restaurant called Cavallone's West in 2003 after nearly two years of major renovations. It was during this time that stories of the ghosts from the past began to surface.

The owner at the time, Rob Degen, had found the place, which was then a biker bar, in 2001 and began renovating the building and updating it to bring it up to code. As an accomplished chef, who had worked for some of the major hotels in Chicago, Degen wanted to expand on his experiences with his other pizzeria, Cavallone's, and open an additional site in the southwest suburbs. When he stumbled across the old brick building, he knew that he had found the perfect place.

During the renovations, Degen noted that some unusual design features were built into the place. One thing that seemed to stand out was the fact that the first floor of the building had five doors leading to the outside, which would offer a quicker than normal exit from any part of the place. In addition, all of the windows on the first floor contained frosted glass with a unique cross hatch pattern that let in light but did not allow anyone to see inside. There were also two staircases leading to the second floor, one in the front and one in the rear. This is not that unusual for a restaurant and bar with an upstairs apartment but there were also two sets of stairs leading down to the cellar. One of them led down from the kitchen area but the other, which is now cut off at the ceiling in the basement, once descended from a small closet in the women's restroom. It had apparently been hidden for years.

There were also obvious openings in the cellar walls that had long been boarded over. Some openings led out toward the street but another led out toward the wooded hill that bordered the backside of the restaurant. There were no windows, or window wells, in the foundation but the ground above the boarded over openings had begun to sink, indicating that perhaps the depressions marked either underground tunnels or chambers. Degen wondered what purpose they could have served.

In the center of the cellar was an unremarkable boiler room. It seemed to offer nothing out of the ordinary except for one of the openings that led out underground and an odd rectangular patch in the concrete floor that looked to have been refilled or patched. Degen would later find out what secrets were hidden under this strange part of the floor.

Next to the boiler room was a walled-in area that seemed to serve no purpose. Once the clutter was removed from the back wall of the area though, a small opening was found under some shelves. If a person crouched down and followed the narrow passage back about eight feet to another opening, he entered a cramped room that was just large enough for a few people to stand. No one knows what the hidden room was built to conceal but based on the amount of melted candle wax that Degen and his workers found on a ledge in the wall, someone frequently used the secret hiding place in the past.

On the main floor, Degen also went about removing some doorbell-like buzzers that were found above each table on the first floor. It was not until he began looking into the building's past that he discovered what these weird buzzers had been used for.

The second floor of the building was like a time capsule of the 1920's. All of the original light fixtures, woodwork and wall coverings were still in place --- as well as some original design features, which were also on the unusual side. At the top of the stairwell was a large foyer area, much like a sitting room, which opened into a large living room with a fireplace and a smaller bedroom. A long hallway then extended the length of the building. It had five small rooms opening off of it and a bathroom that was about halfway down the corridor.

(Left) A photo of the old White Mausoelum in Fairmont Hills Cemetery that I took in 1999.
(Below) The ruins of the mausoleum in 2004. With no warning, the structure was simply destroyed, shortly after Cavallone's West closed down in 2003. Rumors claimed that it was because of the tunnels that connected to the restaurant.

At the end of it was a large kitchen with huge, stainless steel sinks. This would be another area that would reveal its sinister purpose once Degen began delving into the history of the building.

Degen's first exposure to the past of the place came through off-handed remarks and stories that were passed on to him by local residents of Willow Springs. One thing that he heard over and over again was about the connections to Capone. When Degen pressed about the stories, he began to hear tales of gambling, prostitution and murder. When he combined these stories with his own investigations into the history of the building, some of the unusual features of the place started to make sense. He began to wonder if the former owners of the Oh Henry Ballroom were the only ones involved in the construction of the roadhouse.

The solid brick construction, unusual for a roadhouse of the period, and the use of frosted glass for the lower windows, gave the residents privacy from any outside intrusions. The five exits also offered many ways to vacate the place in a hurry if the authorities raided it. If the tunnels beneath it were used as they were in similar establishments of the time, they were escape routes. They also created underground hiding places for guns, contraband and, perhaps, even a dead body or two.

According to legend, one of the tunnels led down the street to the Fairmont Hills Cemetery and, most specifically, to the White Mausoleum that is located there. The mausoleum was the source of many rumors and stories over the years, as it was believed to be haunted. Visitors to the cemetery often claimed that the sound of music could be heard coming from inside of the locked tomb. But could the ghostly music have actually been sounds that were coming through the escape tunnel from down the street? The tomb has since been inexplicably destroyed and its foundation filled with concrete. While the legend of the tunnel will never be proved either way one has to wonder if perhaps the story was started for a reason.

According to the lore, the first floor of the building was used as

A roulette table that previous owner Rob Degen discovered hidden in the basement of the former roadhouse. (Roy Nerad)

a tavern and a waiting room for the brothel that was in operation upstairs. The buzzers that were located above the tables were used to summon customers when it was their turn to sample the wares that bordello had to offer.

The hidden back stairway to the cellar provided quick access to the basement and to the secret room, where gangsters could hide out in case of law enforcement intrusion. It was in this room that Degen discovered a relic of the building from its early years. While cleaning out the cellar, he found an elaborate, Italian-made gaming table, complete with a hidden roulette wheel. The original chess pieces that came with the table, and were used to disguise the table's real use, were also recovered.

Legend also had it that the basement was sometimes used as a temporary holding place for the bodies of men who were murdered for crossing the Outfit. Allegedly, they were taken out a side door into the woods that surrounded the building --- or, in one case, never left the basement at all.

According to an elderly man who came into Cavallone's one night, one such body just might be hidden in the basement. The man recounted how he had been dancing at the Oh Henry Ballroom across the street one night when he was approached by a man who was looking for a couple of strong young men who would dig a hole for him at his nearby building. He also wanted young men who were smart enough not to ask any questions about it. A couple of volunteers were founded up and taken across the street to

The strange spot in the basement that is believed to hide a dark secret about the old roadhouse
(Roy Nerad)

the roadhouse. The man took them into the cellar and showed them where he needed a hole dug, explained the size of it and put them to work. The man told Degen that he and the others had done their work, had collected their pay and left. A couple of years later, he was looking at the newspaper and saw the man who had recruited him to dig the hole. He was a mobster who was on trial for murder.

His blood had gone cold, he said, when he wondered just what had been in that hole.

On the floor of what became the boiler room for Cavallone's was the outline of a concrete patch, roughly three feet by seven feet in size. Degen was curious as to the veracity of the story that the old man told him, so he enlisted the aid of a land surveyor who brought a device into the cellar to see if anything was buried under the patch. The instrument indicated that there was indeed something buried there, a number of feet under the floor. Despite the chilling evidence though, Degen decided to leave whatever was there undisturbed. The oral history of the place seemed to be filled with patrons and employees who never left the building alive and he had to wonder just what else might be found if the restaurant was taken apart by the law. The legends stated that the woods around the place had been used to dump bodies and the tunnels and hidden rooms were used as hiding places for corpses that could not be disposed of right away. Were these merely urban legends? Perhaps, or perhaps not....

In addition to the myriad of apocryphal stories, the place does have its share of documented murders and tragic deaths. At least two of the prostitutes who worked upstairs are known to have fallen to their deaths from second floor windows. They may have been forcibly pushed out, or could have been trying to escape from someone when they could not reach their "safe room", which was the upstairs bathroom.

The building also bore evidence of a knifing that occurred on the upstairs landing, just outside of the door to the brothel's former reception room. Faded bloodstains remained on the wall and discolored the plaster where a murder occurred many years ago.

There is also some evidence that the upstairs kitchen was outfitted to perform illegal abortions for any of the prostitutes who might have become pregnant during these times when contraception, if used at all, was notoriously unreliable. If this evidence is real, there is no way to know how much pain and trauma was enacted in this room in years past --- and what startling manifestations may have been left behind.

And there is also the story of a tragic love affair that led to a double murder in the building, which has left a lasting mark on the property. The story tells of a beautiful, and often in demand, prostitute here who happened to be a girlfriend of one of Capone's mobsters. She didn't love the man though for she was also having a secret affair with the bartender. When her gangster boyfriend found out, he vowed to kill them both. One night, as the bartender went down to the cellar storage area, the boyfriend, who was waiting for him under the stairs, tripped him by reaching through the open steps and grabbing his ankles. Needless to say, the bartender took a tumble and fell to his death. After killing the bartender, the gangster then made his way upstairs to his girlfriend's room. He kicked open her door and beat her to death, leaving her savaged corpse behind in the room.

Not surprisingly, the bloody events of the past have apparently left an impression behind on the building, but no one was really prepared when those events "came to life" and began to make themselves known to the new occupants. Rob Degen, absorbed as he was with his renovation work, never considered that the place might be haunted until several events occurred that convinced him that he was sharing the restaurant with some of its former tenants.

Once the restaurant opened, odd things began to happen. Employees began to experience very odd occurrences when they were alone in some parts of the building. One waitress reported that she was using a bucket of water while mopping the floor and it suddenly started to move on its own! The bucket rolled from one end of the place to the other and clanked against the wall. Another time, a wadded up ball of paper came flying out of the kitchen and hit her in the head when she passed by. Another waitress saw it happen and then two of them went into the kitchen to see who was fooling around. However, the restaurant was closed and there was no one else in the building.

The cellar seemed to be one of the most active areas in the place. There were believed to be several ghosts that haunted this section of the restaurant, including one that caused items to move about on their own and who grabbed at people's pant legs as they walked by. Another waitress told a story of being in the basement one day as she was refilling condiment containers with her back to the liquor storage room. Suddenly, she felt a cold presence behind her and she became so frightened that she was unable to force herself to turn around and look. As she stood there, the sensation became colder and more menacing --- then it passed right through her! The presence became so overpowering that she was knocked to her knees and had to grab a nearby table to keep from falling down. The sensation passed but it was enough to convince her that she never wanted to work in the basement alone again.

The main floor of the restaurant also had its share of unexplained activity, especially around the women's restroom. This was the same room that offered access, via the secret door and staircase, to the cellar. The wooden door to the room had the scars of two small caliber bullets that were fired into it in an attempt to kill a gangster who was fleeing out a window. It was in this bathroom that a female customer complained that whenever she entered the room, the toilet would flush on its own. She also said that she felt very uncomfortable in the room --- and never alone -

Faded bloodstains remain on the wall of this staircase, telling a story in itself of the violent days of the roadhouse.

-- despite the fact that the room was empty and the door was locked.

The front staircase that leads to the second floor was the site of an incident that was so bizarre, and so frightening, that several staff members actually quit because of it. A bartender was heading up the stairs to the second floor apartment to discuss something with Rob Degen when he heard footsteps coming up the stairs behind him. Thinking that another staff member had followed him up, he turned around and was confronted by the large figure of a man wearing a black hat and a long black overcoat. The man was trudging up the stairs, just a few steps behind the bartender. As he watched though, the mysterious man in black vanished before his eyes! The staff member immediately tendered his resignation and never returned to the restaurant.

Some believe that this man may have been the apparition of the gangster boyfriend who brutally murdered the prostitute upstairs many years ago. If it was this man, does his girlfriend haunt the place as well? Perhaps --- for it was in the upstairs bathroom that a new renter in the apartment encountered a ghostly woman. As the tenant emerged from the shower and wiped the steam from the mirror in front of her, she saw the bloody and battered face of a woman behind her, staring at her in the glass. She screamed and turned to see who was there, only to find that she was in the bathroom alone. The woman fled the apartment, later arranging for someone to gather her things and bring them to her. She was never going to set foot in the building again!

Unfortunately, Cavallone's West did not stay around for long, and by the end of 2003, it was closed for business. The former roadhouse remained empty for nearly two years and then, in 2005, it re-opened as its present incarnation, Rico D's. The new establishment is also an Italian restaurant, although with a higher quality fare, and has remodeled again. There have been a number of changes with the property but one thing remains the same ---- it is still a place where a visitor can literally walk back in time and have the chance to come face to face with the building's occupants from days gone by.

The owner of Rico D's, Don Kress, is a genial man and one quick to admit that he was not a believer in ghosts and the supernatural before he opened the business. That opinion changed, he assured me, soon after he opened the place. Since that time, he has had a number of encounters with the ghostly past occupants, including with one of the former prostitutes, who told him that she was pleased with the changes that he was making with the building. He has also encountered the ghost of a little boy, has told of numerous sounds and smells that cannot be explained and has recounted weird tales of windowpanes that somehow plunge three stories to the ground and do not break.

Rico D's remains an odd place and one that is still filled with secrets. Strange things happen here and continue to be discovered, linking the present day to the crime-filled days of the past. Stop in sometime if you get a chance and if nothing else, you'll go away with a good meal. If you are really lucky though, you might find yourself leaving after your own encounter with the unknown.

Rico D's is a place where the past literally comes alive ---- as a historic haunting from yesterday.

4. DILLINGER: LEGEND & LORE

History & Mystery Surrounding the Life & Death of John Dillinger

When all of the known facts about Dillinger are dragged into publicity, it will be found that no desperado in America can approach this bad man's record. There are enough angles on his tribe and its history to wrote a great big book.
Captain Matt Leach, Indiana State Police, 1933

I only wish that I had a mother to worry over me, but she died when I was three. I guess this is why I was such a bad boy. No mother to look after me.
John Dillinger

We do not expect any trouble with our newest prisoner. Of course, I warned the first thing that we would stand for no monkey business.
Indiana Sheriff Lillian Holley --- from whose jail Dillinger escaped with a wooden pistol

I don't smoke much and I drink very little. I guess my only bad habit is robbing banks.
John Dillinger

Shortly after the end of Prohibition, America was plunged into the Great Depression. This era of national poverty gave birth to another breed of criminal: the bank robber. John Dillinger, "Baby Face" Nelson, "Machine Gun" Kelly, Ma Barker, and Bonnie and Clyde were just a few of the bank robbers who made headlines and history during the Depression and they became the last figures of the outlaw tradition, which had been a part of American legend since the end of the Civil War.

Bank robberies had been taking place almost since the time that the first Americans entrusted an establishment with their hard-earned money, but the robbers of the 1930s were different. They were no longer the outlaws of the "Wild West". These bank robbers had the new and novel advantage of motorized transportation. Never before in American crime had outlaws possessed the means to escape so easily from law enforcement officials. Now, they went on the rampage through various states using motorcars.

Most of them got their start thanks to law enforcement's preoccupation with bootleggers, allowing the better-equipped bank robbers to work with little harassment. Many of the jobs made huge headlines because of the amount of loot that was stolen but, as author William Helmer has noted, identification methods were so primitive that newspapers could only report that a group of "unknown strangers" had pulled off a "daring daylight robbery" and had disappeared without a trace. Because of this, some criminals were able to plunder the Midwest with an anonymity that leaves them unknown today, while lesser outlaws became Depression-era celebrities after Al Capone went to prison and the new federal laws unleashed the F.B.I.

This new era gave birth to what are considered legendary criminals today. Many of them not only gained a place on the F.B.I.'s new "Most Wanted" list, but they became folk heroes too. There were few Americans who didn't feel a twinge of jealousy as they saw these freewheeling bank robbers get their revenge on the banks, the wealthy and on the government itself. Stories were claiming that some of these outlaws actually stole from the rich and then gave back part of the money to those who really needed it. And in the 1930's, there were a lot of folks who needed it.

Many of the "folk hero" personas were created by the newspapers which, thanks to the competitiveness of the market in cities like Chicago, were always looking for a headline. The crime magazines and pulps of the day, many of which abandoned fiction for "fact" at a time when gangsters were making daily news, also created them. In some cases, this resulted in making the criminals more recognizable to the general public than to the police. This only made them all the more popular to the people of the era.

John Dillinger

Without a doubt, these folk heroes, bank robbers and stone-cold killers left their mark on the American landscape and many of them died just as they lived --- fast and hard. It's not surprising that many of their stories still linger with us today -- or that some of their ghosts do, too!

PUBLIC ENEMY NUMBER 1

On the evening of July 22, 1934 a dapper-looking man wearing a straw hat and a pin-striped suit stepped out of the Biograph Theater, where he and two girlfriends had gone to see a film called *Manhattan Melodrama* starring Clark Gable. No sooner had they reached the sidewalk than a man appeared and identified himself as Melvin Purvis of the F.B.I. He ordered the man in the straw hat to surrender but the dapper-looking gentleman decided to run instead. Several shots rang out and the fleeing man fell dead to the pavement, his left eye shredded by shots fired by the other agents who lay in wait.

And so ended the life of John Herbert Dillinger, the most prolific bank robber in modern American history and the general public's favorite Public Enemy No. 1 -- or did it?

One of the most famous theaters in the history of Chicago is the Biograph, located on North Lincoln Avenue. It was here that John Dillinger supposedly met his end. The theater has gained a reputation for being haunted, but the story of the ghost seen here actually revolves around the alleyway that is located just a few

117

doors down. But the theater, and the surrounding businesses, has banked on the criminal's name for many years. On the day after the fatal shots were fired, the bar next door placed a sign in the window that read, "Dillinger had his last drink here". For years, theater patrons could examine a window in the box office that described the set-up of Dillinger by the Feds. They could sit in the same seat where Dillinger sat in 1934 and, after the film; they could pass through "Dillinger's Alley". It is here, in what was for many years a dark and dingy passageway, that many people claimed to encounter a ghost ---- a ghost created by the lingering remnants of the life that was cut short on the dirty stones of the alleyway.

But what really happened here? What occurred in the last moments of the life of the man believed to be John Dillinger? To answer the strange and perplexing questions surrounding his possible death, we have to first look at his bloody and violent life.

On the evening that he was killed, Dillinger left the theater in the company of Anna Sage (the famed "Lady in Red") and with a girlfriend, Polly Hamilton. He had recently been hiding out in her North Halsted Street apartment. For months though, Melvin Purvis, the head of the Chicago branch of the F.B.I, had pursued him diligently all over the Midwest. Purvis had lived and breathed Dillinger (and would, after the robber's death, commit suicide) but had narrowly missed him several times at a State and Austin Cafe, at Dillinger's north woods hideout in Sault St. Marie, and at Wisconsin's Little Bohemia, where F.B.I. agents recklessly killed a civilian and injured two others. It was finally at the Biograph where Purvis caught up with Dillinger and put an end to his career.

John Herbert Dillinger was born in Indianapolis in 1903. He came from humble rural beginnings and work dominated his early life. His mother died in 1907 and Dillinger was raised by his older sister, Audrey, and his father, John Wilson Dillinger, who ran a grocery store and maintained several houses that he rented out. Dillinger's father was strict but never had much trouble with his son, who was a quiet child with good grades and who was well liked by friends and teachers. When he was quite young, he proved to be an excellent athlete, especially excelling at baseball.

Dillinger's first brush with the authorities took place when he was in sixth grade. He was charged with stealing coal from the Pennsylvania Railroad yards and selling it to neighbors. He was released into the custody of his father and soon after, the elder

John Dillinger as a young boy. Within a few years, he would have his first brush with the law (U.S. National Archives)

Dillinger packed up his family and moved them to a modest farm outside of Mooresville, Indiana, about 20 miles south of Indianapolis. He reportedly wanted to get his son away from the corrupting influences of the city. It didn't seem to do much good, though. Dillinger refused to help his father on the farm and to return to school. Instead, he took a job back in Indianapolis as an apprentice machinist, driving back and forth to the farm each day on his prized motorbike.

Eventually, just to please his father, he decided to go back to school but dropped out during his first semester at Mooresville High School. However, Dillinger did join the Martinsville baseball team and became known as a remarkable second basemen. He also started dating a young woman named Frances Thornton, his Uncle Everett's stepdaughter. The two of them fell in love and Dillinger asked his uncle for her hand in marriage but he refused, telling John that they were both too young. In truth, he actually wanted the girl to marry a wealthy boy from Greencastle, Indiana.

Angry, Dillinger returned home and on the night of July 21, 1923 he impulsively stole a car from the parking lot of the Friends Church in Mooresville. Hours later, he abandoned it in Indianapolis but fearing arrest, he enlisted in the U.S. Navy. Unknown to Dillinger, the owner of the car, Oliver P. Macy, knew John and refused to press charges. Regardless, Dillinger enlisted under his real name but gave a false St. Louis address when he filled out his paperwork. After basic training at Great Lakes, he was assigned to the *U.S.S. Utah*. He went AWOL several times and was thrown in the brig and when the ship was anchored off Boston in December, Dillinger jumped ship permanently. The Navy listed him as a deserter and posted a reward for his capture but Dillinger made it back to Indiana.

At home, Dillinger met and began courting Beryl Ethel Hovius, 16, and the two of them married in the spring of 1924. They moved in with Beryl's parents but Dillinger spent more time playing baseball and shooting pool than paying attention to his wife and the marriage didn't amount to much.

On the night of September 6, 1924, Dillinger finally stepped completely over the line of the law. Cooking up a plan with a former convict and umpire for the Martinsville baseball team, Edgar Singleton, the two men decided to rob Frank Morgan, a Mooresville grocer who carried his week's receipts home on Saturday nights. They jumped him and hit him over the head, but the 65 year-old man refused to go down. One of the would-be robbers brandished a gun but Morgan knocked it away and a shot was accidentally fired. Dillinger and Singleton, both frightened, took off running.

Morgan's head required 11 stitches but he told Deputy Sheriff John Hayworth that he couldn't identify his attackers. Hayworth looked into the case and came to believe that Dillinger was involved. He took Morgan out to the Dillinger farm and the grocer confronted John. He recalled how the boy had purchased candy from his store and insisted that he wouldn't have hurt him. It couldn't be John, Morgan told the lawman. Hayworth took Dillinger in for questioning anyway and, when his father came to collect him from the county jail, the tearful young man confessed to the hold-up attempt. The prosecutor promised the elder Dillinger that his son would receive a lenient sentence if he threw himself on the mercy of the court. The farmer convinced his son to do so and Dillinger, just 20 years-old, entered a guilty plea. To his surprise, he was fined $100 and sentenced to concurrent sentences of up to 10-20 years in prison. His accomplice, through his attorney, received a change of venue and a much lighter sentence that resulted in his parole in just two years.

Betrayed and angry, Dillinger was sent to the Indiana State Reformatory with no plans to cause trouble, he said, "except to escape." Over the course of the next several years, he tried to break out over and over again, always getting caught. One night, he was found to be missing from his cell and was discovered under a pile of clothing in the laundry. Another time, he made a saw and cut his way out of his cell. He was captured in the corridor. He tried again in 1925 and was captured once more.

About this time, Dillinger met a man who would influence his future career, a bank robber named Harry Pierpont. The soft-spoken ladies' man had been captured after single-handedly robbing a Kokomo, Indiana bank. He and Dillinger became close friends and were soon joined by another young bank robber, Homer Van Meter. The two earned Dillinger's respect by being the toughest criminals in the prison. They spent more time in solitary confinement than in their cells. Eventually, they were both shipped off to the state prison in Michigan City by officials who gave up trying to control them.

The original "Dillinger Gang" met in prison. (Top Row, Left to Right) Prison mugshots of John Dillinger, Harry Pierpont, Russell Lee Clark.

(Bottom Row, Left to Right) John Hamilton & Charles Makley

In 1929, the same year his wife filed for divorce, Dillinger came up before the parole board. He was turned down but, luckily for him, Indiana governor Harry Leslie was sitting in on the hearing. Dillinger had once been playing baseball in the prison yard and had overheard the governor remark that he ought to be playing professional ball. When he knew that he would not be getting out of jail, he asked the board to send him to the state prison in Michigan City because it had a real baseball team. Governor Leslie convinced the board that a move was in order, because it might help Dillinger to find work when he did finally get out. Dillinger was sent to the state prison on July 15 and happily hooked up with Pierpont and Van Meter again.

His friends introduced him to another bank robber, John Hamilton, who began instructing Dillinger on the art of robbing banks. He also met Charles "Fat Charley" Makley and Russell Lee Clark. Both men had been arrested on robbery charges and Clark, especially, was known as a dangerous and brutal man. He had attempted escape several times and had even tried to kill guards on several occasions. He and the others would figure into Indiana's largest prison break (masterminded by Dillinger) four years later and would form a gang of bank robbers who would make headlines around the country.

Since Dillinger would be out of prison before any of the others, he was cultivated as the contact man on the outside. It would be his job to hit a number of small town banks, targeted by Pierpont and Hamilton, and use the funds to finance the prison break. During his last four years inside, Dillinger was a model prisoner, which was all part of the plan. On top of his good behavior, Governor Paul McNutt received a petition from Dillinger's Mooresville neighbors, asking that he be released to help his father on the farm. Even the judge who had sentenced him, perhaps regretting his harsh decision, signed the petition. Dillinger was set free on May 22, 1933 and he immediately rushed to Mooresville, where his stepmother was seriously ill. She died just an hour before Dillinger arrived.

The following Sunday, Dillinger attended church with his father and sat weeping as he listened to the pastor give a pointed sermon on the return of the "prodigal son". When the service ended, he told the minister how much good it had done him -- and, two weeks, later began robbing small banks and isolated stores.

Dillinger recruited a small-time hoodlum named William Shaw and using the list that his friends devised, robbed a bank at New Carlisle, Indiana, netting $10,600. Unfortunately, Dillinger would find that many of Pierpont's targets had gone under during the Depression and he was often met with empty buildings instead of banks that were ripe for the picking. Shaw was arrested a short time later (luckily, he only knew Dillinger as "Dan") and Dillinger recruited Harry Copeland, another bank robber and former convict from Michigan City.

They struck the Commercial Bank at Daleville, Indiana on July 17. Dillinger strolled into the bank, wearing what became his trademark straw boater, and walked up to cashier Margaret Good, who was the only person in the bank at the time. He pulled out a gun and reportedly said: "This is a stick-up, honey."

He then jumped over the railing and entered the vault. Harry Copeland left the getaway car parked in front of the building and also came inside, lining customers up at gunpoint as they entered the bank. Dillinger packed up $3,500 and ordered everyone inside of the vault. Then, he and Copeland casually walked out and drove away. Margaret opened the door from the inside and a short time later, she told police that Dillinger was "the most courteous of bank robbers." His identity as a polite, but daring, bank robber was verified by the other witnesses and now police throughout Indiana were looking for him.

But Dillinger was already in Ohio seeing his new girlfriend, Mary Longnaker, who lived in Dayton. Dillinger took Mary to the World's Fair in Chicago and he chuckled as he photographed a policeman and then asked the cop to snap a picture of himself and Mary.

On August 4, Dillinger and Copeland robbed the National Bank of Montpelier, Indiana. He was thrilled to find $10,100 in the small bank's vault. His next haul would not go so well. Dillinger, Copeland, Sam Goldstine and two other, unknown men hit the Citizens National Bank in Bluffton. Dillinger and Copeland entered the bank and announced that it was a robbery. After going through the teller drawers though, Dillinger demanded to know where the rest of the money was. Bookkeeper Oliver Locher pointed to the bank's vault at about the same time that the alarm went off. One of the lookouts came in and called out that the police

Dillinger and Mary Longnaker at the Chicago World's Fair. The snapshot was taken by an unsuspecting police officer.

were coming but Dillinger ignored him and began filling a sack with small bills. When Dillinger and Copeland didn't come out, the men outside began firing wild shots into the air to discourage the curious. Finally, after collecting only $2,100, they joined the men out on the street. They piled into a sedan and quickly sped away.

Dillinger was discouraged by the small take, still needing much more to finance the Michigan City prison break. He and Copeland decided to try a larger city bank the next time, settling on the Massachusetts Avenue State Bank in downtown Indianapolis. Using Hilton Crouch, a professional racetrack driver as a wheel-man, Dillinger and Copeland entered the bank and immediately began cleaning out the teller drawers. Dillinger stole everything in sight and netted $24,800.

With a major share of this, Dillinger moved to Chicago and bribed the foreman of a thread-making company to secretly place several guns inside of a thread barrel being sent to the shirt shop at the Michigan City prison. It was sealed and marked with a red "X" on the top. Dillinger had earlier attempted to free Pierpont and the others by tossing handguns wrapped in newspaper over the prison walls under the cover of darkness. The guns were supposed to be found, by Pierpont, in the athletic field but were found by other inmates instead and they turned them over to the guards.

While the barrel was being shipped, Dillinger went to Dayton to see Mary Longnaker. Unknown to him, the police had received a tip from the Pinkerton Detective Agency that Dillinger was seeing a Dayton woman and the authorities had tracked Mary down because she was the sister of one of Dillinger's prison friends. Mary's rooming house was staked out and her landlady phoned in a tip to the police when Dillinger arrived. Two detectives, carrying shotguns, broke into Mary's apartment and Dillinger was arrested on the spot.

As things would turn out, Dillinger was in the Lima, Ohio jail four days later, waiting to be indicted for the Bluffton bank robbery, when his friends escaped from the Michigan City prison using the guns that Dillinger had smuggled in to them. Ten men went out the front gates of the penitentiary, driving cars that were stolen from in front of the administration building. The escapees included Harry Pierpont, Charles Makley, Russell Clark, John Hamilton, Edward Shouse, Joseph Fox, Joseph Burns, Jim "Oklahoma Jack" Clark, Mary Longnaker's brother, James Jenkins, and Walter Dietrich.

Pierpont, Makley, Clark, Hamilton, Shouse and Jenkins took one auto and headed for Leipsic, Ohio, where Pierpont's family lived. Somewhere near Bean Blossom, Indiana, a bizarre accident took place. Rounding a corner, the door of the car flew open and Jenkins fell out. Since the police were everywhere, searching for the convicts, Jenkins was left to fend for himself. He walked up the road about a mile and ran into three farmers who were part of a posse searching for the escapees. When Jenkins pulled out a pistol, the farmers blasted him with their shotguns and he was killed.

Before Dillinger had been captured, he left money with Mary Kinder, a contact for the gang. Pierpont used this money to equip his men with new clothes, a new automobile and an arsenal of weapons. He also decided to put together some traveling money by robbing the First National Bank in St. Mary's, Ohio, the hometown of Charles Makley. Inside of the bank, Makley ran into an old friend, W.O. Smith, who was the bank president. He chatted with his friend while Pierpont cleaned out the till. The gang left the bank with $14,000 without ever firing a shot.

On October 12, Pierpont, Makley, Clark, Hamilton and Shouse went looking for Dillinger. They arrived at the jail around 6:20 p.m. that evening, armed with pistols, and walked into the jail office. Sheriff Jess Sarber, his wife, Lucy, and Deputy Wilbur Sharp were reading newspapers after a dinner of pork chops and mashed potatoes. Sarber looked up when the men came in and asked if he could help them. Pierpont replied that they were officials from Michigan City and needed to speak with prisoner Dillinger. Sarber agreed but asked for the credentials. Pierpont pulled out a pistol instead and pointed it at the sheriff's face. "Here's our credentials", he said.

Sarber gasped and put out a hand to wave away the gun. Pierpont fired two shots and hit the sheriff, once in the stomach and once in the hip. He fell to the floor, leaving his wife and deputy to gape in astonishment. Pierpont demanded the keys as Sarber tried to raise himself up. Makley smacked him on the head and he fell back to the floor.

"I'll get the keys," Lucy Sarber screamed. "Don't hurt him anymore!"

At the sound of the first shots, Dillinger knew that his gang had arrived. Pierpont, grinning, unlocked his door and the two men hurried out. As they reached the office, Dillinger knelt down to inspect the damage that had been done to Sheriff Sarber, who had been kind to Dillinger while he had been housed in the man's jail. Regretfully, he left the man behind on the floor. Sarber called out to him and asked why he had to do this, but the bank robber was gone. According to the story, he then looked over to his wife and said "Mother, I believe I'm going to have to leave you." Sheriff Sarber died moments later.

"The Terror Gang", as the press dubbed them, headed for Indianapolis, where Mary Kinder, who had taken up with Pierpont, and Evelyn "Billie" Frechette, who Dillinger had met in Chicago, waited for them. The gang made plans for a string of new bank robberies but first they had to arm themselves. They raided the police arsenal in Peru, Indiana and walked away with machine guns, bulletproof vests, shotguns, handguns, rifles and bags filled with ammunition. To pull off such a daring robbery, Dillinger and Pierpont devised a new approach. Posing as tourists, they came up to a policeman and asked him what preparations the local lawmen had taken in the event that the Dillinger gang came to town. The officer and a desk sergeant proudly gave the men a tour of the arsenal, only to be restrained as the two men began carrying armloads of weapons out to their car.

Chicago became the base of operations for the gang, which Dillinger and Pierpont shared the leadership of. Pierpont was the more experienced of the two, but he encouraged his friend to take the role of leader. Most of the decisions made by the group were made by these two or by Hamilton, who was the "old pro" among them. The idea that there was an actual "Dillinger gang" was a product of the newspapers of the day. It was really more of a criminal community that included several robbers that Dillinger worked with when possible and when the law and luck allowed. The group lived in twos and threes in several apartments on Chicago's north side. None of them drank hard liquor, sticking only to an occasional beer, so as not to draw attention to themselves.

On October 23, 1933, the gang traveled to the Central National Bank in Greencastle, Indiana. Clark stayed behind the wheel of a Studebaker touring car while Pierpont, Dillinger and Makley went inside. Hamilton stayed near the door to watch for suspicious activity on the street. Dillinger and Pierpont had cased the bank several days in advance, pretending to be newsmen, and knew where all of the important areas of the bank were. Dillinger quickly jumped over the counter and began walking through the teller cages, scooping money into a sack while his confederates kept guns pointed at the employees. Makley watched everything with a stopwatch in his hand. At the five-minute mark, Makley called time and Dillinger abruptly stopped filling the sack. He turned, hopped back over the counter and started to walk out. He looked over and saw an old farmer standing at one of the teller's windows. In front of him on the counter was a small stack of bills. Dillinger asked him if the money belonged to him or to the bank.

"It's mine," the farmer nervously replied.

"Keep it," Dillinger said. "We only want the bank's."

The men walked out without firing a shot and drove away. They traveled along back roads, following pre-

Despite having other girlfriends, Dillinger called Evelyn "Billie" Frechette the "love of his life" and often dreamed of escaping to South America with her so they could live in peace.

marked maps, and drove leisurely out of the county. They avoided every single roadblock put up by the state and local police. In the car, Dillinger opened the bag from the bank and found $75,346 -- their biggest haul yet.

About a month later, Dillinger was almost captured in Chicago. He was suffering from barber's itch, a skin disorder, and went to see Dr. Charles Eye for treatment. Edward Shouse, who had been kicked out of the gang for drinking and for making advances toward some of the other men's girlfriends, informed the Chicago police that Dr. Eye was treating Dillinger. They were not quick enough to catch Dillinger though.

On the night of November 15, Dillinger, along with girlfriend Billie Frechette, was on his way to Dr. Eye's office but became suspicious when he saw several cars next to the doctor's office on Irving Park Road. The cops had been dumb enough to park them facing the wrong direction. Dillinger quickly shifted gears and raced off down the street with the police cars in pursuit. Flooring the accelerator of his favorite car, a Hudson Terraplane, Dillinger lost all but one of the police vehicles, which was driven by Sergeant John Artery. With his partner, Art Keller, leaning out the window with a shotgun, Artery pulled up alongside Dillinger's car. They were traveling at a speed of almost 80 miles an hour along Irving Park Road. Keller opened fire on Dillinger but the bank robber did a high-speed turn onto a narrow side street, causing Artery to speed on past. By the time that they had turned around, Dillinger had vanished.

The gang moved on to Milwaukee and made plans for another robbery. On November 20, Harry Pierpont walked into the American Bank and Trust Company just before closing time. Staff members watched in bewilderment as Pierpont unrolled a huge Red Cross poster in the lobby and pasted it over the middle of the bank's large picture window. Moments later, Makley, Dillinger and Hamilton walked in. Makley pulled out a gun and pointed it at head teller Harold Graham -- who proceeded to ask Makley to step to the next window!

Oblivious, Graham didn't realize what was going on until Makley told him to put up his hands; they were robbing the bank. Graham moved suddenly and Makley shot him through the elbow. When he fell, he triggered the alarm button, which did not ring in the bank but in the Racine police department headquarters. Two local policemen were slowly dispatched to the bank but they were in no hurry to get there. The alarm had sounded several times previously when careless tellers had accidentally set it off. When they finally did arrive, Pierpont disarmed them, but one of them was slow to hand over his gun. Makley shot him, attracting the attention of a large crowd outside.

Once the gang had gotten the money together, they needed to get out of the building. By this time though, more people had gathered, including more police officers. Dillinger and the others pushed several women out the front door, using them as shields from the shots that were being fired from across the street. The police, when they saw what was happening, fired high to avoid hitting the women and the other bystanders. The gang left the human shields standing in place and ducked back into the bank.

While the cops were distracted, thinking that the bank robbers were still crouched behind the shields, Dillinger and the others ducked out the back entrance, where Clark was waiting for them with the car. They piled into it, dragging along the bank president and the bookkeeper as hostages. They drove frantically along back roads for about 20 minutes and then let out the hostages before continuing on. The haul from the bank was $27,789.

After that, the gang decided to avoid the harsh Chicago weather and winter in Florida. Packing up, they headed for Daytona Beach, where they rented cottages along the ocean. They played cards, fished, and listened to the radio before becoming bored and heading out to Arizona. Between the time the gang left Dayton Beach and arrived in Tucson, the First National Bank of East Chicago, Indiana was robbed by two unknown men and a policeman named Patrick O'Malley was machine-gunned to death. Dillinger and Hamilton were accused of the crime and Dillinger was said to have been the policeman's killer -- but he always denied it. Billie Frechette, who was interviewed by legendary crime writer Jay Robert Nash before her death in 1969, always maintained that Dillinger never left the gang during this period to commit the robbery that was blamed on him.

Regardless of that, Tucson turned out to be a disaster. Clark and Makley were arrested after a fire broke out in their hotel. They paid a fireman hundreds of dollars to rescue their suitcases but he became suspicious when he noticed one of the suitcases was extremely heavy. He opened it to find a machine gun and several pis-

124

tols. Pierpont, Dillinger, Billie and Mary Kinder were soon identified, arrested, and then sent back east. Dillinger was extradited to Indiana to stand trial for the East Chicago robbery (the one robbery that he probably didn't commit), while Clark, Makley and Pierpont were sent to Ohio to stand trial for the killing of Sheriff Sarber.

Dillinger was jailed in Crown Point, Indiana, which was said to be "escape proof". Armed citizens patrolled the grounds of the jail; ready and waiting in case any of Dillinger's friends decided to break him out. But all of them were also in jail, so he decided to break out on his own. A month after he was locked up, he escaped using a fake gun that he had carved and blackened with shoe polish. The "gun", which looks extremely crude in old photographs, looked real enough to Officer Sam Cahoon and Deputy Sheriff Ernest Blunk when Dillinger waved it at them on the morning of March 3, 1934.

In minutes, he rounded up a dozen guards and made his way down a flight of stairs with a couple of the officers along as hostages. He drove along back roads until he made it into rural Illinois. He let the officers out along the side of the

One of the chummy photos with Dillinger that managed to ruin prosecutor Robert Estill's career.

road and gave them $4 for food and carfare. Dillinger apologized and told them that he would have given them more if he had it.

Dillinger waved as he drove off -- never realizing that, by driving across the state line with the stolen car, he had made his biggest mistake ever. Now, the F.B.I. had joined the hunt.

Dillinger avoided Chicago and moved on to St. Paul, Minnesota. Billie Frechette, who had been freed with Mary Kinder after the Tucson arrests, joined him there. Dillinger started putting together a new gang, including

The wooden revolver that Dillinger allegedly blackened with shoe polish and used to escape from the Crown Point, Indiana jail.

125

(Left) Lester Gillis -- better known as Baby Face Nelson --- and (Right) Homer Van Meter, who was Dillinger's right-hand man. The two of them fought constantly, each jockeying for position in the gang.

Michigan City parolee Homer Van Meter. He also recruited Eddie Green, Tommy Carroll and John Hamilton, who had gone to Chicago instead of Tucson after leaving Daytona Beach. One more man was needed so Dillinger recruited a former Capone gunman named Lester Gillis, who became better known as "Baby Face Nelson", an unhinged killer who had robbed banks all over the Midwest. He was known to be quick on the trigger and killed without mercy and without conscience.

Homer Van Meter had become Dillinger's right-hand man, and he and Nelson argued constantly. Dillinger often had to step between them to keep them from killing one another. Dillinger needed to raise a large amount of cash and needed Nelson to do so, whether he liked the man or not. By this time, Dillinger was planning a permanent escape from the law and he also wanted to help Pierpont, Clark and Makley, who were still in jail awaiting trial.

On March 6, the gang struck the Security National Bank in Sioux Falls, South Dakota and the robbery went off without incident until Nelson spotted an off-duty policeman getting out of a car. He jumped onto a desk and fired several shots though the bank window, wounding the officer. According to accounts, he began to laugh manically and to shout that he "got one of them!"

Meanwhile, Tommy Carroll was outside, standing in the middle of the street with a machine gun. Without firing a shot, he had lined up and disarmed the city's entire police force, including the chief. Thousands of spectators watched the scene, chuckling and laughing and unbelievably, were under the impression that a Hollywood movie was being shot in their town -- and that the bank robbery was just part of the action! Just the day before, a movie producer had been in town spreading the word that he would be filming in Sioux Falls the following day. The "movie producer" had been Homer Van Meter.

The bank robbers piled into a Packard with a sack that was stuffed with $49,000. They raced out of town and after traveling for several miles, Dillinger ordered the driver to stop the car. He and Hamilton got out and sprinkled roofing nails all over the road, which would slow down any pursuit.

Then, Eddie Green was sent out to search for the next target. He found it at the First National Bank in Mason City, Iowa when he learned that the vault contained more than $240,000. The gang arrived at the bank on March 13. Nelson stayed with the getaway car but the gang inside ran into one problem after another. When the bank president, Willis Bagley, saw Van Meter walk in carrying a machine gun, he thought that a "crazy man was on the loose". He ran into his office and bolted the door. Van Meter, knowing that Bagley had the keys to the vault, fired a number of shots through the door, but gave up trying to break in and helped his associates clear out the teller drawers.

Moments later, a guard in a special steel cage above the lobby fired a tear gas shell at Eddie Green. It hit him in the back and almost knocked him down. As he swung around, he fired off his machine gun and several bullets clipped the guard.

At the same time, a female customer, who was missing a shoe, ran out of the bank and down the alley outside, where she ran directly into a short man wearing a cap. She begged him to call for help -- the bank was being robbed. The short man was Baby Face Nelson and he sent her back into the bank.

Meanwhile, John Hamilton was having his own problems. Cashier Harry Fisher had barricaded himself in the locked room with the vault. Since Hamilton could not open the door, he ordered Fisher to start passing money to him through a slot in the door. Fisher began handing him stacks of one-dollar bills.

Dillinger was outside, guarding prisoners on the street. An elderly policeman named John Shipley spotted him from his third-floor office and took a shot at him. He winged Dillinger on the arm and the bank robber whirled around and fired a burst from his machine gun. The bullets bounced off the front of the building and Shipley ducked away unhurt. With that, Dillinger decided that it was time to leave. He sent Van Meter inside to get the others.

Hamilton was still having problems with Cashier Fisher. He could see the stacks of bills on the shelves inside of the vault where Fisher stood. He demanded that the man open the door but Fisher told him that he couldn't do it without the key. Hamilton continued to threaten him with his gun and Fisher continued to load stacks of one-dollar bills into the bandit's bag. He was enraged when Van Meter came inside and told him that they were leaving as he had only about $20,000 in his bag and there was over $200,000 still sitting in the vault! Gritting his teeth in frustration, he turned and ran out of the bank, leaving the crafty Fisher to count his blessings. Hamilton later groaned that he should have shot the man -- just out of spite.

At the same moment that Hamilton ran out of the bank to join the others, Officer Shipley returned to the overhead window and started shooting again. He wounded Hamilton in the shoulder but the bank robber managed to get to where Dillinger and the others were waiting. They had forced 20 hostages to stand on the running boards, fenders and hood of the getaway car, serving as human shields. The bank robbers piled inside and drove slowly away, the car groaning and creaking under all of the extra weight. The police were unable to shoot or try and stop them with all of the hostages on the vehicle so they were forced to follow at a distance. A few miles out of town, Baby Face Nelson climbed out of the car and fired his machine gun in their direction, finally forcing the police to turn back. After following back roads at slow speeds for more than two hours, Dillinger dropped off the reluctant passengers and headed for St. Paul. What should have been a prosperous raid had netted the outlaws a disappointing $52,000.

When the gang reached St. Paul, Dillinger and Hamilton sought medical treatment for their wounds and then decided to lay low for a while. They had no idea that trouble was brewing in town. Local F.B.I. agents had received information that a man named "Carl Hellman" was living in a rooming house somewhere in St. Paul with a woman that was believed to be Billie Frechette. "Hellman" fit the description the agents had of Dillinger and they began working to find the rooming house.

All of this was unknown to Dillinger as he tried to recuperate from his wound. He wrote letters to his sister in Indiana and bemoaned the fact that he was unable to visit. He was worried about his father and could do nothing more than send funds to the family through intermediaries. He also worried about his friends in Ohio -- Pierpont, Clark and Makley -- who were standing trial for the murder of Jess Sarber. Each was tried and Pierpont and Makley both received the death penalty, while Clark was sentenced to life in prison. Dillinger knew there was no way that he could get to them, and this sent him into a depression.

The guards around the Lima, Ohio jail were made up of regular officers, armed citizens, local and state policemen and even Ohio National Guardsmen who had been called up for duty. Heavy machine guns had been mounted on rooftops around the jail and gigantic searchlights were used to illuminate all approaches to the building. The authorities insisted that Dillinger was coming to free his friends with an army of outlaws.

However, Dillinger was far from Ohio and in enough trouble of his own. On the night of March 31, 1934, F.B.I. agents learned that "Carl Hellman" was living at the Lincoln Court Apartments in St. Paul. They arrived

There is no denying that John Dillinger remains an iconic figure in Chicago, and Midwestern, history. For Americans of the time, he was the last great anti-hero and he literally became a legend in his own time. In addition to the stories --- and possibility ---- of his survival after being gunned down by the feds, there have been a number of other myths and legends created around this charismatic bank robber. One has shades of the truth, while the other is merely the product of faulty information and wishful thinking.

So, based on the fact that the man shot down outside of the Biograph really was John Dillinger, here are some of the myths surrounding his death....

One story holds that Dillinger's brain was "stolen" during his autopsy. This story does contain elements of the truth. On the night that Dillinger was shot down, a young medical intern and a resident were forced by the police to conduct the postmortem. The Cook County Medical Examiner was not present at the time but he did sign the report for posterity. The intern and resident did remove Dillinger's brain and they sent it to the pathology department. It seemed like the right thing to do at the time, as some in the medical community still expected to find obvious abnormalities in the brains of criminals. That was the last time that the doctors ever saw it.

A short time later, an undertaker reported that the brain was missing. As no one seemed to have it, the word "stolen" began finding its way into newspaper stories, leading the Dillinger family to threaten a lawsuit against Cook County. It was not so much that the Dillingers needed the brain but that it might end up as a carnival sideshow attraction. They had already angrily turned down offers for Dillinger's entire body. They also knew that during the chaos at the morgue on the night the body was brought there, that three different parties had managed to bribe their way past the police and the crowds to make unauthorized death masks of Dillinger's face. The fact that the brain now seemed to be missing had the family fearing the worst.

Already criticized for the death mask fiascoes, and the general treatment of the corpse, Cook County authorities scrambled to try and solve the mystery of the missing brain but never managed to communicate with each other well enough to keep their stories straight. Coroner Frank Walsh first tried to deny that the brain was missing at all, only to then learn that the Medical Examiner had already acknowledged the removal of "an ounce or two" of the gray matter for scientific testing. Unaware of the Medical Examiner's announcement, a coroner's toxicologist contradicted both of them by reporting that he had half of the brain in a jar of preservative and that he thought the other half had been placed inside of the corpse's stomach, to avoid re-opening the skull. Before that information reached the Medical Examiner, he suddenly remembered having sent the toxicologist two-thirds of the brain and keeping one-third of it in his lab.

GET·DILLINGER!
$15,000 *Reward*
▬ A PROCLAMATION ▬

WHEREAS, that John Dillinger stands charged officially with numerous felonies including murder in several states and his banditry and depredation stamp him as an outlaw, a fugitive from justice and a serious menace to life and property;

NOW, THEREFORE, We, Paul McNutt, Governor of Indiana; George White, Governor of Ohio; F. B. Olson, Governor of Minnesota; William A. Comstock, Governor of Michigan; and Henry Horner, Governor of Illinois, do hereby proclaim and offer a reward of Five Thousand Dollars ($5,000.00) to be paid to the person or persons who apprehend and deliver the said John Dillinger into the custody of any Sheriff of any of the above mentioned states or his duly authorized agent.

THIS IS IN ADDITION TO THE $10,000.00 OFFERED BY THE FEDERAL GOVERNMENT FOR THE ARREST OF JOHN DILLINGER.

HERE IS HIS FINGERPRINT CLASSIFICATION and DESCRIPTION ── FILE THIS FOR IDENTIFICATION PURPOSES.

John Dillinger — age 30 yrs.; wt. 160; ht. 5'8"; build, medium; hair, medium chestnut; eyes, grey; complexion, medium; occupation, machinist. F.P.C. O.S.C. No. 339 FBI

FRONT VIEW

SIDE VIEW

Be on the lookout for this desperado. He is heavily armed and usually is protected with bullet-proof vest. Take no unnecessary chances in getting this man. He is thoroughly prepared to shoot his way out of any situation.

GET HIM
DEAD
OR ALIVE

Notify any Sheriff or Chief of Police of Indiana, Ohio, Minnesota, Michigan, Illinois.

by THIS BUREAU

ILLINOIS STATE BUREAU OF CRIMINAL IDENTIFICATION

On August 3, a wry reporter for the *Chicago Daily News* added up the fractions located in all of the different departments and then complimented the coroner's office on finding more of Dillinger's brain than he had to start with!

After they were convinced that the brain had not been used for devious purposes, the Dillingers dropped their lawsuit. And then, with what must have been to the great relief of Cook County officials, Coroner Walsh announced that whatever portions of the brain had been removed had been destroyed during the tests. None of the tests, he stated, revealed any abnormalities.

Unfortunately, this does not end the story. Years later, someone connected to Northwestern University's Medical School was supposed to have discovered Dillinger's brain, mostly intact, hidden in a laboratory that was remodeled during World War II. One of the professors supposedly kept it for a time as a souvenir, then gave it to a physician friend in another state, who eventually sold it to a Chicago optometrist named ---- or so the story has it --- Dr. Brayne. Truth or legend?

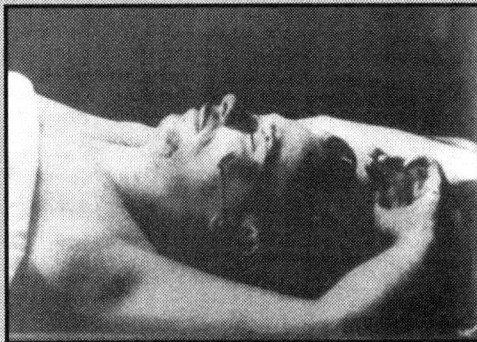

The body at the morgue --- but was it really Dillinger?

This leaves only the story of Dillinger's most private body part --- his allegedly massive penis. The fact that Dillinger was able to easily charm women with his roguish smile, rugged good looks and swaggering self confidence has never been questioned, but how this translated into his having a penis of gigantic proportions will always be a mystery.

Since none of his friends, and certainly none of the many women that he romanced, ever mentioned that his penis was anything other than average-sized, it can only be assumed that this legend was created after a photograph appeared on the front page of the *Chicago Daily News*. The photo, taken while Dillinger's body was on display at the morgue, appears to give his sheet-covered body a very impressive erection, an effect that was actually caused by the position of the dead man's arm. Most other papers that published the photograph had a re-toucher flatten the sheet but enough people saw the original photo that a rumor soon started about the massive size of Dillinger's organ.

Before long, the story took on mythic proportions and soon it was considered general knowledge that the size of the penis had qualified it for display at the Smithsonian Institution, or even at the National Medical Museum, which was located on the Institution's grounds for many years. The story became so widespread that, for decades, both organizations had to print form letters that politely denied that they possessed, much less displayed, any part of Dillinger's anatomy ---- especially his penis.

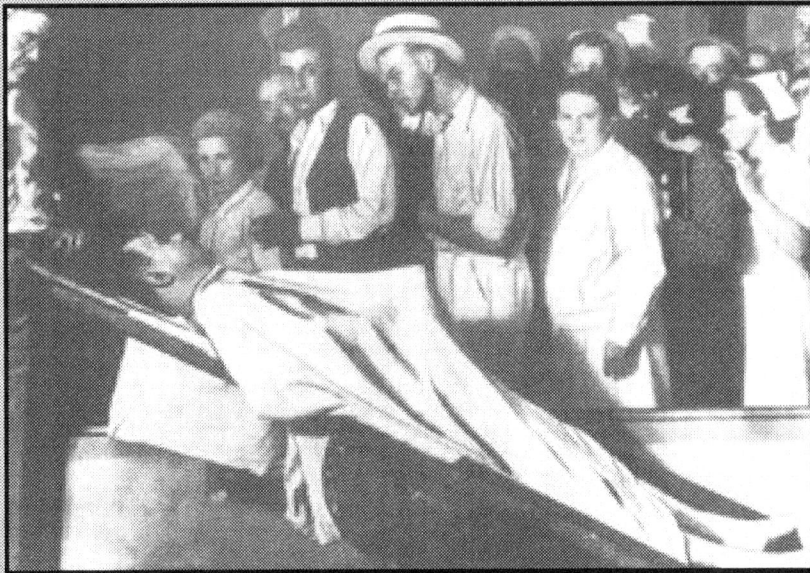

The famous newspaper photo that was taken at the Cook County Morgue. The position of the arm unfortunately started many rumors about the bank robber's sexual endowment.

at the door and Billie answered the knock. She explained that her husband, Hellman, was asleep and that she was not dressed. If they could wait a moment, she would get him up. She then locked the door and ran into the bedroom to tell Hellman/Dillinger that FBI agents were at the door. He got dressed and grabbed a machine gun.

Waiting on the other side of the door, the agents were surprised to see a young man come walking up the stairs to the same door. When they asked who he was, Homer Van Meter stated that he was a soap salesman. The agents asked to see his samples and Van Meter said that he had them out in the car and asked the agents to come downstairs with him. One of them followed him down and when they reached the first floor, Van Meter produced a handgun and shoved it in the agent's face. "You asked for it, so I'll give it to you!" he allegedly said.

With that, the F.B.I. agent ran for the door but Van Meter was laughing so hard that he didn't even fire at him. Instead, he ran outside and jumped on a horse-drawn delivery wagon that was parked at the curb. He donned the driver's cap and whipped the horses down the street.

Wondering what had become of his partner, the second agent also went downstairs to investigate, leaving the door to Dillinger's apartment unguarded. Dillinger, dragging Billie behind him, escaped down a flight of back stairs, firing a burst of bullets down the stairwell just in case. As the pair ran out the back, the second agent hurried after them and opened fire from the back door. Just as Dillinger was getting into the car, a bullet clipped him in the back of the leg and he stumbled into the driver's seat. He slammed the Hudson into gear and backed out of the alley at high speed.

Eddie Green tracked down a doctor to treat Dillinger's leg wound but, by this time, the gang had decided to leave St. Paul. Pat Reilly, a fringe member of the group, told Dillinger about a quiet Wisconsin resort that he knew of called Little Bohemia. It was a remote fishing camp that was not due to open until May and would make the perfect place to lay low for a time. Over the next day or two, they drove into the Wisconsin woods and camped out at the Little Bohemia lodge to plan their next robbery.

Little Bohemia seemed to be just the answer for the gang but somebody talked and soon, Melvin Purvis, the head of the F.B.I. office in Chicago, received a tip from a resort owner in Rhinelander, Wisconsin that Dillinger was at Little Bohemia. Within hours, he moved dozens of agents from Chicago and St. Paul to the forests of Wisconsin. They planned a raid on the lodge for April 22, 1934.

On the night of the assault, Purvis moved his men into position at the front of the lodge just as three men were emerging and getting into a parked car. As the engine started, Purvis shouted for the men to stop but they never heard his warning. Seconds later, the F.B.I. agents unleashed a hail of gunfire and ripped the car apart. Eugene Boiseneau, a Civilian Conservation Corps worker, was killed instantly and his two fishing buddies were both wounded.

Hearing the gunfire outside, Dillinger, Van Meter, Carroll and Hamilton ran out the back of the lodge and disappeared into the woods along the lake. Baby Face Nelson, who was staying in a nearby cabin with his wife, ran outside, fired some random shots at the

Little Bohemia Lodge in Wisconsin, where the F.B.I. missed Dillinger again

agents and also vanished into the trees.

Purvis, believing that Dillinger was still inside the lodge, ordered the assembled agents to continue firing into the building. They pounded the lodge all night long, shattering windows and splintering the walls, floors and ceilings with bullets. When morning came, and there was no resistance, they entered the building to capture the gang's girls, who had been hiding in the basement all night.

Dillinger, Hamilton and Van Meter had stolen a car and had driven to St. Paul. Nelson, after killing an F.B.I. agent while making his escape from another nearby resort, had also stolen a car and headed for Chicago. And Tommy Carroll had stolen yet another vehicle and had taken off for Michigan.

The Little Bohemia fiasco put Purvis and J. Edgar Hoover under the harsh glare of public criticism. They became even more determined to

Melvin Purvis (Left), the man that J. Edgar Hoover (Right) gave the task of getting Dillinger --- dead or alive.

get Dillinger, and Hoover placed a shoot-to-kill order on the bandit's head, along with a $10,000 reward. Another $10,000 was offered by five states in which Dillinger had planned bank robberies. The newspapers screamed Dillinger every day and, over the course of the next couple of months, a half-dozen men who resembled the bank robber were arrested or almost shot. The F.B.I. and local authorities in Chicago, all over Illinois, Wisconsin, Minnesota, and Indiana were looking everywhere for the elusive outlaw.

But Dillinger was nowhere to be found.

In May, Dillinger appeared briefly at his father's farm for Sunday chicken dinner and reportedly told the elderly Dillinger that he was soon going to be leaving on a long trip and his Dad wouldn't have to "worry about him" anymore. Then, he disappeared again.

Dillinger was next reported in Chicago. In preparation for whatever trip he was planning, or perhaps because he knew that his luck would only hold out for so long, he allegedly contacted a washed-up doctor, Wilhelm Loeser, who had done time for drug charges. Dillinger was said to have paid him $5,000 to perform some plastic surgery on his recognizable face, changing the bridge of his nose, getting rid of three moles, a scar and the cleft of his chin. The doctor agreed to the surgery and left Dillinger in the care of his assistant, Dr. Harold Bernard Cassidy, to administer the general anesthetic. An ether-soaked towel was placed over Dillinger's face and Cassidy told him to breathe deeply. Suddenly, Dillinger's face turned blue, he swallowed his tongue and died! Cassidy had just succeeded where F.B.I agents and hundreds of law enforcement officials had failed --- he had just killed John Dillinger.

Loeser immediately revived the gangster and proceeded to do the surgery. Dillinger supposedly had no idea how close he had come to death, at least according to the story and the later testimony of Loeser and Cassidy. Many believe this story to be pure fiction because, while the F.B.I. would later contend that Dillinger had received recent plastic surgery, the medical examiner would be unable to detect any signs of it on the body that was taken to the morgue --- which the F.B.I. claimed was Dillinger!

Which story was true? Did Dillinger receive plastic surgery or not? Loeser and Cassidy maintained that he did. In fact, Cassidy was paid $500 for assisting with the surgery and this payment came from Dillinger himself. Two months after the nearly botched operation, Dillinger met up with Cassidy at the corner of Kedzie and North Avenue. Slouched down in a car with Polly Hamilton, Dillinger handed over five crisp $100 bills and thanked him for his help. Cassidy quickly spent the cash, celebrating a few moments of a bleak and otherwise lonely existence. Loeser and Cassidy were later indicted on charges of harboring a fugitive, but both were given suspended sentences in exchange for their testimony. Cassidy never really recovered from his brush with Dillinger, though. With his medical career in shambles, Cassidy was later reduced to practicing on an Indian reservation during World War II. After the war ended, he returned to Chicago and moved in with his sister. Deeply depressed over his station in life, he committed suicide in July 1946.

But if Dillinger did receive plastic surgery, then why didn't the coroner see any sign of it on the body that was brought to the morgue after the shootout at the Biograph Theater? Could someone else have been mistaken for John Dillinger?

It certainly could have happened that way. On June 30, 1934, word spread that Dillinger came out of hiding again, this time in South Bend, Indiana. Once again though, this seems to be a case of Dillinger getting credit for someone else's bank robbery. The Merchant's National Bank in South Bend was robbed and the local police claimed that Dillinger was the culprit. Eyewitnesses claimed to recognize him and, not only that, they also said that his companions were Baby Face Nelson and Pretty Boy Floyd. This seems impossible, though, as Nelson was on his way to California, unnerved by the Little Bohemia Raid, Floyd was in Ohio and Dillinger was in Minnesota at the time of the robbery.

So, if Dillinger was mistakenly identified in South Bend, could the same thing have happened three weeks later in Chicago?

In early July 1934, Detective Sergeant Martin Zarkovich, of the notoriously corrupt East Chicago, Indiana police department, approached Chicago police Captain John Stege with an interesting deal. Zarkovich claimed that he could, with assistance from a long-time friend and whorehouse madame, deliver Dillinger to the Chicago police. There was only one catch, though --- Dillinger had to be killed, not taken alive. Stege kicked Zarkovich out of his office, refusing to go along with it. "I'd even give John Dillinger a chance to surrender," he told him.

Melvin Purvis had no such qualms, however. When Zarkovich presented his offer to the F.B.I. official, he quickly agreed. Zarkovich's friend, Anna Sage, would agree to set up Dillinger but the FBI had to agree to stop deportation proceedings against her. Purvis agreed, as long as she delivered Dillinger. Ultimately though, Sage would end up being shipped back to Europe as an "undesirable" in 1936.

Chicago madame Anna Sage, who became known as the "Lady in Red". Sage operated a brothel just south of Wrigley Field and often provided a hiding place for Dillinger on the north side.

When Dillinger walked into the Biograph Theater on the night of July 22, 1934, Anna Sage promised her F.B.I. contacts that she would be wearing a red dress (actually, it turned out to be bright orange) for identification purposes. She would be accompanying Dillinger, along with his newest girlfriend, Polly Hamilton Keele. At about 8:30 p.m., Dillinger appeared at the Biograph's box office in the company of two women. He was outfitted in a white summer shirt, gray trousers, white canvas shoes and his usual straw boater hat. He seemed to be completely at ease.

Sixteen F.B.I. agents, cops from East Chicago and Detective Martin Zarkovich waited outside the theater with Purvis for more than two hours, watching for the unknowing Dillinger to exit. Purvis paced nervously, chain-smoked cigarettes and, several times, even entered the darkened theater to be sure that Dillinger was still in his seat. Just before 10:30 p.m., the lights came up, the doors opened and the crowd filed out the doors into the street. Finally, Dillinger left the theater and was spotted by Melvin Purvis, who was standing in front of the Goetz Country

Club, a tavern just south of the theater. Dillinger looked Purvis right in the face as he walked past but, for some reason, despite Purvis being featured in numerous newspaper articles, he did not recognize him.

As the man walked past, Purvis struck a match to light the cigar in his mouth, a signal for the F.B.I agents and the East Chicago police assassins to move on their target. Glancing up the street though, Purvis was shocked to see that two of the East Chicago cops did not see the signal. They had been distracted by several Chicago plain-clothes detectives who, made aware of what was going on, showed up on the scene to make sure that the man who was killed was really Dillinger. According to reports, these men had some doubts about the identity of the

The Biograph Theater in the 1930s

man. Detective Zarkovich, who saw what was happening, hurried across the street to his men.

Meanwhile, two F.B.I. agents were just finishing showing their credentials to the Chicago officers when they spotted the action outside of the Biograph. They immediately started toward Dillinger.

As all of this was taking place, Dillinger allegedly sensed that something was wrong. Polly later reported that she felt his arm tense. He scanned the area around him and slipped a hand into his pocket, where a gun had been hidden. He knew the alley up ahead of him was his best chance for escape so he picked up his pace.

If Dillinger had any doubts about what was about to happen, they disappeared when he reached the mouth of the alley. Several men had fallen into step behind him and he saw two men up ahead with guns in their hands. Moving forward, he turned his head to try and scan the scene behind him and then turning the girls loose, he tried to run. As he clawed for the gun in his pocket, he collided with a woman outside of the alley and was spun part of the way around. He grabbed at the woman and then shoved her away, realizing that she was a civilian. The assassins had no such qualms and they immediately opened fire.

One slug burned through Dillinger's chest at a sideways, downward angle and punched out beneath his left rib. The second slammed into the base of his neck, ripped through his brain and exited beneath his right eye. The impact of the bullets, following his collision with the woman on the street, caused him to spin around like a top. F.B.I. agents continued to fire --- five more times ---- as Dillinger went down in the alley. None of the last bullets struck him but they did shatter a telephone pole that was a short distance behind him.

Dillinger stumbled a bit and then collapsed, falling hard onto his face and elbow. A lens in his eyeglasses shattered and the brim of his straw hat snapped in two. His Colt revolver, its safety still on, remained in his hand. Melvin Purvis reached down and took it from his hand. One of his agents leaned down and heard the man on the ground try to speak. "He mumbled some words I couldn't understand," he later said. "That was the end."

It was later recalled that a long moment of silence seemed to follow the shooting and then chaos broke out. As Dillinger's blood spilled out onto the pavement, automobiles and streetcars came to a halt on North Lincoln Avenue. Passengers, followed by nearby pedestrians, poured into the street, all pushing for a closer look. Within moments, people were shouting the name "Dillinger!"

Above the clamor, the screams of two women could be heard. The first, Etta Natalsky, was the woman that Dillinger had bumped into. A stray bullet, from the gun of either an F.B.I. agent or an East Chicago cop, had passed through the fleshy part of her thigh. The second injured woman was Theresa Paulus, who had been leaving the Biograph with a friend when a bullet from the other direction had clipped her in the hip. Neither one was seriously hurt but, once again, the F.B.I. had claimed civilian casualties while hunting Dillinger.

Two of the agents crossed the alley and ducked into a Chinese Restaurant to place a phone call and announce that Dillinger was dead. They officially informed the local cops that the Department of Justice had "made an arrest" outside of the Biograph Theater.

Back outside, several of the agents hovered over the body as others tried to keep back the surging crowd. Agent Grier Woltz, who had been stationed next to Dillinger, later reported that Dillinger was "still kicking and moving around" on the pavement. He estimated that he lived about three minutes after the shooting and he took one last shuttering breath before he died. No one did anything to try and help him.

Agent Woltz also made one odd observation about the dying man. He later stated that his eyebrows were "discolored and seemed to be painted a heavy, dark brown." No explanation has ever been provided for this.

Polly Hamilton and Anna Sage, curiously, melted into the crowd.

As the two women vanished down the alley, a police van appeared on North Lincoln Avenue. Agent Woltz assisted as Dillinger's bleeding body was lifted onto a stretcher, carried to the van and placed on the floor in back. Five F.B.I. agents climbed in with three Chicago cops and the body was taken to the Alexian Brothers Hospital at 1200 Belden Avenue. Dr. Walter Prusaig turned them away at the door. "This man is dead, " he stated after he placed a stethoscope to Dillinger's chest.

Finally, a Chicago police detective ordered the body to be taken to the Cook County Morgue on Polk Street. A mob scene greeted them when they arrived and curiosity-seekers were allowed to file past the body all night long for one last look at Dillinger.

Little did they know that the man they were looking at might not have been the famous bank robber at all.

AND THEN WHAT HAPPENED?

On July 25, 1934, the man identified as John Dillinger was buried at the Crown Hill Cemetery in Indianapolis and one year later, on July 22, a mysterious woman in black began to appear at his gravesite. This was no ghostly apparition however; she was a living woman who arrived at the cemetery in a large black sedan. She left her car, placed flowers on Dillinger's grave and then vanished back into her car. This unidentified woman made the same eerie, anniversary appearance for many years afterward. Despite surveillance, and the best efforts of the media, no one ever discovered who she was.

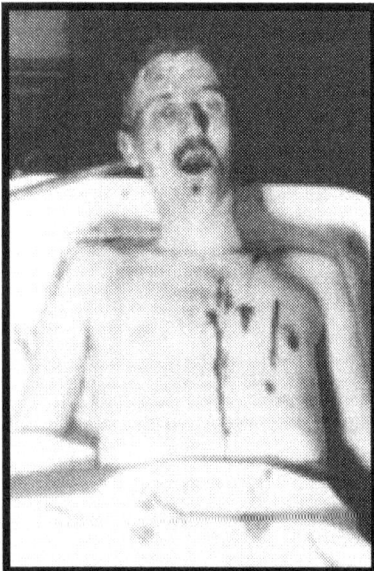

John Dillinger, Sr. declined an offer of $10,000 for the corpse of his son. This was at a time when carnival sideshows traveled the country with such macabre displays as the "death car" of Bonnie and Clyde and the electric chair that claimed the life of killer Ruth Snyder. Dillinger's pickled corpse would have been just par for the course. His father was determined that his son would not fall victim to body snatchers. He had the plot filled with concrete and scrap metal and, to combat souvenir hunters, he didn't place a stone on the grave for two years. This only slowed down the destruction and the stone that was put into place was soon chipped away to nothing. The marker that rests on the grave today is the fourth replacement.

The rest of the Dillinger gang fared little better than their friend John had.

A month after Dillinger's death, Homer Van Meter was gunned

Homer Van Meter was shot to death in a St. Paul alley about a month after Dillinger was killed in Chicago.

down in a St. Paul alley. The local cops trapped him and fired more than 50 shots into him.

A week later, desperate prisoners Charles Makley and Harry Pierpont constructed fake guns from soap, wire, jigsaw puzzle pieces, cardboard tubes and cigarette pack tin foil and tried to bluff their way out of the Ohio State Prison. Makley was shot dead during the attempt and Pierpont was wounded. Less than a month later, the electric chair finished him off.

In late October, Pretty Boy Floyd was killed by federal agents who cornered him on a farm in Ohio. Melvin Purvis led the raid, sealing his status as "America's Number One G-Man".

On November 27, the Feds tracked Baby Face Nelson, Helen Nelson and John Paul Chase to Lake Geneva, Wisconsin. Chase's girl-friend, Sally Blackman, had ratted them out. After a wild car chase, Nelson grabbed his auto-matic and maniacally charged a Hudson touring car that was providing cover for agents Sam

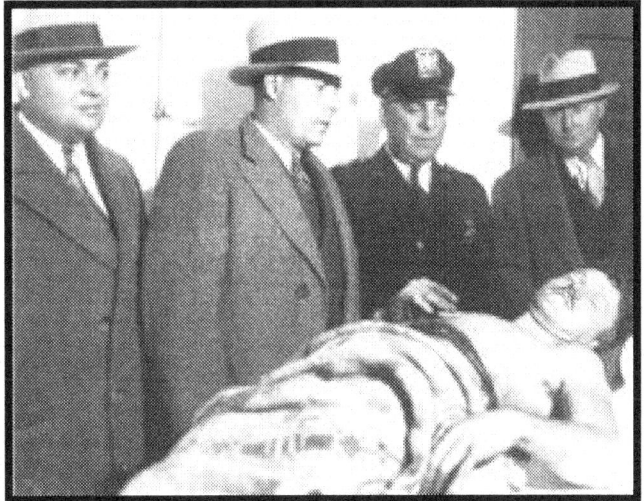

The body of Baby Face Nelson was also placed on display at the Cook County Morgue.

Cowley and Herman Hollis --- two of the men who had headed up Dillinger's assassination at the Biograph. Nelson slaughtered them both. Hit several times, he still managed to escape with Helen and Chase but his nude body, wrapped in a blanket, was found the next day in a ditch 20 miles away. Chase was later captured and sent to Leavenworth and Alcatraz, and was paroled (over the objections of J. Edgar Hoover) in 1966.

Dillinger cohort Russell Clark was imprisoned until 1968. He was let go on a "dying prisoner release" due to lung cancer. He passed away in Madison Heights, Michigan five months later at the age of 70.

The infamous "Lady in Red", Anna Sage, received $5,000 in exchange for giving up Dillinger. She was tricked out of the rest of the reward and was subsequently deported in 1936. Sympathetic newspapers com-plained that the Feds had conned her and then stabbed her in the back, but it was to no avail. A later report stated that she opened a nightclub in Timisoara, Rumania but had to close it when local gangsters tried to shake her down. She escaped to Budapest, and then went to Italy and Egypt before returning to Timisoara. She died there in 1947.

John Dillinger, Sr. eventually accepted invitations to lecture in stage shows, traveling carnivals, sideshows and even at Little Bohemia, where the industrious owner established a Terror Gang Museum. The elder Dillinger was buried beside his son in 1943.

Gang contact Mary Kinder used her notoriety to perform in "Scott Younger's Exhibit of Outlawry", a trav-eling wax museum. She lived until 1981, when she died from a combination of pulmonary edema, heart dis-ease, emphysema and acute respiratory failure.

Billie Frechette also worked on the carnival circuit for a while, talking about her famous boyfriend to rapt audiences. When interest faded, she vanished into history and died from oral cancer in Shawano, Wisconsin in January 1969.

Polly Hamilton worked at Chicago's Ambassador East Hotel as part of the room service staff and then she too disappeared. She was reported to have died at the age of 59 in February 1969.

Beryl Hovius, Dillinger's only known wife, lived the longest out of all of Dillinger's women. She died of a stroke on November 30, 1993 in Mooresville, Indiana, just a mile from the Dillinger farm. She was 87 when she died.

Melvin Purvis resigned from the F.B.I. a year after Dillinger's death so that he could write about his exploits and take advantage of the other opportunities that his fame as "the man who got Dillinger" brought to him. He published a book called *American Agent* in 1936 and began hosting a radio show for children called "Junior G-Men". He also became a newspaper publisher and radio station owner in South Carolina; was briefly engaged to Janice "Toots" Jarratt, a famous New York model; became a JAG (Judge Advocate General) colonel during World War II; and hunted Nazi war criminals for the War Crimes Office in Europe.

And Purvis, as he believed Dillinger did, died by the gun. Depressed over his failing health, he shot himself in 1960. His wife, Rosanne, claimed that he was murdered and while no evidence or motive ever came to light, it seems ironic that his life ended in mystery --- just as John Dillinger's did.

DILLINGER: DEAD OR ALIVE?

Mobs greeted the body of the man believed to be Dillinger at the Cook County Morgue, but the scene at the Biograph Theater remained chaotic. Spectators mobbed Lincoln Avenue outside of the theater. The "extra" additions of the newspapers were already on the streets. "John Dillinger died tonight as he lived, in a hail of lead and swelter of blood," one of them reported. "He died with a smile on his lips and a woman on each arm."

Tradition tells that passersby ran to the scene and dipped their handkerchiefs in the blood of the fallen man, hoping for a macabre souvenir of this terrible event. Others pried bullet fragments from a wooden light pole in the alley until the pole became so unsteady that it had to be removed by city workers. The theater would go on to become a famous, and infamous, location in the days, weeks and even years to come.

And it is at this theater where the final moments of John Dillinger have left a lasting impression. It would be many years after his death before people passing by the Biograph on North Lincoln Avenue would begin to spot a blue, hazy figure running down the alley next the theater, falling down and then vanishing. Along with the sighting of this strange apparition were reports of cold spots, icy chills, unexplainable cool breezes, and odd feelings of fear and uneasiness. Local business owners began to notice that people had stopped using the alley as a shortcut to Halsted Street.

The place certainly seemed haunted. But is the ghost of the man who has been seen here really that of John Dillinger?

Ever since the night of the shoot-out at the Biograph, eyewitness accounts, and the official autopsy itself, have given support to the theory that the dead man may not have been Dillinger. Rumors have persisted that the man killed by the F.B.I. was actually a small-time hood from Wisconsin who had been set up by Martin Zarkovich and Anna Sage to take the hit. Many historians have called this theory "revisionist nonsense", but it's hard to ignore some of the strange facts that have come to light.

To start with, even debunkers have admitted that Zarkovich was a corrupt cop and that he was tied into the mob through Sonny Sheetz, crime boss of Lake County, Indiana. Until Anna Sage had been run out of Lake County in 1927, Zarkovich had been protecting her operation for a percentage of the take and privileges with Sage or one of her girls. Many have pondered the question as to why he would have gone out of the way to set up Dillinger unless he had been asked to for some reason. And why had he insisted that the bank robber be killed instead of captured? Did he owe someone a favor so that he would make sure that "Dillinger" was murdered --- perhaps so the real bank robber could permanently escape?

Some believers in the idea that Dillinger may have escaped have pointed to the odd behavior of the man thought to be the bank robber that night at the Biograph. During the film, F.B.I. agents, including Melvin Purvis, repeatedly entered the theater and walked down the aisles of the auditorium, making sure that Dillinger was still in his seat. It seems hard to believe that Dillinger (if it was him) would not have noticed this careless surveillance. This was a man who had managed to elude capture for years, escaping from what should have been iron-clad traps, and yet he did not notice these obvious and clumsy attempts to check up on him. It's difficult to believe the movie could have been that riveting....

In addition, many also find it odd that Dillinger did not recognize Melvin Purvis when he looked directly in his face as he was leaving the Biograph. Purvis' face had been plastered on almost as many newspaper stories as Dillinger's face had. It seems likely that the clever bank robber would have familiarized himself with the men who were after him, especially Purvis, who had been praised as a "dogged pursuer" and had been well publicized as the G-man in charge of the hunt.

But, for some reason, Dillinger looked right at him, without a flicker of recognition and kept on walking. Could it have been because the man in the straw hat didn't know who Melvin Purvis was? John Dillinger undoubtedly would have, but this man never recognized the federal agent.

Most interesting, though, are the many striking errors in the autopsy report. The dead man had brown eyes while Dillinger's were blue. The corpse had a rheumatic heart condition since childhood while Dillinger's naval service records said that his heart was in perfect condition. He could not have played baseball, joined the Navy or carried out many of his athletic bank robberies with the sort of heart condition that his corpse allegedly had. It's also been said that the man who was killed was much shorter and heavier than Dillinger and had none of his distinguishing marks. The corpse also had a top right incisor ---- a tooth that Dillinger is clearly missing in photographs taken of him around this time.

Police agencies claimed that Dillinger had plastic surgery to get rid of his scars and

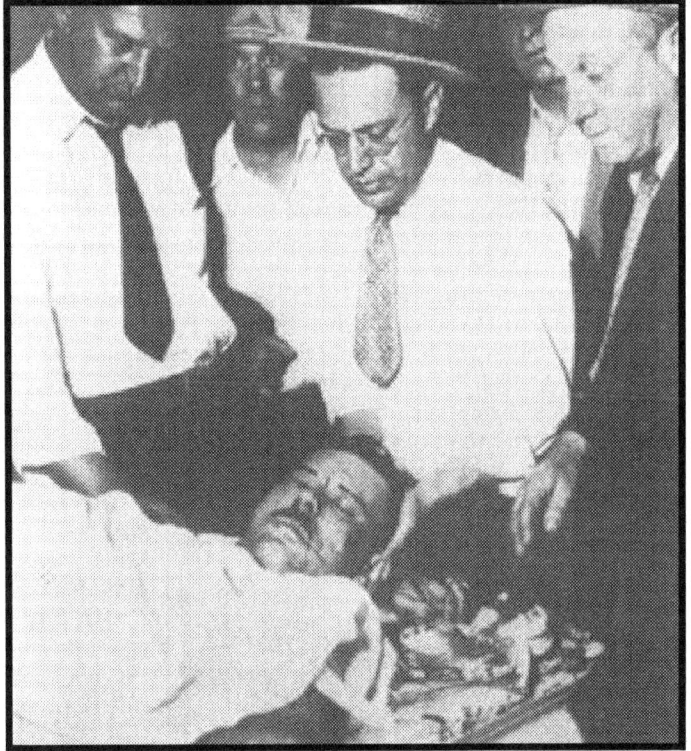

The body said to be the famous bank robber was placed on display, autopsied and repeatedly photographed --- but was it really Dillinger?

moles, but also missing were at least two scars on Dillinger's body. The dead man had not received any plastic surgery, although the F.B.I. stated that Dillinger had undergone surgery to compensate for the obvious facial differences between the dead man and Dillinger. So, which version of the "plastic surgery story" was the truth?

Newspaper reports almost immediately stated that the body was matched to Dillinger by way of a fingerprint card, but there are those who insist that the card was planted in the Cook County Morgue days before the murder. Strangely, the F.B.I. never released the name of the man who allegedly took the dead man's prints and matched them to Dillinger. The signature at the bottom of the fingerprint card was illegible. Of course, there is no proof that the card was actually "planted", and it's this small doubt that debunkers use to dismiss the entire possibility that the F.B.I got the wrong man, ignoring the color of the eyes, the scars and the heart condition.

But if the F.B.I. killed the wrong man, who was he?

There are several possible identities of who may have been killed in Dillinger's place, but it should be noted that Dillinger was not the only member of his gang who may have escaped after being reported dead.

The other was John Hamilton, the "old pro" of the Dillinger gang. Hamilton was believed to have been mortally wounded in the spring of 1934, but the location of his grave remained a mystery for nearly six months. F.B.I. agents eventually located it outside of Oswego, Illinois but the body could not be identified except by prison dental records, which the Bureau declined to release.

The feds had eyewitness accounts and circumstantial evidence to suggest that it was Hamilton, but there was plenty of conflicting evidence as well. Friends and accomplices, whose stories were convincing, insisted that Hamilton had died at a house in Aurora after being shot. Other gang members claimed that he had been buried in an abandoned mine shaft in Wisconsin or in the sand dunes of northern Indiana.

To make things even more confusing, the F.B.I. later received a confidential letter from someone claiming that Hamilton was alive and asking about a possible reward. The letter was filed away. The last thing the Bureau needed was one more dead member of the Dillinger gang still walking around.

Those who believe that Hamilton may have survived his brush with death recall the childhood recollections of his nephew, Bruce Hamilton, Jr., who later remembered a mysterious family trip through several parts of the United States. During this trip, several large sums of cash were obtained. The journey ended with a visit to a small town in Canada and a secret family reunion, where he was told that he met his fugitive uncle, who was very much alive.

The death of Bruce Hamilton's father, who never discussed the trip, and Hamilton's unsuccessful search for another relative who could shed light on the mysterious uncle, left the mystery unsolved.

But it's certainly not the only mystery connected to the Dillinger gang.

The most likely suspect for the man killed in Dillinger's place was a north side man named Jimmy Lawrence. On the night of the shooting, Lawrence disappeared. He was a small-time criminal who had moved to Chicago from Wisconsin in 1930. He had lived in the neighborhood around Lincoln Avenue during the same time that Dillinger had been in prison in Michigan City, Indiana and often came to the Biograph Theater. He

also bore an uncanny resemblance to John Dillinger, which leads many to believe that he may have been killed in Dillinger's place.

A piece of possible evidence to this is a photograph that was taken from the purse of Dillinger's girlfriend, Billie Frechette, after an arrest, which showed her in the company of a man who looked like the person killed at the Biograph. It is a photo that was taken before Dillinger ever allegedly had plastic surgery. Could Jimmy Lawrence have gone on a date to the Biograph, not knowing (thanks to Anna Sage) that the F.B.I. was waiting for him there?

Some writers have suggested this is exactly what happened. Respected crime writer, Jay Robert Nash, an expert on Dillinger, reported in his book *Dillinger: Dead or Alive?* that Dillinger's attorney, Louis Piquett, along with Martin Zarkovich and Anna Sage, rigged the whole affair. According to Nash, Sage was a bordello madame who was in danger of being deported. To prevent this, she went to the police and told them that she knew Dillinger. In exchange for not being deported, she would arrange to have him at the Biograph, where they could nab him. She agreed to wear a bright, red dress so she would be easily recognized. While F.B.I. agents waited, "Dillinger" and his girlfriends watched the movie and

A photograph found in the possession of Billie Frechette, Dillinger's most devoted girlfriend. The photo shows Billie in her younger days, standing next to a man that is not Dillinger, although it looks like him. The man also bears an uncanny resemblance to the man who was shot to death in front of the Biograph and wears a ring just like the one that was photographed on the body.

enjoyed popcorn and soda. When the film ended, the Feds made their move. Nash believes, however, that they shot Jimmy Lawrence instead of Dillinger. He also believes that when they learned of their mistake, the F.B.I. covered it up, either because they feared the wrath of J. Edgar Hoover, who told them to "get Dillinger or else", or because Hoover himself was too embarrassed to admit the mistake.

So, what happened to the real John Dillinger?

According to testimony from a bank robber named James "Blackie" Audett, a friend of Dillinger's, the two of them escaped from Illinois (he was hiding in Aurora at the time) just hours after the shooting at the Biograph. He claimed that they had taken the "northern route", to Wisconsin, Minnesota and then straight west. Dillinger's only regret, he said, was that he had to leave Billie Frechette behind. She was in jail at the time for harboring Dillinger. Audett claimed that he left Dillinger at an Indian Reservation out west, where he later settled down and married a local woman.

Before the shooting, Dillinger had visited his father and left a sum of money with him with which to pay for his funeral. He told his father that he planned to get away so that he would "not have to worry about his son anymore". Dillinger's sister, Audrey, was well aware of the fact that her brother was alive (as were other members of the family) and she corresponded with Audett up until the time of Audett's death.

After leaving Dillinger at the Indian Reservation, Audett was apprehended for his own crimes and sent to serve time on Alcatraz. He was the last prisoner to leave "The Rock" in 1962. Audett claimed that he saw Dillinger on the west coast several times before he was arrested again for a Seattle bank robbery and sent to prison in 1974. He was later paroled into the custody of Jay Robert Nash, who interviewed him extensively about the "posthumous" activities of Dillinger. Audett died of a stroke in 1979 and until the day he died, he claimed that Dillinger was still alive. No amount of persuasion from Nash could get Blackie to tell him where Dillinger was living.

Was Blackie Audett just an old man who was spinning tales to get attention in his last years? Or could he have been telling the truth? Did John Dillinger survive his last run-ins with the F.B.I. and escape to the west to live out his last years in peace? Jay Robert Nash became convinced that Dillinger had gotten away ---- and he wasn't the only one to think so.

In the late 1930s, a federal agent who was passing through Mooresville, Indiana reported that a substantial number of citizens remained convinced that Dillinger had somehow slipped out of the hands of the F.B.I. and had escaped. He also learned that the bank robber's family had received a letter from someone claiming to be Dillinger --- and that it contained enough private information that they were convinced it was genuine.

The agent was unable to learn any details about the letter but it seemed to be common knowledge around town that the Dillingers believed "Johnnie" was alive. Those who had doubts were asked the simple question of how John Dillinger, Sr., a farmer with little money, had managed to pay for his son's elaborate burial, which involved encasing his casket in concrete. Wouldn't this have been very expensive? And well beyond his means?

Some claimed that Dillinger had been killed with thousands of dollars in his pocket and that the money went to his father. This was not the case. The man shot down at the Biograph Theater had the clothing on his back; a pair of white buckskin Nunn-Bush shoes, size 9D; one ruby gold ring; a yellow-gold Hamilton pocket watch; a gold chain and tiny knife attached to the watch; a white handkerchief with a thin brown border; two keys tied with string (one fit Anna Sage's apartment); and a fully loaded, spare magazine for his Colt pistol. The official record stated that Dillinger was carrying $7.70 in his pocket ---- hardly enough to pay for a funeral.

And this always ended the story for me. To be honest, I have long been fascinated with the story of Dillinger and, always enjoying a good conspiracy, I wanted to believe that perhaps he really did get away in the end. Despite the fact that I had been assured several times that this could never really happen, I always wondered about the conflicting autopsy evidence but never thought a lot about it. Then, in 2001, I received a letter from the son of a former police chief who once claimed to know John Dillinger and who got me thinking that maybe there was more to the story of his escape after all. Regardless, it was no longer just a story in a book for me but a real encounter with a very real person.

The letter that I received came from Norm Alder. His father, Norman John Alder (now deceased) had grown up in Loda, Illinois, a small town in Iroquois County, which is south of Chicago and along the Indiana state line. According to the elder Mr. Alder, he had met John Dillinger when he was a small boy in the early 1930s.

When he was eight or nine, Norman would hang around the local tavern in Loda with several friends. The Maddox family owned the tavern and the neighborhood kids often did odd jobs like emptying boxes, sweeping the porch and taking out the trash to earn a little money that could be spent on soda and candy. One day, a new customer showed up in town and claimed to be a farmhand, even though he certainly didn't dress like one. He became friendly with the local boys and, when they got to know him, he introduced himself as "John". He often gave the kids money for candy and played cards with them. One day, he asked if they wanted to play blackjack and most of the boys were excited and agreed, although Norman was embarrassed because he didn't know how to play. Realizing the boy's awkwardness, John took him aside and taught him how the game was played. On many days that followed, John and Norman would sit by themselves and play blackjack.

Then, one day, John suddenly disappeared. The kids were disappointed that their friend never told them goodbye, especially Norman. Not long after though, he was in the Loda post office and happened to see a picture of John on the wall -- it was a "wanted" poster, listing his friend as John Dillinger. Norman later told his son that he knew that it was his friend John without any doubt, even though the John in the picture was missing his mustache. "Dad soon learned that Dillinger was often in the area," Norm Alder wrote, "and that he even had a girlfriend outside of town. Dad's uncle, Earl Alder, ran a service station not far away and he claimed that Dillinger often stopped in for gas."

A few weeks passed and Norman heard the sudden, sad news that his friend John was shot to death by police in Chicago. Notorious bank robber or not, the stranger had been a good friend to the young boy and he was devastated by the news.

A few years later, when Norman was a teenager, he traveled with his parents to visit relatives in Mooresville, Indiana, outside of Indianapolis. His father and his uncle decided to stop in the local barbershop for a haircut, so Norman waited outside for them on a bench in front of the shop. An old man with white hair and a beard was also sitting on the bench and they struck up a conversation. Norman finally got around to asking the man, since this was Dillinger's hometown, if he knew John Dillinger.

"You bet I knew him," the old man replied. "I knew him when he was only this tall." He indicated the height of a small child.

"Then I guess you know that he was shot and killed in Chicago," Norman replied.

"No, he wasn't," the old man told him. "I was at the funeral. It looked a lot like him, but it wasn't him."

"Really? Then where is he?" Norman asked in astonishment.

The old man gave him a shrewd answer before getting up and walking away. "He's on a chicken farm in Wisconsin and that's where he's gonna stay!"

"Many years passed and Dad often wondered about this," Norm Alder finished his story. "He even went into law enforcement himself, serving as police chief for two cities, and he wondered if the Chicago police might really have goofed when they thought they had gotten Dillinger. I enjoyed your account on the Dillinger mystery and hope that now I have gotten a chance to help you tell the whole thing."

Could Dillinger have actually gotten away? It certainly seems possible, despite official denials and the derision afforded to these "conspiracy theories" by many writers in the crime field. Believe it or not though, I believe there are still many unanswered questions about the Dillinger assassination, including the identity of the ghost in the alley near the Biograph Theater, still seen re-enacting the final moments of a life cut short in July 1934.

Is this phantom that of John Dillinger, playing out the last few seconds of his life over and over again? Or could this be the specter of Jimmy Lawrence, doomed to repeatedly run for his life after being betrayed by two women that he trusted?

5. BLOODY MURDER

History & Hauntings from Chicago's Violent Past

Chicago is a place so wicked, vile and abominable that it should be avoided by decent people.
State Tribune Leader --- Cheyenne, Wyoming

They've hung everything on me but the Chicago Fire.
Al Capone

I was born with the devil in me. I could not help the fact that I was a murderer, no more than the poet can help the inspiration to sing -- I was born with the "Evil One" standing as my sponsor beside the bed where I was ushered into the world, and he has been with me since.
H.H. Holmes

It has been said, as I wrote in the foreword to this book, that the deeds of yesterday create the hauntings of today. This is especially true when it comes to murder and crime. The pages of this book have already been filled with horrific murders and violent deaths, many of which have created Chicago hauntings, but the chapter ahead is not one for the squeamish --- or the faint of heart.

The history ahead is dark indeed and the hauntings are perhaps even darker. These manifestations involve a wide variety of strange happenings, from apparitions to phantom footsteps; unexplainable sounds; lights that turn on and off; doors that open and close; eerie smells; sensations of cold chills; the prickling of the skin and touches by unseen hands; and even, in one case, possession by the spirit itself.

Attempts have been made to try and categorize these hauntings but many locations seem to defy this labeling and manifest a variety and combination of types. In fact, it has been my experience that some locations seem to act as a catalyst for activity, causing visitors to manifest their own unconscious phenomena and giving rise to accounts which don't fit into any categories at all. The two different types of hauntings that seem to be most commonly reported are what we call the "traditional haunting" and the "residual haunting", but they aren't alone. They are however, the most likely types of activity to be found at the places we will be visiting in the pages ahead.

The traditional spirit is everyone's classic idea of a ghost. It is a lost personality, or spirit, that, for some reason, did not pass over to the other side at the moment of death. It shows intelligence and a consciousness and often interacts with people. It is the most widely accepted kind of paranormal activity because it is the easiest to understand. It "haunts" a place because of a connection to the site or to the people at the location. This ghost is the personality of a once living being who stayed behind in our world. This sometimes happens in the case of a murder, a traumatic event, or because of some unfinished business which was left in a person's life. At the time of death, this spirit refused to cross over to the other side because of these events. There is also a good chance that this spirit does not even realize that it has died, which could happen if the death was sudden or unexpected. Many Chicago locations seem to involve these "spirits with a purpose". When it comes to murder or violent deaths, it seems that many such confused spirits linger behind.

Another type of haunting that is often reported at crime scenes and murder sites has nothing to do with intelligent, or conscious, spirits at all. It is more common than people think and you might be surprised at how many ghost stories that you have heard over the years just may fit into this category. This haunting is both unexplainable and fascinating ---- and can be downright spooky too!

This type of haunting is called a "residual haunting" and the easiest way to explain it is to compare it to an old film loop, meaning that it is a scene that is replayed over and over again through the years. These hauntings are really just a piece of time that is stuck in place. Many haunted locations experience events that may imprint themselves on the atmosphere of a place in a way that we don't yet understand. This event suddenly discharges and plays itself at various times, thus resulting in a place being labeled as haunted. These "phantom" events are not necessarily just visual either. They are often replayed as sounds and noises that cannot be explained, like footsteps that go up and down the stairs when no one is there. They can also sometimes appear as smells or other sensory events.

Often the sounds and images "recorded" are related to traumatic events that took place at the location and caused what might be called a "psychic disturbance". In other situations, they have been events or actions repeated over and over again to cause the impression. The locations where these hauntings occur act like storage batteries, saving up the impressions of sights and sounds from the past. Eventually, many of these hauntings wear down and fade away, while others continue for eternity.

It's not surprising that many researchers find evidence of residual hauntings at places where great trauma and deaths have occurred. These include both battlefields and of course, crime scenes. These are spots where lives have ended suddenly and with extreme violence. It's as though the dying moments of the victims have left a mark on the place where they breathed their last breath.

THE MURDER CASTLE
H.H. Holmes -- The Monster of 63rd Street

In 1893, Chicago, Illinois was host to a spectacular World's Fair -- The Columbian Exposition -- that celebrated the anniversary of Columbus' discovery of America. It was a boom time for the city and thousands of people came from all over the country to attend. Unfortunately though, the list of those "gone missing" at the end of the fair was extensive and as the police later tried to track down where these people had vanished to -- the trail often turned cold on the south side of Chicago. Everything was not as shiny and beautiful as the advertising for the Exposition's "White City" would have everyone believe, for "a devil" that became known as America's first real serial killer was alive and well on the city's south side, luring visitors to his "hotel", where scores of them vanished without a trace --- never to be seen again.

Today, the neighborhood of Englewood is a part of Chicago but in the late 1800's, it was a quiet, independent community on the southern outskirts of the Windy City. It was a tranquil place and the abode of housewives and shopkeepers. Among these decent folk was a "Mrs. Dr. Holden", as the newspapers mysteriously referred to her, who ran a drugstore at 63rd and Wallace. There was almost too much trade for the woman to handle, as Englewood was rapidly growing, just like so many of Chicago's suburbs were in those days. She was delighted, therefore, to find a capable assistant who said that his name was Dr. Henry H. Holmes. He turned out to be a remarkable addition to the place.

In 1887, being a druggist meant that you were also a chemist and most drugstores were rather crowded places that were stocked with all manner of elixirs and potions. When Dr.

The Devil Came to Chicago -- dashing H.H.. Holmes, the city's most prolific killer

Holmes compounded even the simplest prescription, he did so with a flourish, as if he were an alchemist in the midst of some arcane ritual. His long, pale fingers moved with a surgeon's skill, his handsome face grew intense and his blue eyes grew bright. But he was by no means a socially inept scientist; he was a gentleman of fashion and charming of manner. His politeness and humorous remarks brought many new customers into the drug store, especially the ladies in the neighborhood. In addition, he kept a sharp eye on the account books and was concerned with the profit the store was making. He was, in short, the perfect assistant to the proprietress.

It was not long before Holmes seemed to be more the manager of the store and less the prescription clerk. He began to spend more and more time working with the ledgers and chatting pleasantly with the ladies who came into the place, some of whom took a very long time to make a very small purchase. Dr. Holmes became a familiar figure as he strolled down 63rd Street, the main thoroughfare of Englewood. He appeared to be heading for a leading position in the local business community.

Trade at the drug store continued to improve, making Mrs. Dr. Holden exceedingly happy. But as for Holmes, he was still not satisfied with his lot and he had many plans and visions that drove him onward. Strangely, in 1887, Mrs. Dr. Holden vanished without a trace. A short time later, Holmes announced that he had purchased the store from the widow just prior to her "moving out west". The unfortunate lady had (not surprisingly) left no forwarding address.

Two years later, he acquired a large lot across the street from the drug store and began construction on an enormous edifice that he planned to operate as a hotel for the upcoming Columbian Exposition in 1893. There are no records to say what Holmes decided to call this building but for generations of police officers, crime enthusiasts and unnerved residents of Englewood, it was known simply by one name -- "The Murder Castle".

Henry H. Holmes, whose real name was Herman W. Mudgett, was born in 1860 in Gilmanton, New Hampshire, where his father was a wealthy and respected citizen and the local postmaster for nearly 25 years. Early in life, Mudgett dropped his given name and became known as H.H. Holmes, a name under which he

attended medical school and began his career in crime. He was constantly in trouble as a boy and young man and, in later years, was remembered for his cruelty to animals and smaller children. His only redeeming trait was that he was always an excellent student and did well in school. In 1878, Holmes married Clara Lovering, the daughter of a prosperous farmer in Loudon, New Hampshire and, that same year, he began studying medicine at a small college in Burlington, Vermont. He paid his tuition with a tidy legacy that had been inherited by his wife. Even as a student though, Holmes began to dabble in debauchery.

In 1879, he transferred to the medical school of the University of Michigan in Ann Arbor and, while there, he devised a method of stealing cadavers from the laboratory. He would then disfigure the corpses and plant them in places where it would look as though they had been killed in accidents. Conveniently, Holmes had already taken out insurance policies on these "family members" and he would collect on them as soon as the bodies were discovered.

A few months after he completed his most daring swindle, insuring a corpse for $12,500 and carrying out the plan with an accomplice who would later become a prominent doctor in New York, he left Ann Arbor and abandoned his wife and infant son. Clara returned to New Hampshire and never saw her husband again.

After that, Holmes dropped out of sight for six years. What became of him during most of this period is unknown and later on, even Pinkerton detectives were unable to learn much about his activities in these years, although they did come across traces of his trail in several cities and states. For a year or so, he was engaged in a legitimate business in St. Paul and he gained so much respect from the community that he was appointed the receiver of a bankrupt store. He immediately stocked the place with goods, sold them at low prices and then vanished with the proceeds. From St. Paul, he went to New York and taught school for a time in Clinton County, boarding at the home of a farmer near the village of Moore's Forks. He seduced the farmer's wife and then disappeared one night, leaving an unpaid bill and a pregnant landlady.

In 1885, Holmes turned up in Chicago and opened an office (he was posing as an inventor) in the North Shore suburb of Wilmette. Upon his re-appearance, Holmes filed for divorce from Clara Lovering but the proceedings were unsuccessful and the case dragged on until 1891. However, this did not stop him from marrying another woman, Myrtle Z. Belknap, whose father, John Belknap, was a wealthy businessman in Wilmette. Although the marriage did produce a daughter, it was nevertheless a strange one. Myrtle remained living in Wilmette while Holmes began living in Chicago. John Belknap would later discover that Holmes had tried to cheat him out of property by forging his name on deeds. He would also claim that Holmes had tried to poison him when he was confronted about the fraudulent papers. Myrtle ended the marriage in 1889.

Stories claim that the house in Wilmette where Myrtle lived is haunted today. One has to wonder if the spirit who walks here is that of John Belknap or Myrtle herself. It's possible that her unhappy marriage, and horror as the later crimes of her husband were revealed, has caused her to linger behind.

Shortly after Holmes married Myrtle, he opened another office, this time in downtown Chicago, with the A.B.C. Copier, a machine for copying documents, which was about the only honest device that he was ever connected with. He operated from an office on South Dearborn but the copier was a failure and he vanished again, leaving his creditors with $9,000 in worthless notes.

A few months later, he began working in a drugstore in the Englewood section at the corner of 63rd and Wallace Street. The store was owned by a Dr. Mrs. Holden, an older lady, who was happy to have the young man take over most of the responsibilities of the store. Strangely, in 1887, Mrs. Holden vanished without a trace. Apparently, no one had any reason to doubt Holmes about his "purchase" of her store and she was never found when the police finally began to investigate his activities a few years later.

In 1889, Holmes began a new era in his criminal life. After a short trip to Indiana, he returned to Chicago and purchased an empty lot across the street from the drugstore. He had plans to build a huge house on the property and work was started in 1890. His trip to Indiana had been profitable and, with the help of an accomplice named Benjamin Pietezel, he had used the journey to pull off an insurance scheme. The confederate later went to jail as a result of the swindle, but Holmes came away unscathed.

He continued to operate the drug store, to which he also added a jewelry counter. In 1890, he hired Ned

Connor of Davenport, Iowa as a watchmaker and jeweler. The young man arrived in the city in the company of his wife, Julia, and their daughter, Pearl. The family moved into a small apartment above the store and soon, Julia managed to capture the interest of Holmes. He fired his bookkeeper and hired Julia to take the man's place. Not long after, Connor began to suspect that Holmes was carrying on with his wife, and he was right. Luckily for him, he decided to cut his losses, abandoned his family and went to work for another shop downtown.

Now that Holmes had Julia to himself, he took out large insurance polices on the woman and her daughter, naming himself as a beneficiary. Years later, it came to be suspected that Julia became a willing participant in many of Holmes' schemes and swindles. When he incorporated the jewelry business in August 1890, he listed Julia, along with her friend Kate Durkee, as directors.

By this time, much of Holmes' interest was going into the construction of the building across the street. It was an imposing structure of three stories and a basement, with false battlements and wooden bay windows that were covered with sheet iron. There were over 60 rooms in the structure and 51 doors that were cut oddly into various walls. Holmes acted as his own architect for the site and he personally supervised the numerous construction crews, all of whom were quickly hired and fired, discharging them with great fury and refusing to pay their wages. As far as the police were able to learn, he never paid a cent for any of the materials that went into the building. In addition to the eccentric general design, the house was also fitted with trap doors, hidden staircases, secret passages, rooms without windows, chutes that led into the basement and a staircase that opened out over a steep drop to the alley behind the house.

The first floor of the building contained stores and shops, while the upper floors could be used for spacious living quarters. Holmes also had an office on the second floor, but most of the rooms were to be used for guests -- guests that would never be seen again. Evidence would later be found to show that Holmes used some of the rooms as "asphyxiation chambers", where his victims were suffocated with gas. Other chambers were lined with iron plates and had blowtorch-like devices fitted into the walls. In the basement, Holmes installed a dissecting table and maintained his own crematory. There was also an acid vat and pits filled with quicklime, where bodies could be conveniently disposed of. All of his "prison rooms" were fitted with alarms that buzzed in Holmes' quarters if a captive attempted to escape. It has come to be believed that many of his victims were held here for months before their deaths.

The castle was completed in 1892 and, soon after, Holmes announced that he planned to rent out some of the rooms to tourists who would be arriving en mass for the upcoming Columbian Exposition. It is surmised that many of these tourists never returned home after the fair, but no one knows for sure. The list of the "missing" when the Fair closed was a long one and, for most, foul play was suspected. How many of them fell prey to Holmes is a mystery, but no fewer than 50 people who were reported to the police as missing were traced to the place. Here, their trails ended...

An advertisement for lodging dur-

A rare photograph of Holmes' "Murder Castle", which was constructed in Englewood in 1892. Holmes planned to offer it as lodging during the 1893 Columbian Exposition. (Chicago Historical Society)

ing the fair was not the only method that Holmes used for procuring victims. A large number of his female victims came through false classified ads that he placed in small town newspapers, offering jobs to young ladies. When the ads were answered, he would describe several jobs in detail and explained that the woman would have her choice of positions at the time of the interview. When accepted, she would then be instructed to pack her things and withdraw all of her money from the bank because she would need funds to get started. The applicants were also instructed to keep the location and the name of his company a closely guarded secret. He told them that he had devious competitors who would use any information possible to steal his clients. When the applicant arrived, and Holmes was convinced that she had told no one of her destination, she would become his prisoner.

Holmes placed newspaper ads for marriage as well, describing himself as a wealthy businessman who was searching for a suitable wife. Those who answered this ad would get a similar story to the job offer. He would then torture the women to learn the whereabouts of any valuables they might have. The young ladies would then remain his prisoners until he decided to dispose of them.

Amazingly, Holmes was able to keep his murder operation a secret for four years. He slaughtered an unknown number of people, mostly women, in the castle. He would later confess to 28 murders, although the actual number of victims is believed to be much higher. To examine the details of the story, the reader cannot help but be horrified by the amount of planning and devious detail that went into the murders. There is no question that Holmes was one of the most prolific and depraved killers in American history.

Minnie Williams was believed to be Holmes' willing accomplice -- or was at least aware of some of the crimes that he committed. She lived in the Murder Castle for more than a year and is thought to have witnessed the ends of a number of Holmes' victims.

In 1893, Homes met a young woman named Minnie Williams. He told her that his name was Harry Gordon and that he was a wealthy inventor. Holmes' interest in her had been piqued when he learned that she was the heir to a Texas real estate fortune. She was in Chicago working as an instructor for a private school. It wasn't long before she and Holmes were engaged to be married. This was a turn of events that did not make Julia Connor happy. She was still involved with Holmes and still working at the store. Not long after his engagement became official, both Julia and Pearl disappeared. When Ned Connor later inquired after them, Holmes explained that they had moved to Michigan. In his later confession, he admitted that Julia had died during a bungled abortion that he had performed on her. He had poisoned Pearl. He later admitted that he murdered the woman and her child because of her jealous feelings toward Minnie Williams. "But I would have gotten rid of her anyway," he said. "I was tired of her."

Minnie Williams lived at the Castle for more than a year and knew more about Holmes' crimes than any other person. Police investigators would state that there was no way that she could not have had knowledge about many of the murders. Besides being ultimately responsible for the deaths of Julia and Pearl Connor, Minnie was also believed to have instigated the murder of Emily Van Tassel, a young lady who lived on Robey Street. She was only 17 and worked at a candy store on the first floor of the castle. There is no indication of what caused her to catch the eye of Holmes but she vanished just one month after his offer of employment.

Minnie also knew about the murder of Emmeline Cigrand, a beautiful young woman who worked as a stenographer at the

Keely Institute in Dwight, Illinois. Ben Pietzel went there to take a drunkenness cure and told Holmes of the girl's beauty when he returned to Chicago. Holmes then contacted her and offered her a large salary to work for him in Chicago. She accepted the job and came to the Castle -- but never left it.

Emmeline became homesick after a few weeks in Chicago. She had planned to marry an Indiana man named Robert E. Phelps and she was missing him and her family. Holmes later confessed that he locked the girl in one of his soundproof rooms and raped her. He stated that he killed her because Minnie Williams objected to his lusting after the attractive young woman. Some time later, Robert Phelps made the mistake of dropping by the Castle to inquire after her and that was the last time that he was ever reported alive. Holmes described a "stretching experiment" with which he used to kill Phelps. Always curious about the amount of punishment the human body could withstand (Holmes often used the dissecting table on live victims), he invented a "rack-like" device that would literally stretch a person to the breaking point.

In April 1893, Minnie's property in Texas was deeded to a man named Benton T. Lyman, who was, in reality, Ben Pietzel, the already mentioned accomplice of Holmes. Later that same year, Minnie's brother was killed in a mining accident in Colorado, which is said to have been arranged by Holmes.

A visit to Chicago by Minnie's sister, Nannie, may provide more evidence of Minnie's murderous ways and her willingness to go along with Holmes. In June 1893, Holmes seduced Nannie while she was staying at the Castle and had no trouble persuading her to sign over her share of some property in Fort Worth. She disappeared a month later with an explanation that she had gone back to Texas but, according to Holmes, it had been Minnie who killed her. When Minnie found out that Nannie had been consorting with Holmes, the two of them got into a heated argument. Minnie hit her sister over the head with a chair and she died; then she and Holmes dropped the body into Lake Michigan.

A short time later, Holmes and Minnie traveled to Denver in the company of another young woman, Georgianna Yoke, who had come to Chicago from Indiana with a "tarnished reputation". She had applied for a job at the Castle and Holmes told her that his name was Henry Howard and that Minnie was his cousin. On January 17, 1894, Holmes and Georgianna were married at the Vendome Hotel in Denver with Minnie as their witness! After that, the wedding party (which apparently consisted of the three of them) traveled to Texas, where they claimed Minnie's property and arranged a horse swindle. Holmes purchased several railroad cars of horses with counterfeit banknotes and signed the papers as "O.C. Pratt". The horses were then shipped to St. Louis and sold. Holmes made off with a fortune, but it would be this swindle that would later come back and destroy him.

The threesome returned to Chicago and their return marked the last time that Minnie was ever seen alive. Holmes explained that he believed Minnie had killed her sister in a fit of passion and then had fled to Europe. The police believed him, as he was known for being an upstanding citizen and it was not until much later that he confessed to killing her too. Although her body was never found, it is believed to have joined other victims in the acid vat in the basement.

In July 1894, Holmes was arrested for the first time. It was not for murder but for one of his schemes: the earlier horse swindle that ended in St. Louis. Georgianna promptly bailed him out but, while in jail, he struck up a conversation with a convicted train robber named Marion Hedgepeth, who was serving a 25 year sentence. Holmes had concocted a plan to bilk an insurance company out of $20,000 by taking out a policy on himself and then faking his death. Holmes prom-

Bank robber Marion Hedgepeth

Holmes accomplice -- and unlucky victim --
Benjamin Pietzel

ised Hedgepeth a $500 commission in exchange for the name of a lawyer who could be trusted. He was directed to Colonel Jeptha Howe, the brother of a public defender, and Howe found Holmes' plan to be brilliant.

Holmes then took a cadaver to a seaside resort in Rhode Island and burned it, disfiguring the head and dumping it on the beach. He then shaved his beard, altered his appearance and returned to the hotel, registering under another name and inquiring about his friend, Holmes. When the body was discovered on the beach, he identified it as "H.H. Holmes" and presented an insurance policy for $20,000. However, the insurance company suspected fraud and refused to pay. Holmes returned to Chicago without pressing the claim and began concocting a new version of the same scheme.

A month later, Holmes held a conference with Ben Pietzel and Jeptha Howe and his new plan was put into action. Pietzel went to Philadelphia with his wife, Carrie, and opened a shop for buying and selling patents under the name of B.F. Perry. Holmes then took out an insurance policy on his life. The plan was for Pietzel to drink a potion that would knock him unconscious. Then, Holmes would apply make-up to his face to make it look as though he had been severely burned. A witness would then summon an ambulance and while he was gone, Holmes would put a corpse in place of the "shopkeeper". The insurance company would be told that he had died. Pietzel would then receive a portion of the money in exchange for his role in the swindle but he would soon learn, as so many others already had, that Holmes could not be trusted!

The "accident" took place on the morning of September 4, when neighbors heard a loud explosion from the patent office. A carpenter named Eugene Smith came to the office a short time later and found the door locked and the building dark. For some reason, he became concerned and summoned a police officer to the scene. They broke open the door and found a badly burned man on the floor. The death was quickly ruled an accident and the body was taken to the morgue. After 11 days, no one showed up to claim it so the corpse was buried in the local potter's field. Days later, the police learned that the dead man (Pietzel) had come to Philadelphia from St. Louis and the police of that city were asked to search for relatives. Within days, attorney Jeptha Howe filed a claim with the insurance company, on behalf of Carrie Pietzel, and collected the money. He kept $2,500 and Holmes took the remainder. He later gave $500 to Mrs. Pietzel but then took it back, explaining that he would invest it for her.

The claim was paid without hesitation and everyone got their share of the money, except for Ben Pietzel and Marion Hedgepeth. Holmes never bothered to contact the train robber again, a slight that Hedgepeth did not appreciate. He brooded over this awhile and then decided to turn Holmes in. He explained the scheme to a St. Louis policeman named Major Lawrence Harrigan who, in turn, notified an insurance investigator, W.E. Gary. He then passed along the information to Frank P. Geyer, a Pinkerton agent, who immediately began an investigation.

Ben Pietzel never received his share of the money either, but even if he had, he would not have been able to spend it. What Holmes had not told anyone was that the body discovered in the patent office was not a cleverly disguised corpse, but Ben Pietzel himself! Rather than split the money again, Holmes had killed his accomplice and then burned him so that he would be difficult to recognize. Holmes kept this part of the plan a secret as he and Georgianna were now traveling with Carrie Pietzel and her three children. Carrie believed that her

148

husband was hiding out in New York. The group was seen in Cincinnati and then in Indianapolis on October 1. Carrie was then sent east and the children were left in the care of Holmes and Georgianna. Holmes made arrangements for Carrie to meet him in Detroit, where he assured her that her husband was now hiding. He arrived in Detroit several days before the appointed time and put the three children into a boarding house. Then he went to Indiana, returned with Georgianna, and installed her in a second boarding house. When Carrie arrived, she was lodged in yet another establishment. Then, he began moving about the country, apparently aware that the Pinkerton detective, Frank Geyer, was on his trail. The journey lasted for almost two months but on November 17, 1894, Holmes turned up in Boston alone and was arrested and sent to Philadelphia.

As fate would have it though, he was not arrested for insurance fraud but for the horse swindle that he, Minnie and Georgianna had pulled off in Texas. He was given the choice of being returned to Texas and being hanged as a horse thief, or he could confess to the insurance scheme that had led to the death of Ben Pietzel. He chose insurance fraud and was sent to Philadelphia. On the way there, Holmes offered his guard $500 if the man would allow himself to be hypnotized. Wisely, the guard refused.

Pinkerton Detective Frank P. Geyer

The entire insurance scheme was now completely unraveling. A week later, Georgianna was found at her parent's home in Indiana and Carrie Pietzel was discovered in Burlington, Vermont, where Holmes had rented a small house for her to live in while she awaited the arrival of her family. Holmes had lived at the house with her for several days but had left angry when she questioned him about a hole that he was digging in the back

yard. The police came to believe that he was digging her grave but for some unknown reason, he chose not to kill her. Mrs. Pietzel was arrested and was taken to Philadelphia but was soon released. No charges were ever brought against her.

Detective Geyer was slowly starting to uncover the dark secrets of Henry Howard Holmes, he realized, but even the seasoned Pinkerton man was unprepared for what lay ahead. He was beginning to sift through the many lies and identities of Holmes, hoping to find clues as to the fates of the Pietzel children. At this point, he had no idea about all of the other victims. Holmes swore that Minnie Williams had taken the children with her to London, where she planned to open a massage parlor, but Geyer was sure that he was lying. In June 1895, Holmes entered a guilty plea for a single count of insurance fraud but Geyer expanded his investigation.

Two of Holmes' most tragic victims, Alice & Howard Pietzel, the children of his slain accomplice Benjamin Pietzel. Their remains were eventually discovered through the dogged detective work of Frank Geyer.

149

Throughout his questioning, Holmes refused to reveal any explanation about what had become of Carrie Pietzel's three children: Howard, Nellie and Alice. Fearing the worst, Detective Geyer set out to try and discover their fate -- and his worst fears soon came to realization. In Chicago, Geyer learned that all of Holmes' mail had been forwarded every day to Gilmanton, New York. From Gilmanton, it had been sent to Detroit; from Detroit to Toronto; from Toronto to Cincinnati; from Cincinnati to Indianapolis; and then on from there. He followed Holmes' trail for eight months through the Midwest and Canada, stopping in each city to investigate the house that he had been renting while residing there. In Detroit, a house that Holmes had rented was still vacant and a large hole was found to have been dug in the cellar floor. Geyer was relieved to discover that it was empty.

In Toronto, the Pinkerton searched for eight days before he found the cottage at No. 16 Vincent Street that had been rented to a man fitting Holmes' description. The man had been traveling with two little girls. Holmes borrowed a shovel from a neighbor, which he claimed he wanted to use to dig a hole to store potatoes in. Geyer borrowed the same spade and, when digging in the same location, found the bodies of Nellie and Alice Pietzel secreted several feet under the earth. In an upstairs bedroom, he found a large trunk that had a piece of rubber tubing leading into it; the other end was attached to a gas pipe. Holmes had told the girls that he wanted to play hide and seek with them, tricked them into climbing into the trunk and then had asphyxiated them.

This shocking discovery made Geyer work even harder to find what had become of Howard Pietzel. While questioning the neighbors, he learned that the Pietzel girls had told them that they had a brother who was living in Indianapolis. With this small clue, Geyer went to Indiana and painstakingly searched 900 houses for any clue of Holmes. Finally, in the suburb of Irvington, he found a house that Holmes had rented for a week. The place had been empty since Holmes' occupancy and in the kitchen stove, Geyer found the charred remains of Howard.

Now the door was open for Geyer and Chicago detectives to search Holmes' residence in the Windy City. Geyer was sure that the remaining answers that he was seeking could be found inside of the Castle. He entered the place with several police officers -- and neither Geyer nor the veteran investigators would ever forget what they found there!

Detectives devoted several weeks to searching and making a floor plan of the Castle. The bottom floor had been used by Holmes himself as a drug store, a candy store, a restaurant and a jewelry store. The third floor of the building had been divided into small apartments and guest rooms and apparently, had never been used.

The second floor, however, proved to be a labyrinth of narrow, winding passages with doors that opened to brick walls, hidden stairways, cleverly concealed doors, blind hallways, secret panels, hidden passages and a clandestine vault that was only big enough for a person to stand in. The room was alleged to be a homemade "gas chamber", equipped with a chute that would carry a body directly into the basement. The investigators suddenly realized the implications of the iron-plated chamber when they found the single, scuffed mark of a footprint on the inside of the door. It was a small print that had been made by a woman who had attempted to escape the grim fate of the tiny room.

In addition to all of the bizarre additions to the floor, the second level also held 35 guest rooms. Half of them were fitted as ordinary sleeping chambers, and there were indications that they had been occupied by the various women who worked for Holmes, by tenants during the Fair or by the luckless females Holmes had seduced while waiting for an opportunity to kill them. Several of the other rooms were without windows and could be made airtight by closing the doors. Others were lined with sheet iron and asbestos with scorch marks on the walls, fitted with trap doors that led to smaller rooms beneath, or were equipped with lethal gas jets that could be used to suffocate or burn the unsuspecting occupants.

This floor also contained Holmes' private apartment, consisting of a bedroom, a bath and two small chambers that were used as offices. The apartment was located at the front of the building, looking out over 63rd Street. In the floor of the bathroom, concealed under a heavy rug, the police found a trap door and a stairway that descended to a room about eight feet square. Two doors led off this chamber, one to a stairway that exited out onto the street and the other giving access to the chute that led down to the basement.

The "chamber of horrors" in the basement stunned the men even further. This subterranean chamber was

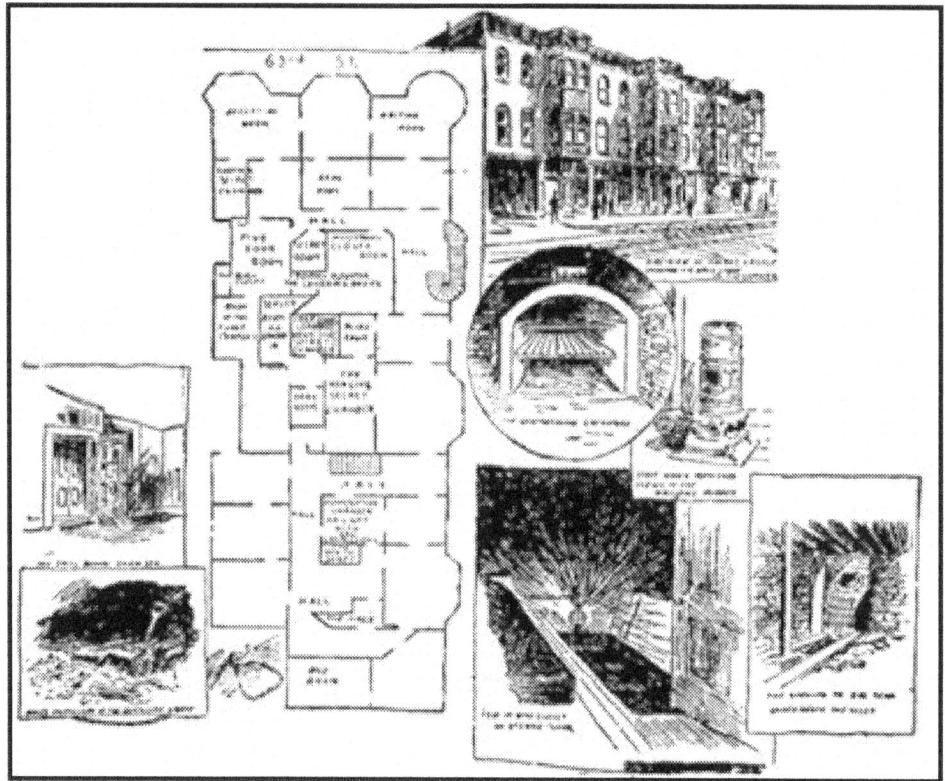

A diagram that appeared in the Chicago Tribune gave readers the chance to see (in lurid detail) the floor plan of Holmes' "Murder Castle", including illustrations of secret passages, the crematory and the quicklime pits.

located seven feet below the rest of the building and extended out under the sidewalk in front. Here, they found Holmes' blood-spattered dissecting table, his gleaming surgical instruments, his macabre "laboratory" of torture devices, various jars of poison, and even a wooden box that contained a number of female skeletons. Built into one of the walls was a crematorium with a heavy iron grate to hold the fire and another grate, fitted with rollers, by which a body could be slid into the flames. The crematorium still contained ash and portions of bone that had not burned in the intense heat. A search of the ashes also revealed a watch that had belonged to Minnie Williams, some buttons from a dress and several charred tintype photographs. Under the staircase, Geyer also found a ball made from women's hair that had been carefully wrapped in cloth.

Buried in the floor, the police found a huge vat of corrosive acid and two quicklime pits, which were capable of devouring an entire body in a matter of hours. A loose pile of quicklime was also discovered in a small room that had been built into the corner. The naked footprint of a woman was found embedded in the pile.

Dozens of human bones and several pieces of jewelry were found and could be traced to Holmes' mistresses. A wood-burning stove in the center of the basement contained scraps of cloth and Ned Connor was summoned to the castle to identify a bloody dress that had belonged to Julia. In a hole in the middle of the floor, more bones were found. After being examined by a physician, they were believed to be the bones of a small child between the ages of six and eight. The fate of Pearl Connor was also no longer in question.

On July 20, some city workers began excavating the cellar and started a tunnel underneath 63rd Street. The hazy smell of gas hung in the air and as the men tore away one wall, they discovered a large tank or metal-lined chamber. As soon as they broke through, the basement was filled with the stench of death, driving the crew back. Noting the metal lining of the tank, they sent for a plumber and he struck a match to peer inside of it. Suddenly, the tank exploded, shaking the building and sending flames out into the basement. The men were buried in piles of debris but no one was seriously injured. The tank was lined with wood and metal and was 14 feet long, although thanks to the explosion, no one will ever know that it was used for. The only clue in the room was a small box that was found in its center. When Fire Marshal James Kenyon opened it, an "evil smelling" vapor rushed out. The gathered men ran, except for Kenyon, who was overpowered by the stench. According to the *New York World*, "he was dragged out and carried upstairs, and for two hours acted like one demented."

Following the excavation, and the discovery and cataloguing of Holmes' potential victims, the "Murder Castle" (as it came to be called) sat empty for several months. Not surprisingly, it drew onlookers and curiosity-seekers from all over the city. The newspapers were not yet filled with stories and illustrations about Holmes' devious crimes but rumors had quickly spread about what had been discovered there. The people of Chicago were stunned that such things could take place ---- and in their glorious city! The Englewood neighborhood watched the sightseers with a combination of fear and loathing, sickened over the terrible things that brought the crowds to their streets.

Then, on August 19, the Castle burned to the ground. Three explosions thundered through the neighborhood just after midnight, and minutes later, a blaze erupted from the abandoned structure. In less than an hour, the roof had caved in and the walls began to collapse in onto themselves. A gas can was discovered among the smoldering ruins and rumors were tossed back and forth between an accomplice of Holmes' burning down the house to hide his role in the horror and the arson being committed by an outraged neighbor. The mystery was never solved but regardless, the Castle was gone for good.

As time passed though, many would claim that the horrific memories still linger at this place. The lot where the Castle was located remained empty for many years until finally, a U.S. Post Office was built on the site in 1938. There would be many in the area who had not forgotten the stories of Holmes' castle ---- or the tales from people who claimed to hear moaning and crying sounds coming from the grounds. This had been a common tale in the community for years and there were those who stated that the ghosts of Holmes' victims did not rest in peace. The ground here was believed to be tainted by the death and bloodshed that had occurred on the spot and the overgrown lot was largely shunned and avoided. Most longtime residents would go out of their way to walk on the other side of the street.

Even after the post office was constructed on the site where so much torture and murder took place, strange things were still reported. Passersby who walked their dogs past the new building claimed the animals would often pull away from it, barking and whining at something only they could see or sense. It was something that remained invisible to their human masters, but which was terrifyingly real to the animals.

In addition, postal workers in the building had their own encounters, often telling of strange sounds and feelings that they could not easily explain. The location was certainly ripe for a haunting and if the stories can be believed, it was, and still is, taking place!

The trial of Herman Mudgett, a.k.a. H.H. Holmes, began in Philadelphia just before Halloween 1895. It only lasted for six days but was one of the most sensational of the century. The newspapers reported it in a lurid and sensational manner and besides the mysteries of the Castle, which were reported at length by several witnesses; Holmes created many exciting scenes in the courtroom. He broke down and wept when Georgianna took the stand as a witness for the state and, eventually, he discharged his attorneys and attempted to conduct his own defense. It was said that Holmes was actually outstanding, clever and as shrewd as an attorney, but it was to no avail. The jury deliberated for just two-and-a-half hours before returning a guilty verdict. Afterward, they reported that they had agreed on the outcome in just one minute but had remained out longer "for the sake of appearances".

On November 30, the judge passed a sentence of death. His case was appealed to the Pennsylvania Supreme Court, who affirmed the verdict, and the governor refused to intervene. Holmes was scheduled to die on May 7, 1896, just nine days before his 36th birthday.

By now, the details of the case had been made public and people were angry, horrified and fascinated, especially in Chicago, where most of the evil had occurred. Holmes had provided a lurid confession of torture and murder that appeared in newspapers and magazines, providing a litany of depravity that compares with the most insane killers of all time. Even if his story was embellished, the actual evidence of Holmes' crimes ranks him as one of the country's most active murderers.

He remained unrepentant though, even at the end. Just before his execution, he visited with two Catholic priests in his cell and even took communion with them, although he refused to ask forgiveness for his crimes. He was led from his cell to the gallows and a black hood was placed over his head. The trap door opened beneath him and Holmes quickly dropped. His head snapped to the side, but his fingers clenched and his feet danced for several minutes afterward, causing many spectators to look away. Although the force of the fall had broken his neck, and the rope had pulled so tight that it had literally imbedded itself in his flesh, his heart continued to beat for nearly 15 minutes. He was finally declared dead at 10:25 a.m.

There were a couple of macabre legends associated with Holmes' execution. One story claimed that a lightning bolt had ripped through the sky at the precise moment the rope had snapped his neck ---- but this was not the strangest one. The most enduring supernatural legend of H.H. Holmes is that of the "Holmes Curse". The story began shortly after his execution, leading to speculation that his spirit did not rest in peace. Some believed that he was still carrying on his gruesome work from beyond the grave. And, even to the skeptical, some of the events that took place after his death are a bit disconcerting.

A short time after Holmes' body was buried, under two tons of concrete, the first strange death occurred. The first to die was Dr. William K. Matten, a coroner's physician who had been a major witness in the trial. He suddenly dropped dead from blood poisoning.

More deaths followed in rapid order, including that of the head coroner, Dr. Ashbridge, and the trial judge who had sentenced Holmes to death. Both men were diagnosed with sudden, and previously unknown, deadly illnesses. Next, the superintendent of the prison where Holmes had been incarcerated committed suicide. The reason for his taking his own life was never discovered. Then, the father of one of Holmes' victims was horribly burned in a gas explosion and the remarkably healthy Pinkerton agent, Frank Geyer, suddenly became ill. Thankfully, though, the diligent detective pulled through.

Not long after this however, the office of the claims manager for the insurance company that Holmes had cheated caught fire and burned. Everything in the office was destroyed except for a framed copy of Holmes' arrest warrant and two portraits of the killer. Many of those who were already convinced of a curse saw this as an ominous warning.

Several weeks after the hanging, one of the priests who prayed with Holmes before his execution was found dead in the yard behind his church. The coroner ruled the death as uremic poisoning but according to reports, he had been badly beaten and robbed. A few days later, Linford Biles, who had been jury foreman in the Holmes trial, was electrocuted in a bizarre accident involving the electrical wires above his house.

In the years that followed, others involved with Holmes also met with violent deaths, including the train robber, Marion Hedgepeth. He remained in prison after his informing on Holmes, although he had expected a pardon that never came. On the very day of Holmes' execution, he was transferred to the Missouri State Prison to finish out his sentence. As time passed, Hedgepeth gained many supporters to his cause, including several newspapers who wrote of his role in getting Holmes prosecuted. In 1906, he finally got his pardon and was released.

Despite the claims that he had made about his rehabilitation, including that he spent each day in prison reading his bible, Hedgepeth was arrested in September 1907 for blowing up a safe in Omaha, Nebraska. He was tried, found guilty and sentenced to 10 more years in prison. However, he was released when it was discovered that he was dying from tuberculosis. In spite of his medical condition, he assembled a new gang and at midnight on New Year's Eve 1910, he attempted to rob a saloon in (of all places) Chicago. As he was taking the money from the till and placing it into a burlap bag, a policeman wandered into the place, realized that a robbery was taking place and opened fire on the thief. Hedgepeth was dead before he hit the floor.

Perhaps Holmes got his revenge after all....

THE SAUSAGE VAT MURDER
Adolph Luetgert & the Sausage Factory Ghost

Drawing of the Luetgert Sausage Factory in 1897 from the Chicago Daily News

The ghost of Louisa Luetgert still walks the neighborhood where her home once stood, or at least that's what the legends of northwest Chicago say. Louisa was the murdered wife of "Sausage King" Adolph Luetgert, a German meat packer who came to the city in the 1870's. Killed by her own husband in one of the most grisly ways imaginable, her ghost not only haunts the area around Hermitage Avenue but the legends say that she hounded her treacherous husband ---- from Joliet Prison to the grave!

Adolph Luetgert was born in Germany and came to America after the Civil War. He lived for a time in Quincy, Illinois and then came to Chicago in 1872, where he pursued several trades, including farming, tanning and, eventually, he started a wholesale liquor business near Dominick Street. He later turned to sausage-making, where he found his greatest success.

After finding out that his German-style sausages were quite popular in Chicago, he built a sausage plant in 1894 at the southwest corner of Hermitage and Diversey. It would be here where the massive German would achieve his greatest success ---- and his continued infamy.

Although the hard-working Luetgert soon began to put together a considerable fortune, he was an unhappy and restless man. Luetgert had married his first wife, Caroline Rabaker, in 1872. She gave birth to two boys, only one of whom survived childhood. Caroline died five years later, in November 1877. Luetgert sold his liquor business in 1879 and moved to North and Clybourn Avenues, where he started his first sausage packing plant in the same building he used as a residence.

Two months after Caroline's death, Luetgert re-married an attractive, younger woman. This did little to ease his restlessness, however, and he was rumored to be engaged in several affairs during the time when he built a three-story frame house next door to the sausage factory. He resided there with his son, and new wife, Louisa.

But Luetgert was still not happy. He often bragged that he had enormous sexual appetites. He carried on with his mistress, Christine Feldt, a wealthy German woman, as well as Mrs. Agathia Tosch, who owned a saloon with her husband on the north side. He later even became involved with Mary Simerling, a household servant who was also his wife's niece. This proved to be the breaking point in his marriage.

His wife, Louisa Bicknese Luetgert, was a beautiful young woman who was 10 years younger than her husband. She was a former servant from the Fox River Valley who met her new husband by chance. He was immediately taken with her, entranced by her diminutive stature and tiny frame. She was less than five feet tall and looked almost child-like next to her burly husband. As a wedding gift, he gave her a unique, heavy gold ring. Inside of it, he had gotten her new initials inscribed, reading "L.L.". Little did he know that this ring would prove to be his undoing.

After less than three years of business, Luetgert's finances began to fail. Even though his factory turned out large quantities of sausages, Luetgert found that he could not meet his supplier's costs. Instead of trying to reorganize his finances though, he and his business advisor, William Charles, made plans to expand. They attempted to secure more capital to enlarge the factory but, by April 1897, it had all fallen apart.

Luetgert, deep in depression, sought solace with his various mistresses. As Matthew W. Pinkerton, of the famous detective agency, later stated: "He was an immoral man and was visited often by women of extremely doubtful character."

Luetgert's excesses, and business losses, took a terrible toll on his marriage. Friends and neighbors frequently heard he and Louisa arguing and their disagreements became so heated that Luetgert eventually moved his bedroom from the house to a small chamber inside of the factory. Louisa soon found out about his involvement with her niece, Mary Simerling, and became enraged. This new scandal got the attention of the people in the neighborhood, who were already gossiping about the couple's marital woes.

"Sausage King" Adolph Luetgert

Luetgert soon gave them even more to gossip about. One night, during another shouting match with Louisa, he responded to her indignation over his affair with Mary by taking his wife by the throat and choking her. Before she collapsed, Luetgert calmed down, after seeing alarmed neighbors looking at him from the parlor window of their home, and he released her. A few days later, Luetgert was seen chasing his wife down the street. He was shouting at her and waving around a revolver. After a couple of blocks, Luetgert broke off the chase and walked silently back to the factory.

Then, on May 1, 1897, Louisa disappeared. When questioned about it, Luetgert stated that Louisa had gone out the previous evening to visit her sister. After several days though, she did not come back. Finally, Diedrich Bicknese, Louisa's brother, came to Chicago and called on his sister. He was informed that she was not there. He came back later and his sister had still not returned. Finding Luetgert at home, he demanded to know where Louisa was. Luetgert calmly told him that his wife had disappeared on May 1 and had never returned. When Diedrich

A drawing of the unfortunate Louisa Luetgert, which appeared in the Chicago Daily News in 1897.

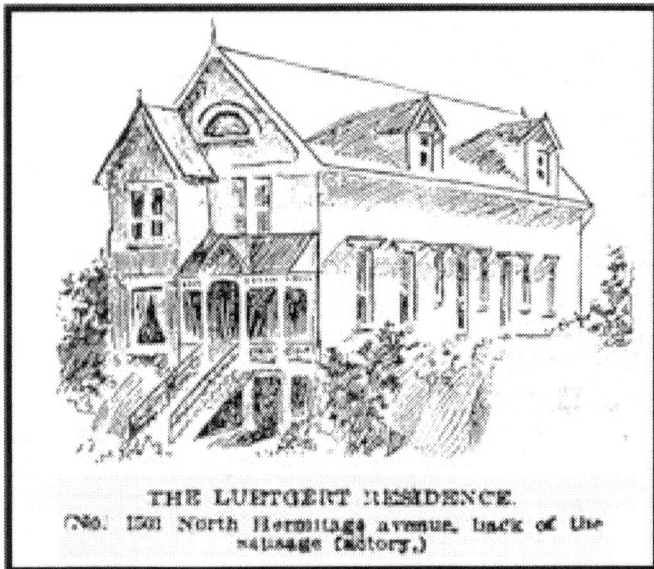

THE LUETGERT RESIDENCE.
(No. 1501 North Hermitage avenue, back of the sausage factory.)

demanded to know why Luetgert had not informed the police about Louisa's disappearance, the sausage-maker simply told him that he was trying to "avoid a scandal" but that he had paid two detectives $5 to try and find her.

Diedrich immediately began searching for his sister. He went to Kankakee, thinking that perhaps she might be visiting friends there, but found nothing and no one who had seen her. He returned to Chicago and when he found that Louisa still had not come home, now having abandoned her children for days, he went to the police. The investigation fell on Captain Herman Schuettler, who was known for being "an honest but occasionally brutal detective".

The detective and his men began to search for Louisa. They questioned neighbors and relatives and heard many recitations about the couple's violent arguments. Captain Schuettler was familiar with Luetgert and had dealings with him in the past. He summoned the sausage-maker to the precinct house on two occasions and each time, pressed him about his wife. Schuettler recalled a time when the Luetgerts had lost a family dog, an event that prompted several calls from Luetgert, but when his wife had gone missing, he noted that Luetgert had never contacted him. Luetgert again used the excuse that as a "prominent businessman", he could not afford the disgrace and scandal. "I expected her to come back," he told Captain Schuettler.

The police began searching the alleyways and dragging the rivers but they also went to the sausage factory and began questioning the employees. One of them, Wilhelm Fulpeck, recalled seeing Louisa around the factory at about 10:30 p.m. on May 1. A young German girl, named Emma Schiemicke, passed by the factory with her sister at about the same time on that evening and remembered seeing Luetgert leading his wife up the alleyway behind the factory.

Frank Bialk, a night watchman at the plant, confirmed both stories. He had also seen Luetgert and Louisa at the plant that night. He only got one glimpse of Louisa but saw his employer several times. Shortly after the couple had entered the factory, Luetgert had come back outside and had given Bialk a dollar and asked him to get him a bottle of celery compound from a nearby drugstore. When the watchman returned with the medicine, he was surprised to find the door leading into the main factory was locked. Luetgert appeared and took the medicine. He made no comment about the locked door and sent Bialk back to the engine room.

A little while later, Luetgert again approached the watchman and sent him back to the drugstore to buy a bottle of

"Honest but occasionally brutal" Detective Herman Schuettler, who went on to become an assistant police chief.

156

Hunyadi water, a medicinal spring water. While the watchman had been away running errands, Luetgert had apparently been working alone in the factory basement. He had turned on the steam under the middle vat at a little before 9:00 p.m. and it was still running when Bialk returned. The watchman reported that Luetgert had remained in the basement until about 2:00 a.m.

Bialk found him fully dressed in his office the next day. He asked whether or not the fires under the vat should be put out but Luetgert told him to bank them at 50 pounds of steam pressure. This was an odd request because the factory had actually been closed for several weeks during Luetgert's financial re-organization. Bialk did as he was told, though, and went down to the basement. Here, he saw a hose sending water into the middle vat and on the floor in front of it was a sticky, glue-like substance. Bialk noticed that it seemed to contain bits of bone but he thought nothing of it. Luetgert used all sorts of waste meats to make his sausage and he assumed that this was all it was.

On May 3, another employee, Frank Odorowsky, known as "Smokehouse Frank", also noticed the slimy substance on the factory floor. He feared that someone had boiled something in the factory without Luetgert's knowledge, so he went to his employer to report it. Luetgert told him not to mention the brown slime. As long as he kept silent, Luetgert said, he would have a good job for the rest of his life.

Frank went to work scraping the slime off of the floor and poured it into a nearby drain that led to the sewer. The larger chunks of waste were placed in a barrel and Luetgert told him to take the barrel out to the railroad tracks and scatter it there.

Following these interviews, Schuettler made another disturbing

The vats in the factory basement. An illustration from the Chicago Daily News in 1897

and suspicious discovery. A short time before Louisa's disappearance, even though the factory had been closed during the re-organization, Luetgert had ordered 325 pounds of crude potash and 50 pounds of arsenic from Lor Owen & Company, a wholesale drug firm. It was delivered to the factory the next day.

Another interview with Frank Odorowsky revealed what had happened to the chemicals. On April 24, Luetgert had asked Smokehouse Frank to move the barrel of potash to the factory basement, where there were three huge vats that were used to boil down sausage material. Luetgert warned him that the potash was very dangerous and that he should avoid contact with it. However, he did need it to be cut up into small pieces.

Frank, along with another employee, crushed the potash with a hatchet and a hammer and were both burned badly on their hands and on their faces. The pieces were all dumped into the middle vat and Luetgert turned on the steam beneath it, dissolving the material into liquid.

Combining this information with the eyewitness accounts from employees and Emma Schiemicke, Captain Schuettler began to theorize about the crime. Circumstantial evidence seemed to show that Luetgert may have killed his wife and boiled her in the sausage vats to dispose of the body. The more that the policeman considered this, the more convinced that he became that this is what had happened.

He and his men started another search of the sausage factory and he soon made a discovery that became one of the most gruesome in the annals of Chicago crime.

On May 15, the search began and it was soon narrowed to the basement and the 12-foot-long, five-foot-deep middle vat that was two-thirds filled with a brownish, brackish liquid. The officers drained the greasy paste from the vat, using gunnysacks as filters, and began poking through the residue with sticks. Here, Officer Walter Dean found several pieces of bone and two gold rings. One of them was a badly tarnished friendship ring and the other was a heavy gold band that had been engraved with the initials "L.L.".

Louisa Luetgert had worn both of the rings.

After they were analyzed, the bones were found to be definitely human ---- a third rib; part of a humerus, or great bone in the arm; a bone from the palm of a human hand; a bone from the fourth toe of a right foot; fragments of bone from a human ear; and a larger bone from a foot. Luetgert would later claim that these were animal bones that he had purchased so that he could boil them down and make soap to clean the factory with. The prosecution would show this was a ridiculous argument. Why would Luetgert spend more than $40 to buy potash and waste materials to scrub down the factory's vats when $1 worth of soap would have done the job?

Adolph Luetgert, proclaiming his innocence, was arrested for the murder of his wife shortly after the search. No body was ever found and there were no witnesses to the crime, but police officers and prosecutors believed the evidence was overwhelming. Luetgert was indicted for the crime a month later and details of the murder shocked the city, especially those on the northwest side. Even though Luetgert was charged with boiling his wife's body, local rumor had it that she had been ground into sausage instead!

Needless to say, sausage sales declined substantially in 1897.

At the trial, Luetgert's mistresses turned on him in the courtroom. Mrs. Agatha Tosch stated that she had asked Luetgert where his wife had gone shortly after she had disappeared. He was in her tavern, gulping down huge quantities of beer at the time. She said that he became pale and very excited and exclaimed: "I don't know! I am as innocent as the southern skies!"

Several jurors were seen shaking their heads. It was obvious to everyone that if Luetgert didn't know what had become of his wife, then he would have no reason to proclaim his innocence for anything.

Mrs. Tosch further told the jury that Luetgert had once told her that he hated his wife. "I could take her and crush her," he said. Another time, she heard him bitterly complain about his need to call a doctor to take care of an ailing Louisa. "If I had waited a little longer," he told her, "the dead, rotten beast would have croaked."

When Luetgert's favorite mistress, Christine Feldt, took the stand, his previously bold demeanor collapsed. He had once told this woman that if she betrayed him, he would not care to go on living. Christine did not feel the same way about Luetgert. She produced all of the poorly written, gushing love letters that he had sent to her and Luetgert blushed when they were read aloud in court.

In her testimony, she stated that Luetgert had given her $4,000 for "safe-keeping" shortly before Louisa's disappearance, but the most damaging evidence came with her production of a bloody knife that Luetgert had also given to her. He left it with her, without explanation, on the day after his wife disappeared.

The trial concluded but ended in a hung jury on October 21 after the jurors failed to agree on a suitable punishment. Some argued for the death penalty, while others voted for life in prison. Only one of the jury members thought that Luetgert might be innocent. A second trial was held and, on February 9, 1898, Luetgert was convicted and sentenced to life imprisonment at Joliet.

Luetgert was taken away to prison, still maintaining his innocence and claiming that he would receive another trial. He was placed in charge of meats in the cold-storage warehouse and officials described him as a model prisoner.

By 1899, though, Luetgert began to speak less and less and often quarreled with the other convicts. He soon became a shadow of his former, blustering persona, fighting for no reason and often babbling incoherently in his cell at night.

But was he talking to himself? Or someone else?

According to legend, Luetgert began to claim that he was talking to Louisa in his cell at night. His dead wife had returned to haunt him, intent on having revenge for her murder. Was she really haunting him or was the "ghost" really just the figment of a rapidly deteriorating mind? Based on the fact that residents of the neighborhood also began reporting seeing Louisa's ghost, one has to wonder if Luetgert was seeing her ghost because he was mentally ill ---- or if the ghost had driven him insane.

Luetgert died in 1900, likely from heart trouble. The coroner who conducted the autopsy also reported that his liver was greatly enlarged and in such a condition of degeneration that "mental strain would have caused his death at any time".

Perhaps Louisa really did visit him after all....

Luetgert was not the only one to suffer in the aftermath of the murder and trial. His attorney, Lawrence Harmon, believed that his client was telling the truth and that he did not kill his wife. He was sure that she had simply disappeared. In fact, Harmon was so convinced of Luetgert's innocence that she spent over $2,000 of his own money and devoted the rest of his life to finding Louisa.

At Luetgert's funeral, Harmon asked to speak. He placed his hand on the sausage-makers coffin and began to read from a type-written letter about which newspaper reporters noted, "the majority of those present appeared to regard the speech as an interesting incident to an entertaining function."

At the conclusion of the letter, which greatly praised Adolph Luetgert as a hard-working, genial man, Harmon became almost overwhelmed with emotion. He dramatically cried out, "I call upon Louisa Luetgert, the missing woman, for whom he suffered without ever uttering an unkind word regarding her, to come forth and remove the unmerited stain from the name of the father of her innocent children..." Harmon paused, looking around and the hundreds of people in the room also looked, as if expecting to see Louisa appear.

Needless to say, nothing happened.

Harmon never stopped believing that Louisa Luetgert was alive and eventually his belief drove him insane. He ended his life in a mental institution.

Attorney Lawrence Harmon
(Chicago Tribune Illustration)

And Louisa, whether she was murdered by her husband or not, reportedly did not rest in peace. Not long after her husband was sent to prison, her ghost began to be seen inside of the Luetgert house. Neighbors claimed to see a woman in a white dress leaning against the mantel in the fireplace. Eventually, the house was rented out but none of the tenants stayed there for long. The place became an object of fear, the yard overgrown with ragweed, and largely deserted.

The sausage factory also stood empty for years, looming over the neighborhood as a grim reminder of the horrors that had visited there. The windows of the place became a target for rocks thrown from the nearby railroad embankment and it often invited forays by the curious and the insane. Only a month after Luetgert's death, a factory caretaker discovered a man in the office, searching the safe and going through the books. The caretaker tried to make the man, later identified as Albert Boyer, leave the place but Boyer produced a hatchet and chased the guard out into the street. A police officer was summoned and he arrested Boyer, asking him to explain his bizarre behavior. "I am looking for Mrs. Luetgert," the man replied, "and I can find her if you leave me alone. She is in the building somewhere and I think she is alive." A court found Boyer insane and he was sent to a mental institution.

In the months that followed his death, Luetgert's business affairs were entangled in legal litigation. The courts finally sorted everything out in August 1900 and a public auction was held for the factory and its grounds. Portions of the property were divided up between several buyers but the Library Bureau Company, which was founded by Dewey Decimal System creator Melvil Dewey, leased the factory itself. The company used it as a workshop and storehouse for its line of library furniture and office supplies. During the renovations, they discarded the infamous vats in the basement.

On Sunday, June 26, 1904, assistant engineer Charles Westerholm was alone in the building and, after starting the building's boilers, climbed the stairs to the fourth floor. He smelled something burning and hurried downstairs to discover that the entire first floor was filled with smoke. Flames were licking up the staircase from the basement. After trying to put out the blaze on his own, Westerholm sounded a fire alarm.

By the time that the horse-drawn fire engines arrived, the flames had climbed to the first floor, spread by the coating of sausage grease that still coated some of the walls and floors. As the fire spread, neighbors panicked and began hauling their prized possessions from their homes. Firefighters manned the 14 engines that arrived on the scene and soon, word spread throughout the north side that the Luetgert factory was on fire. Newspapers estimated that as many as 10,000 people rushed to the scene. The fire department blocked the railroad line next to the building for over an hour and passengers got off the trains and joined the spectators. It was all that the police officers on the scene could do to hold back the crowd.

It took more than three hours to put out the fire. The factory was still standing but everything inside of it had been destroyed. No one had any idea what could have caused the fire but strangely, investigators did believe that it had started in the basement ----- at exactly the spot where Luetgert's middle vat was once located. Fire officials stated: "The source of the fire is a mystery and no one has been able to offer any better explanation than the superstitious folk who have an idea that some supernatural intervention against any commercial enterprise operating at the scene of the murder has been invoked."

Had Louisa's specter returned again?

Despite the damage done to the building's interior, the Library Bureau re-opened its facilities in the former sausage factory. It would go on to change owners many times in the decades that followed. In 1907, a contracting mason purchased the old Luetgert house and moved it from behind the factory to another lot in the neighborhood, hoping to dispel the grim memories ---- and ghost --- attached to it. The part of Hermitage Avenue that intersected with Diversey was closed. By the 1990s, the factory stood empty and crumbling, facing a collection of empty lots that were only broken by the occasional ramshackle frame house. In 1999, though, around the 100th anniversary of the death of Adolph Luetgert, the former sausage factory was converted into loft condominiums and a brand new neighborhood sprang up to replace the aging homes that remained from the days of the Luetgerts. Fashionable brick homes and apartments appeared around the old factory, and rundown taverns were replaced with coffee shops.

Legend has it on the northwest side that Louisa Luetgert still walks. If she does, she probably no longer recognizes the neighborhood where she once lived. They say though, that if you happened to be in this area on May 1, the anniversary of Louisa's death, there is a chance that you might see her lonely specter still roaming the area where she lived and died.

THE CASE OF THE RAGGED STRANGER
Ghosts of One of Chicago's Strangest Murders

There has likely been no other murder case in the country that was as colorfully solved as the Chicago case of the "Ragged Stranger". Over the years, it has been recounted many times in books, in detective magazines and even in a Hollywood movie. There have been a number of different writers who have taken credit for solving the case, and it's likely that this was one time when the press and the police department pooled their resources and brought a killer, a former war hero named Carl Wanderer, to justice.

Wanderer may have been convicted of his crimes but according to legend in the Lincoln Square neighborhood, one of his victims refuses to leave the place where her young life was cut short.

Carl Otto Wanderer was born and raised in Chicago. His parents, German immigrants, taught him the value of a dollar at a young age and, by the time that he was 27, he had saved enough to open a successful butcher shop with his father. His strict upbringing and frugal ways left Wanderer an unhappy and restless young man and in 1916, adventure began to call to him.

The newspapers recounted the raids by Pancho Villa into the southwestern United States and called for volunteers to help pursue the Mexican bandit and his men. Wanderer enlisted in the military and was sent to New Mexico to serve as a cavalry officer under Black Jack Pershing. His experience with the First Illinois Cavalry gave him enough military stature to earn him a promotion to lieutenant with the first units sent to France when the United States entered World War I. He saw action on the western front and returned home, with medals for bravery, in the spring of 1919.

On October 1 of that same year, Wanderer married his sweetheart, a chubby, but attractive, 20 year-old named Ruth Johnson. The couple moved into an apartment shared by Ruth's parents and it was here that any affection that he had for her died. The claustrophobic flat became unbearable, thanks to Ruth's neediness and his nagging mother-in-law, who berated Wanderer about the fact that he didn't have enough money for the couple to get a place of their own. Carl's restlessness got the better of him once more and he began dat-

Carl Wanderer after being brought in for questioning in the case of the "Ragged Stranger", who allegedly murdered his wife in the Lincoln Square neighborhood. (Chicago Daily News)

ing a 16 year-old typist named Julia Schmitt. He often met her at the Riverview Amusement Park while his wife was otherwise engaged.

And then, shortly before Christmas, Ruth happily announced to her husband that she was pregnant. Wanderer would become a father the following summer. Carl accepted the news with dismay and fell into somber, sullen moods. He rarely spoke and avoided coming home. He pondered his options and as it turned out, bided his time, until a plan to rid himself of his problems slowly came to mind.

On June 21, 1920, Ruth and Carl attended an evening performance of a movie called *The Sea Wolf*, a rousing Jack London adventure story, at the Pershing Theater (now the Davis) at Lincoln and Western. As they strolled home afterward, Wanderer later reported seeing a sinister-looking man lurking near Zindt's Drug Store on Lawrence Avenue. According to his story, the man crushed out a cigarette as they passed by and then he followed behind them at a distance.

"Ruth went up ahead of me when we reached the house. She opened the outer door and I heard her fumbling with her keys to the inner door of the hall," Wanderer later told the police. Ruth reached up for the ribbon dangling from the overhead light so that she could find the right key. Carl asked her if she was having trouble and she laughed.

Neither of them noticed the man who followed them into the dark vestibule. The "Ragged Stranger", as this man would come to be known, stepped forward with a gun trained on Ruth. "Don't turn on the light," the man said. "Throw up your hands!"

Before Ruth and Carl could comply with his order, the stranger fired two bullets into Ruth. Wanderer claimed that he heard the man shout out a string of obscenities and he continued to fire. Carl jerked out his own Colt .45 service revolver, which he had started to habitually carry with him, and emptied his clip in the direction of the dark figure. It was later discovered that 14 bullets had been fired in the small vestibule in just several seconds time.

When the smoke cleared, both the stranger and Ruth Wanderer were lying on the floor of the vestibule, sprawled out in pools of blood.

Ruth's mother rushed down to the door to find her daughter had fallen with two bullets in her. Wanderer had gone berserk with rage, smashing his gun and his fists against a man who was lying on the floor. Ruth lived just long enough to utter a few tragic words: "My baby…. My baby is dead."

Detective Sergeant John Norton arrived on the scene just minutes later. By this time, neighbors and onlookers had started to gather around Wanderer, who was covered in the stranger's blood, and Ruth's mother, who cradled her daughter's lifeless body in her arms. Norton pushed his way through. The hulking detective was well-known in the neighborhood, having been shot four times during his celebrated career, and everyone knew that he would get answers quickly in the case. He started off with just one question: Why was Carl Wanderer carrying a gun?

Wanderer had a quick answer: There had been a robbery attempt at his father's butcher shop a short time before, and Carl was carrying his service revolver in case it happened again. He suggested to Norton that perhaps this man could have been involved. A search of the stranger's body turned up just $3.80 and a business card from a traveling circus. There was nothing else on the body, which was taken to Ravenswood Hospital for a check of fingerprints and the inquest. During questioning, Carl decided to embellish his connections with the stranger a little further. He looked familiar to him, Wanderer said, and believed that the man had flirted with Ruth a few nights earlier. She had come home and reported the news to Carl in a near panic, terrified that "the stranger was laying a trap".

The morning editions of the Chicago newspapers jumped all over the story. They told of Wanderer's heroics and exemplary military record, touting his service in New Mexico and during the war. He was a great war hero who had fought to protect America from her enemies, they said, and now this same man had been forced to endure the cold-blooded murder of his wife and unborn child. It was a heartless and horrible crime and the public reacted with shock and outrage.

Carl Wanderer was awarded the status of a hero who had defended the honor of his wife, even though the end result had been tragic. The public expected to see him charged with nothing more than justifiable homicide

Two of the cops involved in the Carl Wanderer Case:

(Left) Detective John Norton

(Right) Summerdale Police Lieutenant Mike Loftus

in the murder of the "Ragged Stranger". He deserved to be left alone to grieve for his family, they believed, and this should be the end of the story.

But little did they know --- the story of the "Ragged Stranger" was just getting started.

Detective John Norton, along with help from legendary crime reporter Harry Romanoff and his editor at the *Chicago Herald-Examiner*, Walter Howey, began to ask some hard questions about Wanderer's story of the murders.

To start with, there was the matter of the two guns that had been used. Both of them were big .45 caliber automatics. Carl Wanderer's gun was explained in that it was his service pistol --- but what about the matching weapon owned by the stranger? Howey and Norton could not understand how he could afford such an expensive sidearm. A man who was down on his luck could have easily hocked the weapon and made a decent amount of money. This should have been preferable to risking a street robbery. It didn't make sense so Romanoff sent a telegram to the Colt firearms company that contained the serial number of the stranger's gun. A reply soon came back. The gun had first been sold in 1913 to Von Lengerke & Antoine Sporting Goods Store in Chicago. The reporter checked with the store and found that Peter Hoffman, a telephone repairman who lived on Crawford Avenue, had purchased the gun.

The next day, Romanoff went to see Hoffman and discovered that he had sold the gun to his brother-in-law several years before. The brother-in-law's name was Fred Wanderer --- he was Carl's cousin. Stunned, the reporter confronted Fred Wanderer with the information about where his gun had ended up. Fred admitted that he had gotten a

Legendary Chicago crime reporter Harry Romanoff

gun from Peter Hoffman but he had loaned it to his cousin, Carl, on June 21 and didn't have it anymore. Suddenly, Fred realized that this had been the day when Ruth had been killed. When this occurred to him, he was so shocked that he fainted.

Romanoff reported the problems with the gun to Detective Norton and Summerdale Police Lieutenant Mike Loftus. Carl Wanderer was brought in for questioning and was confronted with what had been discovered about the gun. Wanderer shrugged it off. Sure, he had been carrying Fred's gun, he told detectives, the other one, which had been used by the "Ragged Stranger", was mistakenly identified as his. As it turned out, this was a possibility. A check with the Colt Company revealed that the other gun had been part of a massive shipment of weapons sent to military training camps during the war. The whole thing, Carl assured them, was all an innocent mistake.

Loftus and Romanoff were not convinced.

While Carl was delayed at the police station, the two men went to the Wanderer's house to speak with Ruth's mother. While Loftus engaged the woman in conversation, Romanoff searched through Wanderer's bedroom and found incriminating photos of Carl and portions of love letters that had been written to Julia Schmitt, the young woman he had been seeing without Ruth's knowledge. When Julia was tracked down, she unraveled Carl's story and the motive for the murder became clear. Carl Wanderer had wanted to get rid of his wife ---- and arranged to have someone carry out the crime.

When confronted with this new information, Wanderer finally confessed.

Carl had grown to hate his wife, he told detectives, and longed to be free of her so that he could marry Julia. He needed to take blame away from himself, so he began hanging around seedy saloons until he met Al Watson (whose real name may have been Bernard T. Ryan), a Canadian ex-soldier who was living in a flophouse on Madison Street, Chicago's skid row. Wanderer told Watson that he was trying to win back his wife's affections and wanted to seem like a hero to her. He would pay him $5 down and $5 on delivery to carry out a robbery. Carl would hand Watson a gun when the couple went into the dark vestibule and then he would slug Carl with it. Wanderer would seem to fight the man off and Watson would run away, restoring Ruth's faith in his hero status.

Watson saw it as a harmless way to make a few bucks so he agreed. That night when Watson came into the vestibule though, Carl did not hand him a gun. Instead, he cocked both weapons and fired at both Ruth and Watson at the same time. After they had fallen, he fired several more shots to make sure they were dead and then went into his "avenging husband act" for Ruth's mother, who he knew would rush to the scene.

Carl Wanderer was twice indicted and twice convicted, once for the murder of Ruth Johnson Wanderer and once for the death of Al Watson. After his first trial, Wanderer was sentenced to serve 20 years, which so outraged editor Walter Howey that he used the editorial might of his widely read newspaper to keep the story alive and to demand a new trial. Public outrage resulted in a second trial --- and a death sentence--- for Wanderer.

While Carl was in jail, awaiting the hangman, he became a favorite subject for doctors, who tried to discover whether or not he was insane when he planned his wife's death, and for reporters, who kept milking a good story. Two of Wanderer's favorite visitors

Editor Walter Howey had been an important part of reporter Harry Romanoff's investigation of the case and he used the power of his newspaper to see that Carl Wanderer was tried a second time for murder.

were Ben Hecht and Charley MacArthur, Chicago's most famous writers from the colorful and sensational journalism era of the early 1900s. They were covering Carl's story for their respective newspapers and visited him often, playing poker with him and becoming quite chummy. They even convinced Carl to read two letters that they had written, hilariously attacking their bosses, from the gallows. The newsmen didn't remember until the last minute that Carl's hands and feet would be bound when he was executed so he couldn't read the letters. They asked him to croon a rendition of "Old Pal, Why Don't You Answer Me?" moments before the drop instead.

On the day of his hanging, Carl was brought to the gallows and to the surprise of everyone present, save for Hecht and MacArthur, Wanderer began to sing. The hangman came forward after the first chorus but Wanderer warned him away with a shake of his head. After the second chorus, even though Carl was still singing, the black shroud was placed over his head. When the song finally finished, he was asked if he had anything to say.

"Christ have mercy on my….", Carl Wanderer began, but never finished his plea. The trap sprung open and Carl shot downwards until the rope snapped tight and instantly killed him.

Charley MacArthur had the last word. He turned to his friend Ben Hecht and said with a sigh: "You know, Ben, that son-of-a-bitch would have been a hell of a song plugger."

The last, broken sentence on the gallows was the last that was ever heard from Carl Otto Wanderer --- but the same cannot be said for his wife, Ruth. The legends of the Lincoln Square neighborhood have it that the house where the ill-fated couple once lived, and where Ruth died, remains haunted by her spirit to this day.

This former residence, located at 4732 North Campbell Avenue, is just a half block from Lawrence and two blocks west of Western Avenue. The place has changed much since 1920. It's been remodeled several times and the number on the house is no longer visible, an oversight that was likely intentional. These days, a wooden gate protects the vestibule leading to the house. It was here where Ruth was heartlessly gunned down.

For many years, the murders that occurred here were widely discussed and few could pass this house without pointing out, often with trembling hands, the place where the murders occurred. As time passed though, and the crime slipped from the public consciousness and took its place among the many other murders in the city, the story of Ruth Wanderer began to fade.

Soon after, stories of the haunting began.

Sources state that, in the years after World War II, regular accounts began to be heard about the sounds of a woman's screams that came from the vestibule of the North Campbell Avenue house. The screams, neighbors claimed, were those of Ruth Wanderer, perhaps re-living her final moments --- perhaps just as she realized that her husband intended to kill her. These same sources relate that the screams still come occasionally even today.

But why does Ruth Wanderer still haunt this place? And why did the spirit wait so long to make her presence known? Most believe the answer to this is that she simply wants people to remember her story, to remember that she once lived and, most heartbreaking of all, to remember the life of her child, who was never allowed to live at all.

CHICAGO'S "THRILL KILLERS"
Leopold & Loeb's Murder for Fun

On an afternoon in May 1924, the sons of two of Chicago's wealthiest and most illustrious families drove to the Harvard School for boys in Kenwood and kidnapped a young boy named Bobby Franks. Their plan was to carry out the "perfect murder". It was a scheme so devious that only two men of superior intellect, such as their own, could accomplish it. These two men were Richard Loeb and Nathan Leopold. They were the privileged heirs of well-known Chicago families who had embarked on a life of crime for fun and for the pure thrill

Chicago's Infamous "Thrill Killers"

(Left) Richard Loeb (Right) Nathan Leopold

These two wealthy young men believed that they were above the law and could murder without consequences. They did so, never believing they would be caught.

of it. They were also a pair of sexual deviants who considered themselves to be "brilliant" ---- a claim that would later lead to their downfall.

Leopold and Loeb have earned a place of infamy in the annals of Chicago crime and will forever be remembered for a horrific murder that left more than one ghost behind.

Nathan Leopold, or "Babe" as his friends knew him, had been born in 1906 and from an early age had a number of sexual encounters, starting with the advances of a governess and culminating in a relationship with Richard Loeb. He was an excellent student with a genius IQ and was only 18 when he graduated from the University of Chicago. He was an expert ornithologist and botanist and spoke nine languages fluently. Like many future killers, his family life was totally empty and devoid of control. His mother had died when he was young and his father gave him little personal attention. He compensated for his lack of fatherly direction with expensive presents and huge sums of money. Leopold was given $3,000 to tour Europe before entering Harvard Law School, a car of his own and a $125-a-week allowance.

Richard Loeb was the son of the Vice President of Sears & Roebuck and while he was as wealthy as his friend was, Loeb was merely a clever young man and far from brilliant. He was, however, quite handsome and charming and what he lacked in intelligence, he more than made up for in arrogance. Both of the young men were obsessed with perfection. To them, perfection meant being above all others, which their station in life endorsed. They felt they were immune to laws and criticism, which meant that they were perfect.

Loeb fancied himself a master criminal detective but his dream was to commit the perfect crime. With his more docile companion in tow, Loeb began developing what he believed to be the perfect scheme. He also constantly searched for ways to control others. Not long after the two became friends, Leopold attempted to initiate a sexual relationship with Loeb. At first, he spurned the other's advances but then he offered a compromise. He would engage in sex with Leopold, but only under the condition that the other boy begin a career in crime with him. Leopold agreed and they signed a formal pact to that affect.

Over the course of the next four years, they committed robbery, vandalism, arson and petty theft, but this was not enough for Loeb. He dreamed of something bigger. A murder, he convinced his friend, would be their greatest intellectual challenge.

They worked out a plan during the next seven months. It was to kidnap someone and make it appear as though they were being held for ransom. They would write the ransom note on a typewriter that had been stolen from Loeb's old fraternity house at the University of Michigan, and make the family of the victim believe that he would be returned to them.

Leopold and Loeb had no such plans though ---- their only plan was to kill their captive as soon as they could ensnare him in their trap.

In May 1924, they rented a car and drove to a hardware store at 43rd and Cottage Avenue, where they purchased some rope, a chisel and a bottle of hydrochloric acid. They would garrote their victim; stab him with the chisel, if necessary; and then destroy his identity with the acid.

The next day, they met at Leopold's home and wrapped the handle of the chisel with adhesive tape so that it offered a better grip. They also gathered together a blanket and strips of cloth that could be used to wrap up and bind their victim. Leopold also placed a pair of wading boots in the car because the boys planned to deposit the body in the swamps near Wolf Lake, located south of the city. They also packed loaded pistols for each of them and looked over the already typed ransom note that demanded $10,000 in cash. Neither of them needed the money, but they felt the note would convince the authorities that the kidnappers were lowly criminals and would deflect attention from people like Leopold and Loeb.

They had only overlooked one thing ---- a victim.

They began discussing their list of possibilities. They first considered killing Loeb's younger brother, Tommy, but they discarded that idea. It was not because Tommy was a family member but only because it would have been hard for Loeb to collect the ransom money without arousing suspiscion. They also considered killing William Deutsch, grandson of millionaire and philanthropist Julius Rosenwald, but also dismissed this idea because Rosenwald was the president of Sears & Roebuck and Loeb's father's immediate boss. They also came close to agreeing to kill their friend, Richard Rubel, who regularly had lunch with them. He was ruled out, not because he was a good friend to them, but because they knew his father was cheap and would never agree to pay the ransom.

They could not agree on anyone but did feel that their victim should be small, so that he could be easily subdued. With that in mind, they decided to check out the Harvard Preparatory School, which was located across the street from Leopold's home. They decided to drive around the school and look for a likely victim. They climbed into their rental car and began to drive. As they searched, Leopold noticed some boys near Ellis Avenue and Loeb pointed out one of them that he recognized ---- 14-year-old Bobby Franks. He was the son of the millionaire Jacob Franks, and a distant cousin of Loeb.

Chosen by chance, he would make the perfect victim for the perfect crime.

Bobby was already acquainted with his killers. He had played tennis with Loeb several times and he happily climbed into the car. Although, at their trial, both denied being the actu-

Bobby Franks, the young victim of Loeb and Leopold. Shown here in a photograph that was taken just a short time before he accepted the fated car ride with the two young men.

167

al killer, Leopold was at the wheel and Loeb was in the back, gripping the murder weapon tightly in his hands. They drove him to within a few blocks of the Franks residence in Hyde Park when Loeb suddenly grabbed the boy, stuffed a gag in his mouth and smashed his skull four times with a chisel. The rope had been forgotten. Bobby collapsed onto the floor of the car, unconscious and bleeding badly.

When Leopold saw the blood spurting from Bobby's head, he cried out, "Oh God, I didn't know it would be like this!"

Loeb ignored him, intent on his horrific task. Even though Bobby was unconscious, he stuffed his mouth with rags and wrapped him up in the heavy blanket. The boy continued to bleed for a time and then died.

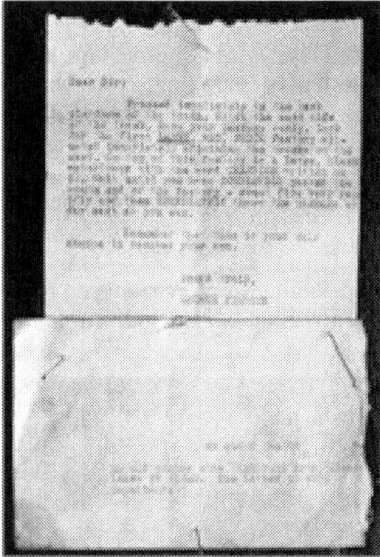

A Chicago Daily News Photograph of the ransom letter that Loeb and Leopold sent to Bobby's father. The letter was typed on a machine that was easily traced to Richard Loeb's old fraternity house.

With the excitement of the actual murder over with, Leopold and Loeb casually drove south, stopped for lunch and then Leopold called his father and left a message for him father that he would be arriving home late that night. They continued driving, waiting for darkness to fall and later stopped for another meal. Eventually, they ended up near a culvert along the Pennsylvania Railroad tracks. It emptied into a swamp along Wolf Lake.

Leopold put on his hip boots and carried Bobby's body to the culvert. They had stripped all of the clothes from his body and then, after dunking the boy's head underwater to make sure that he was dead, they poured acid on his face in hopes that he would be harder to identify. Leopold then struggled to shove the naked boy into the pipe and took his coat off to make the work easier.

Unknown to the killers, a pair of eyeglasses were in the pocket of Leopold's coat and they fell out into the water when he removed it. This would be the undoing of the "perfect crime."

After pushing the body as far into the pipe as he could, Leopold sloshed out of the mud toward the car, where Loeb waited for him. The killers believed that the body would not be found until long after the ransom money had been received. With darkness falling though, Leopold failed to notice the small foot that was dangling out of the end of the culvert.

They drove back to the city and parked the rental car (which had been borrowed under a false name) next to a large apartment building. Bobby's blood had soaked through the blanket that he had been wrapped in and had stained the automobile's upholstery. The blanket was hidden in a nearby yard and they burned Bobby's clothing after they walked back to Leopold's house. Here, they typed out the Franks' address on the already prepared ransom note. After this, they hurried back to the car and drove to Indiana, where they buried the shoes that Bobby had worn along with everything that he had on him that was made from metal, including his belt buckle and class pin from the prep school.

Finally, their "perfect crime" carried out, they drove back to Leopold's home and spent the rest of the evening drinking and playing cards. Around midnight, they telephoned the Franks' home and told Mr. Franks that he could soon expect a ransom demand for the return of his son. "Tell the police and he will be killed at once," they told Mr. Franks. "You will receive a ransom note with instructions tomorrow."

The next morning, the ransom note, signed with the name "George Johnson", was delivered to the Franks, demanding $10,000 in old, unmarked $10 and $20 bills. The money was to be placed in a cigar box that should be wrapped in white paper and sealed with wax. After its arrival, the Franks' lawyer notified the police, who promised no publicity.

Meanwhile, Leopold and Loeb continued with the elaborate game that they had concocted. They took the bloody blanket to an empty lot, burned it, and then drove to Jackson Park, where Loeb tore the keys out of his stolen typewriter. He threw them into one lagoon in the park and the typewriter into another. Later in the afternoon, Loeb took a train ride to Michigan City, leaving a note addressed to the Franks in the telegram slot of a stationary desk in the train's observation car. On the envelope, he had written: "Should anyone else find this note, please leave it alone. The letter is very important."

He got off the train at 63rd Street, as it returned to the city, and rejoined the waiting Leopold. Andy Russo, a yardman, found the letter and sent it to the Franks.

However, by the time that the letter arrived, railroad maintenance men had already stumbled upon the body of Bobby Franks. The police notified Jacob Franks and he sent his brother-in-law to identify the body. He confirmed that it was Bobby and the newspapers went into overdrive, producing "extra" editions that were on the street in a matter of hours.

One of the largest manhunts in the history of Chicago began. Witnesses and suspects were picked up in huge numbers and the "perfect crime" began to unravel. Despite their "mental prowess" and "high intelligence", Leopold and Loeb were quickly caught. Leopold had dropped his eyeglasses near the spot where the body had been hidden and police had traced the prescription to Albert Coe & Co., who stated that only three pair of glasses with such unusual frames had been sold. One pair belonged to an attorney, who was away in Europe, another to a woman, and the third pair had been sold to Nathan Leopold.

The boys were brought in for questioning and began supplying alibis for the time when Bobby had gone missing. They claimed they had been with two girlfriends, "May and Edna". The police asked them to produce the women but the killers could not. Leopold claimed that he had apparently lost the glasses at Wolf Lake during a recent bird-hunting trip. The detectives noted that it had rained a few days before but the glasses were clean. Could Leopold explain this? He couldn't.

Then, two novice reporters, Al Goldstein and Jim Mulroy, obtained letters that Richard Loeb had written with the stolen typewriter --- which had already been found in Jackson Park. The letters matched the type on the ransom note, which was a perfect match for the typewriter that Leopold had "borrowed" from his fraternity house the year before.

Loeb broke first. He said that the murder was a lark, an experiment in crime to see if the "perfect murder" could be carried out. He then condemned, in a long speech, Leopold's perverted sex habits. He also denied being the killer and claimed that he had driven the car while Leopold had slashed Bobby Franks to death.

Hearing this, Leopold told the police that he had been the driver of the car and even posed, with the police detectives, in the driver's seat as if this proved his story was true.

The boys were brought together and were convinced to tell the truth. Loeb had been the killer, Leopold had driven the car but both of them had planned the crime together --- they were both guilty of Bobby Franks' murder.

The people of Chicago, and the rest of the nation, were stunned and soon were crying for the blood of the two killers. It was fully expected that the two would receive a death sentence for the callous and cold-blooded crime. Then, in stepped Clarence Darrow.

After the confession, Loeb's family disowned him but Leopold's father turned to Darrow, America's most famous defense attorney, in hopes that he might save his son. He literally got down on his knees and begged Darrow to take the case. For $100,000, he agreed to seek the best possible verdict that he could, which in this case was life in prison. "While the State is

Famed attorney Clarence Darrow

169

A Chicago Daily News photograph taken during the trial. Loeb and Leopold are near the center of the photo and Darrow is just to the left of the man in front with his head down.

trying Loeb and Leopold," Darrow said. "I will try capital punishment."

Darrow would have less trouble with the case than he would with his clients, who constantly clowned around and hammed it up in the courtroom. The newspaper photographers frequently snapped photos of them smirking and laughing in court and the public, already turned against them, became even more hostile toward the "poor little rich boys".

Darrow was fighting an uphill battle but he brought out every trick in the book and used shameless tactics during the trial. He declared the boys to be insane. Leopold, he said, was a dangerous schizophrenic. They weren't criminals, he railed, they just couldn't help themselves. After this weighty proclamation, Darrow actually began to weep. The trial became a landmark (and some say a bad one) in criminal law. He then began to offer a detailed description of what would happen to the boys if they were hanged, providing a graphic image of bodily functions and physical pain. Darrow even turned to the prosecutor and invited him to personally perform the execution.

Darrow's horrifying description had a marked effect on the courtroom and, especially, on the defendants. Loeb was observed to shudder and Leopold got so hysterical that he had to be taken out of the courtroom. Darrow then wept for the defendants, wept for Bobby Franks ----- and then wept for defendants and victims everywhere. The master manipulator won the case! The defendants were given life in prison for Bobby Frank's murder and an additional 99 years for his kidnapping. The judge stated that neither of them was ever to be paroled, and they were to be kept separated for the rest of their lives.

Ironically, after all of that, Darrow only managed to get $40,000 of his fee from Leopold's father. He got this after a seven-month wait and the threat of a lawsuit.

Leopold and Loeb were sent to Stateville Prison, just outside of Joliet, and as soon as they arrived, the judge's orders were ignored. The "thrill killers" lived in luxury and money was obviously changing hands. Each enjoyed a private cell, books, a desk, a filing cabinet and even pet birds. They also showered away from the other prisoners and took their meals, which were prepared to order, in the officer's lounge. They were also allowed any number of unsupervised visitors and were allowed to keep their own gardens. The doors to their cells were usually left open and they had passes to visit one another at any time.

According to reports, Loeb was the greatest offender of his purchased luxuries at Stateville. He strolled about the prison "as if he owned the place", reports said, and he became feared as a brutal prison rapist. He terrified weaker prisoners and was avoided by the population at large. The guards, as they had been bribed to do, turned their backs on his actions. At some point, Loeb became interested in a young prisoner named James Day and he began offering him extra food, bootleg liquor and cigarettes, which have always been considered "prison currency". Loeb hounded the man, even though Day spurned his advances, and then one day in January 1936,

Day reached his limits.

"He was always after me," Day later stated. "I became desperate. I had to get him off my back."

One morning after breakfast, Day asked Loeb if he could talk with him. Loeb was eating breakfast with Leopold at the time and he said that he would soon be going to take a bath and Day could wait for him in the bathroom. Day waited for him and when he arrived, pretended that he was going to finally give in to Loeb's desire for him. Loeb, who had a straight razor in his hand, instructed Day to take off his clothes and the other man did what he asked. However, when Loeb turned his back, Day attacked him. He managed to get the razor from his hand and turned the blade back on Loeb. He cut and slashed him so many times that he lost all comprehension of the damage that he had done. Loeb, covered in blood, managed to make it out of the bathroom and he collapsed in the hallway. He was found bleeding in the corridor and he died a short time later. It was discovered that Day had slashed him 56 times with the razor!

Loeb's mother rushed to the prison with the family doctor when she heard what had happened and Leopold waited anxiously by his friend's bedside. Loeb opened his eyes only one time. "I think I'm going to make it," he murmured and then moments later, he died.

When Clarence Darrow was told of Loeb's death, he slowly shook his head. "He is better off dead," the great attorney said. "For him, death is an easier sentence."

Leopold lived on in prison for many years and was said to have made many adjustments to his character and some would even say that he was rehabilitated completely. Even so, appeals for his parole were turned down three times. Finally, in 1958, the poet Carl Sandburg, who even went as far as to offer Leopold a room in his own home, pleaded his fourth appeal. Finally, in March of that year, he was released.

"I am a broken old man," Leopold said when he was paroled. "I want a chance to find redemption for myself and help others."

He was allowed to go to Puerto Rico, where he worked among the poor and married a widow named Trudi Feldman Garcia de Quevedo, who owned a flower shop. He went on to write a book about his experiences called *Life Plus 99 Years* and continued to be hounded by the press for his role in the "perfect murder" that he had committed decades before. He stated that he would be "haunted" by what he had done for the rest of his life.

Nathan Leopold died of heart failure on August 30, 1971, bringing an end to one of the most harrowing stories in the history of the city.

But was this really the end?

Many say that it was not, thanks to the fact that at least two restless ghosts from this case continued to walk for many years after their lives came to an end. The spirit with the most horrible connection to the case was that of Bobby Franks, who took nearly 50 years to find peace.

During this time, visitors to Rosehill Cemetery, on the north side of Chicago, often reported seeing the ghost of a young boy standing among the stones and mausoleums in the Jewish section of the graveyard. It is here where the Franks family mausoleum is located, although you will not find its location on any maps of the cemetery and employees are instructed not to point it out to curiosity-seekers. Even so, this tomb can be discovered within the confines of the beautiful burial ground and, starting in the 1920s, maintenance workers and visitors alike encountered the ghostly boy. Many came to believe that it was the ghost of Bobby Franks, unable to rest in the wake of his bloody and violent death.

The Franks family mausoleum in Rosehill Cemetery

The boy was often seen wandering here but only from a distance. Whenever he was approached, the apparition would vanish. These sightings continued for years but, eventually, they seemed to fade away. It's been noted that the encounters ended at nearly the exact same time that Nathan Leopold died in Puerto Rico. Could there be a connection between these two events? It certainly seems possible; perhaps Bobby Frank can now find peace on the other side.

The other ghost of the Leopold and Loeb case, possessing the most tenuous connection to the story, continues to walk today. This is the spirit of master attorney Clarence Darrow.

Darrow was often known in the circles of the law as "the attorney for the damned" because he would take on cases that no one else would touch. He had been born in the farmlands of Ohio in 1857 and his formal education ended after the equivalent of one year in high school. He continued to study law books at night, however, and eventually saved up enough money to attend law school.

He was admitted to the bar in 1878 and later became a well-known corporation lawyer, even though his sympathies were always with the workingman. In 1894, he rejected the business world to defend notorious labor leader Eugene V. Debs for his connection with the Pullman Strike. He also defended radical labor leader Big Bill Haywood on murder charges in 1906 but, in 1910, he was forced to accept a guilty plea on behalf of labor defendants John and James McNamara for bombing a Los Angeles newspaper office. The decision had a shattering effect on the western labor movement. The unions refused to pay his $50,000 fee and the prosecution, spurred on by corporate interests, charged Darrow with jury tampering. Darrow beat the charges but he never took on another labor-related case.

Darrow continued to plead criminal cases and, in 1924, he took on his most famous case with the trial of "thrill killers" Leopold and Loeb. In 1894, Darrow had taken on the case of a convicted murderer who was appealing to a higher court. Darrow lost and the man, Robert Prendergast, was executed. He was the first --- and the last --- Darrow client to be sentenced to death. Darrow would go on to represent more than 50 accused murderers, many of whom, like Loeb and Leopold, were undoubtedly guilty but none of them ever received a death sentence.

During the Leopold and Loeb trial, Darrow earned his place in history as one of the greatest geniuses to ever serve as an attorney. He bypassed a jury trial and focused all of his attentions on the judge, who he managed to sway away from what should have been a certain death penalty decision.

The following year, in 1925, Darrow won worldwide acclaim for his role in the so-called "Scopes Monkey Trial", in which he dueled with former presidential candidate William Jennings Bryan over the theory of evolution. Darrow defended teacher John Scopes in Dayton, Ohio for illegally teaching evolution in a state school. The trial was the first to be covered on the radio. Scopes was eventually convicted, a decision that was inevitable given the time and place, and fined $100 but Darrow clearly won the case against Bryan in the world of public opinion.

During his days of greatest fame, Darrow was living in Chicago's Hyde Park neighborhood on the south side of the city. Living close to Jackson Park and the Museum of Science and Industry, both of which had been constructed for the World's Columbian Exposition in 1893, Darrow often liked to stroll through the area. One spot in the park that he liked in particular was a bridge that overlooked a winding lagoon behind the museum. He often referred to it as having "the prettiest view on Earth" and it would later be named in his honor.

Darrow was always an agnostic when it came to God, as evidenced by his views during the Scopes Monkey Trial, but he had a strong belief in the afterlife. He told his son that, when he died, he wanted to be cremated and have his ashes scattered over the waters of the lagoon in Jackson Park. Legend has it that he also told his son that if there were a way to do so, he would return to the bridge after his death and give some sign from the other side.

Many have wondered why Darrow would have made such a pronouncement but in those days of the late 1920s and early 1930s, the Spiritualist movement was in the midst of its greatest revival. The movement, which is centered around the idea that the dead can communicate with the living, was often featured in newspapers of the time and had attracted the interest of many authors and celebrities of the day. Famous people, like illusionist Harry Houdini, had very publicly made similar plans of trying to communicate with the living after death and perhaps Darrow was inspired by this.

On March 13, 1936, a few days after his death, Darrow's final request was carried out. A group of family and friends gathered on the bridge behind the museum and after a brief ceremony, his ashes were scattered out over the waters of the lagoon. The following year, on the anniversary of Darrow's funeral, most of this same group returned to the bridge and recited speeches and poems in honor of the famous attorney. They waited anxiously for Darrow's promised "sign from the other side" but nothing happened that year, nor the year after that.

The March 13 gathering became an annual event and as time passed, and the original group died out, new revelers came along to take their place. The event became a celebration of the life and death of Clarence Darrow.

No manifestation of Darrow has ever appeared during these gatherings but could the ghost of the great lawyer be appearing at other times instead?

There are many who believe that the phantom has, and does, appear somewhat regularly on a veranda that spans the back of the Museum of Science and Industry. This wide stone area is at the bottom of the steps leading into the rear entrance of the museum and the apparition that appears here is only visible from the site of the Clarence Darrow Memorial Bridge, just across the lagoon. The ghost is reportedly seen dressed in a suit, hat and overcoat and bears a striking resemblance to the attorney. The figure is reported to stand and stare out across the water before disappearing.

Over the years, it has been sighted by literally dozens of people, although none of them have ever gotten close enough to the specter to see it clearly. Whenever it is approached ---- usually by would-be "ghost busters" who are intent on capturing it somehow --- the figure simply vanishes.

Is this the ghost of Clarence Darrow, finally making his presence known from a world beyond our own? There are no other ghostly manifestations connected to this site and certainly none that look like Darrow did in his last days, as he strolled through the park admiring the "prettiest view on Earth."

If it is Darrow, why does his ghost still walk here? Is it because of a promise to return that he had somehow managed to keep or his ties to business in this world that he never managed to complete? We'll never know for sure but one thing that we can say is that this Chicago legend will forever remain a part of the city's long history of crime and punishment.

FAREWELL TO THE GRIMES SISTERS

Have you ever run across a place that just seems to be bad?

Nearly ten years ago, I had the chance to visit such a place for the first time. My "bad place" was a roadway in the southwestern suburb of Willow Springs known as German Church Road. Much has changed here in recent years. New subdivisions have replaced heavy stands of trees, and streetlights now chase away the darkness that once lingered over the old road. I still remember my first visit to German Church Road though; particularly to a low point in the road that once crossed Devil's Creek. This was a spot in the road where the shadows hung long and low and where a chill always seemed to be in the air.

Many have said that this roadway is haunted and, frankly, I can believe that it is. Along this road is where the victims of one of the most horrific unsolved crimes in Chicago history were found.

It was a heartbreaking event that has become one of the region's most puzzling mysteries. It shattered the innocence of Chicago forever and, according to those who have experienced it, left a chilling impression behind.

On December 28, 1956, Patricia Grimes, 13, and Barbara Grimes, 15, left their home at 3624 South Damon Avenue and headed for the Brighton Theater, only a mile away. The girls were both avid fans of Elvis Presley and on that night were on their way to see his film *Love Me Tender* for the eleventh and final time. The

Grimes Sisters Murder Site -- Then & Now

The site on German Church Road where the bodies of the Grimes Sisters were discovered in Jaunary 1956. (Below) The same roadway and site as it looks today.

girls were recognized in the popcorn line at 9:30 p.m. and then seen on an eastbound Archer Avenue bus at 11:00 p.m. After that, things are less certain but this may have been the last time they were ever seen alive. The two sisters were missing for 25 days before their naked and frozen bodies were found along German Church Road, just outside the small town of Willow Springs.

The girl's mother, Loretta Grimes, expected the girls to be home by 11:45 p.m. but was already growing uneasy when they had not arrived 15 minutes prior to that. At midnight, she sent her daughter Theresa, 17, and her son Joey, 14, to the bus stop at 35th and Hoyne to watch for them. After three buses had stopped and had failed to discharge their sisters, Theresa and Joey returned home without them. They never saw the girls again but strangely, others claimed to.

The last reported sightings of the two girls came from classmates who spotted them at Angelo's Restaurant at 3551 South Archer Avenue, more than 24 hours after their reported disappearance. How accurate this sighting was is unknown, as a railroad conductor also reported them on a train near the Great Lakes Naval Training Center in north suburban Glenview around the same time. A security guard on the northwest side offered directions to two girls he believed were the Grimes sisters on the morning of the 29th, hours after they disappeared. On January 1, both girls were allegedly identified as passengers aboard a CTA bus on Damen Avenue. During the week that followed, they were reported in Englewood by George Pope, a night clerk at the Unity Hotel on West 61st Street, who refused them a room because of their ages. Three employees at a Kresge drug store believed they saw the girls listening to Elvis Presley songs at the record counter on January 3.

The police theorized that the girls had run away but Loretta Grimes refused to believe it. She was sure that the girls had gone missing against their will but the authorities were not convinced. Regardless, it became the greatest missing persons hunt in Chicago police history. Even Elvis Presley, in a statement issued from Graceland, asked the girls to come home and ease their mother's worries. The plea went unanswered.

More strangeness would be reported before the bodies of the girls were found. A series of ransom letters, that were later discovered to have come from a mental patient, took Mrs. Grimes to Milwaukee on January 12. She was escorted by F.B.I. agents and instructed to sit in a downtown Catholic church with $1,000 on the bench beside her. The letter promised that Barbara Grimes would walk in to retrieve the money and then leave to deliver it to the kidnapper. She and her sister would then be released. Needless to say, no one ever came and Mrs. Grimes was left sitting for hours to contemplate her children's fate. By that time, it's likely that the bodies of the two girls were already lying along German Church Road, covered with snow.

But if that's true, then how can we explain the two telephone calls that were received by Wallace and Ann Tollstan on January 14? Their daughter, Sandra, was a classmate of Patricia Grimes at the St. Maurice School and they received the two calls around midnight. The first call jolted Mr. Tollstan out of his sleep but when he picked up the receiver, the person on the other end of the line did not speak. He waited a few moments and then hung up. About 15 minutes later, the phone rang again and this time, Ann Tollstan answered it. The voice on the other end of the line asked "Is that you, Sandra? Is Sandra there?" But before Mrs. Tollstan could bring her daughter to the phone, the caller had clicked off the line. Ann Tollstan was convinced that the frightened voice on the telephone had belonged to Patricia Grimes!

And that wasn't the only strange happening to mark the period when the girls were missing. On January 15, a police switchboard operator received a call from a man who refused to identify himself but who insisted that the girl's bodies would be found in a park at 81st and Wolf. He claimed that this revelation had come to him in a dream and he hung up. The call was traced to Green's Liquor Market on South Halsted and the caller was discovered to be Walter Kranz, a 53 year-old steamfitter. He was taken into custody after the bodies were found on January 22 --- less than a mile from the park that Kranz said he dreamed of. He became one of the numerous people who were questioned by the police and then released.

The search for the Grimes Sisters ended on January 22, 1957, when construction worker Leonard Prescott was driving south on German Church Road early one morning. He spotted what appeared to be two discarded clothing store mannequins lying next to a guardrail, a short distance from the road. A few feet away, the ground dropped off to Devil's Creek below. Unsure of what he had seen, Prescott nervously brought his wife to the spot, and then they drove to the local police station. His wife, Marie Prescott, was so upset by the sight of the bodies that she had to be carried back to their car.

Once investigators realized the "mannequins" were actually bodies, they soon discovered that they were the Grimes Sisters. Barbara Grimes lay on her left side with her legs slightly drawn up toward her body. Her head was covered by the body of her sister, who had been thrown onto her back with her head turned sharply to the right. It looked as if they had been discarded there by someone so cold and heartless that he saw the girls as nothing more than refuse to be tossed away on a lonely roadside.

The officials in charge, Cook County Sheriff Joseph D. Lohman and Harry Glos, an aggressive investigator for Coroner Walter E. McCarron, surmised that the bodies had been lying there for several days, perhaps as far back as January 9. This had been the date of the last heavy snowfall and the frigid temperatures that followed the storm had preserved the bodies in a state that resembled how they looked at the moment of death. As the newspapers broke the story on the morning of January 23, both the press and the investigators in the case began to draw connections between the murders of the Grimes sisters and the Schuessler-Peterson mur-

Aggressive investigator Harry Glos. He would eventually be fired for revealing too much about the case and would continue the investigation at his own expense.

ders, which had occurred under similar circumstances in October 1955.

Those murders had sent the region into a panic and the horror felt by parents in Chicagoland was only compounded by the disappearance of the Grimes sisters and the subsequent discovery of their bodies. Like the Schuesslers and Bobby Peterson, the girls had been found naked and dumped in a secluded, wooded area. And also, like the murders less than two years before (still unsolved at the time), the bodies had looked to be mannequins by those who discovered them.

The bodies discovered along German Church Road sent the various police departments into action. A short time after they were found, more than 160 officers from Chicago, Cook County, the Forest Preserve and five south suburban police departments began combing the woods -- and tramping all over whatever evidence may have been there! Between the officers, the reporters, the medical examiners and everyone else, the investigation was already botched. Despite the claims of Lt. Joseph Morris, the head of a special police unit investigating the Schuessler-Peterson murders, who said "We're not going to repeat some of the mistakes that we made the last time", things were already off to a bad start.

And the investigation became even more confusing in the days to come. The bodies were removed from the scene and were taken to the Cook County Morgue, where they would be stored until they thawed out and an autopsy became possible. Before they were removed though, both police investigators and reporters commented on the condition of the corpses, noting bruises and marks that have not been adequately explained to this day. According to a newspaper article, there were three "ugly" wounds in Patricia's abdomen and the left side of her face had been battered, possibly resulting in a broken nose. Barbara's face and head had also been bruised and there were punctures from an ice pick in her chest. Once the bodies were moved, investigators stayed on the scene to search for clothing and clues, but neither was found.

Once the autopsies were performed the following day, all hopes that the examinations would provide new evidence or leads were quickly dashed. Despite the efforts of three experienced pathologists, they could not reach an agreement on a time or cause of death. They stated that the girls had died from shock and exposure but were only able to reach this conclusion by eliminating other causes. And by concluding that the girls had died on December 28, the night they had disappeared, they created more mysteries than they had managed to solve. If the girls had died on the night they had gone missing, then how could the sightings that took place after that date be explained? And if the bodies had been exposed to the elements since that time, then why hadn't anyone else seen them?

Barbara and Patricia were buried on January 28, one month after they disappeared, although their mystery was no closer to being solved than it had been in December.

The residents of Chicagoland were stunned and the case of the murdered girls became an obsession. The local community organized a search for clues and volunteers passed out flyers looking for information. Money was raised to assist the destitute Grimes family (Loretta and Joseph Grimes, an itinerant truck driver were divorced) and eventually the funds paid off Loretta's Damen Avenue home.

The *Chicago Tribune* invited readers to send in theories about the case and paid $50 for any they published. The clergy and the parishioners from St. Maurice offered a $1,000 reward and sent out letters to area residents, hoping that someone might have seen the girls before they vanished. Even photographs were taken of friends of the girls that duplicated the clothing they wore on December 28 in hopes that it might jog the memory of someone who saw them. On the night they saw *Love Me Tender* for the last time, Patricia wore blue jeans, a yellow sweater, a black jacket with white sleeve stripes, a white scarf over her head and black shoes. Her sister reportedly wore a gray tweed skirt, yellow blouse, a three-quarter-length coat, a gray scarf, white bobby sox and black, ballerina shoes. The clothing though, like the girl's killer, was never found.

The killer may have eluded the authorities but it was not because no one was trying to find him. Investigators questioned an unbelievable 300,000 persons, searching for information about the girls, and 2,000 of these people were seriously interrogated which, in those days could be brutal. A number of suspects were seriously considered and among the first was the "dreamer", Walter Kranz, who called police with his mysterious tip on January 15. He was held at the Englewood police station for some time and was repeatedly interrogated and given lie detector tests about his involvement in the murders. No solid evidence was ever found against him, though.

The police also picked up a 17-year-old named Max Fleig as a suspect but the law at that time did not allow juveniles to be tested with a polygraph. Police Captain Ralph Petaque persuaded the boy to take the test anyway and, in the midst of it, he confessed to kidnapping the girls. Because the test was illegal and inadmissible, the police were forced to let Fleig go free. Was he the killer? No one will ever know. Fleig was sent to prison a few years later for the brutal murder of a young woman but whether or not he had any connection to the death of the Grimes sisters remains a mystery.

In the midst of all of this, the police still had to deal with nuts and cranks, more so-called psychic visions and a number of false confessions, which made their work even harder. One confession that they investigated came from a transient who was believed to have been involved in some other murders around the same time period. His confession later unraveled and he admitted that he had lied.

Loretta Grimes prays for the safe return of her daughters. Elvis Presley photos decorate the walls above the bed. (Chicago Daily News)

Eager to crack the floundering case, Cook County Sheriff Joseph Lohman then arrested a skid-row dishwasher named Edward L. "Benny" Bedwell. The drifter, who sported Elvis-style sideburns and a ducktail haircut, had reportedly been seen with the Grimes sisters in a restaurant where he sometimes washed dishes in exchange for food. When he was initially questioned, Bedwell admitted that he had been in the D&L Restaurant on West Madison with two girls and an unnamed friend but he insisted that the owners of the place were mistaken about the girls being the Grimes sisters.

According to the owners, John and Minnie Duros, the group had entered the diner around 5:30 a.m. on the morning of December 30. They described the taller girl, who Minnie Duros said was wearing a coat with the name "Pat" embroidered on it, as being either so drunk or so sick that she was staggering as she walked. The couples sat in a booth for a while, listened to Elvis songs on the jukebox, and then went outside. According to Minnie Duros, "The taller girl returned to the booth and put her head on the table. They wanted her to get into the car, but she didn't want to. The other girl and the two men came back later and I told them to leave the girl alone -- she's sick. But they all left anyway and, on their way out, Barbara said they were sisters."

Lohman found the story plausible, thanks to the unshakable identification of the girls by Minnie Duros: their respective heights, the fact that one of them said they were sisters and, finally, Bedwell's resemblance to Elvis. Lohman believed this might have been enough to get the girls to go along with him. And then, of course, there was Bedwell's confession, which related a lurid and sexually explicit tale of drunken debauchery with the two young women. He made, and recanted, three confessions and even re-enacted the crime for investigators on January 27.

Everyone doubted the story but Lohman. He booked Bedwell on murder charges, but the drifter's testimony was both vague and contradictory and (most likely) his confession had been beaten out of him. On January 31, he testified that he had confessed out of fear of Lohman's men, who had struck and threatened him while he was being questioned. Lohman denied that Bedwell had been beaten and told newspapers that the drifter had lied when he contradicted his confession and added that he considered him the prime suspect in the case, "even more so now than when we first took his confession."

Newspaper photo of the very creepy Benny Bedwell.

Another of the chief investigators in the case, Harry Glos, believed that Bedwell might have been implicated in the murders in some way but that he was a dubious suspect. The case against him further unraveled when Bedwell's "unnamed friend" was identified as William C. Williamson, who ended up in jail on charges of drunkenness soon after his meeting with Bedwell and the two girls at the Duros' diner. He admitted that he was with Bedwell and two girls but denied that they were the Grimes sisters.

State's Attorney Benjamin Adamowski agreed with Harry Glos and ordered the drifter released. All charges against Bedwell were dismissed on March 4 and upon leaving the courtroom, he was re-arrested on a fugitive warrant from Florida for the rape of a 13 year-old girl. The crime he was charged with in Florida closely resembled the one that took the lives of the Grimes sisters but he managed to avoid conviction for it, thanks to the passage of time while he was a fugitive. According to reports, Bedwell's accuser had been held captive for three days before escaping and notifying the police of her abduction and rape. Bedwell later spent time in prison on a weapons charge and after he was released in 1986. He is buried in the Jefferson Barracks National Cemetery in St. Louis.

The dismissal of charges against Bedwell in the Grimes case set off another round of bickering between police departments and various jurisdictions and the case became even more mired in red tape and inactivity. It got even worse when coroner's investigator Glos publicly criticized the autopsy findings concerning the time and cause of death. He shocked the public by announcing that Barbara and Patricia could not have died on the night they disappeared. He said that an ice layer around the bodies proved that they were warm when they were left along German Church Road and that only after January 7 would there have been enough snow to create the ice and to hide the bodies.

Glos also raised the issues of the puncture wounds and bruises on the bodies, which had never been explained or explored. He was sure that the girls had been violently treated prior to death and also asserted that the older sister, Barbara, had been sexually molested before she was killed. The pathologists had denied this but the Chicago Police crime lab reluctantly confirmed it. However, they were angry with Glos for releasing the information because they wanted to keep it secret so that they could use it when questioning suspects.

The coroner, Walter McCarron, promptly had Glos fired and many of the other investigators in the case accused him of being reckless and of political grandstanding. Only Sheriff Lohman, who later deputized Glos to work on the case without pay, remained on his side. He agreed that the girls had likely been beaten and tortured by a sexual predator who lured them into the kidnap car under a seemingly innocent pretense. Lohman remained convinced, until his death in 1969, that the predator who had killed the girls had been Benny Bedwell.

Other theories maintain that the girls may have indeed encountered Bedwell, or another "older man", and rumors circulated that the image of the two girls had been polished to cover up some very questionable behavior on their parts. It was said that they sometimes hung around a bar on Archer Avenue where men would buy them drinks. One of the men may have been Benny Bedwell. Harry Glos, who died in 1994, had released information that one of the girls had been sexually active but later reports from those who have seen the autopsy slides say that there is evidence that both of them may have been. It is believed that Coroner McCarron may not have released this because of religious reasons or to spare additional grief for the family.

Today, veteran detectives believe that there was much more to the story than met the eye. The general consensus seems to be that Barbara and Patricia may have been abducted by a front man for a "white slavery" ring and taken to a remote location in the woods surrounding Willow Springs. They are convinced that the girls were strangled after refusing to become prostitutes. It's also possible that the girls may have been lured into an involvement in the prostitution ring by someone they knew (perhaps one of the older men from the Archer Avenue bar?), not realizing what would be required of them, and they were killed to keep them silent.

Others refused to even consider this and were angered by the negative gossip about the two girls. Some remain angry about this even today, maintaining that Barbara and Patricia were nice, ordinary, happy girls and were tragically killed on a cold night because they made the mistake of accepting a ride from a stranger. They didn't hang around in bars, these old friends maintain; they were simply innocent teenage girls, just like everyone else at that time.

As for myself, I'd like to think these old acquaintances are right. There are few stories as tragic as the demise of the Grimes sisters and, perhaps, it provides some cold comfort for us to believe that their deaths were simply a terrible mistake or the actions of a deviant killer. It can provide us the comfort of knowing that the girls were simply in the wrong place at the wrong time and that such a thing could have happened to anyone. But does believing this make us feel better ----- or worse?

Years passed. As there is no statute of limitations for murder, the case officially remained open but there was little chance that it would ever be solved. The Grimes family saw their hopes for closure in the case slowly fading away. Loretta Grimes passed away in December 1989 and was, by all accounts, a tragic and broken woman.

For the next several years, the investigation continued and more suspects were interviewed. A $100,000 reward was posted but the trail went cold. Then, decades later, hope was raised for the Grimes case when a solution was finally discovered to the Schuessler-Peterson murders from 1955.

Bobby Peterson and the Schuessler brothers could finally rest in peace -- but the same could not be said for Barbara and Patricia Grimes. Despite the new public awareness and police interest in their deaths, the case became cold once again. Apparently, the investigator's theories about a connection between their murders and those of the Schuessler and Peterson boys were not correct after all.

Now, 50 years later, the mystery of who killed the Grimes sisters remains unsolved. Those who still have an interest in the case will sometimes travel down German Church Road and wind up at the low point in this "haunted highway", where the bodies of the two girls were discovered so many years ago. The impact of tragedy is still being felt today, as is the impression of what may have been a depraved killer's most desperate moments.

The bodies of the Grimes sisters were tossed without ceremony at the edge of a ravine, just over a guardrail and only a few feet from the shoulder of the road. A short distance away from this site, its entrance once blocked with a chain, was a narrow drive that once led to a house that was nestled in the trees. Mysteriously, the house was abandoned by the family who lived there soon after the girl's bodies were discovered. Many of the belongings were left behind in the house and toys and furniture lay scattered about the yard for years. Even a 1955 Buick sat rusting in the driveway but it was eventually taken away. At some point, vandals set fire to the house and the owner had to demolish what was left. And while the owner never lived there again, people would occasionally see a tall, gaunt man roaming about the property in the spring and fall, when the trees and brush were thin. It was assumed that he had once occupied the place, but those who saw him were afraid to ask.

Until just a few years ago, the foundation of the abandoned house was still visible and landscaped hedges and a few remaining artifacts served to bear witness that a family had once lived here. Below the concrete slab of the house, a basement remained intact with a water heater, window screens and an old workbench littering the crumbling floor.

Why the family abandoned this house remained a mystery for many years --- until now. In 2005, I was able to interview Charles Werner, who once lived in this house with his family. His father, the "tall, gaunt man" who was often reported on the property, had been the owner and had been present on the day when the bodies of the Grimes girls were found.

"The ravine where the Grimes sister's bodies were found was very nearly the western property line of our house," Charles recalled for me. "My father had purchased the plot from a neighbor in 1947, or thereabouts, when my parents were first married. It was extremely rural at the time and my parents built a fairly large ranch house there. My sister was born in 1949 and I in 1951 and we spent the first years of our lives growing up in this house."

Mr. Werner, Charles' father, owned a successful plastic molding business and typically stayed home during family vacations in order to maintain his business. "It happened," Charles continued, "in January 1957, that my mother had taken the two of us children on our yearly trip to Miami Beach, Florida. My father stayed home. I have a vague recollection --- and I just talked to my sister who confirmed it --- that my mother was extremely agitated reading the Miami newspaper. The paper had reported the Grimes murders, and had detailed the location where the bodies were found. Not surprisingly, this revelation upset my mother to quite a degree. Back in the middle 1950s, the murder of two teenage girls in Chicago would make the front page of papers halfway across the country. It's sad to think of how numb we have become regarding such matters."

Charles' mother telephoned home and was stunned to learn that not only had the bodies been discovered on the road where they lived, but only a few feet from the edge of their propert!. His father had arrived home from work on the night the girls had been found and was "greeted" by sheriff's deputies with guns drawn at the entrance to his driveway. He was questioned about what he may have heard or seen but he was apparently never seriously considered as a suspect.

Charles continued: "I don't recall any major upheaval in our family as a result of the murders. I was young, of course, and naturally, my parents would shield me from the lurid details of such a matter. I do recall friends of my parents breathlessly commenting on the 'Grimes girls' when they would visit. My parents did save the newspaper front pages regarding the story and I still have those to this day. My father's most vivid recollections following the murders involved the sheer number of thrill seekers who paraded past the site in their automobiles and how he had to chase away people who came to our front door asking questions. I admit that I have no memory of these people. As far as I knew, things quieted down and I reverted to the blissful ignorance of my five-year-old life.

"That is, up until the spring of 1957, when we were all 'reminded' of the incident....."

Each day, Charles' sister, who had just turned eight, would take her bicycle down the 500-foot driveway to pick up the mail. Along the driveway was a large clearing and on one afternoon; Charles' sister was surprised to see an unfamiliar automobile parked at the edge of the drive. Three men, apparently from the car, were walking around in the woods just beyond the clearing. They soon noticed her watching them and called out. Quite frightened, she abandoned the idea of getting the mail and hurried back to the house. Charles vividly recalled her entering the house and screaming about the men.

"My mother was never timid," Charles said. "She shooed us into her car, and took off down the driveway toward the clearing. The men were leaving just as we arrived, shooting gravel from under their wheels. My mother told my sister to remember the first digits of the license plate and told me to remember the last digits. We did so, and although the chase rapidly became futile, mother passed along the car make and license to my father, who reported it to the police.

"The men were apprehended and my sister had to appear in court to relate her story. The men denied having been there at all and accused my sister of lying, but the judge apparently believed her. I seem to remember they got off with a small fine for trespassing. I still recall that this outraged my mother who was convinced these men had known something about the Grimes sisters. After all, they were within 50 feet of the crime scene just shortly after the snow cover had completely melted. Were they perhaps looking for some evidence that was left behind?

"We remained living in the house for another two years, through December 1959. My mother wanted us to be in a better school system, so she prevailed upon my father to rent, then purchase, a house in LaGrange, which had excellent schools. I won't deny that the isolation was probably a factor in her decision and certainly the proximity of the murder scene didn't help matters in that regard. I know that it was always my father's intention to move back into the house, perhaps renovate it and add a second floor. He always loved the house and the property, so he was never willing to sell it.

"His intention to move back explains why there were toys in the basement and a workbench still there. We never really 'moved out' completely and he would store things there that we didn't need in our LaGrange home. During the 1960s, he would generally go out there, do maintenance, and mow the lawn on Sunday.

"A building that remains unoccupied for long periods always seems to attract vandals and this house was no exception," Charles continued. "It's a shame to think that each time vandals would break windows, or knock down a door, my father would go out and carefully repair the damage, only to find another problem the next time he went out. Finally, someone actually burned down the house completely. Even then, Dad gathered all of the limestone from the walls and carefully stored it in the garage. Today, at age 92, he still speaks fondly of the property.

"My Dad gifted the property to my sister and me sometime in the 1980s. I bought my sister's share from her shortly thereafter. When I moved to Mississippi with my wife in 1992, I decided there was no chance I would ever build there, so I sold it to a developer. There is a subdivision there now. No doubt most of the owners of those houses have no idea at all that they live merely feet away from what is arguably the scene of the most famous unsolved crimes of 20th century Chicago."

Not surprisingly, the abandoned Werner house gained a reputation for being haunted in the years that followed, likely because of its eerie stillness and its proximity to the place where Barbara's and Patricia's bodies were found. Could this have caused it to become haunted? The idea is not as far-fetched as you might think.

Since the discovery of the bodies, the police have received reports from those who say that they have heard a car pulling up to the location with its motor running. They have also heard an automobile door creak open, followed by the sound of something being dumped alongside the road. The door slams shut and the car drives away. Reports claim people have heard these things -- and yet there is no car in sight!

According to author Tamara Shaffer, there was a young woman who took a number of her friends on a tour of the old Werner house and the murder site one evening. They walked up the path that branched off from the driveway and circled the ruins of the house. Under the light of the moon overhead, they saw a car approaching up the gravel drive from the road. It was a dark vehicle with no lights and it sped past them, drove around the house, and then disappeared. The woman and her friends decided to leave and, as they did, they encountered Willow Springs police officers, who had been called to chase off the "tour group". The chain that had been used to close off the driveway was still hanging in place and the police officers had seen no other car.

Another woman claimed that, in addition to the sounds, she saw what appeared to be the naked bodies of two young girls lying on the edge of the roadway. When police investigated, there was no sign of the corpses.

Many researchers believe in "residual hauntings", which means that an event may cause an impression to be left behind on the atmosphere of a place. It seems possible that the traumatic events surrounding the last ride of the Grimes sisters may have left such an impression on this small stretch of German Church Road. It may have also been an impression caused by the anxiety and madness of the killer as he left the bodies of the young women behind.

But believe in hauntings or not, that choice is up to the reader. But should you ever travel along German Church Road, I defy you to stop along that spot on the roadway where the bodies of Barbara and Patricia were found and I dare you to say that you are not moved by the tragedy that came to an end here.

Without a doubt, I think you will agree ---- this is a dark and haunted place.

A VOICE FROM THE GRAVE
The Teresita Basa Possession

In February 1977, the body of Teresita Basa, an employee of Chicago's Edgewater Hospital, was discovered in her apartment on North Pine Grove. Her naked corpse was found by firefighters under a burning mattress in the bedroom. Her legs were spread apart and a butcher knife had been rammed so hard into her chest that half of the wooden handle had slipped between her ribs. Neighbors had reported smoke coming from beneath her door and investigators realized that her killer had started the fire.

Police detectives were dispatched from the 23rd district to investigate. From all indications, Teresita had been the victim of a random rape and robbery. Unfortunately, this sort of crime was not uncommon in the neighborhood where she lived. Once the officers began to investigate though, they discovered that things were not as they first appeared. They found no evidence at the scene of the crime and there was no sign of a forced entry. It appeared that Teresita had known her killer and had let him into the apartment. They considered looking for a friend, or a boyfriend, who may have raped and killed her. Then, the coroner came back with another odd piece of information. Teresita had not been raped at all and in fact, was still a virgin. A motive for the bizarre crime had just vanished.

Detectives doggedly pursued the case, making lists of suspects and speaking with co-workers and friends of the dead woman. Every one of the suspects managed to come up with an unbreakable alibi and the investigation was stopped dead in its tracks. Days turned into weeks and then weeks into months. The case eventually grew cold as new investigations demanded attention. Detectives never imagined that they would soon get a new lead in the case --- one that would come from Teresita herself.

Teresita Basa was a 48-year-old respiratory therapist who worked at Chicago's Edgewater hospital. She had been born and raised on Negros Island in the Philippines and had come to the United States, where she studied classical music. She was considered a gifted musician and had also studied in Europe at the Royal Conservatory of Music in London. She was pursuing a career in music and worked at the hospital to make ends meet. She spent much of her free time working on a children's book about classical music and, on her nights off, she filled in as a pianist in a local jazz club. Although she was quiet and was slow to make close friends, she lived a full and active life. This life did not include men however. She rarely dated, leaving her co-workers to ponder whether she simply hadn't found the right man or if she had a fear of them. Her lack of interaction with the opposite sex made the investigation into her death all the more perplexing.

As time passed and the inquiries into the murder faded away, Teresita became less and less a topic of conversation among her former co-workers at the hospital. She would never be forgotten but, after many months she was rarely mentioned anymore. This is what made an event that took place in the spring of 1977 even more astonishing.

Murder victim Teresita Basa (Chicago Tribune)

Remy Chua was another respiratory therapist who worked at Edgewater Hospital. Like Teresita, she had been born and raised in the Philippines and had moved to the United States. Her husband, Joe, was a doctor who worked at another local hospital. Although Remy and Teresita had never been close, they had always maintained a friendly relationship. Remy had been shocked and saddened when Teresita had been killed but the other woman was already far from her thoughts a few months after the murder.

Then, one day, Remy was on her break, nearing the middle of her shift, and she went into the employee's lounge to relax for a few minutes. She sat down on the couch and leaned her head back. With her eyes closed, she could see nothing around her but she soon got the distinct feeling that someone else was in the room, watching her. She tried to ignore the feeling. The sensation became so strong that she opened her eyes and saw a woman standing nearby. She wore hospital scrubs and looked very familiar. Then Remy realized why she seemed familiar to her --- the woman was Teresita Basa!

Remy ran out of the room and found a technician in the hallway. She told him what she had seen but he replied that Teresita had been dead for months. Remy continued to insist that she had seen the woman, so the two of them opened the door of the employee lounge and peered inside. The room was empty.

In the weeks following the strange encounter, Remy's husband and friends began to notice a change in her personality. She began to act very moody and sad and one of her co-workers quietly suggested to another one that she was starting to act just like Teresita had. A nurse on staff would also later recall that Remy would sometimes stand transfixed in front of Teresita's old locker. In the cafeteria, Remy moved away from the table where she normally sat with her friends and began sitting alone in the same spot that Teresita used to occupy. Her friends also noticed that Remy would often seem to slip into a daze and would hum little snatches of songs. Co-workers remembered them as being tunes that Teresita often sang. When they mentioned this to Remy, she claimed that she had no idea what they were talking about.

Soon, Remy's personality changes began to cause her to have nightmares that she would vividly recall later. It seemed that whenever she closed her eyes to sleep, Teresita would appear. Before long, she also began to show up when Remy was wide-awake. One morning while she was waiting for a stoplight to change, she saw Teresita standing near her car. In moments, her image was replaced by that of an orderly that Remy worked with at the hospital. His name was Allan Showery and because Remy didn't know him very well, she found it strange that he would appear in her vision. She had never really thought about him before, but lately she had started to feel an intense hatred for the man. She couldn't understand it because he was virtually a stranger and yet she felt her stomach clench whenever he passed her in the hallways.

Remy realized that she had to discuss the situation with her husband. She told him that she had not been sleeping well and that she was having terrible dreams. He had also noticed her personality change and guessed that it had something to do with stress. She was obviously upset about something having to do with Teresita Basa, but what? He couldn't imagine that a ghost was haunting her dreams, but his wife was obviously disturbed. She explained to him that she continually saw the face of Teresita and also that of Allan Showery, an orderly that she barely knew. Joe Chua tried to reassure her. He was convinced that the nightmares would go away.

But they didn't go away and in fact, they became worse. The two faces would appear in her dreams, jolting her awake, and as she became conscious, she would experience the lingering smell of smoke in her bedroom. On a few nights, the smell was so strong that she actually got out of bed to be sure that the house was not on fire.

One afternoon while Remy was in bed trying to rest, Joe called his attorney on the phone. Just as the other man answered, both of them heard a deafening scream from the bedroom. Stunned, Joe dropped the phone and ran into the other room. He found his wife still in a deep sleep on the bed. Remy's parents, who were staying with them at the time, reached the bedroom just moments after Joe did. When they entered, they found the temperature in the room was a good 10 or 15 degrees colder than the rest of the house. They found Remy, still asleep on the bed. Suddenly, she began to rise from the bed with her arms outstretched in front of her. She walked toward her husband and parents and then suddenly fell backwards, collapsing back onto the bed. Joe, assuming that she was sleepwalking, tried to relax her arms into a more comfortable position but they would not budge. They remained stiff and upright, no matter what he did. Thanks to his medical training, it reminded Joe of a corpse that had entered a state of rigor mortis.

Then, Remy began to speak, claiming that she was Teresita Basa. Joe Chua knew that the voice did not belong to his wife. The voice went on to say that nothing had been done about her killer and that Chua should go to the police and tell them that a man came into her apartment and stabbed her. The voice pleaded with him again to talk to the police and then Remy's arms dropped and her eyes flickered open. She had no idea what had just happened.

Joe Chua had never seen anything like it before. He was a man of science, he didn't believe in the supernatural, but he was unable to explain what had just happened to his wife. Finally, Remy's father spoke up and stated that he believed the spirit of Teresita Basa had possessed his daughter.

Several days later, it happened again. Once more, Joe and Remy's parents were present. This time, the voice that came from Remy was even more upset. It demanded to know why Joe had not gone to the police with the information that he had been given. The voice never referred to him as Joe either, as his wife would have, but as Dr. Chua instead, as if he was a stranger. The voice stated that "Allan", a friend from the hospital, had killed her. Remy awoke a short time later and again, had no recollection of what had taken place.

A few days passed and a priest and relatives visited with Remy. Some of them believed that she needed psychiatric treatment, while others, like her father, believed that she was possessed. In the middle of one of her eerie trances, her father had tried to convince the spirit to leave his daughter alone. Teresita (as they had started to believe the voice was) told him that she would not be driven away until her killer was brought to justice.

One evening, Remy again slipped into a trance. She fell down and began to scream that she was burning. She wrapped her arms around her body and cried out. Joe quickly came to her aid. The now familiar voice came from Remy again, demanding that Chua go to the police with the information she had given him. When Chua explained that he was afraid that detectives would not believe him, Teresita replied that it had been a man named Allan Showery who had killed her. She had invited him to her home to fix her television and he had stabbed and burned her. She also said that he had stolen her jewelry and had given it to his girlfriend.

Joe asked how it could be proved that the jewelry was Teresita's and she replied that her cousins would recognize the pieces as family heirlooms. She also went on to give Joe the telephone numbers of her cousins. If he had any doubts remaining about the reality of the supernatural, it vanished with these last words. There was no possible way that his wife could have known the names and telephone numbers of Teresita's family.

On August 8, Chua finally gathered up enough nerve to go to the police with his story about his wife being possessed by the spirit of Teresita Basa. One can only imagine what it must have taken for the respected physician to go to the authorities with a tale that he knew they would find ridiculous. At the precinct house, he was introduced to a detective named Joe Stachula, who had been assigned to the original case. The veteran investigator listened politely to Joe's story, but confessed that he had little faith in its authenticity. However, having nothing else to go on and no other leads to follow, Stachula agreed to at least check out the orderly for a past criminal record.

The detective set to work and put Allan Showery's name into the system. He soon discovered that Showery did have a record. In fact, he had been arrested several times in New York, twice for rape. Further investigation also revealed that complaints had been filed against Showery by relatives whose loved ones had passed away at Edgewater Hospital. It was alleged that Showery had removed and had stolen jewelry from the deceased. After discovering this information, Detective Stachula and his partner, Lee Epplen, brought Allan Showery in for questioning.

During the interrogation, Showery admitted to knowing Teresita and working with her at the hospital. Stachula told him that they had information that Showery was supposed to go to her apartment and fix her television on the night she was killed. Showery admitted that he was but said that he had stopped off in a neighborhood bar on the way. He lost track of time and then, since it was too late to go to Teresita's, went home instead.

Despite the suspect's quick answers, Stachula had a feeling that something was not quite right with the alibi. He pressed a little harder, telling him that they had other information. But Showery insisted that he had never been to Teresita's apartment, even when Stachula told him that a number of people had seen him at the building. He replied that he had carried groceries for her into the lobby, but he had never been up to the apartment itself. When Stachula told him that they would compare his fingerprints to ones that were found in the apartment, Showery changed his story, admitting that he had gone to Teresita's apartment on the night of the murder but only for a few minutes. He didn't have the right tools to fix the television, he said, so he went home. He claimed that his wife would support his story.

Stachula and Epplen left Showery in lock-up and went to his apartment to talk to his wife. He advised Showery to think about his dates and times while they were gone, and see if he could get his story straight. All the while, Stachula had a funny feeling about Showery's version of the events -- and about the weird story told to them by Joe Chua. He and Epplen recalled that "Teresita" had said that Showery had given the jewelry to his girlfriend, not his wife. One of the first things that he asked the woman who answered the door at Showery's apartment was about whether or not she and Showery were married. She admitted that they were only living together but planned to be married soon.

The detectives were happy with the answer and they quickly asked her if Showery had given her any jewelry between January and June. She replied that he had given her an antique ring around the end of February or the beginning of March. It had been a belated Christmas gift, she said. She went to the bedroom and returned with a box containing several other pieces of jewelry. Stachula and Epplen looked at one another and they asked the woman to accompany them back to the police station.

Before leaving the apartment, Stachula asked to use the telephone. He opened his notebook and looked at the list of names and telephone numbers that Joe Chua had given him. Any remaining doubts that he had about the story evaporated as one by one the people on the list answered his calls and said that they were relatives of Teresita Basa. He asked each of them to meet he and his partner at the station house.

As Showery's girlfriend waited with Epplen, Stachula met with Teresita's family. Each of them identified the jewelry that had been taken from Showery's apartment ---- it had been Teresita's. Many of the pieces had been in her family for years.

The detective then took the jewelry into the interrogation room and showed it to Allan Showery. Even when confronted with this evidence, Showery protested his innocence. He said that he had bought the jewelry in a pawnshop but had no receipts for it and could not remember the name of the shop.

His story was interrupted by a knock on the door. Detective Epplen was outside and he led Showery's girlfriend into the room. By this time, Epplen had apprised her of the situation and the look on her face when she saw Showery must have shocked the suspect in a way that the detective's interrogations had been unable to do. As soon as he saw the girl walk in, Showery confessed to having killed Teresita.

On February 21, 1977, Allan Showery had gone to the apartment of Teresita Basa at approximately 5:00 in the evening. Shortly after he arrived there, he inspected her television set and told her that he did not have the necessary tools to fix it. He left and then returned at around 7:30 p.m. As soon as he was admitted to the apartment, he struck Teresita until she was unconscious and left her lying on the floor. He then proceeded to ransack the apartment, taking only $30 in cash but finding her collection of jewelry. After that, he drug Teresita into the bedroom, where he removed all of her clothing and spread her legs apart to make it appear as if she had been raped. He was totally unaware that Teresita was a virgin. Showery then went into the kitchen and took a butcher's knife from a drawer. He plunged the knife into Teresita's chest, narrowly missing a rib. He then covered the body with a mattress and set it on fire. Showery fled the scene just before the firefighters arrived.

The orderly had confessed to the brutal and gruesome crime, but that was not the end of the story. After engaging a lawyer, Showery recanted the confession and, two years later, a trial that was held that ended in a hung jury. He was returned to a holding cell to wait for his new trial date but before it got under way, Showery pled guilty to the murder. The plea came as a complete surprise to both his attorney and the prosecutor, especially in light of the fact that Showery had been claiming that he was innocent of the crime for months. He was later sentenced to fourteen years in prison.

Some have wondered if perhaps Showery had a visitor in his cell one night ---- a visitor who was not of this world. Who knows?

As for Teresita Basa herself, her spirit was never heard from again. She did not return to the Chua family and they were able to live out their lives in peace. They must have wondered why Teresita had chosen them to seek justice on her behalf, but that question remains unanswered. Regardless, the dead woman did find a voice and her murder was finally avenged.

THE CLOWN THAT KILLED
The Dark Legacy of John Wayne Gacy

To everyone who met him, John Wayne Gacy seemed a likable and affable man. He was widely respected in the community, charming and easy to get along with. He was a good Catholic and sharp businessman who, when not running his construction company, was active in the Jaycees and with community volunteer groups. When he was a Democratic Party precinct captain, he had his photo taken with then First Lady Rosalynn Carter. He also spent much of his free time hosting elaborate street parties for his friends and neighbors, serving in community groups and entertaining children as "Pogo the Clown". He was a generous, hard working, friendly, devoted family man, everyone knew that -- but that was the side of John Wayne Gacy that he allowed people to see.

Underneath the smiling mask of the clown was the face of depraved fiend.

John Wayne Gacy was a homegrown monster. Born on St. Patrick's Day 1942 at Edgewater Hospital in Chicago, little Johnny was the second of three children. His older sister, Joanne, had preceded him by two years and two years after his birth came that of his sister Karen. The Gacy children were raised in the Church and all three attended Catholic schools on the north side. Growing up, Gacy was a quiet boy who worked odd jobs for spending money, like newspaper routes and bagging groceries, and busied himself with Boy Scout activities. He was never a particularly popular boy but he was well-liked by his teachers, co-workers and his friends from school and the Boy Scouts. He seemed to have a normal childhood, except for his relationship with his father and a series of health problems that he developed.

When Gacy was 11, he was playing on a swing set and was hit in the head with one of the swings. The accident caused a blood clot in his brain that was not discovered until he was 16. Between the time of the accident and the diagnosis, Gacy suffered from blackouts that were caused by the clot. They were eventually treated with medication. At 17, he was also diagnosed with a heart ailment that led to him being hospitalized several times during his life. He complained frequently about it over the years but no one could ever find a cause for the pain that he claimed to be suffering.

In his late teens, he began to experience problems with his father, although his relationship with his mother and sisters remained strong. His father was an alcoholic who physically abused his wife and berated his children. He was

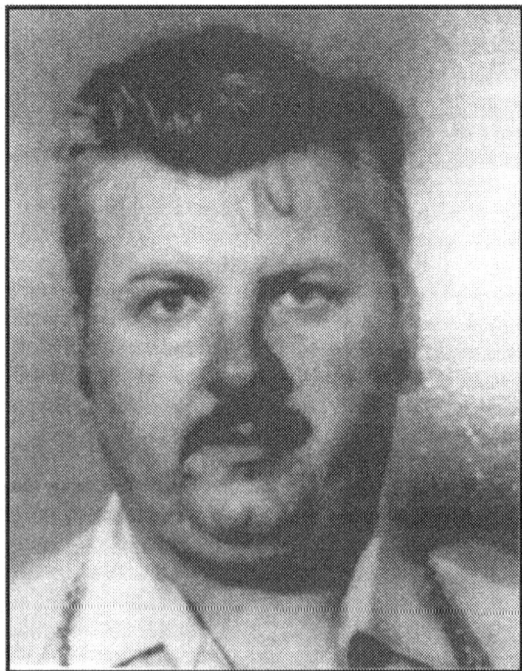

an unpleasant individual, but Gacy loved his father and constantly worked to gain his attention and approval. Gacy Sr. died before his son could ever get close to him.

His growing family problems extended out into his schoolwork and after attending four high schools during his senior year and never graduating, Gacy dropped out and left home for Las Vegas. He worked part time as a janitor in a funeral home and saved his money to buy a ticket back to Chicago. Lonely and depressed, he spent three months trying to get the money together. His mother and sisters were thrilled to see him when he came back.

After his return, Gacy enrolled in business college and eventually graduated. While in school, he gained a real talent for salesmanship and he put it to work in a job with the Nunn-Bush Shoe Company. He excelled as a management trainee and was soon transferred to a men's clothing outlet in Springfield, Illinois. Soon after his move, Gacy's health took a turn for the worse. He gained a great deal of weight and began to suffer more agony from his mysterious heart ailment. He was hospitalized and soon after getting out, was back in the hospital again, this time with back pain. He continued to have problems with his weight, heart and back throughout his life. It's interesting to note that all three of these types of ailments can often be traced to psychosomatic illnesses, and are sometimes assisted more with mental health treatment than by standard medicine. Unfortunately, Gacy never received any.

While living in Springfield, he became involved in several organizations that served the community, including the Chi Rho Club (membership chairman); the Catholic Inter-Club Council (member of the board); the Federal Civil Defense for Illinois; the Chicago Civil Defense (commanding captain); the Holy Name Society (officer) and the Jaycees, to which Gacy devoted most of his efforts and was eventually voted vice-president of the local chapter and named "Man of the Year". Many who knew Gacy considered him to be ambitious and was working hard to make a name for himself in the community. He was an overachiever who worked so diligently that he had to be hospitalized for nervous exhaustion on one occasion.

In September 1964, Gacy met and married a co-worker named Marlynn Myers, whose parents owned a number of Kentucky Fried Chicken restaurants in Iowa. Gacy's new father-in-law offered him a position with the company and soon the newlyweds were moving to Iowa. Life seemed to hold great promise for Gacy and there was no foreshadowing of the horrific events to come.

Gacy began learning the restaurant business from the ground up, working 12 to 14 hours each day. He was enthusiastic and eager to learn, and he hoped to take over the franchises one day. When not working, he was active with the Waterloo, Iowa Jaycees. He worked tirelessly performing volunteer work and he made many friends. Marlynn gave birth to a son shortly after they moved to Iowa and, not long after, added a daughter to the happy family. They seemed to have the picture perfect life --- a loving and healthy family, a good job, a house in the suburbs --- and it seemed almost too good to be true. And it was...

Rumors were starting to spread around town, and among Jaycees members, about Gacy's sexual preferences. No one could help but notice that young boys always seemed to be in his presence. Stories spread that he had made passes at some of the young men who worked in the restaurants but those close to him refused to believe it -- until the rumors became truth. In May 1968, a grand jury in Black Hawk County indicted Gacy for committing an act of sodomy with a teenage boy named Mark Miller. The boy told the courts that Gacy had tricked him into being tied up while visiting Gacy's home and he had violently raped him. Gacy denied the charges but did say that Miller willingly had sex with him in order to earn extra money.

Four months later, more charges were filed against Gacy. This time, he was charged with hiring an 18 year-old boy named Dwight Andersson to beat up Mark Miller. Andersson lured Miller to his car and then drove him to a wooded area, where he sprayed mace in his eyes and began to beat him. Miller fought back, breaking Andersson's nose, and managed to run away. He called the police and Andersson was picked up and taken into custody. He informed the officer that Gacy had hired him to attack the other boy.

A judge ordered Gacy to undergo a psychiatric evaluation to see if he was mentally competent to stand trial. He was found to be competent, but psychiatrists stated that he was an antisocial personality who would likely not benefit from any known medical treatment. Soon after the report was submitted, Gacy entered a guilty plea to the sodomy charge. He received a 10 year at the Iowa State Reformatory, the maximum time for the offence, and entered prison for the first time at the age of 26. Shortly after, his wife divorced him on the grounds that he had violated their wedding vows.

Gacy adhered to all of the rules in prison and stayed out of trouble. Described as a model prisoner, he was paroled after only 18 months. On June 18, 1970, he left his cell and made his way back to Chicago. He moved in with his mother and obtained work as a chef in a city restaurant, settling into the position and trying to get his life back on track.

Gacy lived with his mother for four months and then decided to move out on his own. She helped him to obtain a new house at 8213 West Summerdale Avenue in the Norwood Park Township. Gacy owned one-half of the house and his mother and sisters owned the other. He was very happy with his new, two-bedroom ranch house. It was located in a clean, quiet neighborhood and he quickly went about making friends with his neighbors, Edward and Lilla Grexa, who had lived in the neighborhood since it had been built. Within seven months of moving in next door, Gacy was spending Christmas with the Grexas. They became close friends and often gathered for drinks and card games. The Grexas had no idea of Gacy's criminal past --- or his most recent run-in with the law.

 Just one month before the Grexa's had invited Gacy over for Christmas dinner, he had been charged with disorderly conduct for forcing a young boy, whom he had picked up at the bus station, to perform sexual acts on him. It seems as though once Gacy stepped over the line with Mark Miller, there was no turning back for him. His slide into complete depravity had begun and the earlier problems, leading to jail time, had done nothing to halt his descent. He managed to slip through the system when the new charges against him were dropped, thanks to the fact that his accuser never showed up in court.

In June 1972, Gacy married Carole Hoff, a newly divorced mother of two daughters. Gacy romanced her when she was most vulnerable and she fell for his charm and generosity. She knew about his time in prison but believed that he had changed his life for the better. Carole and her daughters soon settled into Gacy's home and forged a close relationship with the Grexa's. The older couple was often invited over to the Gacy's house for elaborate parties and cookouts. However, they were bothered by the horrible stench that sometimes wafted throughout the house. Lillie Grexa was convinced that an animal had died beneath the floorboards of the place and she urged Gacy to do something about it. He blamed the odor on a moisture buildup in the crawlspace under the house, refusing to reveal the true, and much more sinister, cause for the smell. He would keep this secret for years to come.

In 1974, Gacy started a contracting business called Painting, Decorating and Maintenance or PDM Contractors, Inc. He hired a number of teenage boys to work for him, explaining to friends that hiring young men would keep his payroll costs low. This was not the real reason, though, for Gacy's deviant desires had started to get out of control. He could not longer hide what he was and while he believed that it was all still a secret; it was starting to become very apparent to those who were close to him, especially his wife.

By 1975, Carole and Gacy had drifted apart. Their sex life had ended and Gacy's moods became more and more unpredictable, ranging from jovial to an uncontrollable rage that would have him throwing furniture. He had become an insomniac and his lack of sleep seemed to make his mood swings even worse. And if his personality changes were not enough, his choice of reading material worried her even more. Carole had started to find magazines filled with naked men and boys around the house and when confronted, Gacy casually admitted that they were his. He even confessed that he preferred young men to women. Naturally, this was the last straw for Carole and she soon filed for divorce. It became final on March 2, 1976.

Gacy dismissed his marital problems and refused to let them hamper his need for recognition and success. To most people, Gacy was still the outgoing and hardworking man that he had always been. So many people had experienced divorces that no one thought anything about it. Gacy made up for any lingering questions about him with his natural talent for persuading others to his ideas and thoughts and he always came up with creative ways to get himself noticed. It was not long before he gained the attention of Robert F. Matwick, the Democratic township committeeman for Norwood Park. As a free service to the committeeman, Gacy volunteered himself and his employees to clean up and repair the Democratic Party headquarters. Unaware of the contractor's past and impressed by his sense of duty and dedication to the community, Matwick nominated Gacy to the street lighting commission. In 1975, Gacy became the secretary treasurer but his political career was short-lived. In spite of Gacy trying to hide it, rumors again began to circulate about his interest in young boys.

One of the rumors stemmed from an actual incident that took place during the time that Gacy was working on the Democratic headquarters. One of the teenagers who worked on the project was 16 year-old Tony Antonucci. According to the boy, Gacy made sexual advances toward him but backed off when Antonucci threatened to hit him with a chair. Gacy recovered his composure and made a joke out of it. He tried to convince Tony that he was only kidding and left him alone for the next month.

Several weeks later, while visiting Gacy's home, he again approached Antonucci. He tricked the young man into a pair of handcuffs and then tried to undress him. Antonucci had made sure that he was loosely cuffed though and when he slipped free, he wrestled Gacy to the ground and cuffed the older man instead. He eventually let him go when Gacy promised not to bother him again. That was the last time that Gacy ever made advances toward Antonucci and the boy remained working for the contracting company for almost a year after the incident.

Tony Antonucci would not realize how lucky he had been that day. Others would not fare as well.

Johnny Butkovich, 17, began doing remodeling work for Gacy's company in an effort to raise money for his racing car. He enjoyed the position, it paid well, and he maintained a good working relationship with Gacy until one pay period when he refused to pay Johnny for two weeks of work. This was something that Gacy often did in order to save money. Angered that Gacy had withheld his pay, Johnny went over to his employer's house, with two friends, to collect what was rightfully his. When he confronted him, Gacy refused to pay and a loud argument erupted. Finally, he realized that there was little that he could do and Johnny and his friends left. Butkovich dropped off his friends at home and drove away --- never to be seen again.

Michael Bonnin, 17, enjoyed working with his hands, especially carpentry and woodworking, and often had several different projects going at the same time. In June 1976, he had almost finished restoring an antique jukebox but, unfortunately, the job was never finished. He was on his way to catch a train to meet his stepfather's brother and he vanished.

Billy Carroll, 16, was a long-time troublemaker who had his first run-in with the authorities at the age of 9. Two years later, he was caught with a gun and he spent most of his life on the streets of Chicago, making money by arranging meetings between teenage boys and adult men for a commission. Although he came from a very different background than Michael Bonnin and Johnny Butkovich, all three had one thing in common -- John Wayne Gacy. Like the others, Carroll also disappeared suddenly. He left home on June 13, 1976 and was never seen alive again.

Gregory Godzik, 17, started working for PDM Contractors in order to finance parts for his 1966 Pontiac. He considered it an eyesore but it was a consuming hobby for him. The work that he did for Gacy paid well and he liked it a lot. On December 12, 1976, Gregory dropped his date, a girl he had had a crush on for a while, at her house and drove off towards home. The following day, the police found Gregory's Pontiac but the boy was missing.

On January 20, 1977, John Szyc, 19, also vanished. He had driven off in his 1971 Plymouth Satellite and was never seen alive again. Interestingly, a short time after Szyc disappeared, another teenager was picked up by police in a 1971 Plymouth Satellite while trying to leave a gas station without paying. The boy said that the man he lived with could explain the situation. The man was John Wayne Gacy. He told the officers that John Szyc had sold him the car some time earlier. The police never checked the title, which had been signed 18 days after John's disappearance. Szyc had not worked for PDM Contractors but he was acquainted with Gregory Godzik, Johnny Butkovich and fatally, John Wayne Gacy.

On September 15, 1977, Robert Gilroy, 18, also disappeared. Gilroy was an avid outdoorsman and, on that day, was supposed to catch a bus to meet friends for horseback riding. When he never showed up, his father, a Chicago police sergeant, immediately began searching for the boy. A full-scale investigation was launched but Robert was nowhere to be found.

More than a year later, another young man named Robert Piest would vanish as well. The investigation into his disappearance would lead not only to the discovery of his body but the bodies of Butkovich, Bonnin, Carroll, Szyc, Gilroy, and 27 other young men who suffered similar fates. These discoveries would horrify not only Chicago, but also all of America.

Before Robert disappeared though, a weird event would occur that would later turn out to be a chilling prediction of events to come -- or rather a stunning revelation of events that had already occurred. At a pre-Christmas party that was held on December 2, 1978, a well-known local psychic known as "Florece" (Florence Branson) had been hired to provide cards readings for the guests. The party was held at the home of a contractor associate of Gacy's and Gacy was one of the many in attendance.

The evening was almost over when it came time for Gacy to have his fortune told. Up until this point, the party and the readings had been going well and everyone was having a great time, including the psychic. Then, Gacy approached her for his reading. As soon as he spoke to her, Florece later reported, she sensed something was very wrong with the man. She also said that she became physically ill when she laid out his cards. She was unable to discern any details but knew that there was an evil hiding below the surface of this man. She bluffed her way through the reading, much too frightened to say anything to Gacy.

At the end of the evening, she felt compelled to speak to the hostess about her horrific impressions of Gacy. She told what she had sensed and added that she was afraid of him and that Gacy was "perverted and violent."

The hostess refused to hear such things, as "John" had been a family friend for several years. Florece didn't argue with her, but she was not surprised several weeks later when the story of Gacy and his murderous crime spree made the papers.

Gacy's web of secrets began to unravel with the vanishing of a young boy named Robert Piest. Robert, 15, disappeared mysteriously just outside the doors of the pharmacy where he worked. His mother, who had come to pick him up after his shift, was waiting outside for him when he vanished. He had told her that he would be back in just a minute because he was going to talk to a contractor who had offered him a job. He never returned. She began to get worried but as more time passed, her worry turned to terror. She searched the pharmacy and looked outside but Robert was nowhere to be seen. Finally, three hours after his disappearance, the Des Plaines police were notified. Lieutenant Joseph Kozenczak led the investigation.

The first lead to follow was the most obvious one and officers quickly obtained the name of the contractor who had offered Robert the job. Kozenczak went straight to Gacy's home and, when Gacy came to the door, he told him about the missing boy. He also asked him to accompany him to the police station for some questions. Gacy refused. He explained that there had been a recent death in his family and that he had to attend to some telephone calls, but he agreed to come down later. Several hours later, Gacy arrived and gave a statement to the police. He said that he knew nothing about the disappearance and was allowed to leave with no further questioning.

Something about Gacy did not sit right with Kozenczak, though, and he decided to do a background check on him. He was stunned when he discovered that Gacy had done time for sodomy with a teenaged boy. He quickly obtained a search warrant for Gacy's house and on December 13, 1978, a legion of police officers entered the house on Summerdale Avenue. Gacy was not at home at the time.

From the items that were recovered from the house, it is obvious that Gacy's lusts had finally consumed him. He was still trying to maintain outward appearances but a number of damning items were discovered in the residence that would lead to the discovery of his dark side. Some of the items included a box containing two drivers licenses and several rings, including one that was engraved with Maine West High School class of 1975 and the initials J.A.S.; a box containing marijuana and pills like amyl nitrate; a stained section of rug; a number of books with homosexual and child pornography themes; a pair of handcuffs; police badges; sexual devices; a hypodermic needle and small brown bottle; clothing that was too small for Gacy; nylon rope; and other items. The police also confiscated three automobiles that belonged to Gacy, including a 1978 Chevrolet truck with a snow plow attached and the name "PDM Contractors" on the side, a van with "PDM Contractors" also painted on the side and a 1979 Oldsmobile Delta 88. In the trunk of the car were pieces of hair that were later matched to Robert Piest.

As the investigation continued, the police entered the crawlspace under Gacy's home. They were discouraged by the rancid odor but believed it to be sewage. The earth in the crawlspace had been sprinkled with lime but appeared to be untouched. They left the narrow space and returned to police headquarters to run tests on the evidence that they had obtained.

Gacy was, once more, called to headquarters and was told about the evidence that had been removed from his house. Enraged, he immediately contacted his attorney, who told him not to sign the Miranda waiver that was presented to him by detectives. The police had nothing to arrest him on and eventually had to release him after more questioning about the Piest disappearance. They placed him under 24-hour surveillance but this was the best that they could do.

In the days that followed, friends were called into the station and were also questioned. The detectives were unable to get any information from Gacy's friends that connected him to Robert Piest and all of them insisted that Gacy simply was not capable of murder. He had already told his friends that the police were trying to charge him with murder but that he had nothing to do with it.

In the midst of the investigation, Gacy asked one of these same friends was asked to stop by his house and check on his dog, making sure that the animal had enough food and water. Gacy said that he didn't want to go there because the police were harassing him and trying to pin the crime on him. The friend agreed, borrowed a house key from Gacy and went over to 8213 West Summerdale. Nervous about being seen going to Gacy's house, even though he was sure that his friend had nothing to do with any criminal activities, he decided to go around to the back door instead of walking through the front.

He put the key into the lock and, just as he began to turn it, he heard what sounded like a group of people moaning and crying inside of the house. The groans were so chilling that he immediately closed the door, re-locked it and left. He hurried away from the house and when he returned to the site where Gacy was working, he lied to him and told him that everything in the house was fine, including his dog.

There is no way to know if the sounds the man heard in the house were natural or supernatural. It's possible that one of Gacy's victims was still alive and that his eerie cries sounded like a chorus of moans to the already unnerved friend, but this seems unlikely as, by this time, Gacy had begun disposing of the bodies of his victims in locations outside of his home.

It seems more likely, if this account is true, that the friend may have actually heard the voices of victims whose deaths were yet to be avenged. Could the spirits of some of Gacy's victims have lingered behind in the house -- or at least could some sort of supernatural energy have been impressed on the atmosphere of a place where such horrible and terrifying things had occurred?

The investigation continued and the police became increasingly discouraged by their attempts to gather information from Gacy's friends and acquaintances. Finally, frustrated by the lack of evidence connecting Gacy to the Piest disappearance, the police decided to book him on possession of marijuana.

While Gacy was being charged with possession, the police lab and investigators were coming up with critical evidence against Gacy from the items taken from his home. One of the rings found in Gacy's house belonged to another teenager, John Szyc, who had disappeared about a year earlier. They also discovered that three former employees of Gacy's had also disappeared. Furthermore, a receipt for a roll of film that was found in Gacy's home had belonged to a co-worker of Robert Piest and he had given it to Robert on the day of the boy's disappearance. With this new information, the investigators suddenly began to realize the enormity of the case that was starting to unfold.

Detectives and crime lab technicians returned to Gacy's house again. With everything starting to crumble around him, Gacy finally confessed that he had killed someone but that it had been in self-defense. He said that

Remains are removed from Gacy's home on Summerdale Avenue (Weird Illinois)

he was frightened and had buried the body under his garage. He told the police where they could find the body and investigators marked the gravesite in the garage but they did not immediately begin digging. They decided to search the crawlspace first and, minutes after starting to dig, they found the remains of the first corpse.

That evening, Dr. Robert Stein, the Cook County Medical Examiner, was called in to help with the investigation. He began to organize the search by marking off areas of earth in sections, as would be done with an archaeological site. The excavation of a decomposing body has to be carried out in a meticulous manner in order to preserve the integrity of the evidence so, throughout the night and into the days that followed, the digging progressed under the medical examiner's watchful eye.

On Friday, December 22, 1978, detectives confronted Gacy with the news that digging was being done under his house. With this, the monster finally broke down. He admitted that he had killed at least 30 people and that most of their remains were buried beneath the house. The first murder took place in January 1972 and the second in January 1974, about a year and a half after he was married. He explained that he lured his victims into being handcuffed and then he would sexually assault them. To muffle their screams, Gacy stuffed a sock, or their underwear, into their mouths and would often kill them by placing a rope or board against their throats as he raped them. He also admitted to sometimes keeping the corpses under his bed or in his attic for hours or days before burying them in the crawlspace.

Meanwhile, the police discovered two bodies during the first day of digging. One of these was John Butkovich, who was found under the garage, and the other was in the crawlspace. As the days passed, the body count grew higher. Some of the victims were found with their underwear still lodged in their throats and others were buried so close together that investigators believed they had been killed, or at least buried, at the same time.

By December 28, the police had removed a total of 27 bodies from Gacy's house. Another body had also been found weeks earlier, not in the crawlspace but in the Des Plaines River. The naked corpse of Frank Wayne "Dale" Landingin had been found in the water but at the time, the police were not yet aware of Gacy and his crimes. It would not be until his drivers license was found in Gacy's house that he could be connected to the young man's murder. And he would not be the only victim to be found in the river...

Also on December 28, the body of James Mazzara was removed from the Des Plaines River. His underwear was found stuffed down his throat, linking him to the other victims. Gacy told the police that he had started disposing of bodies in the river because he was running out of room in his crawlspace. Besides that, all of the digging was bothering his chronic back problem. Mazzara was the 29th victim to be found --- but was still not the last.

Much to the horror of the neighbors, the police were still excavating Gacy's property at the end of February. They had gutted the house but had found no more bodies in the crawlspace. Bad winter weather had kept them from resuming the search but they believed that there were still bodies to be found. While workmen began breaking up the concrete of Gacy's patio, another horrific discovery was made. They found the body of a man, still in good condition, preserved in the concrete. The following week, another body was found.

The 31st victim to be linked to Gacy was found in the Illinois River. Investigators were able to learn his identity thanks to a tattoo on his arm, which friends of the victim's father recognized while reading a newspaper article about the grim discovery. The victim's name was Timothy O'Rourke and he was believed to have been acquainted with Gacy.

Around the time that O'Rourke was discovered and pulled from the river, another body was found on Gacy's property, this time beneath his recreation room. It was the last body to be found on the property and, soon after, the house was destroyed and reduced to rubble.

Although the death toll had now risen to 32, the body of Robert Piest was still missing. Tragically, his remains were discovered in the Illinois River in April 1979. The body had been lodged somewhere in the river but strong winds had worked it loose and carried it to the locks at Dresden Dam, where it was finally discovered. An autopsy report showed that Robert had been strangled by paper towels being shoved down his throat.

Police investigators worked hard to identify Gacy's victims, using dental records and other clues, and eventually, all but nine of the young men were identified. A mass burial was held for these unknown victims on June 8, 1981. And while the investigation had ended, Gacy's trial was just beginning.

John Wayne Gacy's murder trial began on February 6, 1980 at the Cook County Criminal Courts Building in downtown Chicago. Jury members, five women and seven men, listened closely as prosecutor Bob Egan outlined the case for them, detailing the short years of Robert Piest's life, his gruesome death, and how Gacy was also responsible for the murders of at least 32 other young men. He told them about the investigation that led to the horrible discoveries under Gacy's house, and noted that Gacy's actions had been carefully planned, and were rational and premeditated. He knew that the defense would work to make Gacy appear insane and Egan needed to counter this as much as possible. When he finished, it was obvious that Egan's statement had a chilling effect on the jury and on the courtroom spectators.

Egan's opening statement was followed by one of Gacy's defense lawyers, Robert Motta, who opposed Egan's statement and insisted that Gacy's actions had been completely irrational and impulsive. He had been insane and no longer in control of his actions. And while most would agree that only a madman would commit the acts that Gacy was being tried for, the legal definition of insanity was much harder to prove. Besides that, prosecutors wanted to make sure that Gacy was kept off the streets -- permanently, if possible -- and only a "guilty" verdict would accomplish this. If Gacy was found to be insane, he would become a ward of the state mental health system with no time limits on the how long he might be incarcerated. In many cases, killers were freed when they were deemed mentally stable enough to re-enter society, only to kill again. Prosecutors did not believe that this type of commitment was just punishment in Gacy's case.

After the opening statements, the prosecution brought their first witness to the stand, Marko Butkovich, the father of Gacy's victim, Johnny Butkovich. He was the first witness on a list that included the family and friends of the victims. Many of them broke down on the stand, recalling their loved ones or recounting their last goodbyes. This testimony was followed by those who worked for Gacy and who survived sexual or violent encounters with him. They spoke of his mood swings and how he tried to trick them into handcuffs, using magic tricks

The most chilling image of Gacy of all --- as his "Pogo the Clown" character
(Chicago Tribune)

193

that he perfected as "Pogo the Clown". The testimony continued for several weeks and included friends and neighbors of Gacy (legitimately shocked at the various clues to his behavior that they had missed over the years), police officers involved in the investigation and psychologists who examined Gacy and found him to be sane. Before the state rested, prosecutors had called some 60 witnesses to the stand.

The defense then took over, never trying to refute the evidence that established their client as a killer but rather to paint him as insane and unable to control his actions. They called friends and family members of Gacy to the stand, including his mother, who testified that her husband would often beat Gacy with a leather strap. His sister told of how she saw Gacy being verbally assaulted by their father on many occasions. Others who testified for the defense told of how Gacy was a good and generous man, who helped those in need and who always had a smile and kind word for everyone. Lillie Grexa even took the stand and spoke of what a wonderful neighbor he was. However, she also said something that turned out to be damaging to the case. She refused to say that he was crazy and instead told the court that she believed him to be a "very brilliant man". One has to wonder if she knew that her statement would conflict with the defense theory that Gacy was insane and out of control.

The defense then called Thomas Eliseo, a psychologist who had conducted interviews with Gacy before the trial. He said that he found Gacy to be extremely intelligent but believed that he suffered from borderline schizophrenia. Other medical experts gave similar testimony, reciting a litany of schizophrenia, multiple personality disorder and antisocial behavior. They also reported that Gacy's mental disorder prevented him from understanding the magnitude of his crimes. In conclusion, each of the experts found him to be insane at the time of the murders and with the testimony of the medical experts; the defense rested its case.

In their closing statements, both sides emotionally argued their case but the jury took only two hours of deliberation to come back with a verdict --- "guilty". Gacy had been convicted of the deaths of 33 young men and had the notoriety of being convicted of more murders than anyone else in American history. He received the death penalty and was sent to the Menard Correctional Center to await execution. After years of appeals, he was put to death by lethal injection on May 9, 1994.

Finally, Gacy's terrifying string of crimes could be relegated to memory -- or could it?

By the spring of 1979, Gacy's home at 8213 West Summerdale had been reduced to ruin. Once the remains of the house were cleared away, it became a muddy, vacant lot and a continuing reminder to the neighborhood of the monster who had once been in their midst. All vestiges of the house, even the driveway and barbecue pit, were hauled away but still the onlookers came, macabre curiosity-seeking tourists who flocked to the once peaceful residential area. Neighbors hoped that, with all traces of the house removed, the line of cars would finally stop. The quiet would return, they believed, once the notoriety of the spot began to fade, warmer weather came and the grass began to grow back over the open scar where the house of John Wayne Gacy had once stood.

Unfortunately though, the grass did not return. Even more than 18 months after the house was destroyed, the land remained strangely barren. Some weeds had started to grow near the front sidewalk but the back of the lot, where the house had stood and where the bodies had been buried, remained completely empty of plant life, despite the fact that there was no logical reason for the soil to be bare.

Those searching for an explanation suggested that perhaps the lime that Gacy had dusted the bodies of his victims with had contaminated the soil in some way but police officers that were involved in the actual recovery of the bodies disputed this. They insisted that Gacy had never used enough lime to cause any damage to the lot. The shallow graves where the bodies lay had been carefully unearthed and then, a backhoe had been brought in to dig down 8 to 10 feet to be sure that nothing was missed. The small amount of lime that had been used would not have survived this and even so, no lime had been used under the garage or in the backyard -- and yet no grass would grow there either.

It was as though the evil deeds that had occurred on the spot had left a supernatural mark on the site, not allowing the grass to grow or the events to be forgotten.

The mystery of the barren soil lasted for a few more years, then the lot was sold, and a new house was built on the site. The new owners even went to the trouble of changing the physical address of the location so that the stigma would be removed. Fortunately for them, their efforts worked and once the construction was completed, the grass began to grow again.

The nightmare, it seemed, was finally over.

HAUNTINGS AT WOLF LAKE
Chicago's "Gangland Graveyard"

Few can deny that there is a "haunting" quality to the ancient woods and swamps around the William W. Powers Conservation Area, better known as Wolf Lake. This area of grasslands, swamps and forest is located south of the city, straddling the Illinois and Indiana border. It is considered perhaps the most notorious region of southern Cook County ---- and with very good reason.

In addition to the many occasions of young children who have drowned in the cold waters of the lake, there have been numerous bodies discovered in these wild, swampy lands. It has been a common thing over the years to see police officers from Chicago and Hammond, Indiana tramping through the woods here in a search for evidence. Wolf Lake has often been referred to as a "gangland graveyard" and a "favorite" place to dump bodies that no one wants found.

Is it any wonder that stories of restless spirits and lonesome ghosts have followed in the wake of the stories of murder and death?

Wolf Lake in the 1920s -- already referred to in the newspapers as a "gangland graveyard", thanks to the number of bodies that had been discovered here

Today, Wolf Lake can be found east of Avenue O and Burnham Avenue between 120th and 134th Streets on the southeast side, but French Explorer Father Jacques Marquette first discovered it in the 1600s. In the days before the Civil War, Lieutenant Jefferson Davis, who went on to serve as the President of the Confederacy, surveyed the region for the U.S. Army Corps of Engineers. It is a place of history and tragedy and has long been linked to the blood-soaked annals of Chicago crime.

During Prohibition days, the most talked-about "one way rides" to Wolf Lake involved two of Al Capone's gunmen, John Scalise and Albert Anselmi, and *Unione Sicilian* president Joseph "Hop Toed" Guinta. Their bullet-riddled bodies were found on May 8, 1929 inside of a car that had been dumped into a ditch on an undeveloped part of Wolf Lake property, just across the Indiana border. Who actually killed these three men remains a mystery to this day.

Some believe that rival gangsters did them in. They had been accused of being involved in the St. Valentine's Day Massacre and had been brought in for questioning by detectives and by the Cook County state's attorney. They were released on bond and it's thought that perhaps gangsters working for George Moran's north side mob may have caught up with them.

Others hold to the theory that the men were taken out by Al Capone himself. It was said that Capone feared that the three men were plotting to move against him and that the three were bludgeoned to death and then shot at a gangland banquet given to celebrate the victory over the Moran gang. Their murders were said to be the real-life counterparts to the "baseball bat bludgeoning" that Hollywood has long been fond of when

Capone gunmen John Scalise (Left) and Albert Anselmi, who were rumored to be dispatched by the boss himself and their bodies dumped near Wolf Lake

portraying Capone on film. The story cannot be verified but, if it happened, the likely location was a nightclub that was located in Hammond, Indiana.

The car was then driven off the road near Wolf Lake, a place where countless other Prohibition murder victims were likely deposited.

In 1935, Wolf Lake became a dumping ground for Wrigleyville Torso Murder victim Ervin Lang. His mother-in-law, Blanche Dunkel and her friend, former stripper Evelyn White, carried out this gruesome bit of carnage. Blanche hated Ervin because he had spurned her after her daughter's death and had recruited White to carry out his murder.

After a night of card-playing and knockout drinks, Blanche left the bloody work to her friend. Evelyn dosed Ervin with ether, tied him securely and then dragged him into a closet where she strangled him to death. The next morning, her estranged husband, Harry Jung, arrived with a saw and the two of them set to work on the corpse.

Evelyn cut off Ervin's legs at the hip so that he would fit into a large trunk that Jung had purchased at a Salvation Army store. They loaded the trunk into Jung's car and then set out for the southeast side, eventually crossing into Indiana to leave Ervin's legs in a roadside ditch near Munster.

The torso was taken to Wolf Lake and dumped into one of the many swamp areas around the lake. Even then, the newspapers referred to the lake as a "gangland cemetery" because of the number of bodies that had been dumped here over the years.

They never expected the body to be found but someone stumbled across the torso just four days later. Blanche and Evelyn were both later convicted and sentenced to prison.

The most famous crime tied to Wolf Lake is the abduction and "thrill killing" of Bobby Franks by Nathan Leopold and Richard Loeb in May 1924. Bobby had been kidnapped from in the fashionable Kenwood section on Chicago's south side and murdered in a rental car by the two young men. Believing that they could carry out the "perfect crime", Loeb struck Bobby on the head with an iron chisel several times and then dumped his body near Wolf Lake. After stripping him of his clothes and pouring acid on his face to hide his identity, they stuffed the body into a culvert underneath some railroad tracks near 121st Street.

Police officers search for clues at Wolf Lake, near the site where Bobby Franks body was discovered in 1924

Within 24 hours, the body of the young boy --- and a pair of eyeglasses that Leopold dropped at the scene --- was discovered. The killers were soon in custody and detectives and prosecutors quickly unraveled the "perfect crime".

The spot where Bobby's body was found is hard to find today, but not impossible. The railroad tracks that once crossed this area no longer exist, but they have been replaced with an asphalt bike trail. The culvert was destroyed many years ago but those who have grown up in the area remember where it once was and can take you to the spot where the traumatic spot where Bobby was discovered.

It is a grim, silent and desperate place and I suppose you can say, it is "haunted" in its own right.

Wolf Lake also became a dumping ground for at least two victims of Chicago serial killer Andrew Urdiales in the late 1990s. Urdiales lived with his parents on the southeast side, at 9709 South Commercial Avenue, and Wolf Lake became a part of his evil psychosis and as Assistant State's Attorney Alison Perona would later describe a connection made by detectives who tracked the killer ---- it was "sex, bondage, lake."

Andrew Urdiales was a loner, an average student and graduated from Thornridge High School in Dolton in 1982 without any fanfare. He had few friends but this didn't stop him from attending a high school reunion many years later and telling a former classmate that he had killed two prostitutes while living in California.

Urdiales had few prospects when he graduated high school, so he decided to enlist in the U.S. Marine Corps. He joined up but not because he was patriotic; he wanted to learn to defend himself and to destroy things. He later confessed to killing five women, and abducting and raping another, while stationed in California. He was promoted five times while serving in the military until, at the rank of corporal, his men refused to take orders from him and he was eventually demoted.

During his time in the Marines, Urdiales fell in love with a 15 year-old girl and she became pregnant. Terrified of her parents, and any military discipline that might befall him, he convinced the girl to get an abortion. He later stated that he loved her "but the law and the state of California and the righteous and the Marine Corps might not see it that way."

Urdiales received an honorable discharge from the Marines and returned to the Chicago area in 1996, just months after killing his last victim in California. He moved into his parent's home on the southeast side and got a job as a security guard. Restless and unable to sleep, he sought psychiatric help from a Chicago veteran's hospital. On April 12, 1996, a veteran's hospital psychologist urged him to "become more open about expressing his anger". Two days later, he claimed his first local victim.

On April 14, Urdiales picked up Lori Uylaki of Hammond and after raping and killing her, he dumped her body into a swampy area along Wolf Lake.

On July 13, he ran into Cassandra Corum at a bar on Michigan Avenue in Hammond. They went for a ride in Urdiales' truck and, not surprisingly, he drove her to Wolf Lake, where they had sex near the spot where Urdiales had dumped the body of Lori Uylaki. Corum said something to make Urdiales mad, although during his trial he could not remember what it was, and he started hitting her in the face. Terrified, Cassie began to panic and tried to get out of the truck. Urdiales had purchased a pair of handcuffs for his security guard job and he pulled them out from under the seat and snapped them around her wrists. Twisting hard, he jerked her arms behind her back and locked the cuffs into place. He then ripped the rest of her clothes off, taped her mouth with duct tape and drove off with Cassie cowering on the seat beside him. He eventually started driving south on Interstate 55, exiting the highway near Pontiac, about 100 miles south of the city. He found his way to a park, where he stopped the truck and removed the handcuffs and duct tape from the naked and terrified young girl. He opened the door, pushed Cassie out and then followed behind her.

A detective later testified that Cassie walked to the back of the truck and turned toward Urdiales. Before she could speak, he pulled out a gun and shot her in the face. She fell to the ground but his rage was not yet satisfied. He pulled out a knife and began stabbing her over and over with it. He put the knife back into the truck when he was finally finished. After that, he carried Cassie's body to a bridge and dropped it into the Vermillion River.

A young woman named Donica Coffman, Cassandra Corum's best friend, later testified that she remembered Urdiales as being a "nice guy". When Cassie turned up missing, she said that Urdiales had cried and had helped her pass out missing person posters.

Urdiales did not wait long to strike again. On August 2, he headed to Chicago's north side, where he picked up Lynn Huber, 22. Urdiales saw her walking with a plastic garbage bag filled with clothes and he asked her if she needed a ride. They traveled in Urdiales' truck until they reached the elevated tracks at 1036 W. Irving Park Road and at that point, an argument broke out between them. Urdiales stopped the truck and Lynn jumped out --- but she was not fast enough. Urdiales grabbed her by the hair and pulled her to the ground. He grabbed his gun and fired at her several times, hitting her only once. Urdiales put the girl back into the truck, tossed her bag of clothing in with her and began driving again. He headed back toward Wolf Lake and told detectives later that it "seemed like the right way to drive". He could not explain the unnatural hold that the lake seemed to have on him.

He drove down the dark roadways around the lake and eventually came to a stop in a secluded area. Lynn was still alive so Urdiales stripped off her clothes, stabbed her multiple times and dumped her body into the murky water. Urdiales then drove away, throwing the clothing that Lynn had been wearing into a dumpster and leaving her bag of extra clothes with the Salvation Army. Exhausted, Urdiales drove back to his parent's home and went to bed.

The Andrew Urdiales case began to unravel on November 14, 1996. That night, Urdiales was stopped by Officer Warren Fryer, a Hammond patrolman, for being parked outside of a drug house with a known prostitute. He called for backup and as officers approached the truck, Fryer described Urdiales as being "cooperative and average". He noticed nothing unusual about him.

As Urdiales was explaining that he had served in the Marine Corps, Officer Fryer spotted his revolver. He loudly stated "gun" to his fellow officers and another patrolman removed it from the truck. It was a snub-nosed, chrome-plated .38 special, fully loaded with six shells. Since Urdiales did not have a gun permit for Indiana, he was arrested and the gun was confiscated.

The police towed Urdiales' truck and in a quick search, they found a sleeping bag and a duffel bag with a roll of duct tape in it. Officer Fryer reported that "the interior of the bed and cab were spotlessly clean. They were as clean as you could wash the outside of your car.... unusual for the norm."

Urdiales fell off the radar for the next six months but, on April 1, 1997, Officer Fryer responded to a complaint about a man and a woman fighting at the American Inn on Calumet Avenue. He was surprised to find that Andrew Urdiales was involved in the dispute and vaguely remembered him from the incident the previous fall. Urdiales was talking to another officer so Fryer questioned the woman involved, a prostitute named Patricia Kelly. Urdiales had accused her of stealing from him.

Kelly said to Officer Fryer: "This guy's kind of kinky. He wants to take me in the back of his pick-up truck to Wolf Lake, handcuff me and (engage in anal sex)."

Fryer, who knew of the bodies of the two girls found murdered there, gave Kelly an immediate response, which he later testified to: "Jeez, Patricia, don't do that. We're finding girls up there dead."

When Officer Fryer returned to the Hammond Police Department at the end of his shift, he conducted a computer search on Urdiales and found his own report from the November 14 seizure of his gun. He prepared a supplemental report and forwarded it to the detectives in the case. Something about Urdiales did not sit well with him, especially his connections to Wolf Lake.

Assistant State's Attorney Alison Perona, who prosecuted the Wolf Lake murders, described Urdiales as a "savage, predatory, cunning killer" who was caught by a "combination of bad luck and good police work. The woman said Andrew wanted her to go to Wolf Lake, let him tie her up and have sex with her," Perona said. "The officer immediately made the connection -- sex, bondage, lake."

On April 7, Hammond detectives contacted Chicago detective Don McGrath about the incident at the American Inn. They also turned over the gun that had been confiscated from Urdiales in November, which McGrath took to weapons expert Robert Smith. After testing it, Smith was able to confirm that it was the same gun used to kill three women.

On April 22, McGrath and his partner, Detective Raymond Krakausky, set up surveillance in an alley just south of Urdiales' parent's home. Urdiales came out about 9:00 a.m., and headed to work. McGrath and Krakausky approached him and told him that they were interested in the November 1996 case in which Urdiales' revolver was seized. Urdiales said the case had been resolved, but agreed to come down to the police station with them to answer some questions.

After seating him in an interview room, McGrath asked him about the gun. Urdiales said that he had purchased it for $300 in Calumet City, about five years earlier. He stated that it had been in his possession ever since. A moment later, the detectives changed the subject of the questions from Urdiales' gun to the murders of Lynn Huber, Lori Uylaki and Cassandra Corum. At first, Urdiales claimed that he did not recognize the photos that he was shown of the three young women but then McGrath told him that bullets used in all three murders were traced to his gun.

Urdiales took off his security badge, loosened his tie and started to untie his shoelaces. "I guess I'm not going to be going to work today," he said.

Andrew Urdiales was indicted and tried for the murders of Lori Uylaki and Lynn Huber in 2002. During his trial, family members and experts testified that mental illness ran rampant on both sides of his family; he had been physically and emotionally abused by his parents and sexually abused by his sister and a male cousin; and that he had been picked on during school and later in the Marines Corps. They also claimed that he was "brain damaged" and that he heard voices that sometimes spoke to him "in code" and led him to "go on missions" so that he could break the code and understand what messages were being given to him.

The jury was not swayed by his claims of insanity, though. Urdiales was convicted and sentenced to death ---- a sentence that was commuted by Governor George Ryan during his mass dismissal of death sentence cases shortly before he left office. In April 2004, Urdiales was tried and convicted in Pontiac County for the murder of Cassandra Corum. He will eventually be extradited to California to face trail for the murders of five other women and the abduction and rape of another.

There are other Wolf Lake legends, curiosities and murders.

On May 22, 1988, off-duty Chicago police officer John Matthews was beaten to death by three men after he ordered them to leave the conservation area after dark. Matthews lived nearby, at 131st Street and Avenue M, and was just trying to keep peace in the neighborhood.

On March 27, 1997, the bullet-riddled body of Antonio Fort was found floating in the lake. The dead man's father was Jeff Fort, the imprisoned gang leader of the former Black P Stone Nation street gang. The murder was never solved.

One of the great oddities of Wolf Lake is the abandoned Nike Ajax missile base that is located near Avenue K and 133rd Street. The missile base, with its 16 launchers, is an unnerving reminder of the Cold War era and its four concrete radar towers, lost in the weeds and underbrush, can still be found a short distance off the main road.

But perhaps the most chilling legends of Wolf Lake are those of the ghosts that have been seen, heard and experienced in the swampy areas and on the shorelines of the lake. Over the years, those who have grown up on the southeast side have told and re-told stories of ghostly figures that have been seen here, wandering the edge of the lake, only to vanish whenever they are approached.

"It's no surprise to me that Wolf Lake is haunted," a long-time resident of the neighborhood told me.

He was just one of the many people on the southeast side that I have interviewed over the years about their ghostly encounters. I have the advantage of the fact that some of my best friends have lived in this area their entire life and frequent visits have led me to a number of people with haunting stories to tell about the dark waters of Wolf Lake.

"I have heard from a lot of people about their encounters," he added. "My sister was driving out near the lake one night with some friends a few years ago and they swear they saw the ghost of a woman."

He explained that they had been in Hegewisch, a small community that is just south of Wolf Lake and his sister and her two friends had gone for a walk in the conservation area, even though it was getting late and

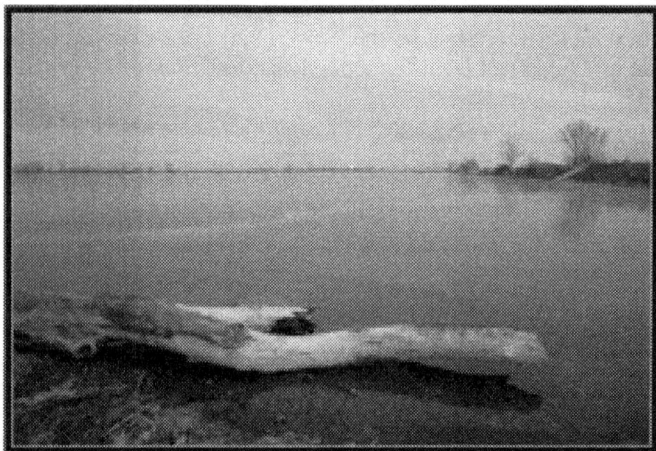

the park is closed after dark. They were hiking in a wet area near the lakeshore when they heard the sound of a woman's voice. Startled, they saw a woman come stumbling towards them. She appeared to be soaking wet. She was wearing a blue dress that clung to her body and her blond hair was plastered down on her head. The girls heard the woman mumbling to herself and she had one hand outstretched in front of her, as though feeling her away along.

Before any of the girls could speak and ask her if she was all right, the woman in the blue dress suddenly vanished. She was simply there one minute and then gone the next.

"Needless to say, they were pretty scared and they didn't stick around there for long," my witness concluded. "I never did hear who this ghost may have been but there have been so many bodies dumped out here, I don't see how anyone could tell."

And the woman in blue is not the only ghost who has been reported around Wolf Lake. Fishermen, outdoorsmen and casual visitors alike have told of weeping women, unexplained screams in the night and, of course, the vanishing hitchhiker of Avenue O. This long stretch of roadway passes through the most secluded and remote areas on the southeast side, passing closer to Wolf Lake than any other road. It offers just about the only access to the recreation area ---- and to the swamps and wet areas that came to be dubbed the "gangland cemetery".

The ghost that has been encountered here is perhaps Chicago's only male phantom hitchhiker. In a city that boasts such restless highway haunts as Resurrection Mary and the Flapper Ghost, male spirits that hitch rides in passing cars seem to be in short supply. The only one that I know of can be found looking for a ride along Avenue O.

According to legends of the neighborhood, the ghost of a man in an old-fashioned looking suit and tie walks the edge of the road here, trying to flag down cars that pass by him at night. He is described as looking very ordinary and not ghost-like at all and most assume that he is someone whose car has broken down on this isolated roadway. The stories say that if a driver stops to offer the man assistance, he always disappears.

One witness claimed that he had encountered the man in 1999. He was driving south on Avenue O and spotted a man in a gray suit and hat walking north in the opposite direction. The man waved at him, apparently trying to get his attention. The driver had just reached an entrance to the conservation area at Wolf Lake, so he pulled in and turned around to see if the man needed help. As he started driving back north, he kept an eye out for the man in the suit. It was starting to get very dark by this time but he knew that there was nowhere to go on the road and that he would quickly come up on the man as he walked along. Strangely, though, the walking man was nowhere to be seen. The driver slowed down, came to a stop and even honked his horn a couple of times --- but the man had vanished.

In 2004, another driver told me of his own encounter with the walking man. "I was driving north on Avenue O and was traveling alongside Wolf Lake when I saw this man in a suit and hat on the side of the road," he told me. "As I passed by him, he turned halfway around and waved both of his arms, as if he wanted me to stop.

"Normally, I would never do this, especially at night, but this guy just looked so normal and well-dressed that I had to think that his car had just broken down somewhere and he needed a ride or a phone.

"Anyway, I stopped and pulled over to the side of the road. It was maybe 30 yards past where I had seen the man but it took me a little distance to slow down. I figured that, since the guy was so intent on waving me down, that he would hurry and catch up to me but he never came. I looked in my rearview mirror but there was no one behind me. I waited a minute or so and then got out of the car. All that I can say is that there was no one back there. I have no idea where the guy went but he was definitely gone."

The witness paused for a minute and shook his head. "I don't think that I have driven that way after dark since then," he chuckled a little nervously. "And, if I ever do, I am never stopping for a hitchhiker again."

I am going to St. Petersburg, Florida, tomorrow. Let the citizens of Chicago get their liquor the best they can. I'm sick of the job ------ it's a thankless one and full of grief. I've been spending the best years of my life as a public benefactor.
Al Capone

BIBLIOGRAPHY & RECOMMENDED READING

Many of the books used for this volume were already collected for my book, *Haunted Chicago* (2003), so I will not repeat those listings here. However, I have listed some of the more relevant and helpful sources below. Please see *Haunted Chicago* for a more complete bibliography list. Thanks!

Asbury, Herbert - Gem of the Prairie (1940)
There have been a lot of books written about Chicago crime but this one still rates as one of my favorites. Asbury writes a compelling account of the city's criminal history, from the early days, right up to the Capone era. It's a great read and one that's tough to put down!

Bielski, Ursula - Chicago Haunts (1998)
Bielski, Ursula - More Chicago Haunts (2000)
Binder, John - The Chicago Outfit (2003)
Burroughs, Brian - Public Enemies (2004)
Caren, Eric C. Collection - Crime Extra: 300 Years of American Crime (2001)
Chicago American Newspaper
Chicago Daily Herald Newspaper
Chicago Daily News Newspaper
Chicago Herald & Examiner
Chicago Sun
Chicago Sun-Times Newspaper
Chicago Times
Chicago Tribune Newspaper
Chicago Public Library
Chicago Historical Society

Cowdery, Ray - Capone's Chicago (1931)
The first book to ever delve into the crime empire of Al Capone, written shortly after he was convicted and sent to prison. An amazing collection of articles and newspaper photos that presents a compelling accounting of recent events at the time. Find a copy of you can!

Demaris, Ovid - Captive City (1969)
Ehhigian, Mars, Jr. - After Capone (2006)
Fraley, Oscar & Eliot Ness - The Untouchables (1957)
Halper, Albert - The Chicago Crime Book (1967)

Helmer, William - Public Enemies (1998)
Helmer, William & Arthur J. Bilek - The St. Valentine's Day Massacre (2004)
Johnson, Curt - Wicked City (1994)
Keefe, Rose - Guns and Roses (2003)
Keefe, Rose - The Man who Got Away (2005)
King, Jeffery - Rise and Fall of the Dillinger Gang (2005)
Kobler, John - Ardent Spirits: The Rise & Fall of Prohibition (1973)

Kobler, John - The Life and World of Al Capone (1971)
This is the first book that I ever read about Al Capone. I found this book some time in the early 1980's and was hooked on the stories from the era and the gangsters of Chicago in general. There have been other books written on Capone, of course, but this one remains my favorite.

Kogan, Herman & Lloyd Wendt - Lords of the Levee (1944)
Lait, Jack & Lee Mortimer - Chicago Confidential (1950)

Larson, Erik -- Devil in the White City (2003)
I was not convinced that anyone could do justice to the story of H.H. Holmes outside of "Depraved", which is mentioned later, but Larson captures the madness and magic of this story in a way that no one else has. The book tells the story of both Holmes and architect Daniel Burnham, the creator of the 1893 World's Fair. If you think (like I first did) that you will only be interested in the chapters on Holmes, think again! This documentary book reads like a novel and if you love Chicago history, you will not be able to put this book down!

Lindberg, Richard - Chicago by Gaslight (1996)
Lindberg, Richard - To Serve and Collect (1991)
Lindberg, Richard - Return to the Scene of the Crime (1999)
Lindberg, Richard - Return Again to the Scene of the Crime (2001)
I have enjoyed all of the books that Richard has written but I can't tell you how excited I was when his first "Return to the Scene of the Crime" book came out. With the city of Chicago doing everything that it has been able to over the years to blot out the crime spots and the gangster era of the city, I have always delighted in the efforts of those who have tried to keep that history alive. Richard (in addition to being a nice guy) has done more than anyone else in my memory to re-create the events of the past in an unbelievably readable form. If you have not read these books -- go out and get them immediately!

Loerzel, Robert - Alchemy of Bones (2003)
Lunde, Paul - Organized Crime (2004)
Matera, Dary - John Dillinger (2004)
Nerad, Roy - Hauntings at Cavallone's West (Ghosts of the Prairie Magazine)(2002)

Nash, Jay Robert - Among the Missing (1978)
Nash, Jay Robert - Bloodletters and Bad Men (1995)
Nash, Jay Robert - The Dillinger Dossier (1970)
Nash, Jay Robert - Dillinger - Dead or Alive (1970)
Nash, Jay Robert - Murder, America (1980)
I have to admit it -- I am a Jay Robert Nash buff. I have long been an enthusiast of his work and while I am perhaps one of the only people with an interest in Dillinger who still lends credence to his theories about Dillinger surviving the shoot-out at the Biograph, I find the story fascinating. If you get a chance to pick up any of his books on the history of American crime, I highly recommend them.

O'Brien, John & Edward Baumann - Teresita: The Voice from the Grave (1992)
O'Shea, Gene - Unbridled Rage (2005)
Sann, Paul - The Lawless Decade (1957)
Schechter, Harold - Depraved (1994)
Scott, Gini Graham - Homicide: 100 Years of Murder in America
Sifakis, Carl - Encyclopedia of American Crime (1982)
Sifakis, Carl - The Mafia Encyclopedia (1987)
Steinke, Gord - Crossing the Line: Mobsters & Rumrunners (2003)
Sullivan, Terry & Peter Maiken - Killer Clown: The John Wayne Gacy Murders (1983)
Wallace, Stone - Dustbowl Desperadoes (2003)

Wright, Sewell Peaslee - Chicago Murders: True Crimes and Real Detectives (1947)
I had no idea how rare this out of print and obscure little book of Chicago crimes stories, penned by a variety of writers, was until someone gave me an autographed copy as a gift. It's a great treat if you ever happen to find a copy of it!

Personal Interviews and Correspondence

Note from the Publisher: Although Whitechapel Productions Press, Troy Taylor, and all affiliated with this book have carefully researched all sources to insure the accuracy of the information contained in this book, we assume no responsibility for errors, inaccuracies or omissions.

Special Thanks to:
Kim Young --- Editing and Proofreading Services
Ken Berg
Adam Selzer
Tom & Michelle Bonadurer
Eddie & Marianne Schaeffer
Mike & Sandra Schwab
Kathy Richardson
Jim Graczyk
& Haven Taylor

ABOUT THE AUTHOR

Troy Taylor is the author of 43 books about history, hauntings and the unexplained in America, including *Haunted Illinois*, *The Ghost Hunter's Guidebook*, *Weird Illinois* and many others. He is the founder and president of the "American Ghost Society", a national network of ghost hunters that collects stories of ghost sightings and haunted houses and uses investigative techniques to track down evidence of the supernatural.

Taylor was born on September 24, 1966 in Decatur, Illinois, a midwestern city that is steeped in legend and lore. He grew up fascinated with "things that go bump in the night" and in school, Taylor was well-known for his interest in the paranormal and often took friends on informal ghost tours of haunted places all over downstate Illinois. He would later turn this interest into his full-time career.

In 1989, Taylor started working in a bookstore and a few years later, he wrote his first book on ghosts. It was called *Haunted Decatur* and delved into the ghosts and hauntings of the city where he grew up. He also created a tour that took guests to places that he had written about in the book. The book became an immediate success and its popularity, along with his previous experiences with ghost hunting, established Taylor as an authority on the supernatural. The book and tour led to media and public appearances and numerous requests to investigate ghostly phenomena.

In 1996, Taylor organized a group of ghost enthusiasts into an investigation team and the American Ghost Society was launched, gained over 600 members in the years that followed. The organization continues today as one of America's largest and most honored research groups.

In 1998, Taylor moved his operations, which now included the American Ghost Society, a history and hauntings bookstore and a publishing company called Whitechapel Press, to Alton, Illinois, near St. Louis. In Alton, Taylor started his second tour company, Alton Hauntings, which also took guests to local haunted places in the small Mississippi River town. He would go on to put the place on the map as "one of the most haunted small towns in America."

Taylor remained in Alton until 2005. By then, he had also established another tour company that arranges overnight stays in haunted places. These tours, including those in Decatur and Alton, were organized under the heading of the Illinois Hauntings Ghost Tours. In 2006, he also launched the Weird Chicago Tours, based on his book from Barnes & Noble Press. Taylor also continued the operation of Whitechapel Press, which specializes in ghost-related titles and has more than a dozen authors working under its banner.

Along with writing about the unusual and hosting tours, Taylor is also a public speaker on the subject of ghosts and hauntings and has spoken to literally hundreds of private and public groups on a variety of paranormal subjects. He has appeared in newspaper and magazine articles about ghosts and has also been fortunate enough to be interviewed hundreds of times for radio and television broadcasts about the supernatural. He has also appeared in a number of documentary films, several television series and in one feature film about the paranormal.

He currently resides in Central Illinois with his wife, Haven, in a decidedly non-haunted house.

WHITECHAPEL PRESS

Whitechapel Productions Press is a small publisher, specializing in books about ghosts and hauntings. Since 1993, the company has been one of America's leading publishers of supernatural books and has produced such best-selling titles as "Haunted Illinois", "The Ghost Hunter's Guidebook" and many others. With nearly a dozen different authors producing high quality books on all aspects of ghosts, hauntings and the paranormal, Whitechapel Press has made its mark with America's ghost enthusiasts.

You can visit Whitechapel Productions Press online and browse through our selection of ghostly titles, plus get information on ghosts and hauntings, haunted history, spirit photographs, information on ghost hunting and much more. by visiting the internet website at:

www.prairieghosts.com

Whitechapel Press is the headquarters for the Illinois Hauntings Tour Co, offering the following ghost tours:

Weird Chicago Tours / Chicago, Illinois
Created by Troy Taylor and based on his book *Weird Illinois* from Barnes & Noble Press, this is an alternative tour of Chicago, offering visitors the chance to see the "other side" of the city. Visit Chicago's most haunted sites, most notorious crime spots, most unusual places and much more! Available all year round!
www.weirdchicago.com

Haunted Decatur Ghost Tours / Decatur, Illinois
Created by Troy Taylor & Skip Huston in 1994, these are the third longest running ghost tours in the state of Illinois! Visit the city's most haunted spots and take a nightime stroll through Greenwood Cemetery! Available April - October!
www.haunteddecatur.com

Alton Hauntings Ghost Tours / Alton, Illinois
Created by Troy Taylor, these tours are an interactive experience that allow readers to visit the historically haunted locations of the city and can be booked every year from April through October.Hosted by Len Adams, Luke Naliborski & Troy Taylor ---
www.altonhauntings.com

Haunted Highways Ghost Tours
Created by authors Troy Taylor these tours offer Haunted Overnight Excursions to ghostly places around the Midwest and throughout the country. Available all year round!
www.illinoishauntings.com

Springfield Hauntings Ghost Tours / Springfield, Illinois
Join us in the Prairie State's haunted Capital City for Springfield's only authentic ghost tours. Experience the hauntings of Abraham Lincoln, the Springfield Theater Center and much more! Available April through October and hosted by John Winterbauer ----
www.springfieldhauntings.com

WEIRD CHICAGO TOUR

THE ALTERNATIVE TOUR OF CHICAGO'S GHOSTS, LOCAL LEGENDS & BEST KEPT SECRETS

www.ingramcontent.com/pod-product-compliance
Lightning Source LLC
Chambersburg PA
CBHW081228090426
42738CB00016B/3221